Superbrands

AN INSIGHT INTO SOME OF BRITAIN'S STRONGEST BRANDS 2010

superbrands.uk.com

Chief Executive
Ben Hudson

Brand Liaison Directors
Fiona Maxwell
Claire Pollock
Liz Silvester

Brand Liaison Manager
Heidi Smith

Head of Accounts
Will Carnochan

Managing Editor
Angela Cooper

Authors
Jane Bainbridge
Karen Dugdale

Proofreader
Anna Haynes

Also available from Superbrands in the UK:
CoolBrands 2009/10 ISBN: 978-0-9554784-8-2

To order further books, email brands@superbrands.uk.com
or call 020 7079 3310.

Published by
Superbrands (UK) Ltd
22-23 Little Portland Street
London
W1W 8BU

Printed in Italy

ISBN: 978-0-9554784-9-9

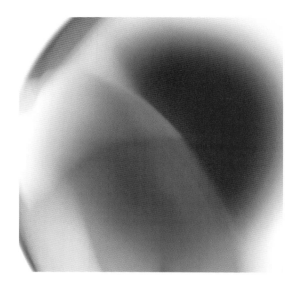  

Contents

Case Studies

Thought Pieces

Appendix

Key

Ⓑ Business Superbrands
Ⓒ Consumer Superbrands

Endorsements

This collection of Superbrands is another inspiring showcase of the power and versatility of branding. The diversity of products and services featured touch all our lives, whether at home or at work. They also stand as testament to the resilience of brands, where they adapt and respond to the changing world around them.

Brands play a crucial role in both the economy and in society, whether in creating and growing markets or in providing more back to society than simply superior performance. In this collection of Superbrands, which the British Brands Group is delighted to support, this contribution is evident for all to see.

This collection demonstrates that brands are in no need of special pleading. Such case studies play a valuable role though in reminding us all how diverse successful brands can be and how they contribute to our lives. In the UK we need the environment for these brands to flourish if we are to compete effectively on the global stage.

John Noble
Director, British Brands Group

As you read through this book you will see an astonishing array of brands and success stories of organisations and companies that, through high quality brand management, have made a major impact on their respective markets.

What I find of value is reading through how they have achieved their positioning and generated both customer loyalty and shareholder value. Last year represented one of the most challenging times for the marketing profession as consumer spending declined, businesses contracted and we all had to fight very hard to minimise the impact of reduced revenues. Those that focused on brand awareness, proper segmentation, quality and delivering exceptional service, by and large, prospered. The brands that have made it into this book are high quality examples of this and we should seek to learn from what they have achieved. I trust you will all be enlightened and motivated by what you read.

Chris Lenton DipM, FCIM, FCCA, FCIS
Chairman, The Chartered Institute of Marketing

As the membership association for marketing and business professionals committed to raising standards in marketing practice worldwide, we are delighted and proud to endorse the Superbrands Annual 2010 and the role it plays in the advancement of marketing.

Whilst 2009 will be seen as a difficult trading year for many organisations, the Superbrands contained within this latest volume demonstrate the value of creating powerful and sustainable brands and the vital role that they play as the world emerges from recession. These organisations demonstrate the value of continuing to invest in building brand equity and the power they have to make a difference to the lives of many stakeholders, and society as a whole.

On behalf of Global Marketing Network, congratulations to those people who have contributed to the achievements contained within this edition and for inspiring of us to create our own Superbrands.

Darrell Kofkin
Chief Executive, Global Marketing Network

At the IDM B2B Marketing Conference 2009 we asked: To survive in times of economic uncertainty, should B2B Marketers be investing in brand or lead generation?

A heated discussion ensued. In a recession it's tempting to concentrate on short term tactical measures and abandon long term strategic goals. Throw in a technology explosion that's put power in the laps of our customers and we've witnessed an era of radical and irreversible change. Brands now find themselves at the centre of discussions that go global in an instant. Peer recommendations (or the opposite) carry more weight than marketing messages, or even expert reviews.

Today, a strong brand, with a cast iron reputation that inspires recommendations, is essential. Our debate concluded that truly successful brands go further. They safeguard both their long term brand strategy, to inspire recommendation, and their short term lead generation, to ensure there are customers to do the recommending! These are the brands you'll find in this book.

Professor Derek Holder F IDM
Managing Director, The Institute of Direct Marketing

About
Superbrands

Published annually since 1995, the Superbrands book investigates some of the strongest consumer and B2B brands in Britain today and establishes how they have managed to achieve such phenomenal success. The 2010 Annual explores the history, development and achievements of 80 much-loved brands, with each case study providing valuable insights into their branding strategy and resulting work.

Brands do not apply or pay to be considered for Superbrands status. Rather, the accolade is awarded to the country's strongest brands following a rigorous and independent selection process; full details are provided on page 180.

This publication forms part of a wider programme that pays tribute to Britain's strongest brands. The programme is administered by Superbrands (UK) Ltd and also features SuperbrandsDigital.com, a national newspaper supplement and regular editorial features throughout the year. The company also hosts regular events which promote networking amongst senior brand owners.

Superbrands was launched in London in 1995 and is now a global business operating in more than 55 countries worldwide. Further details can be found at superbrands.uk.com.

The Superbrands Award Stamps

Brands that have been awarded Superbrands status and participate in the programme are licensed to use the Superbrands Award Stamps. These powerful endorsements provide evidence to existing and potential consumers, media, employees and investors of the exceptional standing that these brands have achieved.

 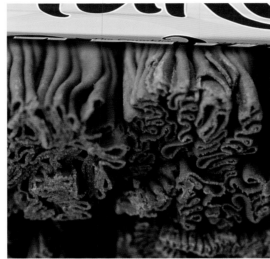 

QUALITY

RELIABILITY

DISTINCTION

acer

Acer was established in 1976 with US$25,000 in capital, 11 employees and the mission to break down the barriers between people and technology. Since then, Acer has successfully grown to become the second largest PC and Notebook brand in the world, with the fastest growth among the top-five players. Today Acer Group employs over 7,000 people worldwide working in 70 countries. In 2008 it achieved revenues of US$16.65 billion.

Product

The company's product portfolio covers diverse areas of IT equipment for both consumers and businesses. Its PC-centric product offering includes mobile and desktop PCs, servers and storage, LCD monitors and high-definition TVs, projectors, and Smartphones.

Sub-brands include the consumer-focused Aspire series, and commercial sector TravelMate and Veriton as well as a Ferrari model from its design partnership with the luxury motor manufacturer.

Most recently it has launched the Timeline series notebooks which balance lightweight credentials with more than 12 hours of battery life for all-day mobile computing.

Market

Over the last decade, Acer has grown from a small scale manufacture with a little known brand into one of the largest PC companies in the word.

Boasting a diverse product portfolio, Acer's success is largely attributed to its Channel Business Model (CBM) and it consistently invests in strategies aimed at the success of its partners.

Acer's commitment to its channel partners extends beyond product placement. By constantly monitoring business trends, Acer can tailor its entire product development and go-to-market strategies to suit the needs of specific target customers, helping the channel, as a result, to grow.

The global PC market grew by 4.2 per cent year-on-year in the third quarter of 2009. In this period Acer achieved a market share of 14 per cent based on total PC shipments, a 26 per cent increase compared with the same quarter in 2008.

Achievements

Acer has grown exponentially in recent years and has evolved into a group with companies which have widespread success. Strategically structured and globally focused, but responsive to the needs of the markets, Acer delivered US$16.65 billion in revenue in 2008. In most recent results, Acer's consolidated revenue

1976	1981	1987	1995	1996	1997
Acer is founded under the name Multitech, focusing on trade and product design.	The Micro-Professor computing tool is launched. About the size of a large dictionary and costing under US$100, the Micro-Professor is an instant hit.	Multitech formally becomes known as Acer, marking the start of Acer's efforts toward creating a strong brand name.	The Acer Aspire transforms the company from an anonymous PC manufacturer into a trendsetter. With its breakthrough design, the Aspire instantly becomes successful.	Acer introduces the Nuovo Notebook PC, featuring the innovative power management system, Heuristic Power Management, that is able to learn the user's specific behaviour, and then distributes power accordingly.	The company acquires Texas Instruments' notebook division.

was US$5.2 billion in the third quarter of 2009, the best yet recorded by the company, representing a 5.3 per cent year-on-year growth, which is significant considering other major players were recording negative growth in revenue in the same period. This was also a significant period for Acer as it moved from being the third, to the second largest PC brand in the world with 14 per cent global market share.

Acer has achieved this unrivalled success not only by adopting a successful CBM strategy but by investing heavily in R&D to continue to gain recognition for its products that lead the market in terms of innovation, technology and design. The Acer Aspire 5738DG 3D notebook and Acer Aspire Z5610 AIO PC have been named as Honourees for the CEA's (Consumer Electronics Association) Innovations 2010 Design and Engineering awards in the Computer Hardware category. The Innovations programme has become an international hallmark for the best designed products in consumer technology.

The Acer S243HL LCD monitor won the 2010 iF product design award from the International Forum Design out of a potential 2,486 products.

Acer is dedicated to developing integrated sustainability and CSR strategies and is committed to being a global PC and IT player which embeds CSR as a key priority.

The five focal points of its environmental objectives are to fortify its Environmental Management System (EMS), strengthen green product development, expand product recycling and processing services and strengthen green supply chain management and environmental communication platforms.

Recent Developments
In terms of results and product innovation, 2009 was a significant year for Acer. In respect to key results, Acer successfully pushed forward to become the second largest PC brand in the world. In terms of product

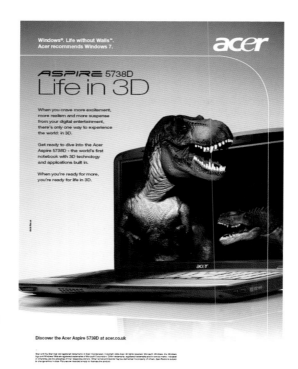

innovation Acer introduced the world's first; 3D notebook (Aspire 5738DZG), 24 inch 3D Monitor (GD245HQbid), ION based PC (Aspire Revo R3600) and the Liquid Smartphone with Qualcomm Snapdragon™ processor based with Android™ 1.6. Other recent innovations include the new Aspire and TravelMate Timeline range which deliver eight plus hours of battery life from a single full charge, giving the benefit of all day computing.

Promotion
Acer has always believed that sports and technology share the same ideals: strength, passion, competitiveness, coherence, skill and the determination to overcome new challenges. Acer's ability to identify strategically-favourable alliances has helped make its brands recognised outside the IT industry.

Acer has implemented high profile sponsorships which represent the spirit of the Acer brand and coherent ideals. Recently Acer announced that it was the official worldwide partner of the Olympic Movement in the computing equipment product category for the 2010 Olympic Winter Games in Vancouver and for the 2012 Olympic Games in London. This sponsorship is part of the TOP programme which was created in 1985 and is managed by the IOC. It is the only sponsorship with the exclusive worldwide marketing rights to both the Winter and Summer Games.

The Olympic Games will offer Acer a wide reaching stage to showcase its prowess in technology and innovation. As a worldwide TOP partner of the Vancouver 2010 Olympic Winter Games, Acer is providing more than 6,500 computing devices and more than 100 engineers and technicians to support the flawless management of one of the most complex sporting events in the world.

Other key sponsors include, Scuderia Ferrari, FC Internazionale Milano and London Wasps.

Brand Values
In 2006, Acer celebrated 30 years of long term growth in the fast-paced IT industry. The Acer Group remains firm in its commitment to develop easy-to-use and reliable products.

Its mission is 'Breaking the barriers between people and technology' through the creation of empowering hardware, software and services. It is committed to designing IT products that improve usability and add value to its customers' needs – be it at work or leisure.

It also believes that innovation is not the mere creation of new technologies and solutions, but the guarantee that users receive the benefits of these developments, and feel truly empowered.

acer.co.uk

2001	2003	2007	2008
Acer adopts a new corporate identity to symbolise its commitment to enhancing people's lives through technology.	The next-generation Empowering Technology platform is launched, integrating hardware, software and service to provide easy-to-use, dependable end-to-end technologies.	Acer completes the acquisition of Gateway, eMachines and Packard Bell.	Acer implements a multi-brand strategy which exploits the brand awareness of the companies in the group (Acer, Packard Bell, Gateway and eMachines).

American Express is a diversified global travel, financial and network services company founded in 1850. American Express is a leader in charge and credit cards, Travellers Cheques, travel and business services. Through its Global Commercial Card group (GCC), American Express provides payment solutions and expense management services to mid sized and large companies across the globe.

Market

American Express has more than 88 million cards in circulation globally and in 2008 US$683 billion was spent using American Express products. In the same year, American Express reported an income of US$2.7 billion, created through its leading global payments and travel offering. GCC alone contributed seven million cards and US$129 billion of spending activity.

In the UK, GCC is the largest commercial card provider in the market. Being a specialised company focused on business-to-business (B2B) payment and expense management solutions, American Express is able to offer companies the opportunity to simplify their day-to-day procedures, increase productivity and control when, where and how funds are spent.

American Express offers UK customers not only local expertise but access to international solutions through its global network with its footprint spanning across 130 countries.

Product

With almost 40 years' experience in the UK, American Express is the largest Commercial Card provider. Delivering expense management and payment solutions, American Express' breadth and depth of products are delivered via an extensive network of account management, sales and implementation teams. American Express is therefore positioned to provide medium, large and global companies as well as UK public sector organisations with comprehensive expense management programmes.

Identifying opportunities for customers to make significant savings possible through process efficiencies and compliance is key to American Express. It is this capability that enables American Express to deliver high quality programmes. Expense management

programmes are designed with a company's business requirements in mind. From Corporate Cards, to Business Travel Accounts, to Purchasing Solutions, GCC product suite aims to be all encompassing and flexible.

Committed to servicing its customers' commercial payment needs, American Express

completed the acquisition and integration of GE Corporate Payment Services into its business. With the acquisition of the vPayment technology, American Express has broadened its payment solutions capabilities to service the growing B2B payments arena, providing end-to-end tailored expense management and payment solutions. The vPayment technology allows a company to control payments and tailor them to any supplier by issuing a unique account number for every transaction which allows set amounts and dates to be specified for easy reconciliation.

Achievements

American Express strives to be at the forefront of customer service by providing exceptional products and services to its customers. American Express' employees are known for going the extra mile – literally. On occasions, customers have received a helping hand from employees, who have even personally delivered emergency replacement cards and travel documents. American Express has also helped to locate Cardmembers and help them make contact with their families in times of crisis.

The vision of American Express is to be one of the world's most financially successful and most respected companies. Every year since 2001, American Express has been listed in the top 25 in Interbrand's Best Global Brands survey. In 2009, the Interbrand study valued the brand at more than US$14 billion, achieving its goal of being the most valuable brand in the financial services category.

American Express was also recognised in 2009 as the Best Business Card Provider

1850	1896	1958	1965	1966	1978
American Express is established in New York and quickly becomes one of the most successful express delivery businesses in the US.	American Express opens its first offices in London. Mark Twain is among the first customers to visit the new office.	The charge card is first introduced.	American Express becomes the first company in the industry to safeguard Cardmembers against fraud.	American Express Corporate Card is first introduced.	American Express launches emergency card replacement, a benefit pioneered by American Express.

in the UK by Business Moneyfacts as well as third Best Large Company to Work For in the UK by The Sunday Times. American Express is also a member of Stonewall's Diversity Champions programme, which is Britain's good practice forum.

Recent Developments
American Express continues to expand its commitment to its customers through the development of industry-leading products that deliver greater value. In 2009, American Express and British Airways launched the British Airways American Express Corporate Card Plus in the UK. This is the latest addition to their successful co-brand programme that

offers mid-sized companies and their employees access to significant benefits.

Also in 2009, American Express won the right to sell payment solutions to the UK Public Sector as part of the Buying Solutions framework. In response, American Express launched a number of co-branded Government Procurement Cards (GPC) to cater for the sector's unique requirements. One product in particular, which is also the latest in American Express' product innovations, is the Defined Expense Card. With a fixed spending and time limit set at application, the card counts down its balance throughout its lifetime, reducing administrative and out-of-pocket expenses associated with ad hoc or project based business expenses.

Promotion
The longer term marketing strategy for GCC is to drive awareness of its B2B payment capabilities and comprehensive expense management solutions. Branching out, American Express is driving its focus on savings derived from consolidating business related expenses away from conventional forms of payment to the more efficient, cost saving B2B payment solutions. Complementing its traditional focus on travel and entertainment expenses, its solutions focus on holistic expense management, rather than the products alone.

Brand Values
American Express is committed to delivering its brand promise of World-Class Service and Personal Recognition. 'World-Class Service' recognises that American Express is a premium brand, delivers prestige and has global reach. 'Personal Recognition' conveys that American Express will treat customers as unique individuals.

Extraordinary customer care, peace of mind globally, superior business intelligence, and broad-based innovation further define the values of the brand.

americanexpress.co.uk

1991	2006	2008	2009
The celebrated Membership Rewards programme is launched.	The British Airways American Express Corporate Card is launched in the UK.	The Platinum Corporate Card is introduced in the UK.	The British Airways American Express Corporate Card Plus is launched in the UK. GCC wins the right to sell payment solutions to the UK public sector and launches co-brand Cards.

Autoglass® is a leading consumer automotive service brand, providing vehicle glass repairs and replacements to more than 1.5 million motorists every year. With the widest reaching auto glazing network in the UK and Ireland, Autoglass® has 109 branches nationwide and 1,300 mobile service units operating 24 hours a day, 365 days a year. Autoglass® is part of Belron® group, operating in 28 countries with a team of more than 10,000 highly skilled technicians.

Market

Over the last 20 years, windscreens have evolved to play an integral role in modern automotive design and today's cars typically use 20 per cent more glass than in the 1980s. Windscreens can also incorporate complex technology such as rain sensors, wire heating and satellite navigation components. The latest BMW 3-Series, for example, has 26 variations and the 5-Series has 21. Specialist skill is required to ensure they are repaired and replaced to the highest safety standards and that's where Autoglass® excels. The company is the UK's market-leading auto glazing expert.

Product

Quite simply, Autoglass® fixes broken vehicle glass on any make, model or age of vehicle. The company operates a 'Repair First' philosophy ensuring that wherever possible, its technicians will repair a chipped windscreen rather than replace it so that the existing seal doesn't have to be disturbed; a safe solution that saves time, money and is better for the environment.

If the damage is beyond repair, Autoglass® will replace the windscreen. It only uses glass manufactured to OEM standards, whether sourced from original manufacturers or other suppliers, ensuring that each replacement windscreen is as good as the original and a perfect fit for the vehicle. It also uses one of the quickest drying bonding systems for safety and customer convenience. As part of its commitment to the environment, Autoglass® reprocesses any laminate screens it removes.

Appointments can be made by phone or online and customers can choose to take their vehicle into their local branch or arrange for one of the company's 1,300 mobile technicians to come to a location of their choice.

Achievements

Thanks to its focus on delivering first-rate service, in 2009 Autoglass® topped its category at the inaugural Institute of Customer Service (ICS) Customer Satisfaction Awards. Autoglass® was also the top performer in the Services sector of the ICS UK Customer Satisfaction Index, which asked more than 24,000 people to rate how companies and organisations performed in 12 key public and private sectors.

1958	1982	1983	1990	1994	2002
FW Wilkinson is founded. In 1973 it becomes Autoglass Ltd and opens headquarters in Bedford.	Autoglass becomes part of Belron®, the world's largest vehicle glass repair and replacement company, extending its UK service into all five continents.	Autoglass Ltd merges with Bedfordshire-based Windshields Ltd and becomes Autoglass Windshields, rebranding to Autoglass in 1987.	The windscreen repair service is launched.	Autoglass® becomes a registered trademark after a seven year IP registration process.	Carglass Ireland rebrands to Autoglass®.

Other accolades include a number of independent awards, including two National Training Awards, a Glass Training Ltd (GTL) Commitment to Training Award and the Insurance Times Training Award. In addition, Autoglass® holds ISO 9001 quality certification and is exclusively recommended by the AA.

Because a windscreen accounts for 30 per cent of a vehicle's structural strength, Autoglass® places considerable emphasis on training its technicians to ensure every screen is fitted safely. It remains the only company in its industry to have achieved accredited status from Thatcham and the Institute of the Motor Industry (IMI) for its National Skills Centre in Birmingham and its Startline Induction and Repair training programmes.

Recent Developments

Autoglass® has demonstrated its commitment to raising standards within its sector by becoming the first to introduce the Automotive Technician Accreditation (ATA) scheme. Under the ATA, technicians work towards three accreditation levels dependent on knowledge, skills and experience, ultimately leading to Master Auto Glazing Technician status.

Autoglass® takes an innovative approach to delivering work of the highest standard. The newly introduced Ezi-wire, for example, helps technicians safely remove the glass from the windscreen and enables them to carry out their job both safely and professionally.

The Lil' Buddy, an innovative lifting and positioning device introduced in 2008, has delivered many benefits and has encouraged more women to consider a career as an auto glazing technician; Autoglass® now employs 11 female technicians.

During 2008, Autoglass® established a team of 'home workers' to provide greater flexibility for its customer contact centre workforce, enabling it to maintain call quality throughout peak periods of demand.

Promotion

Autoglass® became a household name in the 1990s after becoming the main sponsor of Chelsea Football Club. Since then it has invested in a number of high profile brand campaigns to ensure it remains at the forefront of motorists' minds.

In 2005 Autoglass® launched the Heroes radio campaign, using real Autoglass® technicians to explain the benefits of repairing windscreen chips. The campaign has become the most successful in Autoglass® history, helping to boost brand recognition and drive contacts via the call centre and website up by 20 per cent.

The campaign took double honours at the 2007 Media Week/GCap Radio Planning Awards, winning the award for Outstanding Campaign Above £250,000 and the Grand Prix for Most Outstanding Radio Planning. In 2008 it went on to win the Effectiveness Award for Campaign with Best Results.

In April 2008 the firm brought the award-winning radio concept to TV with a super-heavyweight campaign. The advert shows real life Autoglass® technician Gavin, the popular voice of the company's radio campaign, explaining the importance of getting windscreen chips repaired and highlighting the quality and safety benefits of the Autoglass® service. This campaign has continued into 2009, delivering record numbers of enquiries.

2009 has also seen Autoglass® further develop the Heroes concept with the firm's new van livery and website now featuring a variety of technicians from a range of regions across the country.

Brand Values

The Autoglass® vision is to be the natural choice through valuing its customers' needs and delivering world-class service. Its brand values are to be caring, expert, professional, innovative and to have integrity.

autoglass.co.uk

Things you didn't know about Autoglass®

Autoglass® doesn't just repair chipped windscreens; it has even repaired a chip on the viewing glass at the tiger compound at Glasgow Zoo.

The jingle used in the Heroes adverts has been translated into 12 different languages and is now used by Belron® subsidiaries in 18 countries.

During 2008, the Autoglass® 'Repair First' philosophy resulted in savings of more than 13,200 tonnes of CO_2 equivalent emissions and 5,200 tonnes of waste glass.

2005	2007	2008	2009
Autoglass® launches the Heroes radio campaign, using real Autoglass® technicians to explain the benefits of repairing windscreen chips.	Autoglass® becomes the first windscreen repair and replacement company to offer online booking at autoglass.co.uk.	Autoglass® launches its first ever TV adverts and Lil' Buddy is introduced into its workforce.	The Heroes campaign is extended to the website and outdoor advertising with the introduction of new van livery. Ezi-wire is also introduced into the Autoglass® workforce.

B&Q is the largest home improvement and garden centre retailer in the UK, with 331 stores and 33,500 employees. B&Q strives to be the first place people think of when they think of home improvement and the only place they need to go. The company is part of Kingfisher plc, Europe's leading home improvement retail group and the third largest in the world.

Market

The UK home improvement sector is worth £26 billion a year and B&Q is the market leader, with a 14.8 per cent share. B&Q has annual retail sales of £3.8 billion and an average of three million customers every week (Source: Kingfisher plc Annual Report 2008/09).

Key competitors include home improvement retailers such as Homebase, Wickes and Focus DIY, garden centre retailers such as Wyevale, and general retailers such as John Lewis, Marks & Spencer and Tesco.

Product

B&Q offers more than 40,000 home improvement and garden products for the homemaker, occasional to serious 'DIYer', and trade professional. The company also offers planning, design and fitting services.

B&Q own-brands include leading names such as Cooke & Lewis (bathrooms and kitchens), Colours (interior décor), Performance Power (tools) and entry-level brand, B&Q Value.

The company has recently launched One Planet Home, a range of 4,000 eco products that help customers reduce their environmental impact. Products include insulation, water saving showerheads, peat-free compost, water butts, clothes lines, LED Christmas lights, energy saving light bulbs and minimal VOC paint.

Achievements

B&Q takes a positive approach to the challenges that social responsibility presents, and has developed solutions that not only address its environmental and social impact but also add value to the business and build the brand's reputation.

The company's corporate social responsibility programme is spearheaded by a partnership with sustainability charity BioRegional. Launched in 2008, the three-year partnership will see B&Q move towards becoming a One Planet Living business, guided by the 10 principles of sustainability developed by BioRegional and WWF.

According to BioRegional, B&Q has made 'huge progress' in the past twelve months with achievements including an almost 50 per cent reduction in waste sent to landfill (two-year figure); a reduction in emissions from distribution, home deliveries and car travel; a 10 per cent reduction in water usage (two-year figure); a seven per cent reduction in fuel usage by retail logistics; and a 65 per cent reduction in the number of plastic bags used.

1969	1982	1990s		2001	2002
Richard Block and David Quayle found B&Q and open the first store in Southampton. Ten years later the company goes public and has 26 stores.	FW Woolworth acquires B&Q before a takeover by Paternoster (later known as Kingfisher). A period of growth sees B&Q operating 155 stores by 1984.	B&Q begins to move away from its depot format, opening its first B&Q Warehouse in 1995, in Aberdeen. The following year its first store in Taiwan opens.	Towards the end of the 1990s, acquisitions and mergers include NOMI (Poland's leading DIY retailer), Castorama (the French number one), and Dickens and Screwfix (the UK's largest hardware mail order business).	B&Q launches diy.com and opens its largest ever store; the Yangpu store is B&Q's third store in Shanghai and fourth in China.	B&Q opens its first store in the Republic of Ireland. The following year its 100th B&Q Warehouse opens in Northern Ireland.

The latest ad campaigns feature 'B&Qers' (B&Q staff) – including plumbing, gardening and design experts with long trade careers behind them – talking about their knowledge-base, how they can help, and their understanding of the challenges customers face.

B&Q is one of just a few organisations to hold the Carbon Trust Standard and in 2008, was awarded chain-of-custody certification for both the Forest Stewardship Council (FSC) and Programme for the Endorsement of Forest Certification (PEFC) schemes.

Furthermore, in 2008 B&Q was awarded the Gallup Great Workplace Award for employee engagement for a third year – the only UK-based organisation to win the award.

Recent Developments

B&Q has revitalised its online store to include nextday.diy.com, an exclusive service giving customers the opportunity to purchase from 12,000 products and have them delivered to their home the next working day. A new range of furniture is also set to launch online at diy.com.

In-store, an £18 million investment will provide new and improved kitchen, bathroom and bedroom showroom ranges over the coming months. A new selection of appliances will also go on sale, including top branded white goods.

B&Q will introduce seven new stores during 2009, including its greenest-ever venture which opened its doors in February. The store, in New Malden, is anticipated to have half the carbon footprint of equivalent sized B&Q sites and carries the company's biggest range of One Planet Home products.

The first B&Q One Planet Living Awards are also set to take place during 2009. The awards are open to organisations across the UK and Ireland that are working on projects to enhance the local community or reduce their impact on the environment. Forty winners will share a prize fund of £100,000, with the overall winner receiving £10,000 to help fund its project.

Promotion

With a history of classic advertising featuring the well-known strapline, 'You can do it if you B&Q it', today B&Q's promotional campaigns focus on two key marketing strengths: expertise and price.

The campaigns are backed by a price positioning that aims to set B&Q apart from its competitors, with the B&Q price promise assuring customers that they won't find a product cheaper elsewhere; if they do, B&Q will refund the difference and give the customer a further 10 per cent discount on the lower price.

In May 2009 B&Q announced its biggest price investment campaign to date, knocking £15 million off the price of thousands of products and launching its first customer privilege card to add further value to the shopping experience.

Brand Values

B&Q aims to be a company of 'friendly experts' in home and garden improvement, providing customers with expertise in a helpful, open and motivating way – as only B&Q people know how.

diy.com

Things you didn't know about B&Q

B&Q has featured in the Where Women Want to Work Top 50 listing in The Times for three years.

In February 2009, B&Q sold one million rolls of loft insulation for £1 each. The promotion will save 12,000 tonnes of CO_2 every year, which is equivalent to taking 4,800 cars off the road.

In a May bank holiday weekend, B&Q sells some 25 million plants, half a million bags of compost, 30,000 screwdrivers, 200,000 paint brushes, 15,000 'relaxer' chairs and 100,000 litres of decking stain.

B&Q is 40 years old in 2009; the company started with one store called Block & Quayle in Southampton in 1969.

2004	2006	2007	2009
B&Q announces a four-year partnership with the British Olympic Association to sponsor Team GB. In 2005, it sponsors solo around-the-world sailor, Ellen MacArthur.	B&Q launches an energy efficiency campaign to encourage its customers to make improvements around the home to save energy – and money.	B&Q relaunches its decorative brand, Colours, with a new range of paints, wallpapers, curtains and soft furnishings.	B&Q begins a one-year sponsorship of 4homes, Channel 4's property portfolio, and opens its most environmentally friendly store in New Malden, London.

Barclaycard is a global payment company delivering market leading levels of new technology and innovative business solutions. Founded in 1966, Barclaycard is one of the few businesses that facilitates the making, taking and managing of payments for companies of all sizes. It is one of Europe's leading commercial card issuers and one of the UK's largest payment processors.

Market

Barclaycard has a total of 11.9 million cardholders in the UK and 23.7 million worldwide. Barclaycard credit cards can be used to pay for goods and services in more than 28 million locations in more than 200 countries as well as 600,000 ATMs and banks worldwide.

Barclaycard, part of Barclays Global Retail Banking division, is a leading global payment business which helps consumers, retailers and businesses to make and accept payments flexibly, and to access short term credit when needed. The company is one of the pioneers of new forms of payments and is at the forefront of developing viable contactless and mobile phone payment schemes for today and cutting-edge forms of payment for the future.

Product

Barclaycard has more than 88,000 retailer/merchant relationships and processes card transactions for them. In 2008, just over 2.3 billion purchases were made with credit and debit cards through 184,000 of Barclaycard's customer outlets in the UK.

Barclaycard has 128,000 commercial customers, including the UK Government, who it has issued with over half a million credit and charge cards. Barclaycard is also Europe's number one issuer of Visa commercial cards and offers a range of payment solutions to meet a variety of business needs, including innovative and secure online payments.

Barclaycard's business presence is split into two business units, Barclaycard Commercial and Barclaycard Payment Acceptance.

Barclaycard Commercial provides; purchasing cards, corporate cards and award winning solutions such as Barclaycard Hotel Tracker and the Barclaycard Commercial Visa CodeSure Card. These solutions help it meet, and exceed, the needs of its customers and ensure that it gives as customisable an approach as possible. Barclaycard Commercial is also part of the framework to provide The Government Procurement Card. International solutions will be developed in 2010 to offer customers in areas of Western Europe the opportunity to

1966	1967	1977	1986	1990	1995
Barclaycard is launched – the first all-purpose credit card in Europe.	Barclaycard becomes the first ATM card used in the UK.	Barclaycard becomes a founder member of the international Visa system and launches the business element as the Barclaycard brand.	Barclaycard launches the UK's first credit card loyalty scheme, Profile Points.	Barclaycard MasterCard launches.	With the launch of Barclaycard Netlink, Barclaycard becomes the first UK credit card company to have a presence on the internet.

take advantage of the benefits of a Barclaycard commercial charge or purchasing card.

Barclaycard Payment Acceptance continues to offer market leading solutions and technologies. Accepting both credit and debit cards, Barclaycard caters for all segment needs. Barclaycard Payment Acceptance takes payments in multiple currencies and caters for all businesses from market traders to conglomerates. New terminal solutions now accept contactless cards and integrate with online shopping carts and other e-commerce solutions.

Achievements

Barclaycard has been recognised industry wide for making and taking payments as well as for advertising, design and innovation, winning many business nominations and awards.

In 2008, it won both the Best Technology Innovation of the Year and the Best Industry Innovation of the Year with Barclaycard's contactless technology.

In 2009, it won Best Business Travel Product for its Hotel Tracker product at the Business Travel Awards and at the Oscards Awards 2009, it received the Most Innovative Commercial Card accolade for the Barclaycard Commercial Visa CodeSure card. Also in 2009, it was the winner of the Best Use of Visa Innovation for the Barclaycard Commercial Visa CodeSure card at the Visa Europe Member Awards.

For 2010, Barclaycard has been shortlisted for Best Business Card Programme and Best Industry Innovation of the year for the Becta programme at The Card Awards.

Recent Developments

Barclaycard is at the forefront of promoting contactless technology. New and innovative card readers let customers pay for products that cost under £15 in less than a second using a traditional card or even a mobile phone. As well as terminals being enhanced to meet the increasing demands of contactless technology, Barclaycard has also been a pioneer of new contactless platforms which are set to revolutionise the world of global payments.

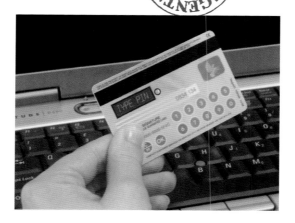

Barclaycard is continuing to push boundaries in innovation to meet the needs and demands of all sizes of businesses. For the first time ever, Barclaycard implemented Visa CodeSure technology in a business card programme. This means that a keypad, an LCD screen and a battery with a three-year lifespan are all incorporated into a standard payment card. This card significantly reduces levels of fraud.

Promotion

Barclaycard has moved away from traditional product advertising placing an emphasis on the core brand message as well as functional excellence.

Barclaycard has successfully launched contactless technology in traditional and digital media channels. The 2009 'Waterslide' campaign, which was recently voted as one of the top ads of the decade, raised the profile of Barclaycard as a payments brand as well as educating customers about contactless technology. The new advertising campaign for 2010 looks at building on the success of the previous year with an emphasis placed on Barclaycard being a global payments brand.

The Barclaycard 'Waterslide Extreme' iPhone game became the number one free download in 57 countries within two weeks of launching. It has had more than seven million downloads to date worldwide and is the most successful free branded app ever in the history of iTunes. Movement into additional services such as music payment has also further highlighted the total brand value.

Barclaycard also promoted the brand in the US for the first time, with a promotional campaign in Times Square and the re-branding of partner cards to show the Barclaycard logo.

Brand Values

Barclaycard has always been a customer centric organisation aiming to provide confidence, convenience and control in financial services. The brand is focused on constantly improving by thinking ahead, so that smart and innovative solutions can be designed to suit the ever changing needs of all customer segments. Barclaycard's goal is to ensure that customer experiences are as seamless and easy as possible through excellent customer service and simple payment solutions.

barclaycard.co.uk/business

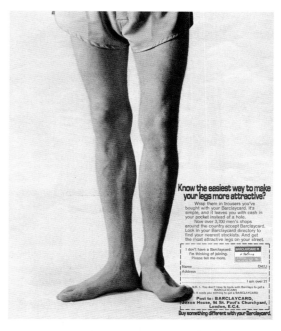

Things you didn't know about Barclaycard

One in five UK credit cards is a Barclaycard.

Barclaycard has issued over four million contactless credit cards in the UK.

Barclaycard's first foray overseas was in Germany in 1991. Today, Barclaycard International operates in more than 60 countries across Europe, the US, Africa, Asia and the Caribbean.

Barclaycard staff have always been willing to be hands on when required. In 1969, head of marketing, John Lawson's legs were used in a photo shoot when the photographer decided that the legs of the model employed for the shoot were too good and wanted some more ordinary legs. All the men present were ordered to drop their trousers and Lawson was selected.

2007	2008	2009	
Barclaycard launches the first contactless card.	Barclaycard launches a new visual identity which includes redesigning the current card range as well as introducing a new multicoloured logo and typeface.	Barclaycard launches the first ever Visa CodeSure card, a card which has an LCD screen, keypad and battery and will help minimise fraud for card-not present transactions.	Also in 2009, Barclaycard moves into music sponsorship and ticketing with the launch of Barclaycard Unwind.

BBC

The BBC is the world's best-known broadcasting brand and today's digital BBC plays a key civic and cultural role in UK life. As an organisation funded by the universal licence fee, the BBC's mission in meeting its public service remit is to inform, educate and entertain. BBC content is watched and listened to via 10 UK-wide network television services, 10 national and 47 Nations & Regions radio stations, and can also be accessed online and via the Red Button.

Market

Broadcasting in the UK is in the middle of a radical transformation, courtesy of digital technology. Around 21 million households already receive digital multichannel television and radio services from a range of suppliers such as Sky, Virgin Media, Freeview, Tiscali and BT Vision (Source: BARB) and 61 per cent of homes have a broadband connection (Source: Screen Digest). By 2012, every home in the UK will receive digital-only television. The original terrestrial public service broadcasters – BBC, ITV, Channel 4 and Five – are now multiplatform, multimedia brands operating 24 hours a day, seven days a week. The BBC reaches the vast majority of the UK audience.

The BBC licence fee makes a significant contribution to UK investment in the creative industries; more than one-third goes straight to external contracts including investing in independent production. Each year, the licence fee adds £6.5 billion to the UK economy (Source: PricewaterhouseCoopers). The BBC is currently increasing its focus on partnerships with the rest of the UK media in order to share the benefits of the licence fee. For example, in 2008 the BBC and ITV agreed to explore sharing regional news footage and premises where appropriate.

Product

The BBC is thought of primarily as a creator of high-quality content and programming. The product offering is a complex mix with 19 major television, radio and online public service brands.

Today's BBC television and radio brands, particularly BBC One, BBC Two and BBC Radio's 1, 2, 3, 4 and 5 live, attract large terrestrial audiences. These channels are complemented by digital brands, BBC Three, BBC Four, BBC HD, BBC News, BBC Parliament, CBBC, CBeebies and BBC Alba on television (supplemented by BBC Red Button) and BBC Radio 1Xtra, BBC 5 live sports extra, BBC 6 Music, BBC Radio 7 and the Asian Network on digital radio. The online destination bbc.co.uk is also a recognised brand leader in the UK.

The BBC's Nations & Regions services for England, Scotland, Wales and Northern Ireland produce original content for UK audiences as well as extensive local programming. To ensure it embraces talent from across the UK, the BBC is developing a new creative hub in Salford; by 2016, 50 per cent of production will originate outside London.

The BBC actively develops new talent and supports training opportunities. BBC Blast is a youth creativity service that aims to inspire

1922	1927	1932	1936	1953	1960
British Broadcasting Company (BBC) is formed by a group of leading wireless manufacturers.	The BBC gains its first Royal Charter, ensuring its independence from government, political and shareholder interference.	The BBC moves to the world's first purpose-built radio production centre, Broadcasting House in Portland Place, London.	The BBC opens the world's first regular service of high definition television from Alexandra Palace, north London.	On 2nd June, around 22 million people watch the Queen's coronation live on the BBC – a historic event that changes the course of television history.	BBC Television Centre opens – the world's first purpose-built television building. Authorisation is given for a new channel and BBC Two launches in 1964.

13-19 year-olds through online resources, television and face-to-face activity. For adults, BBC Raw is an interactive site to help independent learners improve their basic skills.

The BBC is required to generate additional revenues to reinvest in its core public service. BBC Worldwide, for example, sells on programmes and footage and is the UK's number one international television channel broadcaster.

Achievements
In 2008/09 the BBC received more than 150 programme-related awards across television, radio and new media. These included 30 BAFTAs, 31 Royal Television Society (RTS) awards, 20 Sony Golds for radio and two Webby awards for its online service. BBC iPlayer has gone from strength to strength since its launch, winning 20 marketing and technology awards.

The BBC takes its operational responsibilities seriously and in 2008, was awarded Gold status in the Business in the Community Corporate Responsibility Index.

Recent Developments
The BBC was granted a new 10-year Royal Charter at the end of 2006 that defined expectations of the corporation in a digital, on-demand world; audiences increasingly expect to access programme content 'anytime,

anywhere, anyhow'. In response, BBC iPlayer was launched at the end of 2007 – a free service letting viewers in the UK catch up on more than 400 hours of BBC programming. Furthermore, Freesat launched in May 2008 as a national free-to-view satellite service with ITV, offering up to 200 channels, full interactivity and high definition broadcasts.

Promotion
The trademark block letters of the BBC master brand are associated worldwide with high-quality programmes and services. Subsidiary brand identities for channels and services are regularly refreshed to reflect market changes and audience research. In 2008, the English Regions brands were aligned with a contemporary new look and feel to ensure greater consistency and increased audience relevance.

The BBC aims to help its audiences find content they will enjoy by producing integrated communications campaigns. In 2008, one of its biggest campaigns centred on the Olympic Games and specifically targeted younger audiences. Working with Gorillaz creators, Damon Albarn and Jamie Hewlett, an animated campaign was produced based on the Chinese folklore, 'Monkey: Journey to the West'. The

trails generated close to 50 press articles carrying 100 visible key messages and achieved 1.3 million hits on YouTube.

Designed to build excitement and anticipation, the BBC One Christmas campaign featured Wallace & Gromit and comprised a specially created set of BBC One idents as well as an online game, mobile downloads and preview clips. 'Wallace & Gromit – A Matter of Loaf and Death' was 2008's highest rating TV programme with a 53 per cent audience share, peaking at 14.4 million.

In addition, events and new technologies are used to further engage with audiences. In 2008, BBC Radio 1's Big Weekend festival featured acts such as Madonna and Usher and was attended by 30,000 people. A unique online application gave those who couldn't attend the festival a link to a secret web page, where an exclusive video of The Fratellis performing could be accessed. The application reached 60,000 unique users. The event was also broadcast on the BBC's Big Screens in key locations across the UK.

Brand Values
The BBC exists to serve the public interest and through its mission to inform, educate and entertain, must promote six public purposes as outlined in its Charter. The BBC seeks to be independent and impartial in all of its content.

bbc.co.uk

1967	1990s	2007	2008
Colour broadcasts begin on BBC Two and are extended to BBC One in 1969.	BBC's online transformation begins as bbc.co.uk goes live in 1991. The decade also sees the launch of BBC Radio 5 and the forerunners to digital TV channels BBC Three and BBC Four.	Digital expansion continues with the launch of BBC iPlayer, a service letting people catch up on BBC TV and Radio they've missed.	The first full digital switchover takes place in Whitehaven. BBC Alba and BBC HD are launched.

Part of

The BMRB (British Market Research Bureau) Omnibus is a market leader and one of the most established omnibus services in the country. Its clients include Government departments, media owners, high street outlets, food retailers, consumer goods manufacturers as well as financial companies. Omnibus research surveys carry more than one client and are set up to run to a specified schedule with consistent samples.

Market

With recent consolidations, there are now only three market research companies in the UK able to offer Online, Face to Face, and Telephone Omnibus surveys. These players, namely Ipsos MORI, GfK NOP and TNS/BMRB Omnibus, are able to run short questionnaires to large-scale sample groups, achieving reliable results with a fast turnaround. Data on market sizing, awareness, brand trackers and attitudes can be gathered.

Product

The BMRB Omnibus is a weekly survey which interviews 2,000 different adults, Face to Face every week. The sample is representative of the population of Great Britain by age, sex, social grade and region. It is regarded as being the most accurate survey available for the price in the country – hence its use by so many social research clients.

The BMRB Omnibus team also manages a full range of projects across telephone and online methodologies and can provide a comprehensive global omnibus service.

The BMRB Omnibus is used to place questionnaires for the Target Group Index, the largest independent survey encompassing the use of products, services and media consumption.

BMRB Omnibus prides itself on delivering high quality research and is committed to continually improving and maintaining standards. It is independently audited twice-yearly by Marketing Quality Assurance (MQA) and is certified as working to the ISO 9001:

2008, and ISO 20252 the new international standard for market research.

This policy on quality enables the organisation to promote and support a management system and environment that is designed to continually improve performance, increase efficiency and share BMRB Omnibus' expertise internally.

Achievements

The most recent full-year data shows the BMRB Face to Face and Telephone Omnibus surveys have 24 per cent market share – one of the leaders in the market.

The BMRB Omnibus Consumer Confidence Survey is provided free of charge to BMRB Omnibus clients and to other companies in the WPP Group (of which BMRB Omnibus is a part). Thus it is used for forecasting by major ad agencies, consultancies and other market research companies in the Group. In addition, some of BMRB Omnibus' clients use the Consumer Confidence as classifications for their own tracking studies.

Recent Developments

Following the acquisition of TNS by the WPP group, BMRB has been merged into TNS with the BMRB Omnibus becoming part of the TNS Omnibus department – making it the largest in the UK.

BMRB Omnibus continues as a brand within TNS with its own portfolio of blue chip clients.

Promotion

Omnibus research is one of the most straightforward market research techniques which can be commissioned by clients with a basic understanding of research. Once a

1933	1934	1939	1969	1987	1997
The British Market Research Bureau is set up, making it the longest established research agency in Britain.	One of the earliest and largest studies on newspaper readership for the Daily Herald is carried out.	BMRB is one of the first agencies to conduct major surveys for Government, including a survey for the Ministry of Food to monitor wartime rationing.	BMRB develops the Target Group Index (TGI), which has since become a standard trading currency for the UK media sector.	BMRB joins WPP Group plc.	It becomes the first to conduct Multi-Media Computer Aided Personal Interviewing (MM CAPI) nationally.

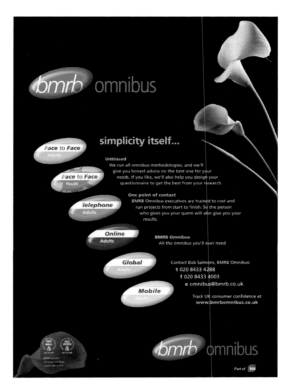

client has used an omnibus methodology it tends to stay in their mind as a potential information gathering option. Therefore, the BMRB Omnibus promotional strategy has two strands. Firstly, to educate non-users about the opportunities provided by omnibus research and secondly, to remain front of mind amongst past and present users.

The main source of promotion is via marketing and research trade press advertising as well as mailshots of the Omnipresence newsletter. This publication contains case studies, product information, ratecard costs and contact details.

Another key promotional tool is the BMRB Omnibus website. The main aim of which is to provide information on how omnibus surveys work and what they can do. Information is presented in an accessible way, free of 'research jargon'.

Brand Values

BMRB Omnibus aims to be the 'blue chip' provider in the marketplace. It strives to achieve this by ensuring that all the surveys it runs conform to the highest possible research standards.

The organisation's culture is client-focused and is comprised of highly trained executives with high quality standards. By offering the full suite of omnibus services and having executives who are able to offer the best possible advice, the BMRB Omnibus strives to provide the 'highest quality' unbiased omnibus service available. It also seeks to be the 'provider of choice' for the media and social research sectors by providing added value and specialist expertise in these areas.

bmrb-omnibus.co.uk

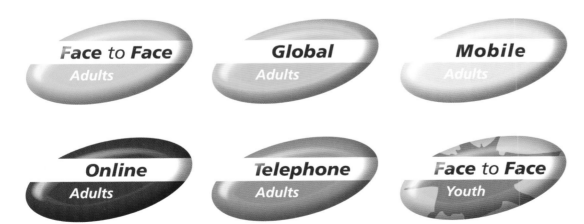

	2005	**2007**	**2009**
Also in 1997, BMRB conducts its first web-based research project – a readership survey for The Lancet.	BMRB wins two of the four BMRA (British Market Research Association) Research Business Effectiveness Awards.	BMRB and Henley Centre HeadlightVision launch the Institute for Insight in the Public Services (IIPS).	BMRB Omnibus is merged into TNS.

Things you didn't know about BMRB Omnibus

Research from the BMRB Omnibus has been used as admissible evidence in court cases.

Data from the BMRB Omnibus can be merged with the Target Group Index to give comprehensive information on the usage of products and media services as well as media consumption.

Every other major omnibus supplier has sub-contracted work to the BMRB Omnibus.

The BMRB Omnibus works to the highest possible quality controls available in the research industry.

BSI Group is a global independent business services organisation delivering standards-based solutions to help organisations improve their performance, manage risk and make their operations sustainable. BSI does this through the development of standards; the assessment and certification of management systems and medical devices; testing and certification of products and services; software solutions; and training services.

Market

BSI works with clients operating in a myriad of sectors, including communications, construction, engineering, electronics, retail, food and drink, healthcare, agriculture, consumer goods, banking and the public sector. In order to compete and inspire their customers' trust, BSI's clients – which include 75 per cent of FTSE 100 companies, 42 per cent of Fortune 500 companies as well as 42 per cent of companies listed on the Hang Seng – rely on BSI's independence and expertise in delivering standards-based solutions, which cover every aspect of the modern economy. BSI's certification mark and Kitemark® are respectively seen as one of the best quality assurance marks and safety marks to be gained.

Product

BSI's standards-based solutions help organisations to successfully implement best practice, manage business-critical decisions, mitigate risk, increase business performance, achieve operational excellence and make businesses sustainable.

BSI is the UK's National Standards Body and at the heart of its work is the development of standards which help make life more efficient, easier, fairer and safer – making the world a better place. BSI works with businesses, consumers and the Government to represent a spectrum of interests and to make sure that British, European and international standards are useful, relevant and authoritative. Standards are developed and regularly updated by external experts through a process of consensus, with the goal of establishing blueprints for excellence.

BSI is also one of the world's largest certification bodies for assessing and certifying management systems. It has certified 68,000 locations in more than 120 countries and is market leader in the UK and North America. BSI's testing and certification services ensure that products and services meet safety and performance requirements – from vehicle bodywork repairs to fire extinguishers and respiratory equipment. This work is exemplified by BSI's Kitemark®, one of the UK's most trusted quality marks. BSI also provides CE marking for products that need to comply with European Directives in order for them to be sold in the EU.

BSI's software solutions help organisations manage their governance, risk and compliance.

Entropy Software™ provides auditable solutions to improve environmental, social and economic performance.

The healthcare and medical devices sector is an important part of BSI's business. As a highly respected, world-class Notified Body, BSI is dedicated to providing stringent regulatory and quality management reviews and product certification for medical device manufacturers around the world.

Achievements

BSI employs more than 2,300 staff and in 2008 generated a turnover of £202.3 million. It services clients in 120 countries and assists nations such

1901	1903	1929	1953	1979	1992
BSI Group is founded as the Engineering Standards Committee (ESC). One of the first standards to be published is to reduce the number of sizes of tramway rails.	The Kitemark® is first registered as a trademark.	The ESC is awarded a Royal Charter and in 1931, the name British Standards Institution (BSI) is adopted.	In the post-war era, more demand for consumer standardisation work leads to the introduction of the Kitemark® for domestic products.	BS 5750, now known as ISO 9001, is introduced to help companies build quality and safety into the way they work. The Certification mark is also introduced.	BSI publishes the world's first environmental management systems standard, BS 7750 – now known as ISO 14001.

as Albania, Serbia and Sierra Leone in developing their emerging standardisation infrastructures.

BSI produces an average of 2,000 standards annually and has recently published the world's first standard for risk management, BS 31100, and business continuity management, BS 25999. The internationally recognised quality management systems standards, ISO 9001, started life at BSI in 1979 as BS 5750. ISO 9001 is recognised as the world's most successful standard having been adopted by more than 982,000 organisations in 176 countries. The world's most widely accepted environmental standard, ISO 14001, started in a similar way.

BSI has won a number of recent awards including, in 2008, a Continuity, Insurance & Risk (CIR) Award for Industry Advancement for its work in developing BS 25999, and Fleet News Awards' 'Best Safety Initiative' for the Thatcham BSI Kitemark® scheme for vehicle bodywork repair. In 2009, BSI's Kitemark® was also recognised as a Business Superbrand in its own right, for the third consecutive year.

Recent Developments
In 2007 BSI and Thatcham developed PAS 125, a specification for vehicle bodywork repair, with the related Thatcham BSI Kitemark® scheme providing independent

certification that a bodyshop is competent to safely repair vehicles. Another automotive sector development is the Kitemark® scheme for Garage Services which ensures that the standards of PAS 80, for the servicing and repair of vehicles, are met and maintained.

BS 8901, the world's first standard for sustainable event management, was also published in 2007. This standard now forms part of London 2012's sustainability guidelines and was implemented by organisers of the United Nations Conference on Climate Change in Copenhagen (COP15) in December 2009.

Following the wide take-up of PAS 2050, a standard methodology for the measurement of the embodied greenhouse gases in products and services, BSI began development in 2009 of a new standard designed to enable a consistent and comparable approach to carbon neutrality claims. The Department of Energy and Climate Change and household names such as Marks & Spencer, Eurostar and The Co-operative, are involved and PAS 2060 is expected to help restore consumer confidence in the credibility of carbon neutrality claims and encourage increased action on climate change.

BSI is contributing to the development of the world's first brand valuation standard – ISO/DIS 10668. It specifies the requirements for procedures and methods of monetary

brand value measurement. Aimed at both brand consultants, and finance and marketing professionals, publication of the final standard is expected in summer 2010.

Promotion
In May 2009, BSI created the 'one BSI' vision, in place of its existing three-divisional structure and associated sub-branding. BSI's activities are now sold and branded under the BSI master brand identity.

In 2009, BSI overhauled its global recruitment communications in order to convey the variety and versatility of careers at BSI. The new 'employer' brand identity, BSI Careers, has been implemented globally with a unified logo, graphical language, tone of voice and strapline which ensures consistency and aligns the employer brand to the overall BSI brand.

The majority of BSI's marketing activities are now delivered electronically and in 2009 BSI developed a presence on YouTube and social networking sites including Twitter. BSI's business magazine, Business Standards, also has a dedicated online presence reaching a wider business community than its 92,000 print readership can reach. Public relations also plays a key role in promoting BSI activities.

Brand Values
Integrity, innovation and independence are the values at the core of the BSI brand, supporting the organisation as it strives towards its vision of inspiring confidence and delivering assurance to all customers. BSI continually endeavours to deliver its brand values, with the aim of building a powerful, globally recognised brand, satisfying the needs of all stakeholders.

bsigroup.com

2006
BSI acquires German certification company NIS ZERT, UK and Canadian-based software solutions company Entropy International Ltd and Australia's Benchmark Certification Pty Ltd.

2007
BSI publishes the world's first standard for business continuity management, BS 25999-2, and BS 8901 for sustainable event management.

2009
BSI acquires the Supply Chain Security Division of First Advantage Corp in USA, Certification International S.r.l, an Italian Certification company, and the

German healthcare certification and testing company EUROCAT. Also in 2009, BSI abolishes its divisional structure to create a single unified BSI brand.

BT operates in over 170 countries and is one of the world's leading communications services companies. It is a major supplier of networked IT services to Government departments and multinational companies. BT is the UK's largest communications service provider to consumer and business markets and is made up primarily of four customer-facing lines of business: BT Retail, BT Global Services, Openreach, and BT Wholesale.

Market

BT operates in a thriving, multi-trillion pound industry that spans the whole world. In recent years the global communications market has been focused on convergence, whereby the boundaries between telcos, IT companies, software businesses, hardware manufacturers and broadcasters have become intertwined to create a new communications industry – driven by the relentless evolution of technology and insatiable customer demand for innovative communications solutions.

Product

BT provides a wide range of world-class communications solutions for all types of business organisation – from sole trader start-ups to multi-site global enterprises. The company's vision is to be dedicated to helping customers thrive in a changing world, through easy to use products and services that are tailored to their needs.

For business customers, traditional products such as calls, analogue/digital lines and private circuits are combined with products and services such as networking and network management, broadband, mobility, CRM, applications management and hosting as well as desktop services.

In the UK, BT Business customers have benefited from a number of firsts in the communications market. BT was the first provider to launch free mobile broadband as part of an all-inclusive offer and the BT Business One Plan was the UK's first

'triple play' bundled package for broadband, fixed-line and mobile services. Meanwhile, BT Tradespace was the first ever business social networking site to launch in the UK, helping companies interact with their customers as well as each other. As a result, more than one million small businesses in the UK rely on BT Business to deliver their communications services.

For larger enterprises, governments and multinational corporations, BT Global Services provides networked IT products, services and solutions. This includes a range of specialist network-centric propositions such as high performance networking, applications management, outsourcing and managed services. In September 2009, BT Global Services was rated the 'global leader of global leaders' in the networked IT services market by leading industry analysts, Ovum.

1984	1991	2003	2005	2006	2008
BT is privatised making it the only state-owned telecommunications company to be privatised in Europe.	British Telecom is restructured and relaunches as BT.	BT unveils its current corporate identity and brand values, reflecting the aspirations of a technologically innovative future.	Following the Telecommunications Strategic Review (TSR), BT signs legally-binding undertakings with Ofcom to help create a better regulatory framework.	Openreach launches and is responsible for managing the UK access network on behalf of the telecommunications industry.	BT becomes the Official Communications Services Partner and a Sustainability Partner for the London 2012 Olympic and Paralympic Games.

Achievements

BT has successfully transformed itself in recent times. It has evolved from being a supplier of telephony services to become a leading provider of innovative communications products, services, solutions and entertainment products. BT's business customers range from multinational, multi-site corporations to SMEs and start-ups.

More than 80 per cent of the FTSE 100 and 40 per cent of Fortune 500 companies rely on BT for networking, applications and system integration. The National Health Service, Procter & Gamble, PepsiCo, BMW, Emirates, Fiat, Microsoft, Philips, Unilever and the Colombian Government are just some of the organisations working with BT to maximise the power of networked IT and communications services.

BT has been a driving force behind the success of 'Broadband Britain'. Thanks to the company's investment, nearly every home in Britain now has access to broadband and in September 2009, BT announced plans to more than double the availability of its fastest fibre broadband service. The £1.5 billion programme is the UK's largest ever investment in fibre-based, super-fast broadband and will deliver a range of services for customers, giving them top speeds of up to 100 Mb/s with the potential for speeds of more than 1,000 Mb/s in the future.

BT has a Royal Warrant to supply communications, broadband and network services for Her Majesty the Queen. In 2009, The Sunday Times ranked BT as one of the UK's top 10 Best Green Companies, for its achievements in carbon reduction and corporate social responsibility. BT is developing the UK's biggest corporate wind power project outside the energy sector. BT Carbon Clubs are encouraging employees to raise awareness of how energy savings can be made at work, in homes, schools and in the wider community. Its solar energy installations at its US headquarters in California has also won BT awards further afield.

Recent Developments

In recent years, BT has transformed itself from a narrowband company to a broadband one. It has now embarked on the next stage of its transformation, moving from being a hardware-based business to becoming a software-driven company. This means instantly delivering new software services for customers at the push of a button rather than through a process involving screwdrivers, rewiring and customer visits. This will dramatically increase the speed at which BT can design new services and deliver them to its customers.

BT also continues to roll out its 21st Century Network (21CN), the world's most advanced next generation network.

Promotion

BT is the Official Communications Services Partner for The London 2012 Olympic and Paralympic Games, and a Sustainability Partner. This puts BT at the heart of the biggest event the UK will stage in the next decade. BT is integral in helping London to stage a 'Digital Games', and is responsible for providing key communications services to the operational workforce and at Games venues. In addition, BT has exclusive marketing rights to use the London 2012 brand within its category.

In October 2009, BT held its third annual Small Business Week, championing commercial, industry and government support for the country's 4.7 million-plus smaller enterprises. In partnership with the British Chambers of Commerce, Business Link, the ACCA, NatWest, Growing Business and everywoman, the week of events included roundtable discussions, web seminars and advice clinics all dedicated to supporting local and home-based small businesses across the UK.

Brand Values

BT's corporate identity defines the kind of company it is today – and the one it needs to be in the future. Central to that identity is a commitment to create ways to help customers thrive in a changing world. To do this, BT focuses on 'living' its brand values which are as

follows: Trustworthy – doing what it says it will; Helpful – working as one team; Inspiring – creating new possibilities; Straightforward – making things clear; Heart – believing in what it does.

The BT strapline – Bringing it all together – aims to convey leadership in the way in which BT enables global business customers to profit from convergence.

bt.com

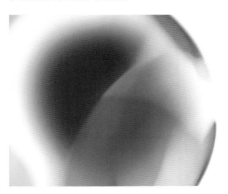

Things you didn't know about BT

Thanks to BT, more homes in Britain now have access to broadband than have access to mains water.

More than 40 per cent of Fortune 500 companies are BT customers.

The world's top 10 global stock exchanges depend on BT infrastructure.

BT Conferencing is the number one provider in Europe; the use of conferencing has reduced BT's own carbon footprint by 100,000 tonnes of CO_2.

BT's partnership with UNICEF is bringing education, technology and communication skills to children from poor socio-economic backgrounds in Brazil, South Africa and China.

2009

BT becomes a Premier Partner of the Cultural Olympiad with the launch of the National Portrait Gallery/BT Road to 2012 project – commissioning 100 brand new photographs over the next three years showing the people behind the London 2012 Olympic and Paralympic Games.

Also in 2009, the BT Tower was updated with a 360 degree LED screen wrapping the 36th and 37th floors. This giant information band launched to celebrate 1,000 days until the opening ceremony of the London 2012 Olympic Games, with a pyrotechnic display from the BT Tower.

Cadbury

Cadbury is the UK's leading confectionery company and holds number one or two positions in over 20 of the world's 50 biggest confectionery markets. Its origins can be traced back to 1824 when John Cadbury opened a shop in Birmingham selling tea and cocoa. Since then Cadbury has expanded its business through a programme of organic and acquisition growth and now creates brands people love in over 60 countries.

Market

Cadbury is a strong pure play confectionery company with excellent market positions. Its global business is split into seven business units with Britain and Ireland generating 23 per cent of Cadbury's revenue and North America being responsible for a further 23 per cent.

It has the largest and most broadly spread emerging markets business of any confectionery company with a strong presence in India, the Middle East and Africa as well as South America. Its business in emerging markets has grown from less than 20 per cent of its turnover in 2002 to around 38 per cent today and this is expected to grow to 45 per cent by the end of 2013.

Product

Cadbury has 13 focus brands globally including Cadbury Dairy Milk, Flake, Creme Egg and Green & Black's in chocolate; Trident, Dentyne,

Hollywood and Bubbaloo in gum; and Halls, Cadbury Eclairs, Bassett's and The Natural Confectionery Co. in candy.

Available in 33 countries worldwide, Cadbury Dairy Milk is the company's flagship

brand and is at the heart of its success. When Cadbury Dairy Milk chocolate was first introduced in the early 1900s, it made an immediate impact quickly becoming the market leader; and this success story continues today with it being the biggest confectionery brand in the UK.

Achievements

Cadbury has won a number of awards in recent years. In December 2009 it was voted in the top five of Management Today's 'Most Admired Companies' survey and also received the top Community and Environmental Responsibility award. The business was also named as one of the Top 50 Great Places to Work in the UK and was also listed in a number of other markets including Ireland, Portugal, Brazil, Colombia, Peru and Venezuela in this well known annual survey.

Among its other accolades in 2009 was the Editor's Choice award in the CorpComms

1824	1847	1879	1905	1919	1969
John Cadbury opens his shop in Birmingham. Apart from selling tea and coffee, he also sells hops, mustard and a new sideline – cocoa and drinking chocolate.	John Cadbury is joined by his brother, Benjamin and Cadbury Brothers becomes the family business.	Having outgrown the Bridge Street factory, the Cadbury Brothers move their manufacturing operations to Bournville.	Cadbury's Dairy Milk is introduced with a new recipe using fresh milk. By the mid 1920s it is market leader.	Cadbury Brothers merges with JS Fry & Sons of Bristol.	Cadbury Group Ltd merges with Schweppes Ltd and Cadbury Schweppes plc is listed on the London Stock Exchange.

awards for its groundbreaking Cadbury Dairy Milk going Fairtrade campaign. It also received Business in the Community's Community Mark and was voted 2009 Green Supplier of the Year in The Grocer awards. Cadbury's UK marketing director Phil Rumbol was also ranked number one in Campaign's Top 10 Marketing Directors for 2009.

Recent Developments

Cadbury views corporate social responsibility and sustainability as key to its future success and has embedded sustainability commitments into its business strategy.

In January 2008 the Cadbury Cocoa Partnership was established with the United Nations Development Programme, local governments, NGOs, farmers and communities. It aims to secure the economic, social and environmental sustainability of around one million cocoa farmers and their communities in Ghana,

record of community involvement, volunteering and support at the Sydney 2000 Olympic Games, the Manchester Commonwealth Games in 2002 and the Melbourne Commonwealth Games in 2006.

Cadbury's share of profits from the single have gone to the charity CARE International, one of the Cadbury Cocoa Partners, to fund education programmes in Ghana's cocoa growing communities.

Cadbury Wispa was re-launched in 2008 after consumers campaigned online to bring it back; followed by a campaign to bring back Wispa Gold, which was then launched for a limited period in September 2009. The Wispa Facebook group now has more than 700, 000 fans. Approximately 65 million Wispa bars and 20 million Wispa Gold bars were sold in 2009 alone. This made Wispa the number one selling chocolate bar in the UK for 2009.

Brand Values

Cadbury is guided by a 'Performance Driven, Values Led' culture. The company's values are performance, quality, respect, integrity and

India, Indonesia and the Caribbean through a £45 million investment set to run for 10 years.

Cadbury launched Fairtrade certified Cadbury Dairy Milk bars in the UK in July 2009 making it the first mass market chocolate bar to gain certification from the Fairtrade Foundation.

The company is extending its commitment to Fairtrade by confirming that new markets – Canada, Australia, New Zealand and Japan – are to receive Fairtrade certification for its Cadbury Dairy Milk brand by early 2010. This commitment will quadruple the amount of Fairtrade cocoa bought from Ghana under Fairtrade terms in 2010 and see around 350 million bars of Fairtrade Cadbury Dairy Milk sold globally.

Cadbury is proud to be the Official Treat Provider to the 2012 Olympic and Paralympic Games. The company already has a successful

Promotion

The world of brand building is undergoing a revolution and Cadbury is right at the forefront, both on and offline. Today's brands are built in places beyond our TV screens and Cadbury is leading the way in opening doors for consumers to interact with its brands. A great example is the creation of Cadbury Dairy Milk's 'A Glass and a Half Full Productions' which has set a new dynamic in advertising. The first offering, Gorilla, which didn't actually feature chocolate, became the most watched advert ever and swept the board at the advertising Oscars.

Gorilla has since been followed by Trucks, Eyebrows and in 2009 the launch of Cadbury's first ever music video – Zingolo – by Ghanaian music superstar, Tinny. The video, which was also shown as a TV ad, is a five minute celebration of Ghana and Cadbury's move to Fairtrade.

responsibility. Cadbury believes that 'doing good is good for business' and this, inspired by its founders, is still at the heart of its brands today.

cadbury.com

Things you didn't know about Cadbury

Cadbury Dairy Milk was first produced in Bournville in 1905.

A bar of Cadbury Dairy Milk is sold around the world every two seconds.

The largest chocolate bar in the world – a giant block nearly 9ft high, 4ft wide and weighing 1.1 tonnes – was made by Cadbury Dairy Milk in 1998.

The total weight of Cadbury Dairy Milk produced in one year is equivalent to 51,641 minis or 7,230 Indian elephants.

In 24 hours, Cadbury's Bournville factory can produce 1.2 million Cadbury Creme Eggs, 5.5 million blocks of chocolate and 17 million Cadbury Dairy Milk Buttons.

1989	2002	2003	2009
Bassett and Trebor are acquired and merged together in 1990.	Cadbury acquires Dandy, owner of the Stimorol gum brand.	Adams Confectionery is acquired for US$4.2 billion, making Cadbury the leading worldwide confectionery company and the world's number two in chewing gum.	Cadbury announces Fairtrade certification for Cadbury Dairy Milk in Britain and Ireland.

As the only chartered professional body dedicated to management and leadership, the Chartered Management Institute (CMI) is committed to raising the performance of business by providing the necessary skills to address new practices and challenges. Through engaging with the wider management community, the CMI provides training and development, disseminates knowledge and promotes best practice.

Market

The essential skills required to survive and prosper in the modern business environment are constantly changing, impacting significantly on the way in which organisations structure and develop themselves and their managers.

The Chartered Management Institute helps to set and raise standards in management by encouraging development in order to improve performance. The breadth and depth of the Institute's offering is unrivalled in the marketplace and caters for individuals and employers in a variety of sectors across a number of distinct markets: training and development, qualifications and management consultancy.

Product

The Institute is committed to supporting managers across the globe throughout

their careers and learning, from individuals seeking to enhance their careers to employers looking to develop staff and training bodies seeking accreditation.

CMI members have access to a comprehensive online information resource as well as books, articles, journals and trade publications via the Management Information Centre.

Regional and branch events offer opportunities to develop new skills and network with likeminded professionals, while the online Continuing Professional Development service allows members to assess their needs, plan their development and record their progress.

ManagementDirect is an online support facility which uses videos and podcasts, featuring business leaders' real-life experiences, to bring subject matter to life. Members can search by topic or content – or even by the amount

of time they are able to devote to finding the required information.

The online media centre presents the latest news on management and leadership as well as providing access to research, reports, policy, management facts and figures and information on current topics. The CMI's network of Approved Centres in the UK and overseas enables organisations to deliver and access their choice of qualifications from a comprehensive range of full certificates, diplomas and S/NVQs.

Achievements

For more than 60 years, the Chartered Management Institute has been supporting individual managers and developing organisations. It is the only institution dedicated to management and leadership to acquire 'Chartered' status, granted in 2002, and is home to the Management Standards Centre, the government-recognised

1947	1951/52	1987	1992		1995
The British Institute of Management (BIM) is formed.	The UK's first ever Diploma in Management Studies is introduced by the BIM and the Ministry of Education.	The BIM, in conjunction with other bodies, issues two pivotal reports – The Making of British Managers and The Making of Managers.	BIM and the Institution of Industrial Managers (IIM) merge to form the Institute of Management (IM) and the transfer of the Awarding Body status of the IIM to the new	Institute is approved by the (former) National Council for Vocational Qualifications (NCVQ), now the Qualifications and Curriculum Authority (QCA).	The Institute of Management publishes 'Test your management skills' – the world's first validated general management aptitude test.

standards setting body for management and leadership.

The Institute is seen as the leading body for developing and promoting best practice in management and leadership. Its research agenda continues to produce data that identifies the management skills needed now and in the future and demonstrates the impact of management and leadership on individual and organisational performance. The research benefits those within the workplace, those delivering development needs, the media and key policy makers.

As the 'champion' of management, the CMI is regularly consulted on a range of management and legislative issues and frequently engages in discussion with government and senior business leaders.

Awarded by the CMI, Chartered Manager status offers independent recognition and endorsement of an individual's management and leadership credentials. It has been cited, by independent analysis of Labour Force Survey data, as a route towards higher earnings potential and greater employability.

Recent Developments

The Institute's recent focus has centred around the launch of independent research based on Labour Force Survey (LFS) data. The LFS demonstrates how professionalism pays – namely, how membership of professional bodies and undertaking professional qualifications has a direct impact on earning power and employability. CMI believes that driving up the demand for professionalism in the UK has immense potential; not only can individuals benefit at a personal level but the spill-over effect as they influence colleagues can have a significant impact on UK productivity.

CMI is aware that the skills required for an organisation to succeed and prosper

are constantly changing. The Institute has therefore begun to implement a number of strategic initiatives to address evolving workplace conditions; a supporting role aimed at equipping managers and organisations with the necessary tools to tackle new challenges as they arise.

Looking forward, continued investment in new and media-rich resources features heavily in the brand's future plans, as does the rolling out of a new group membership package, aimed at making it easier for employers to engage their managers with the range of products and services available within the Institute. A particular emphasis is also placed on extending collaborative working and partnership relations that will see relationships with higher education establishments forged in order to engage potential career managers earlier.

There is a growing recognition of the need to raise awareness and understanding of the Chartered Management Institute through continued investment in integrated marketing activities, not only to help promote its future pivotal role in establishing and reviewing management and leadership standards but also to ensure a world-class benchmark of best practice.

Promotion

Promotion of the Institute to raise the brand profile remains vital and takes place through a full range of marketing and promotional activities, from branch events and regional conventions to more targeted PR activities. Brand marketing activities focus around three key areas: opinion forming, influencing and brand building.

A recent campaign – 'However do you manage?' – focused on individuals and employers within the management community and highlighted the totality of the Institute's offering by directing respondents to a purpose

built micro site from where resources aimed at improving management skills could be downloaded. The campaign theme was used across the Institute's PR activities and was also rolled out across various advertising media, from national press to adverts on the London Underground and online advertising.

During 2008, media coverage (both traditional and more innovative) has promoted the Institute's work to more than 197.5 million people. National coverage, specifically, increased by 53 per cent with mentions in over 40 items of broadcast news.

Brand Values

The Chartered Management Institute is built around key brand values that look to develop, support and recognise the skills and achievements of managers. It works with employers to identify and promote the necessary management and leadership skills to drive performance, through a combination of innovation and authority. The Institute looks to influence stakeholders to address the challenges faced by today's managers and leaders and in doing so, aims to provide guidance to help managers choose the most appropriate strategy for their business.

managers.org.uk

Things you didn't know about Chartered Management Institute

The first Chartered Manager programme was launched in September 2003.

Companions form the highest level and most exclusive membership of the Institute. Involvement is by invitation only to leaders who have demonstrated outstanding management and leadership achievement in substantial organisations. There are currently around 1,000 Companions.

CMI holds events throughout the year, the highlight of the calendar being the annual National Conference which focuses on key management and leadership challenges.

2000	2002		2010
The IM accredits its 250th approved centre to deliver IM management qualifications.	The IM's management qualifications are recognised as part of the UK's National Qualifications Framework for Higher Education.	Also in 2002, The IM is granted a Royal Charter, perhaps the key achievement of all, and is renamed the Chartered Management Institute (CMI).	The CMI names the UK's 1,000th Chartered Manager.

A UTC Fire & Security Company

Chubb is a name that has been synonymous with security and fire protection for nearly 200 years, integrating the best manpower and technology to provide a truly integrated solution. It supplies systems and services to most of the FTSE 100 companies as well as the highest levels of Government, defence, banking and industrial companies.

Market

Not surprisingly, Chubb has become one of the most respected brand names in the fire safety and security solutions market. A name that gives confidence and trust to the customers its serves. The company's strengths are underpinned by a global infrastructure, a highly skilled and experienced workforce, a diverse range of quality products and services as well as a reputation for service excellence.

Product

Formerly associated with locks and safes, Chubb now delivers solutions that include the latest electronic security technology,

monitoring and response services, fire protection and detection apparatus, and fire suppression systems. Chubb's ability to integrate its products and services into tailored, comprehensive solutions, makes it uniquely positioned to meet a broad range of customer requirements.

Chubb invests extensively in service innovation and technical development. By combining in-house design expertise with components sourced from some of the world's leading

technology suppliers, Chubb is able to remain at the cutting-edge of system design and service advancement. In recent years Chubb has introduced customers to a number of breakthroughs, such as new wireless technologies, Remote Video Response (RVR) and the increasing trend towards Integrated Security Management (ISM).

Achievements

From inventing the Detector Lock in 1818, to launching one of the first dedicated CCTV monitoring centres in 1999, Chubb's rich history of innovation continues today. Chubb was one of the first national security installers to adopt European Norm (EN) Standards for the installation of monitored alarm systems when British Standards were phased out in 2005. In 2007 it was awarded a Business Commitment to the Environment Award for its groundbreaking extinguisher recycling programme, which continues to process more than 500,000 units every year.

The company prides itself on having an in-depth understanding and knowledge of specific market sectors, with the ability to solve the particular problems businesses face. Its proposition is based on defining and

1818	1835	1870s	1945	1997	2000
Charles and Jeremiah Chubb respond to the increasing demand for greater security by inventing the original secure lock mechanism, patented as the Detector Lock.	The Chubb brothers patent the burglar-resistant safe.	A Time Lock mechanism is developed for protecting vault and safe doors. Although the designs have since been refined, the basic principles of security and quality have remained the same.	Chubb expands its operations overseas and extends its product range into fire protection.	Chubb is sold to Williams plc.	In August, Chubb's Lock Security Group is acquired by Assa Abloy, a Swedish-based lock manufacturer. In November, Chubb de-merges from Williams plc to become Chubb plc.

developing appropriate solutions closely with its customers, liaising with the police, insurers and various trade and industry bodies.

The result is that Chubb is responsible for protecting many of the world's most prestigious and vulnerable sites, from Westminster Abbey to the British Museum. It has experience that spans all types of premises in all sectors, regardless of size or location – from the smallest shops, to the largest airports. Protecting people, infrastructure and assets is Chubb's core business.

Recent Developments

Chubb's Remote Video Response (RVR) service is at the forefront of remote CCTV monitoring. The service remotely monitors CCTV video images from sites over IP networks and provides specialist security protection for large, open and vulnerable sites.

With the advent of Chubb's AFx system, integrated security is no longer only specified for large public sector organisations, such as the Ministry of Defence. More and more Chubb customers are choosing to integrate their security requirements onto a single platform in order to benefit from improved cost efficiencies, greater control and increased flexibility.

The Chubb ControlMaster1000 fire detection system has the potential to integrate with building systems and CCTV, and is showcased at the Schools for the Future project at the Building Research Establishment. The system design was based on the Chubb Resonance fire detection system, which protects the Eiffel Tower.

Web-based fire risk assessment and fire safety training complement Chubb's traditional range of fire protection and fire detection services.

Promotion

Chubb is positioned as the UK's leading brand for security and fire protection. It not only provides bespoke solutions for businesses of all types and sizes, but also commits to keeping customers informed of any legislative changes that could affect the security or fire systems they are operating. This includes running educational seminars and publishing informative guides to support communities

across the UK. In addition, since 2003 Chubb has sponsored the Scouts Fire Safety Badge to help educate children about fire safety issues.

Brand Values

The Chubb brand is one of the most recognised and most valued security and fire brands in the world. Throughout its history, the company has demonstrated an ability to perform in new sectors and to incorporate new technologies in

order to provide the most advanced and cost effective solutions.

Trust, integrity and strength are Chubb's core brand values. With the backing of its parent company, United Technologies Corporation (UTC), the Chubb brand is set to get even stronger. Quality is at the centre of every service Chubb provides, with guaranteed product quality, service levels and response, leveraging the advantages of a national network and local understanding.

Chubb is a national name – delivering at a local level – committed to service excellence.

chubb.co.uk

Things you didn't know about Chubb

In UK prisons, the phrase, 'Chubbing-up for the night' is a commonly used euphemism for 'locking-up for the night'.

The reputation of the Chubb brand has led to it being used as the generic term for security mortice locks, regardless of who the actual manufacturer is.

Chubb is the only national security company able to offer customers the complete security service including installation, maintenance, monitoring and response services.

The Chubb Keyholding service responds to more than 300,000 alarm activations each year.

More than 75,000 Scouts have passed their Fire Safety Badge since 2003.

The Chubb logo was originally designed to represent the front of a mortice lock.

2003	2005	2007	2009
In July, Chubb plc is acquired by United Technologies Corporation (UTC).	In April, UTC acquires Kidde plc, forming UTC Fire & Security, the number two global player in the fire safety industry.	In July, UTC increased its share of the UK fire and security market by purchasing Initial Fire and Security, and integrating them into Chubb's UK business.	UTC Fire & Security employs more than 43,000 people in 30 countries, with a family of leading global brands including Kidde, Lenel and Chubb.

Clear Channel Outdoor is the world's largest outdoor advertising company with close to one million displays in more than 50 countries across five continents. Clear Channel Outdoor UK is the UK's leading outdoor advertising company, providing more than 60,000 advertising opportunities across its premier brands: Clear Channel Billboards, Clear Channel Adshel and Clear Channel Pinnacle.

Market

The outdoor advertising market was worth £938.7 million in the UK in 2008, which represents nearly 10 per cent of display ad spend, according to the Outdoor Advertising Association (OAA). Clear Channel Outdoor's main competitors are JCDecaux, CBS Outdoor and Primesight.

Product

Clear Channel Adshel is the UK's leading supplier of 6-sheet advertising with 65 per cent of the UK roadside market. In addition, Clear Channel Adshel offers point of sale opportunities at some 300 Sainsbury's supermarkets and in more than 80 UK shopping malls.

Clear Channel Billboards is the market leader in quality 96-sheet billboards and provides national, high quality 48-sheet billboards across the UK.

The company's Pinnacle division offers market-leading premium advertising on more than 200 special high-profile sites such as London's Cromwell Road, Piccadilly Circus and M4 Towers.

Achievements

Clear Channel Outdoor UK's managing director, Rob Atkinson, received one of the media industry's highest accolades at the Campaign Media Awards in November 2009. Voted for by the industry through an interactive poll, Atkinson was named Best Sales Leader.

Clear Channel Outdoor's (CCO) revolutionary proof of posting system – WAVe (Wireless Activity Verification) – was named Private Sector Project of the Year at the UK IT Industry

Awards in 2009. WAVe provides proof-of-posting and peace of mind for advertising clients and has set an industry standard. It also enables CCO to improve its community and advertiser service by ensuring instantaneous reporting of any damage to bus shelters and billboards.

Clear Channel has also worked hard for more than 10 years to ensure high standards of environmental management, and is now recognised as the leading outdoor company in the field for sustainability.

Clear Channel Outdoor was named one of the UK's Top 50 Green companies for the second consecutive year in 2009 by The Sunday Times, was highly commended at the Green Business Awards in 2008 and 2009 and was a finalist at the National Energy Efficiency Awards 2008.

A longstanding commitment to LPG fuels and greener fleets secured the Green Fleet Award 2006 and the Fleet Hero Award 2007.

1936	1967	1996	1998	2004	2006
More O'Ferrall is founded.	The Adshel brand is launched.	The company is rebranded as the More Group.	Clear Channel Communications acquires the More Group. Town & City billboard is bought and the Sainsbury's contract is won.	The company wins the malls POS contract.	The company is rebranded as Clear Channel Outdoor. It buys Van Wagner in the UK and launches the Pinnacle brand.

Recent Developments

In 2009, William Eccleshare was appointed as president and chief executive officer of Clear Channel International, making him responsible for all of its business outside of the Americas.

Also in 2009, the company retained two of its major contracts without having to go to tender: Sainsbury's and Birmingham International Airport (BIA) – the UK's second largest airport outside London. CCO retained the exclusive contract to sell advertising at Sainsbury's

enhanced advertising opportunities, including the sponsorship of the airport's new 230m International Pier. When complete, the pier will allow an advertiser to target more than 4.3 million passengers in the first year alone.

Among Clear Channel's new products is its digital mall network with more than 100 HD portrait displays in busy malls including the Trafford Centre in Manchester and Merry Hill in the West Midlands. The network is expanding rapidly throughout the UK. Another highly successful new format is the national dry-posted 96-sheet billboards. The dry-posting system uses a frame that clamps the single sheet firmly in place with Velcro strips behind to give a guaranteed flat and high quality presentation. This system means clients get faster posting and coverage. The process enables campaigns to be re-posted three times over 12 months and the posters are made from 70 per cent recycled material which can be safely converted into energy after use.

In Glasgow the company has worked with the city to provide the new pedestrian tourist

Brand Values

The values of leadership, innovation, quality, flexibility, and accountability illuminate everything the company does and says. They inspire the business to focus on services such as WAVe proof of posting and on the environmental management work and charity support that the company undertakes. The company provides high quality products and services that benefit its clients, partners and communities, and helps to set new standards for the whole sector.

clearchanneloutdoor.co.uk

UK stores in a partnership that dates back to 1998. This deal means that the point-of-sale estate will increase by 50 per cent; the company currently has 1,800 6-sheet panels outside the stores. Further to which, the BIA deal means that Clear Channel is able to offer

'wayfinding' system which includes 149 maps and more than 300 new ad panels on premium free-standing units across the city.

Promotion

Clear Channel Outdoor not only communicates with its key audiences advertisers, agencies and other stakeholders, but also seeks to promote the outdoor advertising industry as a whole. In partnership with Media Week, Clear Channel launched the Outdoor Planning Awards in 2007, now in their fourth year. Clear Channel has also championed creativity in outdoor advertising through the Student Design Awards, which it has been running for more than 20 years. Clear Channel also provides research and insight to help advertisers and is a strong supporter of Postar, the audience research body for the out-of-home advertising industry.

Things you didn't know about Clear Channel Outdoor

Bus shelters were once built solely by local councils. By the early 1970s the bus shelter revolution began with advertising company Adshel installing panels in shelters in Leeds. It supplied them free, in return for the right to display advertising on them. Local councils often benefit from a revenue share of the advertising, which helps mitigate council tax.

For the eighth consecutive year Clear Channel Outdoor UK has posted more than one million Adshel posters. The one-millionth posting for 2009 was completed at 8.43am on 21st October at a site in Renfrew, Scotland. All Adshel posters are recycled.

Clear Channel's flagship Piccadilly Lite site is the only flexible advertising opportunity offered at the iconic Piccadilly Circus location. The site, which measures 23m by 2m, reaches a young, affluent audience in excess of 2.2 million per fortnight.

Clear Channel Outdoor in the US has an agreement with the FBI to display 'wanted' messages on all of its digital billboards across the country. Since the agreement was formed in 2008, it has led to the apprehension of 13 criminals as a result of information displayed on its networks.

2008	2009		2010
The digital roadside network is formed and the Interact mobile services division is launched. The company is acquired by Bain Capital Partners LLC and Thomas H Lee Partners L.P.	Clear Channel Outdoor launches the digital malls network and national dry-posted billboards.	Also in 2009, WAVe proof of posting technology is launched.	Clear Channel expands its digital mall network nationwide.

CNN is the world's leading global 24-hour news network, delivered across a range of multimedia platforms. Launched in 1985, the channel's output comprises its trademark breaking news, business and sports news, current affairs and analysis, documentary and feature programming.

Market

Since CNN pioneered the genre of 24-hour news, the pan-regional news market has expanded to include more than 100 news channels worldwide. CNN has remained at the forefront of this increasingly competitive market, warding off competition from domestic and pan-regional news services, with its growing international newsgathering operation and intricate network of regionalised services and affiliates.

CNN's clear cross-platform leadership in reaching premium audiences (Source: Ipsos Business Elite Europe, European Media and Marketing Survey and Global Capital Markets Survey 2009), positioning the network well to embrace the new media challenges of an increasingly converged world.

CNN continues to attract a range of high profile advertisers with its cross-platform ad sales offering, one of the most comprehensive and innovative in the industry. Online is currently the fastest-growing driver of the ad sales business while TV remains strong, drawing major clients such as Abu Dhabi, Philips, Skype, Nokia, Zenith Bank, Qatar Foundation, Vestas, Finnair, Rolex and The Greek National Tourism Organisation.

Product

CNN's global news group currently consists of nine international networks and services, five international partnerships and joint ventures as well as eight US-based services. Available in six languages, the channel's joint ventures include CNN Chile, CNN-IBN, CNN Turk, CNN+ in Spain and Japan's CNNj, as well as a number of websites including CNN.co.jp in Japan and CNNenEspanol.com.
While breaking news remains CNN's

trademark, its feature programming line up caters to a wide range of audiences, covering business, sport, lifestyle and entertainment, compelling documentaries and special landmark programming.

Throughout the year, CNN's best known faces, including its chief international correspondent, Christiane Amanpour and Richard Quest, front prime time programmes such as Amanpour and Quest Means Business as well as special documentaries.

Achievements

In 2009, CNN International won an Amnesty International Media award in the International Television and Radio category, for World's Untold Stories: The Forgotten People in which presenter Dan Rivers highlighted the on-going persecution of the Rohingya people.

In addition, CNN freelance cameraman Talal Abu Rahma received the Martin Adler Prize at the Rory Peck Awards 2009 for his work in Gaza and CNN's World's Untold Stories documentaries. One Woman's War and Wedlocked were both short-listed for awards at the Monte Carlo TV Festival.

In 1980 CNN launched as a single US network available to 1.7 million homes. Twenty-nine years later, CNN's 24 branded networks and services are available to more than two billion people worldwide across television, radio, online and mobile in more than 200 countries and territories via six languages.

CNN has become synonymous with breaking news, acting as a visual history book for the world. As stories from across the globe have hit the headlines, CNN has been there from

1980	1985	1989	1995	1997	1999
CNN launches on 1st June as a single US network; the brainchild of media entrepreneur Ted Turner, it becomes the first round-the-clock news channel.	CNN International launches, along with live 24-hour transmission to Europe.	CNN becomes available worldwide, 24 hours a day, with transmission via a Soviet satellite to Africa, the Middle East, the Indian subcontinent and South East Asia.	CNN.com, the world's first major news website, is launched. This is followed by the all-encompassing international edition.	CNN launches a regionalisation strategy with the guiding philosophy, 'Global reach, local touch'.	CNN Mobile launches, the first mobile telephone news and information service available globally with targeted regional content.

Tiananmen Square and the 11th September terrorist attacks to the death of Michael Jackson and the global credit crunch.

In March 2009, 20 staff with the help of CNN's parent company Turner Broadcasting, raised funds to travel to Mali for a two week project to help build a new village school.

On the commercial front, CNN International Advertising Sales won two Internationalist Magazine Gold awards in 2009 for Innovation in its global brand campaign My South Africa, created for South African Tourism.

Recent Developments

CNN has a strong heritage of offering extensive coverage and analysis of international events and stories of global importance. It continues to invest in intelligent and compelling feature and documentary programming across all digital platforms, setting the standard for forging unique audience connections that truly engage consumers worldwide.

In the past 14 months CNN International has launched nine programmes which make up its new European primetime line-up uniting Christiane Amanpour, Richard Quest, Becky Anderson, Fionnuala Sweeney, Michael Holmes, Stan Grant, Jim Clancy, Isha Sesay and Hala Gorani in a schedule that between them covers a diverse spectrum of business and current affairs programming, breaking news and behind-the-scenes reportage in distinctive formats. This, alongside the network's existing feature and documentary slate, confirms CNN's evolution into much more than a multimedia 24-hour rolling news channel.

CNN's programming investment continues in 2010 with the introduction of a new primetime schedule for Asia Pacific.

With an eye on changing consumer trends, CNN embraces the range of emerging, non-linear distribution outlets to maximise its presence across all platforms.

In October 2009 the network unveiled a re-vamped website with cutting-edge design, extensive integrated video, customisation options and greater opportunities for its audience to be involved. The re-launch of CNN.com also meant incorporating CNN's continually growing citizen journalism initiative, iReport, for the first time. There are now 375,000 'iReporters'.

In September 2009, CNN launched a commercial self-service online storefront: CNN Wire Store which enables, journalists,

publishers and media organisations worldwide, to license CNN story content through a web-based service.

In 2009, CNN continued to invest in its international newsgathering operation and now has bureaux in 47 major cities around the world with the most recent addition being a regional newsgathering hub, opening in the United Arab Emirates.

With a network of over 1,000 broadcast affiliates worldwide, CNN International broadcasts upwards of 90 per cent of its programmes exclusively for a global audience.

Promotion

Since launch, the CNN logo has been one of the world's most instantly recognised

brands and is promoted via select marketing opportunities and partnerships.

In September 2009, CNN International (CNNI) unveiled a new tagline: Go Beyond Borders, replacing Be the First to Know, which debuted in March 2001. Go Beyond Borders is an articulation of the network's shared values and commitment to delivering intelligent news in a connected world. CNNI now uses this tagline not only as a marketing message, but also as a content filter; every day CNN International's news coverage promises to go beyond the expected.

Brand Values

For 30 years, CNN has stood by the news values of accuracy, intelligence, transparency and diversity. The network's commitment to digital integration also ensures that its audiences get access to CNN 'whenever, wherever and however'. CNNI is the genuine international news source, delivering intelligence for an interconnected world.

CNN is global in its reach and continually aims to break new ground and go beyond expectations. To go beyond borders is to demand excellence and dedication. It demonstrates that stories and people are not defined or limited by geography, and neither is CNN.

CNN's viewers do not define themselves by the colour of their passports and Go Beyond Borders speaks directly to their aspirations and expectations. It also reflects the changing world, as news is consumed across an increasing number of platforms.

Transparency and diversity are vitally important to CNN's viewers; they expect their news source to challenge and question, as well as deliver truly international reporting and perspectives.

cnn.com/international

Things you didn't know about CNN

Sheikh Mohammed, the Ruler of Dubai, tweeted about meeting CNN International's EVP and managing director, Tony Maddox, for lunch while CNN was in town for the launch of CNN Abu Dhabi in November 2009.

According to the latest industry research, less than four per cent of CNN's audience are expatriates.

CNN is now available on every multichannel television platform in the UK.

CNN's European headquarters, in the heart of London, were opened by the Queen in 2001.

2006	2007	2008	2009
CNN launches its citizen journalism initiative, iReport.	CNN launches across major IPTV and VOD outlets including YouTube and CNN.com is redesigned to incorporate video, text and images within its storytelling page.	iReport.com is born; an online incarnation of iReport, it is the company's first unfiltered, uncensored user-generated content website.	CNN international launches eight new programmes which make up its new European primetime line-up and the tagline Go Beyond Borders replaces Be the First to Know.

The Coca-Cola Company is the world's largest beverage company and the leading drinks brand worldwide, with a brand value of US$66.7 billion (Source: Business Week/Interbrand Best Global Brands 2008). In Great Britain, Coca-Cola and sugar-free diet Coke are the country's two biggest soft drinks and in 2006, Coca-Cola Zero was added to the family. The classic contour bottle has become synonymous with the brand and is an instantly recognisable icon the world over.

Market

Coca-Cola remains one of the most successful brands in the world today. Ongoing brand and product innovation continue to reinforce its leadership in the soft drinks category.

In Great Britain in 2008, retail sales of Coca-Cola grew by 3.6 per cent to reach a value of £514.5 million and in 2009, the brand experienced its best January to date (Source: ACNielsen w/e 3rd January 2009).

Coca-Cola Great Britain's portfolio of brands for the Coca-Cola trademark achieved a combined revenue of £970 million in 2008 (Source: ACNielsen). Coca-Cola Zero was the trademark's most significant launch and innovation in the last 20 years and is now worth £56.2 million (Source: ACNielsen w/e 17th January 2009).

Product

There are three core products in the Coca-Cola trilogy: Coca-Cola, introduced more than 100 years ago;

diet Coke, launched almost 30 years ago; and Coca-Cola Zero, launched three years ago. The Coca-Cola Company aims to provide consumers with a range of products that are relevant to their needs. As an example of this, in 2008 easy-to-hold 'grip' bottles were rolled out across all 500ml PET bottles.

Achievements

As Coca-Cola remains at the pinnacle of global brand recognition, the Company is able to utilise its relationship with consumers to make an impact beyond the soft drinks market. 2008 saw Coca-Cola build on the success of its 'Talent from Trash' initiative, rewarding football fans for recycling by giving them the opportunity to win cash for youth development programmes within The Football League. 'Talent from Trash' won a number of environment and marketing awards during 2008, including Best Green Outdoor Campaign (over £50,000) at the Green Awards and Best Waste & Recycling Project at the edie Awards for Environmental Excellence.

Recent Developments

In 2009, Coca-Cola Great Britain celebrated the first anniversary of Coke Zone. This innovative website was developed to reward and engage with Coca-Cola trilogy drinkers as well as attract a new generation of consumers

1886	1893	1915	1919	1984	2006
Coca-Cola is invented by John Styth Pemberton, a pharmacist in Atlanta, Georgia. Asa Candler acquires the business in 1888.	The famous signature 'flourish' of Coca-Cola is registered as a trademark. By 1895, Coca-Cola is available in every US state.	The Coca-Cola contour bottle, made from Georgia green glass, appears for the first time. A unique 3D trademark protects it from a growing army of imitators.	The business is sold to Ernest Woodruff. In 1923 his son becomes president of the company, declaring that Coca-Cola "should always be within an arm's reach of desire".	diet Coke is launched – the first brand extension of Coca-Cola in Great Britain.	Coca-Cola Zero becomes the third brand in the Coca-Cola family in Great Britain.

to the brand. Offering a range of content such as rewards and money-can't-buy prizes, CokeZone.co.uk is the leading FMCG brand website and boasts nearly half a million members with visitors browsing the site for an average of more than nine minutes.

Promotion

Coca-Cola has become known for innovative, relevant marketing campaigns and famous for iconic advertising. In Great Britain in 2008, it continued to invest heavily in maintaining awareness across the Coca-Cola, diet Coke and Coca-Cola Zero brands.

As a key sponsor of the Olympic Games, Coca-Cola launched a limited edition bottle designed by iconic photographer, Rankin. On-pack promotion to support the sponsorship included the chance to win a 'dream' experience. Keeping on the sporting theme, Coca-Cola also continued its sponsorship of The Football League, amplified with successful campaigns such as 'Win a Player, Buy a Player' and 'Find the Next Rooney'.

Coca-Cola continued to communicate the 'Coke Side of Life', reminding people of the iconic heritage of the drink. 2008 saw the TV debut of Coca-Cola's award-winning 'Video Game' creative, portraying the hero of a gritty video game spreading happiness by handing out bottles of Coke. The 'Coke Side of Life' messages were reinforced with two summer campaigns: 'Pemberton', focusing on the heritage of Coca-Cola and 'Intrinsics', bringing to life the taste and refreshment of an ice-cold Coca-Cola.

Finally, the Christmas season saw the return of two well-known TV ad campaigns: 'Holidays are Coming' and 'Greatest Gifts'. These were supported by nationwide outdoor ads and on-pack promotions offering consumers the chance to win festive-themed prizes and rewards via the Coke Zone website.

Meanwhile, 2008 saw diet Coke go back to its roots with campaigns aimed at its key audience: young women. The diet Coke City Collection was launched, comprising four limited edition bottles designed by Patricia Field, New York stylist to the stars. Sold exclusively in Selfridges, the designs embodied today's modern women: confident, glamorous, sexy and in charge of their own lives.

Elsewhere, Coca-Cola Zero – dubbed 'bloke Coke' – continued to communicate with young men. In its first collaboration since launch, Coke Zero began a multimillion-pound global partnership with the James Bond film, Quantum of Solace. The integrated communications campaign, which ran across more than 30 markets, included TV, cinema, digital and outdoor activity as well as on-pack promotion and an exclusive 007 inspired original glass bottle in Great Britain.

Coca-Cola Zero also launched 'Coke Zero Street Striker', a competition judged by Wayne Rooney to find the nation's most skilful street footballers with the final shown on Sky One.

Brand Values

The brand values of Coca-Cola have stood the test of time and aim to convey optimism, togetherness and authenticity. Coca-Cola is not political but aims to bring people together with an uplifting promise of better times and possibilities. These values make Coca-Cola as relevant and appealing to people today as it has always been and underpin the loyalty, affection and love that generations have felt for the brand. The Coca-Cola Company's reputation for strong marketing ensures that this connection remains as powerful as ever.

coca-cola.co.uk

Things you didn't know about Coca-Cola

The Coca-Cola Company markets more than 400 brands worldwide, with 20 in the UK alone, providing over one billion servings of sparkling and still beverages every day.

Coca-Cola has been an official partner of the Olympic Games since 1928 – the longest running sports sponsorship in history.

Coca-Cola was originally sold as a soda fountain drink – produced by mixing Coca-Cola syrup with carbonated water.

conqueror

Now in its 122nd year, Conqueror is recognised worldwide as a symbol of premium quality paper for business and creative communications. One of the very few paper brands to be requested by name, its reputation for quality and professionalism is acknowledged across the 120 countries in which it is available.

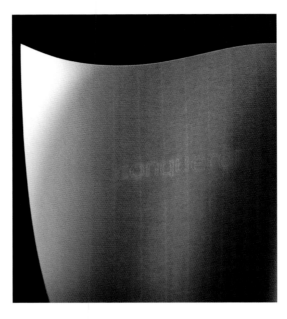

Market

In today's digital age, paper continues to be used as a key communication tool which helps companies promote a positive business image. Conqueror is a long-established mark of quality and supports all companies and organisations in generating cut-through messages.

As companies face increasing environmental pressures, many are looking for ways to reduce their carbon footprint – as a result end users now actively choose products which can support this objective. The Conqueror range is constantly adapted to meet these changing market demands, resulting in a product which boasts the highest environmental credentials. The visual impact and tactile quality of Conqueror also help end users to promote core values such as excellence, professionalism and style.

Product

Conqueror products are renowned for helping a range of users to achieve standout in the ever crowded marketplace – whether it's printers, designers or end-users. The paper offers a multi-functional, sustainable solution which guarantees performance across the latest print processes. Constant monitoring of fashion trends means that Conqueror also offers creativity and quality for materials requiring an eye-catching finish, such as brochures, annual reports, promotional materials or packaging.

Within the extensive range, a selection of innovative and contemporary colours, finishes, textures and watermarks are available, as well as co-ordinated boards and envelopes. The quality and versatility of the stock guarantee a look and feel of effortless style and professionalism combined with impeccable environmental credentials.

Achievements

With a constant focus on product development to meet new market demands, Conqueror has embraced change. From traditional beginnings during the era of pen and ink, through to the modern multiple print and digital communication technologies, Conqueror has continued to deliver high quality results across a variety of applications. With brand awareness levels at more than 70 per cent in the UK, Conqueror is one of the few paper brands requested by name and remains synonymous with quality business stationery.

Recent achievements include the development of a new set of environmental credentials which mean that Conqueror now boasts a complete green offer. It achieved full FSC certification in 2007 and launched a new range of premium 100 per cent recycled papers at the beginning of 2009. This last range has been developed through a unique post-consumer paper pulp developed at the company's Greenfield mill, enabling Conqueror to boast the cleanest 100 per cent recycled paper. At the end of 2009, Conqueror became CarbonNeutral® in Denmark, Norway, Sweden, Finland, Iceland, Austria, Benelux and Switzerland, in addition to the UK and Germany where this certification had already been achieved.

Conqueror also continues to achieve best-in-category performance, cementing its status as one of the most well-known and favoured paper brands. Blind and branded tests have proven that Conqueror is consistently chosen as the best quality and overall preferred sheet of paper.

1888	1945	1960s	1990s	2001	2004
Conqueror paper first rolls off the paper machine at Wiggins Teape. Conqueror Laid is born.	Changes in the production of Conqueror are developed, as well as quality control and specialised colour matching.	Conqueror continues to develop and grow its export business.	Arjowiggins Appleton group is formed from the merger of Wiggins Teape with the French paper manufacturer Arjomari and the US manufacturer, Appleton Papers.	A new, contemporary, stylised logo and identity based on the Conqueror name is launched. Innovative iridescent papers are also added into the range.	Conqueror Digital Multi Technology is introduced as the only fine paper that is printable on offset and digital presses.

Recent Developments

Conqueror has remained at the cutting-edge of the paper industry by continuing to drive forward new product innovation. Not only has the brand responded to increased demand for sustainable products, but it has encouraged customers to take a significant step forward in reducing their company's carbon footprint with minimal effort and investment.

In 2007, Conqueror became the first CarbonNeutral® fine paper brand in Europe, with full FSC certification across the range. The 2009 addition of premium 100 per cent recycled papers which offer incomparable levels of whiteness and brightness, makes Conqueror an ideal choice for companies with more stringent Corporate Social Responsibility (CSR) policies, communicating their environmental commitment without compromising on quality. At the end of 2009, Conqueror clearly reflected its international green credentials by becoming CarbonNeutral® in 12 countries across Europe. Conqueror is also supporting the Longwangtan Hydro Power Project in China as well as the Dutch Sterksel Biogas Project.

Promotion

A 'push-pull' marketing strategy has been developed successfully for Conqueror, focusing on distribution partners, printers, designers and end-users. A strong emphasis is put on brand awareness and brand building, with the wide range of applications at the heart of any campaign. Promotion of the brand is underpinned by a global communications strategy, which delivers a consistent image and clear, targeted messages, tailored to key audiences.

Direct mail was the main driver in the 2007 'Blank Sheet Project', along with online and press advertising. Developed to promote Conqueror's CarbonNeutral® status and FSC certification, the campaign was aimed at SMEs, CEOs, CSR directors, existing customers and printers, encouraging businesses to share ideas about easily achievable steps that can be taken to help reduce carbon emissions.

In 2008, Conqueror was supported by an extensive national press and online advertising campaign, incorporating a refreshed Conqueror CarbonNeutral® logo and a newly created strapline: It says who you are. The campaign was designed to reflect the high quality of the range and to demonstrate how small steps, such as using an environmentally friendly paper for business communications, can be used to send a positive message to stakeholders.

In June 2009, Conqueror worked with illustrator Damien Weighill and design agency Blast to launch a new campaign, Endless Possibilities. The campaign took an original approach to paper marketing by providing a free resource of more than 300 original illustrations for designers. Campaign materials included a 236-page book and a website which showcased the illustrations, supported by a special edition set of A2 posters. While Conqueror is a leading business communications brand, it also offers a strong range of creative options. The aim of the campaign was to inspire designers to think of the possibilities available when using Conqueror while providing them with a useful tool for their daily work. The final idea incorporates web and print, with content that will allow designers to really engage with the brand. The campaign was a winner at the 2009 Benchmark Awards. Organised by Design Week, these awards aim to set a standard in the recognition of excellence in brand communications.

Brand Values

Conqueror has a rich heritage in providing high quality, distinctive papers. It is renowned for reliability in both professional and creative communications. Indeed, recent customer research commissioned for Conqueror revealed that the brand has the highest awareness and usage levels amongst its competitive set in the UK and throughout the world.

The same research also found that the paper is perceived as a trusted, high value brand that can enhance a company's image. This cements Conqueror's position and commitment to deliver ultimate attention, interest and impact for image conscious businesses, ensuring customers feel valued.

Ongoing investment in research and development aims to maintain Conqueror's position at the forefront of the paper industry, meeting increasing demand for exceptional performance whilst maintaining its relevancy in today's market.

conqueror.com

co₂nqueror® 2NEUTRAL
Your choice of environmentally friendly business stationery says a lot about you.
It says who you are.
ARJOWIGGINS

2007	2008	2009	
Conqueror becomes CarbonNeutral® in the UK, whilst also using pulp from FSC certified sources across the entire range.	Conqueror becomes CarbonNeutral® in Germany.	Conqueror launches a premium 100 per cent recycled offering in response to market demand for sustainable papers which deliver the highest possible quality.	Also in 2009, Conqueror becomes CarbonNeutral® in 12 countries across Europe.

COSMOPOLITAN

British Cosmopolitan launched in 1972 and has remained one of the dominant magazine brands in the UK ever since. Having recently celebrated its 37th birthday, Cosmo attributes this success to the brand DNA, consistency of voice and an ongoing ability to innovate and evolve for its generation. Cosmo believes that relevance counts for more than heritage because a consumer purchase of a magazine is an act of trust – 'You know something I don't'.

Market

The magazine market has come a long way since Cosmopolitan launched in February 1972.

Today, despite the unprecedented levels of competition, Cosmo consistently delivers an average circulation of more than 450,000 every month and, able to command a premium price, continues to deliver the highest retail sales value of all monthly magazines.

At more than 1.7 million, Cosmo's readership is 32 per cent greater than that of its nearest competitor. What's more, 947,000 readers are unique to Cosmo, choosing not to read any other competitor magazine (Source: NRS July-December 2008). The Cosmo reader accounts for £1 in every £12 spent on beauty and £1 in every £12 spent on fashion in the UK (Source: TGI October 2007-September 2008). Furthermore, research commissioned in 2008 – entitled 'Come Closer' – proved Cosmopolitan to have the highest ad engagement among its competitors.

Product

For the British reader, Cosmopolitan aims to be a life and relationship bible. Through its pages the reader is able to observe life and more importantly, change her life. The USP of Cosmo is to 'Inspire women to be the best they can be'. As a result, readers can feel engaged, empowered and able to achieve anything they want.

Cosmo's core business is the magazine, but an extended family includes Cosmopolitan Bride and cosmopolitan.co.uk. The brand has also diversified into other areas, such as licensed merchandise carefully selected to fit with its personality. The Cosmopolitan Collection includes beauty accessories, handbags, luggage, soft furnishings and bedding. Cosmopolitan has also produced a significant number of books on relationships, sex, beauty and emotional well-being.

Achievements

Since 1972, Cosmopolitan has established an enviable campaigning heritage across a variety of issues, from equal pay and sexual health to motivating political engagement on the rights of rape victims. Considered an authority on a wide range of subjects, Cosmo's spokespeople are widely used by the press for comment.

In February 2002, Cosmopolitan celebrated its 30th birthday and was praised highly in the comment of the day in The Times leader column: 'Cosmo is bigger than a magazine; it is a brand, an empire, a state of mind.'

Cosmo has been recognised with a number of prestigious awards, including the British Society of Magazine Editors (BSME) Innovation of the Year in 2003 for the magazine's Rapestoppers Campaign. The magazine also received the BSME Women's Magazine Editor of the Year accolade in 1991, 1993, 1999 and

1972	2002	2004	2006	2008	2009
British Cosmopolitan launches with an issue price of 20p. The first issue – supported by Saatchi & Saatchi – sells out in three hours.	Cosmo introduces a travel-size format, offering consumers more choice.	Cosmo appoints London ad agency CHI for the first above the line campaign since launch.	The Cosmo website launches – cosmopolitan.co.uk. The following year Louise Court is appointed as editor and Cosmopolitan celebrates 35 years.	The Cosmo Online Fashion Awards are launched and cosmopolitan.co.uk is redesigned.	The Cosmo Fragrance Awards are launched.

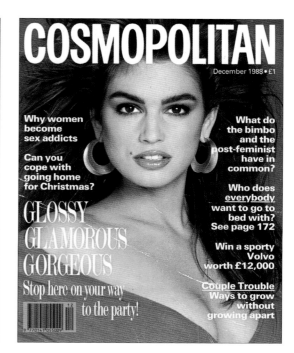

2001, as well as the Periodical Publishers Association Consumer Magazine of the Year in 1992. In both 2004 and 2006, Proctor & Gamble (P&G) awarded Cosmo its Beauty Award for the magazine that has best supported the beauty and grooming industry and then in 2007, the P&G Beauty Consumer Award.

Most recently, Cosmopolitan took joint Gold for Most Effective Promotional Campaign by a Major Magazine at the 2009 Association of Circulation Executives Press Awards.

Recent Developments
Cosmopolitan.co.uk is an online life, love, sex and relationships bible and was relaunched in April 2008 with a major new design, which aims to enhance and expand the Cosmopolitan magazine reader's experience, creating a powerful online community of women.

The redesigned site sees the introduction of new daily content, clear navigation and greater user interaction. Users can upload images of their partners to compete in Boyfriend Wars,

share their secrets in the Cosmo confessions booth, put problems to the public vote with Moral Dilemma and go behind-the-scenes at Cosmo cover-shoots through Cosmo TV – alongside the customary mix of fashion and beauty that Cosmo is known for and, of course, the Naked Centrefold.

A famous editorial and event property, the Naked Centrefold supports the testicular and prostate cancer charity, Everyman, raising research funds and awareness. In 2006 it celebrated its 10th anniversary.

In such a dynamic marketplace, a business strategy that keeps the brand fresh, modern and relevant is essential. Cosmopolitan has risen to the challenge by continuing to evolve its popular 'Awards' formula.

The Cosmo Beauty Awards, launched in 2003, have become an ultimate buying guide for the consumer and are used extensively by the trade as a powerful brand endorsement of 'best in class'. Building on their success – and in response to recent growth in the fragrance market – 2009 sees the launch of the Cosmo Fragrance Awards.

In 2008 the launch of the Cosmo Online Fashion Awards took place. Judged by a panel of celebrities, Cosmopolitan readers and fashion experts, the awards celebrate the best in online fashion retailing.

The Ultimate Women of the Year Awards for fun, fearless females, sponsored by Olay, are now in their fourth year. More than the average celebrity awards, Cosmo rewards the most 'fun, fearless females' in all walks of life, from celebrities to readers, bound by their inspirational qualities.

Promotion
Cosmopolitan remains the industry benchmark in magazine publishing. To its readers, Cosmo is as relevant today as it was in the 1970s, 1980s and 1990s. In the 2000s, Cosmo has developed a travel-size version to offer choice and convenience at the newsstand.

Working with key beauty and fashion houses that share the same brand synergy, Cosmopolitan creates effective partnerships that can raise its brand awareness in relevant markets, beyond the newsstand.

As a truly multi-platform media brand, Cosmopolitan can connect with its readers over and above the magazine through online, events, surveys, reader polls, subscribers, e-subscribers, text and email.

Brand Values
The Cosmopolitan mission is to celebrate fun, glamour and passion for life, inspiring young women to be the best they can be. It achieves its aim of being a magazine for a 'fun, fearless female' via eight core editorial pillars: relationships, sex, men, real-life stories, beauty and fashion, careers, emotional health and well-being issues, and campaigns. Of these editorial pillars, 'relationships' is unique to Cosmo and is the crucial element that enables a trusted and more intimate relationship with the brand's readers.

cosmopolitan.co.uk

Things you didn't know about Cosmopolitan

Cosmopolitan is the world's biggest magazine brand, with 60 international editions, published in 34 languages and distributed in more than 100 countries. It is sector leader in 43 markets.

Every month, Cosmo's reach extends to more than 100 million readers across the globe (Source: hearstmagazinesinternational.com).

Cover stars have included Jerry Hall, Elizabeth Taylor, Farrah Fawcett, Paula Yates, Bob Geldof, Boy George and Claudia Schiffer, Madonna and Yasmin Le Bon, Beyoncé and J.Lo.

COSTAIN

Costain is an international engineering and construction group with a reputation for innovation and technical excellence founded on more than 140 years of experience. As one of the UK's premier engineering and construction companies, it is playing a key role in building a critical infrastructure for the nation's future.

www.adderley.net

Market

Costain is at the forefront of the construction industry's effort to meet the challenges facing Britain today. With a rapidly increasing and ageing population, Britain's frontline services, energy and transport infrastructure are being overhauled to provide the necessary capacity for future generations. Costain's ongoing success in securing numerous high-profile and sector critical projects, such as the £297 million Evaporator D project at Sellafield, one of the largest nuclear projects in the UK, and the £397 million Greater Manchester Waste contract, the largest waste service contract in Europe, continue to strengthen its brand and market position within this highly complex and competitive sector.

Product

Costain's primary markets are water, highways, rail, energy and processing, nuclear, waste management, health, education, retail, marine and airports. Costain anticipates future investment in major infrastructure, and environment-related projects and is well placed to seize the opportunities that will be presented by these, including Crossrail, high speed rail links, new nuclear power and waste schemes, and airport expansions.

Across all sectors the Costain product is defined by excellent design and the quality of its workmanship. Costain succeeds in delivering challenging projects through an uncompromising adherence to specification and procedure and by utilising its experiences and extensive knowledge at all stages of a project. Innovation, initiative and teamwork combined with high levels of technical and managerial skills have kept the company ahead in a complex and competitive marketplace, ensuring that Costain has become 'the construction brand'.

Achievements

A strong performance in 2008 bolstered the Costain Group's market position providing a platform for further growth. A landmark set of results saw a profit before tax up 17 per cent to £23.1 million (2007: £19.8 million) and a record order book, up 25 per cent at £2.0 billion (2007: £1.6 billion) driven by 87 per cent repeat business

1865	1933	1951	1971	2007	2008
Richard Costain, a 26 year-old builder from the Isle of Man, sets up a construction business in Liverpool.	Costain floats as a public company, with a share capital of £600,000.	Costain builds the Skylon and Dome of Discovery for the Festival of Britain.	Costain becomes the first contractor to win the Queen's Award for Export Achievement.	St Pancras International station, a Costain joint venture project, is officially opened by HM The Queen.	St Martin-in-the-Fields church in Trafalgar Square is reopened by HRH The Prince of Wales after a major two-year renovation contract by Costain.

from existing customers, highlighting the success of Costain's 'Being Number One' strategy.

The signs of growth in 2009 were positive, with three major Highways contract wins and the securing of the Severn Trent Water AMP5 contract from 2010 to 2015.

The Costain Group was named 2009's Major Contractor of the Year by New Civil Engineer magazine, retaining the prestigious award that it had won the previous year. The Costain Group also won the Supreme Award at the Construction News 2009 Quality Awards which is given to the construction company that records the best overall Awards performance. Costain was short-listed six times and won two categories – Training and Corporate Social Responsibility.

As organisation's ethical and environmental credentials come under increasing scrutiny, Costain has embraced Corporate Responsibility (CR) as defining the way it does business. It has demonstrated its commitment towards CR through the continued work of its own CR committee and as a member of Business in the Community (BITC), a HRH Prince of Wales charitable organisation which inspires, engages, supports and challenges businesses to operate responsibly. In 2009 Costain achieved a Silver ranking in BITC's CR index with a score 15 per cent above the sector average.

Recent Developments

Costain has continued to successfully implement its 'Being Number One' strategy, which is centred on leadership through focus and excellence leveraging the Group's core brand values, to develop market-leading positions in its primary sectors. Nowhere is the success of this strategy better reflected than in the utilisation of its expertise in emerging markets such as waste management and highways maintenance. Costain's Riverside Resource Recovery Facility project at Belvedere, in London reached a significant milestone in 2009 with over one million man hours worked without a single reportable accident.

Costain has become the market leader in highways operations and maintenance in the UK and is now responsible for maintaining approximately a third of the UK's motorway

network. Significant highways projects which Costain is currently undertaking include the M25 Bell Common Tunnel refurbishment, the A34 Wolvercote Viaduct replacement and the M53 Bidston Moss Viaduct refurbishment.

Costain's energy and process division has continued to deliver specialist expertise in nuclear design, process modularisation, and underground gas storage at complex projects such as the Stublach Underground Gas Storage Facility in Cheshire.

Promotion

Costain utilises a variety of communication channels to promote itself ranging from advertising in key technical and business-focused publications, to sponsorship of industry related events and through it new online news service hosted at www.costain.com.

As part of Costain's ongoing brand awareness programme, the Group launched in October 2009 an industry leading online news service.

A continued commitment to enhancing the presentation of Costain's sites and deliver a consistent brand image remains a key promotional activity.

Brand Values

Costain's brand, corporate values and reputation are hugely important to the business. They set the standards by which Costain does business and have allowed the Group to attract quality customers, suppliers and people, enabling it to achieved continued growth. The company's seven brand values are – Customer focused; open and honest, Safe and environmentally aware, Team players, Improving continuously and therefore the Natural choice.

costain.com

Things you didn't know about Costain

When complete, Costain's Greater Manchester Waste Authority contract will service one-twelfth of the UK population.

One million vehicles travel through Costain highway works every day.

Costain reduced its business mileage by 12 per cent in 2008.

St Martin-in-the-Fields church, in London's Trafalgar Square, was the subject of a major renovation and restoration project which was carried out by Costain and completed in 2008. In 2009 the project received five prestigious awards including the British Construction Industry Awards top prize in the Conservation category, the Heritage Award for Buildings from the Institution of Structural Engineers, the English Heritage Award for Sustaining the Historic Environment, The Royal Institute of British Architects Award 2009 and the Design for London – Public Space Award 2009.

CRABTREE & EVELYN®

Founded in 1970, Crabtree & Evelyn has evolved from a family-run business to a successful international company, recognised worldwide for its fragrances, naturally-based bath and body care products, and gourmet foods. Long before the 'natural' and 'wellness' movement became popular in the toiletries industry, Crabtree & Evelyn was introducing formulas made with fruit, flower and plant essences, and inspired by English heritage.

Market

Crabtree & Evelyn operates primarily in the health and beauty market, which remains buoyant as consumers increasingly seek products to indulge and restore themselves.

Its strategic goal is to establish its name as one of the most respected natural body care brands in the world. Today Crabtree & Evelyn has a presence in 40 countries and products are sold in approximately 350 stores worldwide, with 42 branded stores in the UK.

Product

Crabtree & Evelyn's product range comprises fine fragrances, bath and shower gels, soaps, home spa solutions, body lotions and creams, hand and foot treatments as well as home fragrance in the form of candles, diffusers and oils. Its products span more than 30 separate collections, each with its own scent, style or benefit-giving properties.

In addition, Crabtree & Evelyn has worked with British food producers for more than 30 years to offer its customers a range of gourmet grocery items, including preserves and marmalades made in Somerset, biscuits and cookies baked to traditional family recipes, and a selection of teas and herbal infusions.

Across its portfolio, the company continues to launch new products using top quality ingredients and fragrances from around the world. Crabtree & Evelyn aims to create products and gifts that transform the rituals of daily life into pleasurable experiences, and

1970	1977	1990	1994	2002	2005
Products are sold under the Crabtree & Evelyn name for the first time.	Crabtree & Evelyn's first store opens in the US, in Philadelphia. Three years later, its flagship store opens in London.	The Evelyn Rose, developed by David Austin, launches at the Chelsea Flower Show.	Crabtree & Evelyn designs a range of toiletries for British Airways Concorde and First Class passengers.	Hand Recovery, Crabtree & Evelyn's first patent-pending hand care product, is launched.	Crabtree & Evelyn USA signs an agreement with Hilton Hotels Resorts & Spa North America to supply in-room amenity products.

its product formulas have earned the brand a loyal customer base.

Achievements

A significant milestone for Crabtree & Evelyn was the launch of its first ever patent-pending product, Hand Recovery, in 2002. This benefit-driven product, along with Hand Therapy, was an instant hit and has gained a strong customer following.

Launched in 2006, the India Hicks Island Living range contains both home and body products as well as indulgent products such as scented candles, fragrance diffusers and other treasures. In April 2008, the signature Spider Lily fragrance from the India Hicks Island Living collection won the UK's most prestigious trade beauty accolade: the CEW (UK) award for Best New Women's Fragrance in the Prestige/Limited Distribution category.

Recent Developments

October 2008 saw the launch of Aromatherapy Distillations, a body care and home collection that combines the benefits of essential oils with natural ingredients. The range is divided into three sensory benefits – Relaxing, Revitalising and Purifying – and contains luxurious body and home products. Created in collaboration with an aromatherapist and international perfumers, the essential oil blends have been designed to treat the senses while benefiting the skin.

In March 2009, Crabtree & Evelyn's creative partnership with British style icon India Hicks saw the launch of India Hicks Island Night, the

second successful fragrance range inspired by India's island life. India worked closely with Crabtree & Evelyn to develop the collection and was involved at every stage, from fragrance and formulation to packaging and design. A musky scent of orchids, jasmine, orange blossom nectar and green island palms, the collection contains luxurious body products, candles and unique etched glass home fragrance diffusers. The Island Night collection has been granted the Royal Warrant by HRH The Prince of Wales.

Autumn 2009 will see the UK launch of an innovative new age defying hand care product, designed to work in collaboration with the brand's established Hand Therapy formula.

Promotion

In 1994, Crabtree & Evelyn designed a range of toiletries for British Airways Concorde and First Class passengers. Since then, sampling on airlines and in hotels has proved a successful way of introducing customers to the brand. Currently, Hilton Hotels worldwide provide their customers with toiletries that have been designed exclusively for the chain by Crabtree & Evelyn.

The Crabtree & Evelyn Privilege Card Program rewards regular customers by offering discounts, incentives, gifts-with-purchase, and various other promotions and offers. A further incentivised VIP status complements a large database of customers.

In addition, Crabtree & Evelyn provides a customised gift service programme, catering to meet the needs of its customers' special requirements when buying a gift for business associates, family or friends.

Brand Values

The Crabtree & Evelyn philosophy is to continually strive for excellence across all areas of the business, with the aim of consistently offering customers the very best products united with outstanding customer service.

crabtree-evelyn.co.uk

Things you didn't know about Crabtree & Evelyn®

One La Source® Hand Recovery product is sold somewhere in the world every minute.

Evelyn was the first perfume to be created using a single, specially developed rose, grown by specialist breeders David Austin Roses. Using headspace technology, it took eight years, 30,000 seedlings and hundreds of cuttings to identify the perfect specimen.

The Gardeners range, designed for use by both men and women, was created to honour the work of John Evelyn, who wrote one of the first important works on conservation.

Selected Crabtree & Evelyn products hold the Royal Warrant from HRH The Prince of Wales, granted in recognition of its services as a supplier of fine toiletries.

2006	2007	2008	2009
Crabtree & Evelyn announces its first spokesperson and creative partnership, with India Hicks.	Crabtree & Evelyn launches its first co-branded line, India Hicks Island Living, with features appearing in key publications such as Vogue, Red and Sunday Times Style.	CEW (UK) names Spider Lily Eau de Toilette – from the India Hicks Island Living range – Best New Women's Fragrance in the Prestige/Limited Distribution category.	Crabtree & Evelyn launches its Aromatherapy Distillations and India Hicks Island Night ranges.

Strength in a new era

Passion to Perform

Deutsche Bank has established itself as a leading global corporate and investment bank, supported by a private client franchise with undisputed leadership in the home market and a strong Asian growth engine. The bank competes to be the leading global provider of financial solutions, creating lasting value for its clients, its shareholders, its people and the communities in which it operates.

Market

In a tumultuous year for the financial industry, Deutsche Bank has responded exceptionally well to unprecedented conditions. While many banks have struggled to weather the crisis, Deutsche Bank has stood out among its global peers for its greater financial strength, stability and leadership, which have enabled it to make a quick return to profitability.

Corporate, institutional and private clients have recognised that Deutsche Bank will be a long term winner among global banks. Since the financial crisis began, Deutsche Bank has increased its market share in many asset classes and regions. Deutsche Bank also acted as financial adviser to HM Treasury on its measures to stabilise the UK financial system.

Product

Deutsche Bank is one of the most global banks and offers its clients a broad range of products and services.

The Private Clients and Asset Management Division comprises three areas: Private and Business Clients, which provides private clients with an all-round service encompassing daily banking, investment advisory and tailored financial solutions; Private Wealth Management, which caters for high net worth clients, their families and select institutions worldwide; and Asset Management, which combines asset management for institutions and private investors.

The Corporate and Investment Bank (CIB) comprises Global Markets and Global

Banking. Global Markets handles all origination, trading, sales and research in cash equities, derivatives, foreign exchange, bonds, structured products and securitisations and occupies a leading position in foreign exchange, fixed-income and equities trading and derivatives. Global Banking comprises Global Cash Management, Global Trade Finance and Trust & Securities Services and handles all aspects of corporate finance, including advising corporations on M&A and divestments, and support with IPOs and capital market transactions.

Achievements

Deutsche Bank continues to win accolades for its performance across all product disciplines and regions. In the Euromoney Awards for Excellence 2009, Deutsche Bank won 15 awards, including Best Risk Management House and Best Bank in Germany. As well as FX, debt and equity awards, Deutsche Bank was also named Best Investment Bank in the UK.

Deutsche Bank achieved further success in The Banker awards and was named Most Innovative Bank for FX and Most Innovative Bank for Retail Structured Products.

Recent Developments

In line with all of the world's major banks, Deutsche Bank embarked on a de-risking and de-leveraging programme to strengthen its capital base. During 2009, the Bank reduced its balance sheet assets and increased its Tier 1 capital, without loss of earnings power. Deutsche Bank also took advantage of new

opportunities, investing in growth and global reach, while keeping costs down. The Bank adapted to the new market conditions, providing relevant products and services for clients and leading the way in developing investment products for the new market environment. With a strong and consistent management team, Deutsche Bank remains well placed to continue to seize the new opportunities available.

1870	1872	1926	1970s	1989	2009
Deutsche Bank is founded in Berlin to support the internationalisation of business and to promote and facilitate trade relations between Germany, other European countries, and overseas markets.	The first international branches open, in Yokohama and Shanghai, and trade relations begin with the Americas. The following year the first London branch opens.	Deutsche Bank arranges the merger of Daimler and Benz, takes on advisory roles for BP in a major UK deal, and advises on and finances the £2.6 billion London Underground Financing.	Deutsche Bank pushes ahead with the globalisation of its business: Deutsche Bank Luxembourg S.A. is founded and offices open in Moscow, Tokyo, Paris and New York.	Deutsche Bank takeover UK merchant bank Morgan Grenfell, a milestone in its presence in the City.	The Bank now offers financial services in 72 countries throughout the world with more than 78,530 employees.

Promotion

Deutsche Bank's communication initiatives leverage its renowned brand icon introduced in 1974, the symbol for growth in a stable environment, designed by graphic artist, Anton Stankowski. Real momentum was created through the global brand campaign 'Winning with the Logo', introduced in March 2005. The concept gives the logo a physical presence and places the brand icon centre stage, becoming Deutsche Bank's tangible face for globally aligned communication of its corporate story. Brand monitor surveys consistently show Deutsche Bank as one of the most widely recognised global brands.

Deutsche Bank's brand and visual identity have recently been evolved to match the Bank's ambition and confidence. The new concept (that was approved by the Management Board in October 2009) is underpinned by three core elements: The iconic logo now stands alone on all communications materials and delivers a premium, consistent and confident look and feel. The Bank's new corporate design will be supported by a defined brand personality highlighting Deutsche's unique characteristics;

passionate, precise, confident and agile minded. The final element is the development of Deutsche Bank's existing claim, 'Passion to Perform' which will appear in a handwritten style to demonstrate the passion that it promises. This format also emotionalises the claim, giving a sign of commitment to all stakeholders.

Deutsche Bank actively embraces its role as a corporate citizen. It regards Corporate Social Responsibility (CSR) not as charity, but as an investment in society and in its own future. Deutsche Bank's goal as a responsible corporate citizen is to build social capital. The Bank leverages its core competencies in five core areas of activity: through social investments, it aims to create opportunities; with its involvement in art and music it fosters creativity; via its educational programme, it enables talent; through its commitment to sustainability it ensures long term viability, and the Bank's employees regularly commit themselves as Corporate Volunteers in their local community.

The Bank's foundations and charitable institutions play a key role, firmly anchoring its CSR activities around the world. From an annual global CSR budget of roughly 80 million euros, about 12 per cent was dedicated to the UK. Projects have included Playing Shakespeare with Deutsche Bank, a major partnership with Shakespeare's Globe Theatre to increase access to and understanding of Shakespeare for young people to a wide range of employee volunteer programmes in disadvantaged areas of London. The Bank has more than 70 non-profit partner organisations and its projects indirectly benefit more than three million individuals each year.

Brand Values

Deutsche Bank's claim, 'Passion to Perform' has always been much more than a marketing slogan or advertising strapline, it defines the way that the Bank does business. Through the consistent delivery of the claim and personality Deutsche Bank aims to live its brand promise of excellence, relevant client solutions and responsibility to all stakeholders.

db.com

DURACELL®

Duracell® has been providing people around the world with portable power for more than 40 years. The world's number one selling AA and AAA battery brand (Source: Nielsen June 2007-June 2008), Duracell® provides a variety of personal power options to give consumers the best value for their power needs. The Duracell® Bunny is an important and enduring symbol of the brand; created in 1973, it has become one of the world's most successful brand icons.

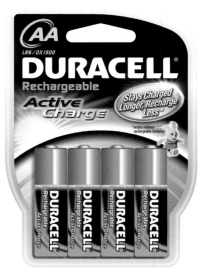

Market

Duracell® is the leader in the battery market (Source: IRI/GFK last 12 months March 2009) and with a 54 per cent share, Duracell®'s sales are not only steady, but growing. In February 2009, total alkaline market sales were worth £282 million (Source: IRI/GFK).

In recent years, there has been substantial growth in AA and AAA batteries (or 'cells'), primarily fuelled by sales of high-tech gadgets such as digital cameras, MP3 players and other devices which require portable power solutions (Source: Euromonitor 2008).

Product

Over the past 40 years, Duracell® has built a reputation for manufacturing and supplying superior batteries that consistently lead the market in performance, quality and innovation. Duracell® recognises that different devices demand different levels of power and offers a range of products to ensure consumers can select the right battery for each device.

The two pillars of its portfolio are Duracell® Plus, the core line, and Duracell® Ultra, its premium offering. In 2008 the entire Duracell® alkaline range had a significant performance upgrade. Duracell® Plus now has a longer life than its predecessor, while Duracell® Ultra has been upgraded to become the brand's most powerful alkaline battery ever.

In addition to developing its core product portfolio, Duracell® is committed to excellence within the rechargeable sector. As a brand, Duracell® has made full use of its extensive research and development skills to bring to market a range of rechargeable products. The full range features family-sized and compact chargers, including the premium one hour charger which charges four AA or AAA cells in one hour.

Duracell® also offers a range of speciality batteries for watches and electronic, security, photo lithium and photo devices.

1920s	1950s		1964	2000s	
Scientist Samuel Ruben and a manufacturer of tungsten filament wire, Philip Rogers Mallory, join forces to form Duracell® International.	Ruben improves the alkaline manganese battery, making it more compact, durable and longer lasting than anything before it.	Eastman Kodak introduces cameras with a built-in flash unit that need the added power provided by alkaline manganese cells but in a new size, AAA – this puts alkaline cells on the map.	Duracell® introduces its AAA battery. Soon, the consumer market for Duracell® batteries rockets.	Duracell® continues to lead the way with product innovation, reflected in the Duracell® Plus and Ultra batteries.	Duracell® launches its Best Ever Formulation across the AA/AAA alkaline portfolio and a refreshed design of the entire product line-up.

Achievements

Duracell® has continued to be recognised and rewarded for its portfolio of products. 2009 saw Duracell® Ultra win Product of the Year in the Battery category while independent consumer reviewer Which? bestowed Duracell® Ultra AAA, Duracell® Plus AA and AAA, and Duracell® ActiveCharge AA with its Best Buy accolade.

2009 builds on the success of the last few years, which have seen several Duracell® products recognised by consumers as 'products which genuinely enhance their lives'; in 2008, Duracell® Mini Charger won the Battery Product of the Year accolade after 12,008 consumers were surveyed and in 2007, an independent survey of 10,049 consumers chose PowerPix – a specialist digital camera battery – as the best innovation of the year in the Battery category.

Recent Developments

In its ongoing quest to innovate and add value for consumers, Duracell® has upgraded its formulation across all AA and AAA alkaline products as well as improving the functionality, user comfort and design across its product portfolio, including cells, rechargeables and torches.

The technology behind Duracell® Ultra AA and AAA cells has been improved and specifically designed to make them the longest lasting Duracell® alkaline batteries in all devices. Duracell® Ultra cells now have a new High Performance Cathode (HPC), with new superconductive graphite and an ultra pure and higher level of manganese dioxide (the active ingredient) ensuring the best ever performance from Duracell® alkaline batteries.

Not only has the all-important formulation of the AA and AAA alkaline batteries been improved but the packaging has also been redesigned. The entire Duracell® portfolio is now set to feature a new 'Planets' identity, giving strong standout and a cohesive look across the range.

Promotion

As an active partner in the summer music festivals, Duracell® Powerhouse has appeared at the top UK festivals for the past three years, playing music into the early hours after the bands finish. Duracell® Powerhouse reinforces the brand's connection with music and the key music consumers who are known for their use of high-tech digital devices. Music downloads also form a key part of the brand's music partnership. Following the success of its iTunes collaboration in 2007, in which a free music download was given away with every promotional pack purchased, Duracell® made the campaign accessible to more music consumers by partnering with Universal Music in 2008.

Duracell® recognises the opportunities within the market and is the first major brand in the UK to invest in a significant above the line print advertising campaign for rechargeable cells, driving awareness among consumers.

Brand Values

As the world's number one selling battery brand, Duracell® provides a variety of personal power options to give consumers the best value for their power needs. Thanks to its long history of innovation and its focus on best serving the needs of the consumer, Duracell® continues to set the standard for portable power. Through the Duracell® Technology Center, the company continues to invest in ways to enhance the performance of its alkaline and specialty batteries.

duracell.com/uk

Things you didn't know about Duracell®

The name 'Duracell' is a portmanteau for 'durable cell'.

The Duracell® bunny made his first appearance in a US advert in 1973.

A Duracell® battery appears in the film The Matrix. It is used by Laurence Fishburne's character, Morpheus, to illustrate how humans are being used as a power supply.

Eddie Stobart

Eddie Stobart forms the road haulage element of the Stobart Group, a fast developing public limited company with wide-ranging multimodal transport interests. As it approaches its 40th year, the UK's best known logistics brand employs more than 5,500 people at more than 40 sites, operates around six million sq ft of premium warehousing capacity, and has a fleet approaching 2,000 trucks.

Market

In the notoriously hard-pressed road haulage sector, the iconic 'Eddie Stobart' name is one of the brand's greatest strengths. Highly competitive pricing and renowned levels of customer service and efficiency, combined with 95 per cent brand recognition throughout the UK, have ensured that Eddie Stobart is not only keeping pace, but expanding and increasing in profitability. The UK logistics market remains highly fragmented with Stobart Group having a market share of around two per cent. Group turnover for the year ending 28th February 2009 increased significantly to £431 million with a healthy profit of £23.9 million.

Product

Eddie Stobart is a logistics specialist and, as part of the Stobart Group, has full transport service encompassing road, rail, sea and air services as well as warehousing and full distribution logistics offerings.

Achievements

In an ever-more environmentally conscious world, road transport is an increasingly contentious issue due to its CO_2 emissions. Eddie Stobart has been at the forefront of the sector's responses to environmental considerations; Stobart Group was one of the first businesses to train drivers in the Safe and Fuel Efficient Driving (SAFED) techniques that can reduce fuel consumption by as much as 10 per cent.

A proactive approach has also been taken to address the traditional haulage problem of 'empty miles', as a result of which, Eddie Stobart now has the best fleet utilisation figures in the industry, currently 85 per cent compared to the industry average of 72 per cent. Through incisive planning, shared capacity solutions and more strategic developments, Stobart Group is committed to pursuing efficiency even further. Indeed, it is in the midst of high level negotiations to

1950s	1960s	1980	1992	2001	2004
Eddie Stobart establishes an agricultural contracting business in the Cumbrian village of Hesket Newmarket.	The Company incorporates to form Eddie Stobart Limited in order to fully develop its transport and distribution interests.	The business relocates to Carlisle. The fleet, numbering just eight vehicles, consists mainly of tippers but rapidly develops to include the more versatile artics.	Eddie Stobart is voted Haulier of the Year by the Motor Transport Industry, testimony to its dedication and hard work in revolutionising the sector.	Rapid, sustained growth results in a fleet of 900 vehicles and 2,000 staff operating from 27 sites and delivering a turnover of £130 million.	The company is acquired by WA Developments International. A major rebrand takes place, from vehicle liveries to clothing, heralding a new era for the business.

introduce a new environmental trailer design that could cut the number of trucks on Britain's roads by as much as 13 per cent.

Recent Developments

While traditionally strong in ambient transport, strategic development and intelligent acquisitions have allowed Eddie Stobart to make a seamless move into the chilled market. The business now has a dominating – and increasing – presence in the crucial FMCG sector.

In October 2009 Stobart Rail launched a groundbreaking Iberian service in collaboration with rail giant, DB Schenker. This dedicated weekly train, which links the fruit and salad

growing areas of southern Spain with the UK's major grocery retailers, comprises 30 chilled containers each controlled and monitored using the latest satellite technology; ensuring produce arrives in exceptional condition. The five rail services will save 29.6 million road kilometres per year, cutting annual CO_2 emissions by 27,510 tonnes.

Promotion

Despite an enviable level of public awareness, the Eddie Stobart branding underwent significant changes in 2004, heralding a new era for the business. The development saw a complete reworking of corporate colours and the logo itself, while vehicle livery took on a simpler, more cost effective design.

Today, this look is the driving identity for the parent Group, flexible enough to be applied to the ever-expanding range of transport options without polluting the brand or reducing recognition. While the recognisable green and white livery plays a pivotal role in public awareness, the brand's impressive profile can also be attributed to an ongoing marketing and promotional drive that extends throughout the business' culture. The Company operates its own Members' Club with some 20,000 dedicated followers and retails a wide variety of branded merchandise.

Brand Values

Since its inception, the Eddie Stobart brand has built its reputation through a commitment to courteous drivers, its high quality fleet and exceptional levels of service. Today, adapting to society's changing needs, the Company has added exemplary employment and environmental practices to its core principles and is working to achieve its vision of building a fully multimodal transport offering for its customers.

stobartgroup.com

Things you didn't know about Eddie Stobart

Every Stobart vehicle is individually identified by a girl's name that is unique within the fleet.

A Stobart vehicle makes a delivery somewhere in the UK every 5.5 minutes, on average.

Recent surveys show that when driving on Britain's major roads a Stobart vehicle is passed, on average, every 4.5 minutes.

The total distance travelled by the Stobart fleet each day is equivalent to travelling to the moon and back.

2005/06	2007	2008	2009
Eddie Stobart wins its first Tesco Distribution Centre contract. Stobart Rail freight services are launched and a new central control site is built at Warrington.	Eddie Stobart merges with Westbury Property Fund in a £138 million deal that sees the formation of the public limited company Stobart Group.	The business expands to a total workforce in excess of 5,000 and a fleet numbering around 2,000 vehicles.	A groundbreaking Iberian rail freight service is launched in collaboration with DB Schenker.

Save today. Save tomorrow.

EDF Energy is the UK's largest supplier of electricity to British businesses. The company recognises it has a particular responsibility to take care of the environment and its Climate and Social Commitments represent the biggest package of environmental and social initiatives of any UK energy company. EDF Energy is the largest generator of low carbon electricity in Britain.

Market

EDF Energy operates in both the B2C and B2B energy supply markets and generates approximately one fifth of the nation's electricity from its nuclear, coal and gas power stations, as well as combined heat and power plants and wind farms. EDF Energy's diverse business customer base ranges from public sector organisations to high street retailers and 75 per cent of the top construction firms.

There are three key challenges facing the energy industry and its customers. Firstly, price volatility and affordability. The outlook for energy prices remains challenging. Particularly at this time of economic uncertainty, managing energy costs is crucial to the survival of many businesses and energy companies have a special duty to care for their most vulnerable domestic customers.

sustainability partner

Secondly, security of supply. The phasing out of fossil fuels and closure of many existing power stations has produced a growing need for new sources of energy, known as an 'energy gap'. In response, EDF Energy is supporting the Government's commitment to develop a diverse energy mix, including low-carbon technologies such as nuclear and renewables.

Finally, climate change. Carbon reduction through energy efficiency is taking hold as consumers and businesses realise that saving energy is a highly cost effective way to substantially reduce their carbon footprint. Legislation and national targets are bringing this to media attention.

Product

EDF Energy believes that businesses have four main requirements from their energy supplier and has developed its products and services to answer them.

The company offers a range of knowledge and insight services to help its customers

1990	1998 – 2002	2003	2006	2007	
The UK electricity market is privatised.	London Electricity, SWEB and SeeBoard are merged.	The EDF Energy brand is launched in the UK.	One Planet and One Community Ambassadors programmes – an EDF Energy employee champion scheme – are launched. EDF Energy becomes the first UK energy supplier to introduce a Social Tariff.	EDF Energy's Climate Commitments, the most significant package of environmental initiatives adopted by any major UK energy company, is launched.	EDF Energy becomes a sustainability partner of the London 2012 Olympic and Paralympic Games.

better understand how the energy markets work, current wholesale energy prices and the regulations affecting their business.

Energy costs affect different organisations in different ways. EDF Energy provides its customers with a selection of energy supply contracts so they can manage their energy purchasing in a way that fits their in house skills and appetite for risk.

Administration can be tedious and costly, so EDF Energy helps its customers simplify their billing and payment arrangements and provides easy access to their account information.

EDF Energy also helps its business customers to save energy to reduce their costs and meet their carbon reduction targets. Services include its free Energy Efficiency Toolkit; Energy View to track energy use against targets online; and complete energy saving programmes designed by its Energy Services team.

Achievements
EDF Energy has achieved Platinum status in the Business in the Community (BITC) Corporate Responsibility (CR) Index. The company attained an overall score of 99 per cent, making it a sector leader in the CR Index.

The company was awarded the Green Apple Award for its Energy Efficiency Toolkit, an interactive resource pack that provides businesses with a step-by-step guide to developing an energy saving strategy and many of the tools required to implement it.

In 2009, EDF Energy was ranked as the number one electricity provider for major business energy users in an independent customer satisfaction survey conducted by Datamonitor. In the same year, it achieved the Carbon Trust Standard, a mark of excellence awarded to organisations for measuring, managing and reducing carbon emissions year-on-year. This recognised EDF Energy's achievement of reducing its own carbon emissions by 26 per cent since 2006.

Recent Developments
In its Climate Commitments, EDF Energy has committed to lower the carbon intensity of its legacy electricity generation by 60 per cent by 2020. It set up a joint venture with its French sister company, EDF Energies Nouvelles, to

create EDF Energy Renewables. This has seen the two companies combine their skills, expertise and resources in order to develop opportunities for renewables development in the UK.

It is building a highly-efficient combined cycle gas turbine (CCGT) power station in West Burton which is capable of producing 1.3 GW – enough electricity to supply approximately 1.5 million homes. EDF Energy has also announced longer term plans to build four new nuclear power stations – subject to the right investment framework – which will produce low carbon electricity on a large scale.

In 2009, EDF Energy merged with British Energy and became the largest UK generator of low carbon power.

Promotion
In 2008, EDF Energy launched a campaign to help businesses prepare for new government legislation related to reducing carbon emissions – the Carbon Reduction Commitment (CRC) Energy Efficiency Scheme.

The campaign's aims were to help educate customers about the scheme and build credibility for the energy supplier as a provider of energy saving services.

The campaign spoke about the new obligations businesses faced in a positive, enabling way,

contrasting the alarmist, scaremongering tactics employed by many others. Amongst other activities, EDF Energy ran workshops called Café Energy, in which its CRC experts explained the mechanics, risks and opportunities of the upcoming legislation. In just over a year nearly 1,000 business customers attended a workshop.

EDF Energy has since won contracts to deliver energy saving programmes for dozens of its larger business customers, many of whom are household names. A particular highlight was EDF Energy's inclusion in the Building Energy Efficiency Programme (BEEP) in December 2009. BEEP is designed to enable public sector organisations to retrofit buildings with energy conservation measures easily and quickly, and is supported by the Mayor of London.

Brand Values
EDF Energy's brand values, which it shares with the other members of the EDF group, are: respect for individuals, respect for the environment, excellent performance, social responsibility and integrity.

edfenergy.com/business

Things you didn't know about EDF Energy

Waste ash from its coal-fired power stations is processed to be reused by the cement and construction industry, preventing more than 200,000 tonnes of ash being sent to landfill.

'Team EDF' consists of 20 athletes who are training for the London 2012 Olympic and Paralympic Games. The athletes are all sponsored or employed by the EDF Group.

EDF Energy's chief executive, Vincent de Rivaz, was awarded the Prince of Wales Ambassador Award for 2009. This recognises individuals whose leadership and commitment to responsible business has driven change inside their own company and inspired other organisations to take action.

2008		2009	
The company's Social Commitments, a set of pledges focusing on safety, energy affordability,	security of supply, employee development and community investment, is launched.	EDF Energy merges with British Energy and becomes the largest UK generator of low carbon power.	EDF Energy launches Green Britain Day in partnership with London 2012, the Eden Project and Global Action Plan.

ExCeL LONDON

An ADNEC Group Company

ExCeL London has staged more than 2,800 events since 2000. More than five million people from 200 countries worldwide have visited, experiencing everything from sporting events, gala dinners and religious festivals to award ceremonies, conferences and exhibitions. ExCeL London is home to some of the UK's leading exhibitions, including World Travel Market, Grand Designs Live and, as well as events for blue-chip corporate clients, government organisations and associations.

Market

ExCeL London is one of the UK's premier venues for exhibitions, events and conferences, a market currently worth £20 billion.

The venue operates across the sector, and markets itself as able to handle almost any event imaginable. Its two large halls, totalling 65,000 sq m, can be divided up or used in their entirety. ExCeL London also offers an additional 25,000 sq m of meeting space and is set in a 100-acre waterside campus, including more than 30 bars and restaurants, five onsite hotels and a host of additional services.

ExCeL London has built a client list which includes BP, Tesco, Barclays, Toyota, Microsoft®, NHS, AstraZeneca, BMW Mini and Coca-Cola. It has also announced some major wins including the European League against Rheumatism Annual Congress (12,000 delegates), the European Society of Cataract & Refractive Surgeons (6,000 delegates) and the European Federation of Orthopaedics & Traumatology (8,000 delegates).

Product

ExCeL London is a £300 million international venue located on a 100-acre, waterside campus in Royal Victoria Dock. It is the largest and most versatile venue in London, boasting 90,000 sq m of available multipurpose space, compared to the 65,000 sq m offered by its nearest competitor.

The Platinum Conference Suite can stage conferences and dinners for between 400-1,100 delegates, whilst an additional 45 meeting rooms – many with dockside

views – can cater for between 20-200 delegates. There are five onsite hotels, providing 1,400 bedrooms, ranging from budget to four star, 4,000 car parking spaces and three on-site DLR stations – linking to the Jubilee line. London City Airport, which is five minutes away from ExCeL London, offers over 350 flights a day, from more than 29 European destinations and a business flight to New York.

Achievements

ExCeL London has received many industry accolades over the years, and in 2009 was awarded Best Venue Support and the Green Award at the Exhibition News Awards, as well as Best Venue at the aeo awards. It was also awarded Business Tourism Venue of the Year and Best Corporate Event for the G20 Summit at the Visit London Awards in 2009.

The venue has the additional accolade of being at the forefront of London's Thames Gateway

regeneration, and will play host to seven events and five Paralympic events during the 2012 Olympic Games.

On 2nd April 2009 The London Summit was hosted at ExCeL London, with the aim of restoring stability and stimulating economic growth across the globe by world leaders including the G20. This historic event, which saw unprecedented publicity on a global scale, required a world class venue that could meet its stringent demands on high security, flexibility and adaptability of event space, together with a quality assured service at all levels.

ExCeL's green credentials have come to the forefront in the last few years. Developments include a Materials Recycling Facility (MRF) onsite and colour coded bins for all events. The MRF is able to recycle paper, cardboard, plastic, wood and glass. The venue also has the UK's largest and only commercial wormery.

1855	1950s	Mid 1960s	1981	1988	1990
The Royal Victoria Dock site, on which ExCeL London now sits, is opened by Prince Albert as a working dock.	Traffic through the Royal Dock reaches its peak.	Containerisation and other technological changes, together with a switch in Britain's trade following EEC membership, leads to the Royal Dock's rapid decline.	The dock finally closes.	Architect Ray Moxley is approached by the Association of Exhibition Organisers (aeo) to locate and design a new exhibition and conference centre within the M25.	A turning point is reached when the 100-acre Royal Victoria Dock site is found.

Food waste is collected from the kitchens and preparation areas and delivered to the wormery, where all types of food waste is naturally recycled into productive, nutrient rich soil. In the last year ExCeL has reduced its gas consumption by 64 per cent and electricity by 17 per cent. This has led to a 33 per cent reduction in CO_2 emissions. The wormery and other initiatives have led to ExCeL recycling 80 per cent of its waste on and offsite. ExCeL was ranked 44th in The Sunday Times Top 60 Green Companies in 2009. Furthermore, the Government body which gives venues energy performance operating ratings, awarded ExCeL with a 'C' category, showing that it was rated as 34 per cent more energy efficient than any other venue of a similar type.

Recent Developments

In October 2009, ExCeL launched ICC London ExCeL, the official identity of the venue's £165 million Phase 2 investment by owners ADNEC

(Abu Dhabi National Exhibitions Company), with endorsement from Visit London, the GLA and Mayor of London, Boris Johnson. The launch coincided with a new commitment from the city to attract more large scale conferences and events with ICC London ExCeL representing the first purpose built large scale convention venue in London. ICC London ExCeL is set to open in May 2010, on time and on budget.

This represents a new era for business tourism in London with the establishment of a Business Tourism Working Group in the capital also with the full support and backing of the Mayor of London.

The ICC London will provide a greater sense of arrival at the east end of the venue, an increase in total event space from 65,000 sq m to just under 100,000 sq m. This will include a 5,000-seat semi-permanent auditorium, extra conference and meeting rooms, mezzanine

casual dining, production kitchens and additional underground parking. There are also plans for a 252 bedroom four star hotel to be built and completed by January 2012, as well as possible plans for a leisure and entertainment district. This would make full use of the waterside location and could include a further hotel as well as bars, restaurants and a music club.

Promotion

The marketing team targets two distinct audiences – the exhibitions industry and the conference and events market.

UK exhibition organisers are targeted via a variety of communication channels, including e-bulletins, sales literature, PR and the ExCeL London website. The venue also undertakes as much face-to-face marketing as possible, through organiser forums, corporate hospitality and strategy days with key organisers.

Unique to the exhibitions campaign is an award-winning marketing and PR support package, tailored for trade and consumer show organisers. Benefits comprise inclusion in 'what's on' materials, local PR, support

with exhibitor days and familiarisation trips as well as contra-deals with local organisations, London and UK wide partners and media partners.

The conference and events marketing campaign targets both UK and international event planners and is very much focused on promoting the venue in the context of London, a key city in Europe. To this end, much of the international activity is executed in conjunction with Visit London where the destination and the venue are jointly promoted.

ExCeL London also exhibits at international shows and is involved with key industry bodies, hospitality events, speaking at industry seminar programmes and organising UK, European and US road shows, as well as press and client familiarisation trips.

Brand Values

ExCeL London is more than an events venue. It's an organisation that promises its clients and staff 'space to perform'. This promise is underpinned by a commitment amongst staff to deliver the ultimate environment in which events can flourish; a blank canvas providing creative inspiration and flexibility; a meticulous approach to every aspect of a project; a caring attitude to the environment and to its neighbourhood.

excel-london.co.uk

Things you didn't know about ExCeL London

ExCeL London is a 2012 Olympic Games venue and will be hosting: boxing, wrestling, judo, tae-kwon-do, weight lifting, fencing and table tennis, as well as five Paralympic sports.

ExCeL London hosted The London Summit 2009; Stability, Growth and Jobs, with 20 Heads of State including Barack Obama.

ExCeL London's economic impact on London in 2008 was more than £750 million and this is expected to rise to £1.6 billion in 2011 once Phase 2 is completed.

1994	2000	2008	2009
The London Docklands Development Corporation launches an international competition to appoint a preferred developer, which is won by the ExCeL London team.	ExCeL London opens in November, as one of Europe's largest regeneration projects.	ExCeL London announces it will build Phase 2 to expand its event space by 50 per cent and include a Convention Centre for London with a 5,000 seater auditorium.	The Mayor of London, Boris Johnson and Visit London endorse and launch ExCeL's Phase 2 expansion as London's first International Convention Centre (ICC).

FAIRY

Fairy is Britain's number one dish cleaning brand and has been a regular and trusted household feature since it first appeared in 1898 on a bar of soap. Today the brand represents a range of products renowned for their cleaning ability and caring nature. More than 13 million UK households buy a total of 150 million bottles of Fairy each year, which equates to 57 per cent of the total market (Source: IRI May 2009).

Market

The dish cleaning market contains sink and dishwasher sectors, with Fairy leading the total category in household penetration, volume and value sales (Source: IRI May 2009).

The value of this market continues to increase by three per cent per year, driven by the launch of premium products such as Fairy for Dishwashers; the future is bright for Fairy with a wealth of new product development in the wings.

Product

During the 1950s, most people used powders and crystals to wash dishes and it was Fairy that launched the first liquid version: Fairy Liquid. By the end of its first year on the market, six out of 10 people in the UK had bought it.

The Fairy brand has stood for 'trust' and 'sparkling performance' for more than 100 years. Fairy is an iconic household emblem and has maintained market leadership for over 50 years thanks to its brand attributes

New richer Fairy. Outstanding grease cutting power means it can last up to 8 weeks! So just how large do you think a loaf of bread would have to be to last as long?

New richer Fairy. Twice the grease cutting power means it can last up to 8 weeks! So just how big do you think a carton of milk would have to be to last as long?

of unbeatable performance and value: lasting up to 50 per cent longer than the next best selling brand (Source: Independent Laboratory Testing). Fairy does not produce products for other brands or retailers.

Today the Fairy range consists of Fairy Liquid Original, Apple, Lemon, Pink Petals and Fresh Lavender; Fairy Antibac, which provides the additional benefit of controlling the growth of germs on sponges; and Fairy Clean & Care, which helps keep hands moisturised.

The Fairy portfolio also encompasses a dishwasher range with Fairy for Dishwashers

(regular and Platinum), Fairy Rinse Aid and Fairy Machine Cleaner – as well as Fairy non-biological laundry products.

The newest addition to the Fairy family is Fairy Platinum, the only dual-action dishwasher tablet on the market that not only leaves dishes 'sparkling clean' but also maintains dishwasher cleanliness. The new tablets help prevent the build up of limescale in the dishwasher, while providing Fairy's best ever degreasing formula.

Achievements

Fairy is the UK's top selling household brand (Source: IRI) and became the UK's fastest

1898	1930	1987	1997	2003	2006
Fairy Soap launches through Thomas Hedley & Sons.	Procter & Gamble acquires the brand and Fairy Baby trademark.	Lemon-scented Fairy Liquid is introduced alongside Fairy Original. Two years later, a Fairy non-biological laundry product launches for sensitive skin.	Fairy Liquid with antibacterial agents is introduced.	Fairy Powerspray launches, for tough, burnt-on stains, adding £9 million to the category.	Fairy Active Bursts for Dishwashers launches, and Fairy sales top £120 million.

growing non-food brand in the grocery sector when turnover topped £120 million behind the launch of Fairy Active Bursts for Dishwashers (Source: Nielsen). In 2007 it was voted Dishwasher Product of the Year.

Fairy Liquid Fresh Lavender was voted Washing Up Product of the Year in 2008 and Fairy Clean & Care was voted Household Cleaning Product of the Year in 2009.

Fairy Liquid has consistently received Best Buy accolades from Which? magazine, while its top cleaning results together with its kindness to skin have seen Fairy certified by the British Skin Foundation.

Recent Developments

The past few years have seen a steady stream of product development from the Fairy brand, beginning with the introduction of Fairy Powerspray in 2003, designed to remove tough, burnt-on food from dishes.

In 2006 Fairy introduced the first of its Fairy for Dishwashers range of products. A revolutionary all-in-one detergent plus liquid, Fairy Active Bursts required no unwrapping prior to use to provide unbeatable cleaning and convenience. The Dishwasher range was bolstered in 2007 with the introduction of Fairy Rinse Aid and Fairy Machine Cleaner. Within its launch year, Fairy for Dishwashers became the second best selling dishwashing range (Source: IRI 2009), with 90 per cent of independent repairmen recommending it (Source: GSAT 2006).

2008 saw the biggest Fairy Liquid development to date with the introduction of the pampering range, Fairy Clean & Care. This was followed by the introduction of an improved Fairy Liquid formula in 2009, to provide its best ever

degreasing power and the longest lasting liquid on the market, therefore offering the best value for money. At the same time, Fairy updated the bottle to a new ergonomic and stylish design. It was last changed in 2000 when the signature white bottle was replaced with a transparent version for the first time.

Fairy also led the way in the dishwasher market, introducing Fairy Platinum in the same year. A breakthrough innovation, it is the first dual action tablet that leaves 'sparkling' dishes and a visibly cleaner dishwasher.

Promotion

Fairy Liquid TV advertising campaigns first began in the 1950s. This led to a host of celebrity endorsements, including actress Nanette Newman with the much-loved line, 'hands that do dishes can feel soft as your face with mild green fairy liquid'.

In recent years, Fairy's advertising has seen chefs Ainsley Harriott, Anthony Worrell Thomson and Gary Rhodes front the brand together. The use of glamorous spokespeople such as Jodie Kidd, Helena Christensen and Louise Redknapp has enabled Fairy to talk to a younger audience.

Brand communications emphasise unbeatable performance and value due to product mileage. Its FAIRYconomy campaign, for example, highlights the value benefits of its longer lasting formula to the consumer's pocket and the environment, with fewer bottles required.

Fairy supports a number of charities and has been the UK's number one fundraiser for children's charity, Make-A-Wish, over the last five years. Its corporate social responsibility policy also means that it donates products for use during natural disasters, such as the 2007 south coast oil spillage, as it is recognised by

the RSPB as the best product for cleaning birds following oil spills.

Brand Values

Fairy is a family-oriented brand with strong links to the kitchen and the role of mealtimes within families. It is also associated with environmental and sustainable organisations such as the RSPB, WWF, Energy Saving Trust and Wastewatch. Its products are concentrated in order to produce less packaging waste, bottles are recyclable and the dishwasher range is designed to be used in short cycles and at lower temperatures. Fairy is also part of the Future Friendly programme, a partnership between brands and leading sustainability experts that is aimed at inspiring people and enabling them to live more sustainable lives.

fairy-dish.co.uk

Things you didn't know about Fairy

The Fairy baby that has appeared on all of the brand's products since the 1930s is called 'Bizzie' and has been reproduced as a figurine by Royal Doulton.

Fairy Liquid first went on sale in the UK in 1960 and since then, more than 4.8 billion bottles have been bought by UK consumers – enough to circle the earth 2,400 times.

Every minute, 579 bottles of Fairy are produced, which equates to more than 10 million gallons of Fairy Liquid in a year.

One bottle of Fairy Liquid washed 14,763 dirty plates – a world record.

2007	2008	2009	
Fairy Active Bursts is awarded Dishwasher Product of the Year, and the Machine Cleaner and Rinse Aid products are launched.	Fairy launches Fairy Clean & Care in a new bottle design; the range provides the dual benefits of helping to keep hands soft and moisturised while leaving dishes 'squeaky clean'.	Fairy launches Fairy Platinum, the unique dual action dishwasher tablet that leaves 'sparkling' dishes and a visibly cleaner dishwasher.	Also in 2009, Fairy Liquid improves its formula and changes the bottle design. The new formula delivers its best ever degreasing power and longest lasting washing up liquid.

Express

FedEx Express is the world's largest express transportation company with a comprehensive global air and ground network dedicated to secure and timely delivery to more than 220 countries and territories worldwide. FedEx Express employs more than 140,000 people throughout the world; all committed to delivering more than 3.1 million packages safely to their destinations every day, each with the responsibility to make every customer experience outstanding.

Market

Despite increasingly challenging global economic conditions, for the first quarter of FY 2009/10 FedEx Express delivered revenues of US\$4.92 billion and an operating income of US\$104 million.

Better-than-expected FedEx International Priority volume, decisive management actions and dedicated team members helped drive financial performance above initial expectations. FedEx believes wise investment and careful cost management will contribute to FedEx Express emerging a stronger, more profitable company as the global economic recovery takes hold.

Product

FedEx Express offers time-definite, door-to-door, customs-cleared international delivery services and can deliver a wide range of time-sensitive shipments, from urgent medical supplies, last minute gifts and fragile scientific equipment, to bulky freight and dangerous goods. Each shipment sent with FedEx Express is scanned 17 times on average, to ensure that customers can track its precise location by email, on the internet or by telephone 24 hours a day. FedEx Express aims to treat each package as if it was the only one being shipped that day. In addition to the international product range offered by FedEx Express, FedEx UK now provides customers with

a wide range of options for domestic shipping. Within the UK this includes time-definite, next day and Saturday delivery services. All services are supported by free and easy-to-use automation tools, allowing customers to schedule pick-ups and track their packages online.

Achievements

FedEx Express, which started life in 1973 as the brainchild of its founder and current chairman, president and CEO Frederick Smith, has amassed an impressive list of 'firsts' over the years. FedEx Express originated the overnight letter, was the first express transportation company dedicated to overnight package delivery and the first to offer next-

1971	1973	1977	1984	1989	1994
Frederick W Smith buys the controlling interest in Arkansas Aviation Sales and identifies the difficulty in getting packages delivered quickly; the idea for Federal Express is born.	Federal Express officially begins operations with the launch of 14 small aircraft from Memphis International Airport. It delivers 186 packages to 25 US cities on its first day.	Air cargo deregulation allows the use of larger aircraft (such as Boeing 727s and McDonnell-Douglas DC-10s), spurring Federal Express's rapid growth.	Intercontinental operations begin with service to Europe and Asia. The following year, Federal Express marks its first regularly scheduled flight to Europe.	With the acquisition of the Flying Tigers network, Federal Express becomes the world's largest full-service, all-cargo airline.	Federal Express officially adopts 'FedEx' as its primary brand, taking a cue from its customers who frequently refer to Federal Express by the shortened name.

day delivery by 10.30am. FedEx Express was also the first express company to offer a time-definite service for freight and the first in the industry to offer money-back guarantees and free proof of delivery. In 1983 Federal Express (as it was then known) made business history as the first US company to reach the US$1 billion revenue landmark inside 10 years of start-up, unaided by mergers

or acquisitions. This illustrious history has resulted in many awards and honours. In 1994 FedEx Express received ISO 9001 registration for all of its worldwide operations, making it the first global express transportation company to receive simultaneous system-wide certification and in 2008 FedEx Express and FedEx UK were granted the highly-regarded ISO 14001 2004 certification for environmental management for the UK. ISO 14001 2004 is considered to be the most important environmental standard in the world. In 2009

FedEx ranked seventh in Fortune magazine's World's Most Admired Companies.

Recent Developments

FedEx Express has expanded its international shipping portfolio to provide customers with more choices and reach, when shipping packages worldwide. FedEx Express has launched FedEx International Economy and FedEx International Next Flight. The International Economy service is now offered from more than 90 countries and territories, prior to this global expansion it was only available from 16 countries and territories. This service is a door-to-door, customs-cleared, day-definite delivery service that is an economical alternative for less urgent shipments but comes with the same quality, service and reliability expected from FedEx Express.

The FedEx International Next Flight service, available from the UK and Ireland is a premium service offering 24/7 expedited shipping with a Money Back Guarantee to more than 220 countries and territories worldwide. This product is designed for customers with critical, rush shipments that require, for example, out of hours pick-up and delivery.

Promotion

FedEx Express launched its latest Global Advertising Campaign, FedEx Delivers to a Changing World, in October 2009. The campaign positions FedEx as the service provider that business can count on, against the background of the recent economic challenges and the changing market conditions. The campaign uses a multimedia approach, combining print with online

advertising to reach the audience of decision makers responsible for choosing international express shipping companies.

Brand Values

The FedEx corporate strategy, known to FedEx Express employees as the 'Purple Promise', is to 'make every FedEx experience outstanding'. The Purple Promise is the long term strategy for FedEx to further develop loyal relationships with its customers. The FedEx corporate values are: to value its people and to promote diversity; to provide service that puts customers at the heart of everything it does; to invent the services and technologies that improve the way people work and live; to manage operations, finances and services with honesty, efficiency and reliability; to champion safe and healthy environments; and to earn the respect and confidence of FedEx people, customers and investors every day.

fedex.com

Things you didn't know about FedEx Express

FedEx Express Air Operations has an Air Fleet of over 650 aircraft and serves 375 airports worldwide.

In 2007 FedEx Express donated a retired Boeing 727 from its fleet to the Air and Space Museum at Le Bourget Airport. The donation took place during the 47th International Paris Air Show. Before its final flight to Paris, the 727-100F provided FedEx Express with more than 18 years of service, transporting packages to destinations around the world.

FedEx Express has been known to transport many unusual items, from dolphins to helicopters.

2000	2006	2008	2009
The company is renamed FedEx Express to reflect its position within the overall FedEx Corporation portfolio of services.	FedEx Express builds its service capabilities in Europe by acquiring UK domestic express company ANC, rebranded as FedEx UK in 2007.	FedEx Express celebrates its 35th year and is now the world's largest express transportation company, operating 650 aircraft and a ground fleet of over 44,500 vehicles.	FedEx Express takes delivery of its first Boeing 777 Freighter (777F) which have impressive operational efficiencies and environmental benefits.

FERRERO ROCHER

Ferrero Rocher is among the UK's biggest names in premium confectionery and is the world's best selling boxed chocolate (according to Euromonitor 2007). Since it launched in 1982, the brand's recipe for success has centred on offering a distinctive product experience, underlined by a commitment to connect with consumers.

Market

The UK confectionery market is worth £4.5 billion, making it the largest confectionery market in Europe (Source: Nielsen Scantrack December 2008).

Within the gifting segment, UK consumers have been 'saying it' with chocolates to the tune of £700 million. Indeed, over the past two years, value sales have grown by almost seven per cent (Source: Nielsen). During 2008, more than 80 per cent of households bought boxed chocolates (Source: Nielsen Homescan 52 w/e December 2008).

The market for boxed chocolates is seasonal, with around two-thirds of sales occurring during the Christmas period. Other key trading periods such as Easter and Mother's Day are becoming more important, growing their value contribution every year.

Ferrero Rocher operates within the increasingly competitive premium boxed chocolates market. During 2008, growth in the premium sector outstripped overall market growth by 15 per cent (Source: Nielsen).

Product

Introduced by Michele Ferrero – creator of well known and popular brands such as Kinder Surprise, Bueno, tic tac and nutella – Ferrero Rocher was launched in the UK in 1982. Today, it is recognised as the world's biggest selling boxed

chocolate (Source: Euromonitor 2007) and is now sold in more than 40 countries across five continents.

Inside each individually-wrapped Ferrero Rocher is a whole roasted hazelnut surrounded by an 'indulgent' filling, encased in light, crispy wafer, all wrapped in milk chocolate and chopped hazelnuts. It is this distinctive 'layered' experience that has come to define Ferrero Rocher.

Today, Ferrero Rocher is available in a number of formats to meet different consumer needs and occasions. The best-selling pack is the 16-piece sharing box, closely followed by the 24-piece gift version with its diamond-effect finish. The range is completed by a four-piece token gift box, a flow pack for personal indulgence and seasonal offerings such as the Ferrero Rocher Easter Egg and a Valentine's Day heart-shaped box.

Achievements

Instantly recognisable, Ferrero Rocher has become an iconic brand in the boxed chocolate market. Synonymous with gifting and entertaining, consumers recognise Ferrero Rocher as 'standing out from the crowd' (Source: Ferrero Qualitative Research).

In a mature and competitive market, the brand continues to inspire enthusiasm. In 2008 sales reached a 24-year high (Source: Nielsen) and loyalty levels exceeded those for any other brand in the boxed chocolate category (Source: Millward Brown).

1946	1950s	1982	2006	2007	2009
Originally a master patissier, Pietro Ferrero founds the Ferrero Company in Alba, Italy.	Michele Ferrero takes over the reins and masterminds well known brands such as Kinder Surprise, Bueno, tic tac and nutella.	Ferrero Rocher is launched in the UK, France and Germany.	Ferrero Rocher launches its 'share something special' campaign.	Ferrero Collection and Ferrero Raffaello are launched in the UK. The following year, Ferrero Rondnoir is launched.	The company is still owned and run by the Ferrero family, now in its third generation.

Ferrero Rocher accounts for one in every six pounds spent on boxed chocolates, a figure that rises to one-third of spending in the category by Ferrero loyalists during the Christmas sales period (Source: Nielsen Homescan MAT December 2008).

Recent Developments

As part of the brand's continuous revitalisation, in 2006 a need-states segmentation and portfolio development programme was put into motion to future-proof Ferrero Rocher's success. The strategy reflects the shift in UK socialising habits from more formal occasions – embodied by the brand's famous 'Ambassador' advertising – towards altogether more relaxed gatherings with family and friends.

Opportunities to develop the Ferrero product offering were also identified to meet different consumer needs. In 2007 a gifting assortment, Ferrero Collection, was added to the range followed closely by Ferrero Raffaello, a creamy and light confection. Ferrero Rondnoir was introduced in time for Christmas 2008 to tap into more self-indulgent occasions.

Promotion

To update Ferrero Rocher's image and move away from the powerful adstock created by the 20-year 'Ambassador' campaign, a radical new creative that looked and felt very different was required; in 2006 the 'share something special' proposition was born.

The intention was for consumers to have a positive feeling about the brand and to instinctively understand how Ferrero Rocher fits into their socialising. Indeed, at pre-testing the new campaign scored nine in the Millward Brown Link Awareness Index (compared to a UK average of just six) and a persuasion index score that placed it in the 'ideal' percentile. A relevant updating of the brand was underway.

Heavyweight TV investment in the run-up to Christmas has always been central to Ferrero Rocher's success, and a category-beating share of voice (SOV) was secured for the new creative's launch. SOV dominance has now continued for seven consecutive years, with Ferrero Rocher most recently achieving 34 per cent (Source: MEC September-December 2008).

To complement the television advertising, a print campaign was developed across premium women's magazines and specialist food publications while a micro site, sharesomethingspecial.com, featured expert tips and advice for organising special get-togethers. National and regional PR was also used to further amplify the campaign.

In-store, standalone point of sale displays were developed to communicate the 'share something special' message and an extensive national sampling campaign was implemented to draw consumer attention to the taste of Ferrero Rocher.

The campaign has achieved a marked increase in consumer engagement with the brand. Indeed, three years on, Ferrero Rocher's brand equity has seen a sustained increase across all key measures including modernity (up 23 per cent) and likelihood to use (up 26 per cent) (Source: Millward Brown).

With Ferrero Rocher successfully revitalised, the full family of Ferrero specialities was highlighted in 2008. The enlarged Ferrero range (including Ferrero Rocher, Ferrero Collection, Ferrero Raffaello and Ferrero Rondnoir) was introduced to its target consumers through sponsorship idents for Channel 4's Desperate Housewives series. An extensive print campaign accompanied the TV work, along with experiential sampling. Consumers engaged positively with the range creative and sales have built incrementally.

Brand Values

By reflecting the contemporary values of light-heartedness and relaxed friendship that are close to consumers' hearts when socialising, Ferrero Rocher and the new Ferrero range – with its sense of mystery – aim to become their first choice for special sharing and gifting. Only top quality ingredients are used across the range.

ferrero.co.uk

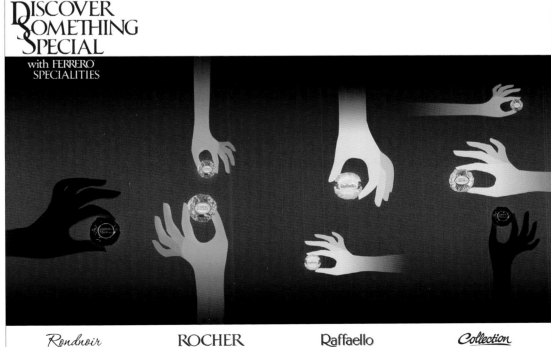

DISCOVER SOMETHING SPECIAL with FERRERO SPECIALITIES

Rondnoir   ROCHER   Raffaello   Collection

Things you didn't know about Ferrero Rocher

Ferrero Rocher is sold in more than 40 countries across five continents.

More than 3.6 billion individual Ferrero Rocher are produced each year. When lined up, this equates to circumnavigating the world twice.

Ferrero Rocher's advertising still features in top 20 ad-recall lists some 20 years after it was first aired.

flybe.

Flybe is the UK's number one domestic airline, carrying more domestic passengers than any other airline and operating four times as many domestic routes than anyone else. Following Flybe's acquisition of BA Connect in 2007, the airline created a business that, in the last financial year, carried seven million passengers and generated revenues in excess of £500 million.

airports, with routes to key European centres including Paris, Düsseldorf, Frankfurt and Milan. The airline's network is made up of 75 per cent domestic UK routes, 15 per cent business and 10 per cent leisure. It is also the largest scheduled airline at Belfast City, Birmingham, Cardiff, Exeter, Inverness, the Isle of Man, Jersey, Manchester and Southampton.

For the business travel market, a key part of the airline's offering is Flybe Economy Plus. As well as free executive lounge access across its network, this offers a range of additional features such as shorter minimum check-in times, fully changeable tickets and a generous baggage allowance.

In addition, its aircraft maintenance division, Flybe Aviation Services, is the largest regional engineering maintenance centre in Europe, operating a network of supporting line stations across the UK and Europe and was voted Aviation Week's 2009 Overhaul & Maintenance European Airline MRO of the Year.

Carrying a higher percentage of business passengers than any other UK low cost airline, Flybe has invested £2 million in its business travel product to maintain passenger loyalty and attract new custom: five of its 11 Executive Lounges are less than two years old and more than 69 CUSS self-service check-in kiosks have been installed at airports across the UK.

Achievements
Flybe has chalked up 30 years of continuous operations, evolving from its Jersey European roots into a successful, innovative market

leader within the low cost airline industry. It continues to differentiate itself in the crowded airline marketplace by focusing on a strong regional business model, offering 'affordable travel on your doorstep'.

Flybe entered into a historic franchise agreement with Scottish regional airline Loganair in 2008, the deal being the first of its kind ever for a UK low cost carrier. The move demonstrated Flybe's commitment to extending its quality low fare model throughout the UK, increasing accessibility to geographically isolated regions.

Market
The boom in budget airlines over the past decade has led to regional air travel becoming more popular. This has resulted in the market becoming highly competitive, with tight margins. It is a challenging market, with huge swings in the price of oil, rising taxation on air travel, higher airport charges and pressure from environmental groups; all factors that are impacting the aviation sector.

Product
Flybe currently operates from a total of 68 departure points; 37 UK and 31 European

1979	1991	1993	2000	2003	2006
Jersey-based entrepreneur Jack Walker founds Jersey European. The airline is taken over by the Walkersteel Group in 1983.	Jersey European gains its first London route from Guernsey to London Gatwick.	The Business Class service is launched and Jersey European is named Best UK Regional Airline at the Northern Ireland Travel and Tourism Awards, for two consecutive years.	Jersey European changes its name to British European, becoming Flybe two years later.	Flybe is voted Most Recommended UK Low Fares Airline by Holiday Which? It goes on to be named 'Most Popular UK Domestic and France-bound Airline' in 2005.	Flybe becomes the first airline to offer online check-in to passengers carrying hand and hold baggage, along with functionality for online flight changes.

Flybe has also been highly successful in driving ancillary revenue, being the first airline in the world to charge for hold baggage and reward hand baggage-only passengers.

Significantly, the airline has also spearheaded efforts to reduce the environmental impact of air travel. Investing more than US$2 billion in new aircraft since 2006, it was the first airline to take delivery of the new Embraer 195 jet aircraft. Its performance features include greater fuel efficiency and a reduction in noise levels. This 14-aircraft order – in addition to 60 Bombardier Q400 turboprop aircraft – now allows Flybe to boast one of the youngest and most environmentally sensitive fleets in the world. This enabled it to reduce fuel consumption by more than 50 per cent per seat by the end of 2009.

In line with this commitment, Flybe was the first airline in the world to introduce an aircraft eco-labelling scheme. Passengers booking via the internet now receive a detailed breakdown of fuel consumption, carbon emissions and noise patterns.

Recent Developments
The recently introduced Flybe Connections offers a one-stop booking service, enabling customers to book multiple connecting Flybe flights that incorporate those of its franchise partner, Loganair, in a single transaction, effectively creating an additional 117 flight options.

Another new innovation is the Flybe Spend & Fly MasterCard. The only UK low cost carrier loyalty programme open to all passengers and operating under the 'Spend Once, Fly Free' maxim. This provides passengers with added

value across a range of rewards. The card is integrated with Flybe's Rewards4all frequent flyer scheme.

Flybe was the only UK airline out of 150 leading UK companies to sign the Government's Skills Pledge in 2007 and, in 2010, will open its new state-of-the-art Flybe Training Academy at its Exeter headquarters.

Promotion
Along with its high frequency retail advertising and online activity, customer relationship marketing is central to Flybe's long term strategy to increase customer loyalty. Operating a highly segmented database and personalised communications approach, its online frequent flyer programme Rewards4all

Visit your customer. If you don't your competitors will. That's the real bottom line.

- High frequency business traveller schedules
- Over 500 flights a day across the network
- Serving 63 destinations from 34 UK airports
- Supporting over 7000 jobs in the UK regions

flybe.com
Powering regional business

provides generous benefits to its regular travellers. In addition to this, Flybe has just launched a hard-hitting advertising campaign, targeting the business traveller, titled Business is Better Face to Face.

Supporting and championing the local communities in which it operates is key to Flybe's operation. Part of this commitment is reflected in its football sponsorship with Exeter City, Southampton and Inverness Caledonian Thistle football clubs. Other corporate social responsibility programmes include the Flybe Local Hero Award programmes, the appointment of Flybe Ambassadors and its partnership with Cancer Research UK.

Brand Values
Flybe's brand is built on a vision to be modern, different, environmentally and socially responsible, transparent and customer-driven. Its commitment and contribution to regional economies, investment in local communities, advocacy for regional 'on your doorstep' services and strong regional heritage, all support the Flybe identity. Alongside this, innovation and providing a comprehensive, high quality customer service offering remain key to the ongoing development and success of the brand.

flybe.com

Things you didn't know about Flybe

Last year Flybe staff and passengers raised £153,373 for its nominated charity, Cancer Research UK.

Flybe could fill 15 Olympic-sized swimming pools with all the bottles of mineral water it sells in a year.

Each year Flybe's aircraft fly a total of 44.4 million kilometres.

The fleet uses 1,800 aircraft tyres per year.

2007	2008	2009	2010
Flybe acquires BA Connect, becoming Europe's largest regional airline. It also launches a frequent flyer programme, Rewards4all, and the world's first airline eco-labelling scheme.	Flybe announces a landmark franchise agreement with Loganair, while Flybe Connections creates 117 new route options across an expanded network.	Flybe's chairman and CEO, Jim French wins the Regional Leadership award at the Airline Strategy Awards and the Special Merit for Commitment to the Environment at the Budgie Awards.	A new state-of-the-art teaching centre, the Flybe Training Academy is due to open at its Exeter headquarters.

Good Housekeeping

Good Housekeeping launched in 1922 and has remained one of the UK's most enduringly successful magazines. Good Housekeeping is an international brand with 16 editions around the world including publications in China, Russia, Indonesia, Chile and Central America – selling more than six million copies worldwide every month.

Market

There are more than 3,000 magazines in the UK market, seven of which compete directly with Good Housekeeping.

In 2008 the women's interest magazine market became more competitive than ever, as the credit crunch began to bite and consumers cut back on non-essentials. However, Good Housekeeping has managed to maintain its leadership in this mature market, outselling its competitors with copy sales of more than 425,000 (Source: ABC July-December 2008).

Furthermore, Good Housekeeping boasts the largest subscription base of a magazine in the women's interest market, with 53 per cent of its readers currently subscribing to the title on a monthly basis. Recent orders have seen subscriptions hit a record high of 224,347 copies.

Product

Good Housekeeping aims to be lively, inspirational and an essential read for women in the 21st century, focusing on what really matters in life. It sets out to be the magazine readers trust most, providing expertise and attention to detail, delivered in a positive and accessible way – giving readers access to the 'best of everything'. Good Housekeeping's remit is to provide its readers with a wealth of information and advice, keeping them up-to-date and balancing practical solutions with achievable inspiration in a no-nonsense format.

Good Housekeeping is the only women's interest magazine with an independent consumer research centre, the Good Housekeeping Institute (GHI), established in 1924. The GHI was founded to provide readers with unbiased, independent research findings on consumer products.

In 2000, the GHI launched an accreditation scheme that allows manufacturers and retailers of food and non-food products to apply for access to use the GHI Approved logo – the benchmark for quality. Only after a consumer product has passed a series of rigorous Consumer Quality Assessment tests can the GHI Approved logo be used for marketing, PR and advertising purposes during a 12-month period. The GHI currently has more than 50 accredited products, bringing the trust and authority of the Good Housekeeping brand to a consumer audience that reaches far beyond the pages of the magazine.

Bringing the Good Housekeeping brand to life further, more than 30 reader events are organised annually, ranging from gardening evenings to cookery demonstrations and beauty workshops to fashion shows. Every year more than 10,000 readers have the opportunity to meet the people who work on the magazine and share in their expertise.

Achievements

In November 2008, The National Magazine Company's editorial director, Lindsay Nicholson, returned to the day-to-day editing of Good Housekeeping. A winner of the prestigious Mark Boxer lifetime achievement award presented by the British Society of Magazine Editors, Lindsay previously edited Good Housekeeping from 1999 to 2006 when it was named Magazine of the Year by the Periodical Publishers Association.

With her return to the magazine coinciding with an increasingly uncertain economy, Lindsay undertook the first major overhaul of the magazine's content in 10 years in order to reflect readers' current concerns. Underpinning the project was a clear belief: "In good times people love Good Housekeeping. In tough

1922	1994	2000	2006	2008	2009
British Good Housekeeping launches. Two years later, the Good Housekeeping Institute (GHI) is set up to provide unbiased advice on the best consumer products available.	Good Housekeeping achieves its highest ever ABC figure – selling an average of 518,435 copies a month (Source: ABC July-December 1994).	The GHI launches an accreditation scheme.	Good Housekeeping celebrates its 1,000th issue.	The launch of allaboutyou.com takes place.	As an alternative to the main issue, the ecologically inspired smaller issue size returns, last seen during World War II.

times, they depend on it." Given that the magazine had already survived four major recessions and a World War, she turned to the archive copies for inspiration. The resulting redesign, which made its debut with the May 2009 issue, features classical typography and more copy-heavy pages, delivering up to 25 per cent more information per page. Not only representing greater value for money for readers, it is also a more ecologically sound use of paper stocks.

Additionally, new columns were introduced, covering emotional issues, modern etiquette and household tips from the former head of the GHI, Aggie MacKenzie. Consumer advice provided by the GHI was expanded and a new campaign launched within the Food pages, encouraging readers to recognise that 'it's cheaper to make it yourself'.

Recent Developments
In 2003 Good Housekeeping launched its own range of branded products, the Good Housekeeping Essentials range. Established to add value to everyday life, every item is selected for its innovative and user-friendly design and tested and approved by the GHI. To complement the bakeware and utensil ranges already available, a woodware range was launched in June 2005 and a cookware range was launched at the end of 2008.

A new 'content rich and community driven' website, allaboutyou.com, was launched in April 2008. Representing the key editorial pillars of the magazine, the site provides an extensive database of tried and tested recipes.

Promotion
Core to Good Housekeeping's promotional strategy is working closely with its editorial teams to reinforce the brand's values and ensure that readers' needs are met; focus groups and reader panels provide valuable insight into the magazine's readership. The magazine also endeavours to work closely with third parties to enhance its position both on the newsstand and within the existing subscriber base. Good Housekeeping has seen a steady and consistent subscription growth over the years and in more recent times has tested innovative direct marketing techniques, with significant growth through online channels.

Brand Values
The Good Housekeeping brand is built upon the values of trust, expertise and authority, aiming to be progressive while maintaining its integrity as a consumer champion.

allaboutyou.com

Things you didn't know about Good Housekeeping

In the UK, Good Housekeeping sells one copy of the magazine every seven seconds (Source: ABC July-December 2008).

Good Housekeeping was the first magazine to publish a 'handbag' size. The reduced size was run during the paper shortages of World War II, when the information in Good Housekeeping was deemed by the government to be vital for the war effort.

Good Housekeeping was the first British women's magazine to publish an interview with Michelle Obama.

Over 45,000 recipes have been developed in the GHI since its launch. It would take someone eating three meals a day, more than 40 years to try all the recipes.

Cover stars have included Oprah Winfrey, Jane Fonda, Twiggy, Jamie Oliver and, in May 1937, George VI.

Heathrow **express** ⊗

Serving the world's busiest international airport and carrying more than five million passengers per year, Heathrow Express is one of the most successful high-speed air-rail links in the world. The service carries more than 16,000 passengers a day on the 15-minute journey between Heathrow Airport and central London.

Market

Every year, more than 65 million passengers pass through Heathrow Airport. Compared to many other international airports, Heathrow has historically been one of the hardest to get to, with passengers travelling to and from London facing a long journey by tube or risking traffic congestion by car or taxi.

Heathrow Express was one of the first to offer a premium, dedicated and high-speed airport train service, giving passengers an easy, reliable and fast option for travelling between the city centre and airport. It reaches the airport in just 15 minutes, with services to Terminal 5 taking a further six minutes, compared to around 55-60 minutes by London Underground and 30-45 minutes by taxi.

Product

Heathrow Express is a dedicated and non-stop, high-speed, air-rail link that operates daily between Heathrow Airport and central London, departing every 15 minutes. Every day 150 services run from London Paddington to Heathrow Central (Terminals 1 & 3) and Terminal 5. Passengers wishing to travel to Terminal 4 can change at Heathrow Central and board the free inter-terminal rail service, which arrives in three minutes.

The Heathrow Express cabins are designed to be level with the platform, making it easier to get luggage onboard. All cabins are climate controlled with modern accessible toilet facilities, ergonomically designed seating and generous luggage areas with onboard televisions to keep customers entertained throughout their journey. There are also Quiet Zones on the trains where the use of mobile phones is prohibited and Express TV is not in use. The First Class cabins deliver a high-end travel experience with leather-trimmed seats, complimentary copies of the FT, personal tables as well as quicker and easier access to the terminals.

Heathrow Express is a unique rail company as it is the only non-franchised mainline railway service operating in the UK, having been paid for by Heathrow Airport owner BAA.

Achievements

Since its launch in June 1998, Heathrow Express has established itself as a favoured route for both business and leisure passengers. On commencement of the service in 1998, it was estimated that approximately 3,000 journeys would be removed from the roads every day, a saving to the UK economy in terms of time – compared to the use of tube, taxi or bus – of more than £444 million.

1991	1998	2001	2007	2008	2009
The Heathrow Express Railways Act gives BAA the power to construct the Heathrow Express.	Heathrow Express is officially launched by the Prime Minister, Tony Blair.	Heathrow Express places an order for five new carriages, costing a total of £6.5 million.	In partnership with T-Mobile and Nomad Digital, a WiFi Hotspot service is introduced, providing passengers with 2Mbps internet access throughout the entire journey.	Heathrow Express launches services to Terminal 5, introduces e-ticketing, and launches its biggest multimedia campaign to date: 'The Airport is closer than you think.'	Heathrow Express introduces Flight Information Display Screens and Airline Self Service Check-In at Paddington. The WiFi service is now offered free to all customers.

Heathrow Express has also extended its global reach by becoming the first ever air-rail link to sign a deal with travel technology provider Amadeus. The deal means that travellers in more than 215 geographic markets can book Heathrow Express tickets at the same time as booking their flights and accommodation.

Heathrow Express has won a host of awards and has been recognised internationally as one of the most successful airport rail services. Its corporate identity, developed by Wolff Olins, is among the most comprehensive branding and design projects ever undertaken in transportation. This was recognised when the project became the 2000 Grand Prix Winner of the Design Business Awards.

Heathrow Express has worked hard to translate its customer service ethos into action and in 2006 was judged to have the Customer Service Team of the Year at the National Customer Service Awards. Since 2007, Heathrow Express has repeatedly secured a double first by topping the poll in the independent National Passenger Satisfaction Survey and has recently achieved the highest score in the survey's nine-year history. In 2009 Heathrow Express maintained its high position with a 92 per cent satisfaction rating.

Recent Developments
Heathrow Express is an innovative media owner and is constantly looking for ways to give other businesses commercial access to its hard-to-reach business audience.

In January 2007, Heathrow Express launched the first ever motion picture videowall advert in Europe. Four hundred and fifty 'frames', each holding an individual printed image, were installed on the train tunnel walls, covering a total distance of 1,500ft. Seen from a train travelling at 70mph this created a 15-second moving image advert.

Heathrow Express has also enhanced its groundbreaking onboard television service,

Express TV, which was created specifically to cater for the Heathrow Express passenger. It delivers a personalised live BBC news and world weather bulletin covering domestic, international and business news, as well as travel clips and entertainment programmes.

The company continues to innovate to meet customer needs and in 2008 launched an e-ticketing service. Tickets can be sent to mobile phones, in the form of a barcode, allowing passengers to book and board the service without having to queue for paper tickets.

In December 2009 Heathrow Express made London Paddington station the first UK railway station to offer Flight Information Display Screens and Airline Self Service Check-In. The machines, located at the Heathrow Express ticket office, are easy to use with touch screen facilities, allowing customers to print their boarding pass and view their flight information before they even arrive

at Heathrow Airport. Customers can proceed direct to the baggage drop, helping them save time and feel more at ease on their journey.

Promotion
Heathrow Express' biggest multimedia campaign, 'The Airport is closer than you think' was launched in 2008 and saw a series of idents run worldwide on Sky News to complement press, outdoor and digital advertising. The campaign set out to reinforce Heathrow Express as the fastest way to the airport. Press advertising featured in key UK business titles while an international campaign ran at JFK Airport in New York as well as Frankfurt, Schipol and Dublin airports.

The company uses below-the-line media to target its audience, investing in customer relationship marketing to boost frequency of use amongst its most loyal customers and developing marketing relationships with airlines at Heathrow Airport. For example, Heathrow Express partnered with British Airways to provide BA Executive Club members with complimentary tickets when booking flights online. Partnerships are communicated

via membership packs, media activity and email newsletters.

Brand Values
Heathrow Express' key brand values are speed, frequency and certainty; recent research has shown that these are the service benefits most required by customers.

For both business and leisure customers, Heathrow Express aims to provide high levels of comfort and customer service. However, different aspects of the brand's personality are highlighted for each market. For the business traveller, the brand is portrayed as fast, frequent, reliable and convenient. When speaking to the leisure market, the brand is reflected as not being overly formal or austere while being fast, reliable, convenient, approachable and family friendly.

heathrowexpress.com

Things you didn't know about Heathrow Express

Since launching, Heathrow Express has not only carried more than 50 million passengers, but has also regenerated enough energy to have boiled 400,000,000 kettles.

The Heathrow Express carbon-efficient electric trains are fitted with electrical regenerative brakes, a mechanism that reduces vehicle speed by converting some of its kinetic energy into another useful form of energy.

Heathrow Express was the first rail service in the UK to introduce onboard televisions, at its launch in 1998.

Heathrow Express trains are purpose-built and can travel at speeds of up to 100mph.

As it celebrates its 30th year, Highland Spring continues to be the leading UK-produced brand of bottled water (Source: Zenith Bottled Water Report 2009). Highland Spring is the only major bottled water brand to have its catchment area certified organic by the Soil Association. For more than 20 years, Highland Spring has been protecting its land in the Ochil Hills, Perthshire, keeping it free from pesticides and pollution to provide consumers with 'the water from organic land'.

Market

Packaged water has been one of the fastest growing and best performing soft drinks categories over the past 10 years. The short term market is, however, a challenging one. In the face of an overall volume decline in 2008, driven by a global economic slowdown and a poor British summer, imported brands have suffered the most while British brands show the greatest resilience.

Highland Spring produces more than 240 million bottles of water per year and in 2008 recorded a sales turnover of £54.2 million.

Product

The entire water catchment area for Highland Spring, extending to approximately 1,000 hectares, is certified organic by the Soil Association. The land has been kept free from pesticides and pollution for more than 20 years, with no farming, agricultural spraying, building or habitation permitted within the protected area from which the water is drawn.

Highland Spring launched new-look packaging across its range from April 2009, and the new designs vividly illustrate the brand's organic and environmental credentials.

Mindful of its environmental responsibilities, in 2008 15 million PET bottles made from 25 per cent recycled material were produced as part of Highland Spring's environmental programme. The aim is to increase use of recycled PET to 50 million bottles in 2009.

Highland Spring remains the only bottled water brand recognised by the Eco-Management and Audit System (EMAS). EMAS recognises organisations that go above and beyond legal compliance in order to continually improve their environmental performance.

Achievements

In 2008, Highland Spring continued its trend of outperforming the market, seeing its volume share rise to 8.6 per cent, drawing it closer than ever before to the market leader, Evian (Source: Zenith 2008).

Highland Spring is the number one sparkling water brand in the UK, outperforming its nearest competitor by more than two to one (Source: Zenith Bottled Water Report 2009).

1979	1993	1998	2001		2004
Highland Spring Ltd is formed.	Highland Spring displaces Perrier from the number one slot and wins the contract to supply bottled water to British Airways worldwide.	Highland Spring becomes the official water supplier to the World Snooker Association.	Highland Spring becomes the first British brand of bottled water to have its land certified organic by the Soil Association.	Throughout 2001 the brand continues to innovate, pioneering the children's bottled water market.	Highland Spring celebrates its 25th anniversary.

Now, that's true love.

www.thewaterfromorganicland.com — The water from organic land

Against an overall market decline of 5.5 per cent to 2,055 million litres, Highland Spring's sales fell by just 1.4 per cent (Source: Zenith 2008).

Highland Spring bypassed Volvic to be ranked second in the take-home market and was the fastest growing brand among major multiples. It also won share in both the impulse and on-premise markets. It remains the leading UK-produced brand of bottled water, and is first in doorstep deliveries and the cash and carry sector. (In the latter, its volume sales are greater than those of the next three brands combined.) A pioneer of children's bottled water, Highland Spring continues to lead the sector.

In the same year it was the 'most trusted' British bottled water brand, according to consumer research (Source: NOP November 2008) and was recognised as the leading ethical bottled water brand by The Good Shopping Guide in 2007, 2008 and 2009.

Recent Developments

Highland Spring is leading the way in communicating the benefits of bottled water and healthy hydration. A founder NATURAL HYDRATION COUNCIL member of the Natural Hydration Council (NHC), together with Danone and Nestlé, it is providing information to help consumers make informed choices, free from media myth and misinformation. The NHC will continue to research and promote the environmental, health and other sustainable benefits of natural bottled water. A major advertising campaign in 2009 spearheads this initiative.

In 2009 Highland Spring acquired premium Scottish brand, Speyside Glenlivet Natural

Mineral Water. Bottled at source on the Crown Estate of Glenlivet, it is drawn from Scotland's highest spring. The brand is found in some of the world's most distinguished hotels, from London's The Dorchester to The Ritz in Paris.

Promotion

2009 sees a major development in Highland Spring's brand communication strategy.

Having successfully communicated its unique rational credentials as the first bottled water to be drawn from land certified organic, Highland Spring is setting out to make an emotional connection with consumers via a high profile national press campaign. Using iconic cinematic moments of 'unconditional giving', featuring some of Hollywood's most treasured stars, the campaign conveys the idea that choosing to give someone Highland Spring is an act of 'true love'.

Underpinning this is a refreshed web presence that further communicates Highland Spring's organic and environmental credentials.

As advocates of a healthy, active lifestyle, the company strives to promote the link between active sport and good hydration and has a comprehensive sports sponsorship portfolio.

Highland Spring is the exclusive drinks sponsor of Britain's number one tennis professional, Andy Murray and his brother, Jamie Murray – a former Wimbledon doubles champion. Highland Spring is the official bottled water supplier to the Lawn Tennis Association and also supports initiatives promoting tennis as a fun and healthy pursuit for all ages.

The brand sponsors Scottish cyclist and Olympic gold medallist Sir Chris Hoy and is the official water supplier to high profile rugby teams and athletics events. It also sponsors top golf and snooker professionals.

Highland Spring's sports sponsorship portfolio aims to inspire and motivate young Britons to get involved in sport and develop healthy hydration habits.

Brand Values

Highland Spring is an iconic Scottish brand. The water is drawn from an underground spring in the Ochil Hills in Perthshire, Scotland.

As guardian of the land, the company goes to great lengths to protect its source, ensuring the water is as pure as possible.

Highland Spring is committed to protecting the wider environment and developing its business in a sustainable, eco-friendly way.

highland-spring.com

Things you didn't know about Highland Spring

Highland Spring is the first bottled water to have the land from which it is drawn certified organic.

Highland Spring is a founder member of the Natural Hydration Council.

Highland Spring's packaging is 100 per cent recyclable.

2006	2007	2008	2009
The first national TV advertising campaign is rolled out.	Highland Spring is revealed as the exclusive drinks sponsor to British tennis star Andy Murray and his brother, former Wimbledon doubles champion, Jamie Murray.	Highland Spring signs a major sponsorship partnership with Sir Chris Hoy, multi-gold medal winner at the Beijing Olympics.	New packaging is launched and classic Hollywood stars are used to promote 'the water from organic land'.

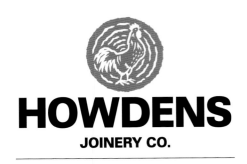

HOWDENS
JOINERY CO.

MAKING SPACE MORE VALUABLE

Howdens Joinery was founded in 1995 in order to serve the needs of small builders undertaking routine joinery and kitchen installation work. By 2009 it had become one of the UK's leading suppliers of kitchens and joinery products to the trade. Howdens has achieved this by creating a strong entrepreneurial culture within its depots, a close relationship with its customers and a range of kitchens specifically designed to meet the needs of modern living.

Market

Howdens operates within the trade or 'done for you' kitchen market, its core customer base comprising local builders and skilled professionals. The company has always believed that project management by the local builder is the best solution for installing a kitchen; it has experience in bringing together products, services and local trades in order to deliver a project on time, on budget and to a high standard. The introduction of additional legislation governing materials and services, combined with increasingly 'cash rich, time poor' and design-savvy end-users, has seen this market grow dramatically.

Howdens helps builders to manage their businesses by guaranteeing product availability from local stock with rigid cabinets that are ready to install, saving builders time and money as well as allowing them to plan effectively. Its versatile and scaleable supply chain ensures its depots, and in turn the customer, receive a high level of service. Specifically within the trade sector, key competitors are Jewson, Travis Perkins, Magnet Trade and Benchmarx.

Product

Howdens sells kitchens – encompassing appliances, accessories, handles, worktops, sinks and taps – and joinery, such as doors, flooring, stairs and hardware. A free survey and Computer Aided Design (CAD) service, which includes a site visit, is also available. The company has the UK's largest kitchen range available from stock and ensures its portfolio remains informed by new product development. As all depots hold stock locally they are also able to offer local delivery when and where required.

Achievements

Since it was established in 1995, Howdens has demonstrated strong growth with a turnover exceeding £750 million in 2009. In 15 years it has expanded from 14 depots to more than 460, supplying 234,000 building trade professionals as well as over 300 local authorities and housing associations with around 400,000 complete kitchens each year. In 2003 Howdens also set up Houdan Menuiseries in France with a further 11 depots.

In September 2007, a partnership between Howdens Joinery and Leonard Cheshire Disability was named 'Best Corporate Partnership' at the Third Sector Excellence

1995		1999	2002	2003	2004
Howdens Joinery starts trading in October with 14 depots, supplying trade professionals locally from stock.	The depots stock joinery, hardware and 11 kitchen ranges, plus appliances, sinks and taps, worktops and accessories.	Howdens Joinery opens its 100th depot.	Howdens Joinery opens its 250th depot.	Howdens Joinery opens 11 depots in France under the name Houdan Menuiseries.	Howdens Joinery sets the standard in the trade kitchen market with its new format high quality Kitchen Brochure. The partnership with Howdens and Leonard Cheshire is formed.

Awards. The research partnership aims to develop affordable, attractive and practical kitchen products for people with physical disabilities. In 2007, six kitchen activity centres were created, donated and installed in Leonard Cheshire homes across the UK. It is an area with significant potential for ongoing product development and both Howdens and Leonard Cheshire Disability are committed to building their relationship in order to further benefit local communities. In addition, Howdens has developed a highly accessible kitchen collection called 'Inclusive Kitchens', which is sold through its depots.

Recent Developments

Since the autumn of 2007, Howdens has operated two mobile display vehicles, which highlight products aimed at the social housing market and showcase new products. The trailers are able to travel to depots and customers' premises to create maximum impact and support localised marketing activities. In addition, the company's fleet of more than 400 delivery trailers has been rebranded to create further brand awareness.

Howdens has been awarded FSC and PEFC chain of custody certificates for a number of joinery products and a selection of its kitchen ranges. It will continue to strive for certification on additional ranges and products.

Product development remains key to the company in order to ensure its continued growth. By offering products that are both affordable and in line with the latest design trends for the home, Howdens aims to meet changing market needs head on.

As consumers become ever more design conscious, increased emphasis is placed on building brand awareness further, so that the Howdens name is recognised and recommended not only by builders but also by end-users themselves.

Promotion

Howdens puts the relationship between local depots and builders at the heart of its promotional strategy. As such its kitchen and joinery brochures, alongside other literature, are specifically designed to help builders in discussion with their own customers. Local marketing is key and the depots tailor their promotional activity to meet customer needs. Many depots also provide donations to local charities and community projects, including sponsorship of grassroots football and rugby teams.

More recently, Howdens has developed a website to showcase the company and its

complete range of products, and for the first time in its history, in 2008 began to undertake consumer and trade advertising campaigns. These ventures have been carefully considered to raise brand awareness and help the local depot and local builder in selling Howdens products to end-users.

In 2009, Howdens introduced a series of Truly Local books, published quarterly, to tell the stories behind their customer relationships and to show how the business is an integral part of the local community.

Brand Values

Howdens is guided by the aim of providing small builders with kitchen and joinery products of the highest quality, at the best price and from local stock. The company attributes its success to the strength of the depots' relationships with their customers and the breadth of the market they serve; the quality and range of Howdens products; the ability to service customers from local stock; and the opportunity to streamline the business around supplying one customer, the small builder.

howdens.com

Things you didn't know about Howdens Joinery

Howdens sells 400,000 complete kitchens every year.

Four million kitchen cabinets are manufactured annually by Howdens.

Howdens prints more than 1.5 million kitchen brochures each year.

Howdens makes charitable donations to over 1,500 good causes each year.

2006	2007	2008	2009
Howdens Joinery launches a market leading Joinery Brochure featuring doors, joinery and flooring.	The Howdens website launches in April. A mobile Contract trailer launches to assist the depots in promoting their products and services. The 400th depot opens.	The first Howdens Joinery branded delivery trailers go on the road. The first consumer and trade advertising campaign launches.	The Lamona brand of appliances, sinks and taps launches, which is exclusive to Howdens Joinery. There are 462 depots across the UK supplying over 40 kitchen ranges from stock.

The ICAEW is a world leading professional accountancy body, providing representation, qualifications and support to more than 134,000 members in over 160 countries. Founded in 1880 the ICAEW has a long track-record of working in the public interest with governments and regulators. Many of the frameworks and standards that guide the modern accountancy profession were developed in conjunction with the ICAEW.

Market

During periods of economic uncertainty, people making business decisions need the knowledge and support of finance professionals, trained to provide objective and impartial advice at the highest levels. ICAEW's members challenge people and organisations to think and act differently. The training and professional development they receive equips them to be capable of providing leadership and direction to organisations of all sizes across economic sectors. Collectively ICAEW members make a major contribution to economic activity as well as to the effective operation of markets.

Chartered accountants work across the full breadth of the economy, using their expertise in business, practice and the public sector to drive efficiency. For example, in 2009 more than 84 per cent of the FTSE 100 members' boards included an ICAEW member. The organisation licensed 4,100 audit firms and its members working in private practice were a first port of call for many of the SMEs that constitute the backbone of the UK economy.

The ICAEW's flagship professional qualification, the ACA, attracts talented people from a variety of backgrounds. While the majority of its students are graduates it encourages access to the profession through a variety of routes and it is possible to qualify as a Chartered Accountant straight from school.

Product

The ACA is widely regarded as one of the leading global business and finance qualifications, recognised and valued across industry sectors. The ICAEW offers ACA training through more than 3,000 authorised training offices around the world, from the UK to Malaysia, Pakistan, Russia, China, Cyprus and the United Arab Emirates, as well as through partnerships with leading education providers in other countries.

Characterised by its technical rigour, ethical focus, international outlook and multidisciplinary approach, the ACA is designed to reflect modern global accounting practices. Once qualified, members are entitled to call themselves 'chartered accountants' and to use the designatory letters ACA (Associate of the Institute of Chartered Accountants in England and Wales). To retain ACA status, members must participate in continuing professional

1880	1893	1919	1930	1970	1999
A new professional body, The Institute of Chartered Accountants in England and Wales (ICAEW) is created by Royal Charter.	Chartered Accountants' Hall, in the City of London, is completed and opened by the ICAEW's president Edwin Waterhouse. It goes on to become a Grade II listed building.	Mary Harris Smith is admitted to the ICAEW, becoming the first female chartered accountant in the world.	Sir William Plender of Sundridge (ICAEW president, 1929-1930) becomes the first chartered accountant to receive a peerage.	The extended and new building at Chartered Accountants' Hall is opened by Her Majesty Queen Elizabeth The Queen Mother.	Dame Sheila Masters is the first woman to become president of the ICAEW.

Over 84% of FTSE100 companies have an ACA on their board.

With an ACA the whole world's calling.

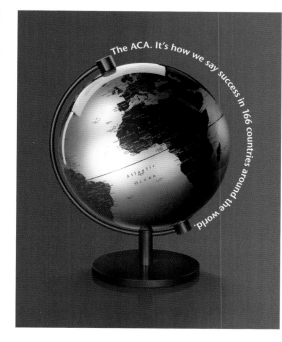

The ACA. It's how we say success in 166 countries around the world.

development every year to ensure their skills and knowledge remain up-to-date and relevant. As well as the ACA, the ICAEW provides a range of additional qualifications across various disciplines such as corporate finance (CF), charity accounting (DChA), and International Financial Reporting Standards (IFRS certification). To widen access to the profession, the CFAB qualification was introduced in 2008 to allow individuals without formal qualifications the opportunity to be certified in the foundations of finance, accounting and business.

Achievements

A key part of the organisation's role is to encourage and promote informed debate on the future of the profession as well as the economic sectors it supports. Its thought leadership activity in areas such as tax, auditing, financial services and corporate reporting feeds directly into the public policy debate both in the UK and increasingly internationally. For example, in 2009 it was commissioned by Government to undertake an in-depth analysis of the bank lending environment for small businesses. Its G20 submission advocated the importance of convergence of financial reporting standards which became one of the key recommendations of the Denver summit.

The ICAEW also works extensively with organisations such as the World Bank to encourage the profession in developing economies such as its recent project with the Bangladesh Government, intended to raise standards across the country's fledgling accountancy profession.

Closer to home its financial capability initiative encourages members to work with schools and colleges to help deliver personal finance education through a structured programme of outreach. This initiative is intended to help young people develop the basic skills needed to manage their personal finances.

Recent Developments

The ICAEW has also recently launched the Business Sustainability Programme (BSP), which allows businesses to educate their staff on social and environmental issues; and the first peer-to-peer leadership network, the Financial Talent Executive Network (F-TEN). Aimed at the next generation of finance leaders in business and practice, F-TEN is designed to help employers retain their best talent and develop their leadership capabilities. The Narrowing the Gap programme is designed to help businesses recruit and retain the best female financial talent, as well as helping individuals returning to the workforce after a career break. The programme is supported by the ICAEW's dedicated recruitment portal www.icaewjobs.com – an all-encompassing career resource for members that showcases the opportunities available to ACAs worldwide.

Promotion

An international advertising programme was launched in October 2009 to reinforce the premium positioning and global appeal of the ACA qualification. This campaign built on the success of the 2008 campaign which demonstrated a measurable shift in positive perceptions among the ICAEW's key stakeholders, as well as increased recognition of the ACA. Advertisements feature in national and trade press, online, and in transport hubs.

Brand Values

The ICAEW has a clear vision – to inspire business confidence in the UK and internationally. Its mission is to deliver on its Charter obligations. Its strategy is to focus on premium positioning for member services, qualifications, reputation and influence, delivered through partnerships and international growth.

Building on its leadership position in the UK, the organisation is focused on representing and supporting the profession across the world.

icaew.com

Things you didn't know about ICAEW

The ICAEW is the only international professional body to be invited to join the World Economic Forum in Davos.

The ICAEW is a founding member of the Global Accounting Alliance (GAA), which has more than 775,000 members.

ICAEW Library and Information Service holds the largest collection of UK accountancy auditing and taxation resources in the world.

The Business Confidence Monitor, a quarterly report from the ICAEW, is drawn upon as an accurate barometer of business thinking by the UK Government and the Bank of England.

Many of the founding fathers of the 'Big Four' accountancy firms were early presidents of the ICAEW – such as Arthur Cooper, William Deloitte, Edwin Waterhouse and William Peat.

2006	2007	2008	2009
The ICAEW is appointed by the European Commission to study the implementation of IFRS throughout the European Union.	The ICAEW wins a £1 million tender from the World Bank to raise standards across the accountancy profession in Bangladesh.	ICAEW chief executive Michael Izza chairs the committee recommending to the Chancellor an independent valuer for Northern Rock.	A new, modern business centre and restaurant are launched to support members.

Imperial Leather has been in consumers' bathrooms for generations. Today, while we're still all familiar with the original Imperial Leather bar of soap and its little metallicised label, the brand has grown to the extent that at any given moment, thousands of people all over the world are using a product from Imperial Leather's extensive washing and bathing range.

Market

Imperial Leather is a key player in the UK's personal washing and bathing market. In 2009, this market was worth an estimated £492 million (Source: Nielsen March 2009) and is in slight growth year-on-year.

With more than one in five UK homes now having two or more bathrooms (Source: GB TGI BMRB 2006/07) and UK consumers living busier lives (for example, making more visits to the gym) there has been an increase in shower usage occasions while bath usage has decreased. Imperial Leather, with its extensive portfolio of affordably luxurious, feel good, rich lathering products, is well positioned to continue to tap into this growth.

Product

Imperial Leather's product range includes shower gels, Foamburst shower gels, bath foams, hand washes, deodorants and talcum powder as well as its famous bars of soap. The range is aimed at the whole family, with products designed to give a trusted, feel good, luxurious washing and bathing experience at an affordable price.

Achievements

When Imperial Leather launched its innovative Foamburst range in 1998, it was the first shower product in a can that dispensed as a gel and transformed into a mass of rich creamy lather. This market-leading development has proved to be hugely popular with men, women and children alike.

Ten years on, Imperial Leather continues to launch innovative products. 2008 saw the introduction of Skinbliss, an ultra-mild moisturising bodywash targeted specifically at young women looking for an indulgent shower experience. It offers significantly softer, smoother skin in comparison to the leading shower gel (Source: Skin Investigation Technology December 2007). Skinbliss won Bronze in the Best Bath and Shower Launch category at the 2008 Pure Beauty Awards, with judges praising its moisturising ability.

Over the last year, more than one in three people in the UK purchased at least one Imperial Leather product (Source: TNS) – the equivalent of more than 17 million people. It is now the leading washing and bathing brand in many key markets across the globe and can be found in countries including the UK, China, Australia, Nigeria, Greece and Indonesia.

1768	1938	1940s	1950s-60s	1970s	1998
Russian nobleman Count Orlof challenges perfumers, Bayleys of Bond Street, to create a perfume that embodies the distinctive aroma of the Russian court.	Imperial Leather is brought to the UK by Cussons, introducing the British public to the 'Eau de Cologne Imperiale Russe' fragrance.	Manufacturing operations expand rapidly. Marjorie Cussons, the pioneering daughter of the company's founder, is responsible for energising public interest in the brand.	Production expansion continues with the addition of manufacturing sites in Manchester and Nottingham.	Shower gel is introduced to the product range.	The innovative Foamburst shower product range is launched, packaged in a rust-free can rather than a bottle.

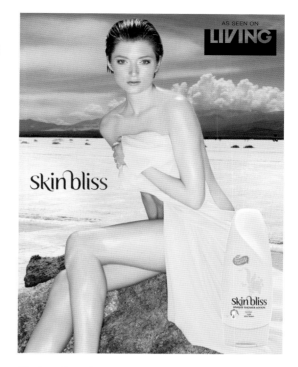

Promotion

Imperial Leather was one of the first brands in washing and bathing to recognise the potential and power of advertising.

By 1946, Cussons was spending £100,000 supporting the brand – an enormous sum at the time. Predominantly choosing to advertise in the popular women's magazines of the day, Imperial Leather's advertising campaigns used a series of specially commissioned paintings featuring orchids, tropical fish, miniature gardens and roses. Furthermore, Marjorie Cussons, the marketing-minded daughter of the company's founder, introduced gift sets at key purchasing periods.

During the 1950s, cinema's popularity led Cussons to place commercials on the big screen, in advance of the featured presentation, to convey the brand's everyday luxury credentials.

The brand was also one of the first to commit to TV advertising. Imperial Leather's first TV commercial aired in 1959 and featured a mother and daughter using Imperial Leather. It is this investment by Imperial Leather and other similar brands that led to the coining of the phrase 'Soaps' in relation to advertiser-funded TV drama.

The famous Imperial Leather 'Family' campaign was launched in the 1970s. Whether travelling across the Russian Steppes in the Imperial Train or flying high in their Imperial Leather Spaceship, the family always found time to enjoy a luxurious soak in their decadent mobile bathroom.

The brand's latest TV campaign celebrates 'the hug', showing people from all walks of life 'getting closer to the ones they love'. The campaign also gives consumers the opportunity to send a personalised e-hug via the internet, with more than a quarter of a million people using the service at Imperial Leather's huggableskin.co.uk website during the campaign launch.

To support the launch of Skinbliss, 2008 saw the launch of the 'Skin Is In' creative. An outdoor, fashion-led campaign, it featued 20ft images of Imperial Leather's Skinbliss model displayed in city centre locations across the UK. The brand enhanced its fashion strategy by sponsoring an episode of Britain's Next Top Model, filmed in the Argentinian Salt Lakes, a first for Imperial Leather.

Brand Values

Imperial Leather is a leading quality washing and bathing brand aimed at families. The brand understands the importance of the family bond and believes in developing quality products for everyone at an affordable price.

imperialleather.co.uk

In the UK the brand has moved its manufacturing to a new multimillion-pound facility in Agecroft, with significant improvements in efficiency of production and enhanced benefits for the environment.

Recent Developments

In 2008 Imperial Leather relaunched its entire range with a contemporary design and livery, further embracing its family-oriented positioning.

This followed on from the successful launch of the brand's Limited Edition range of shower gels and bath foams in 2006. Further Limited Edition products were introduced in 2007, followed in 2008 by Hawaiian Spa and Icelandic Spa variants. 2009 sees the launch of a new Limited Edition range inspired by the feel of luxurious fabric against the skin – Sumptuous Satin and Sensuous Silk. With a creamy blend of textures and complementary fragrances, the products are designed to leave skin feeling soft, pampered and smooth.

Things you didn't know about Imperial Leather

Contrary to popular belief, the metallicised label on each soap bar should face downwards not upwards, to keep the bar fresh in the soap dish.

The shape of the Imperial Leather bar has not changed since its inception; it was developed to mirror that of saddle soap used by the Russian Imperial household to clean its riding tack.

More than 60 million bars of Imperial Leather soap are sold every year. If these were placed side by side they would stretch the entire length of the Great Wall of China.

2000s	2002	2008	2009
Imperial Leather collaborates with The Tussauds Group, sponsoring 'Bubbleworks' at Chessington World of Adventures and 'The Flume' at Alton Towers.	Imperial Leather is a key sponsor of the Manchester Commonwealth Games.	Manufacturing moves to a new, multimillion-pound facility in Agecroft, improving production efficiency and reducing its environmental impact.	PZ Cussons opens a £26 million innovation centre in Manchester, demonstrating its continued commitment to forward thinking and local industry.

INVESTORS IN PEOPLE

Investors in People is a flexible, easy to use framework which helps organisations transform their business performance and boosts the productivity of the UK economy. It improves the ways in which organisations manage and develop their people. The framework is outcome focused, outlining what needs to be achieved, never prescribing how. Investors in People focuses on identifying organisational priorities, applying the framework in a tailored way to deliver them.

Product

At the heart of Investors in People is The Standard. It comprises 39 outcome-based evidence requirements which follow the 'plan, do, review' cycle. This allows organisations to build up a complete picture of how they are managing their people and where they can make improvements. Organisations need to meet these 39 evidence requirements in order to be recognised as an Investor in People and permitted to display the laurel logo and plaque.

In May 2009, following extensive consultation with customers, Investors in People launched an extended framework offering greater breadth and depth of expertise. This was introduced alongside a more tailored approach to delivering business support shaped around organisational needs. This new approach is focused on listening to the organisation's

priorities and applying the framework towards meeting objectives giving in-depth feedback on the issues that matter most.

The extended framework provides customers with more scope for continuous improvement and stretch. It offers deeper and more

challenging evidence requirements where relevant. To celebrate progress, additional Bronze, Silver and Gold recognition have been introduced to acknowledge additional achievement beyond The Standard.

Investors in People offers a number of free online support tools, including Interactive. This tool is built around five management practices that relate directly to the Investors in People framework. It is designed to guide organisations through development activities so that they can establish a clear understanding of their current strengths, and prioritise areas that require further focus.

Market

Born out of the recession of the early 1990s, Investors in People was launched by business, for business. Since then thousands of employers throughout the UK have worked with the Investors in People framework in conjunction with expert advisors and assessors to enhance their performance and meet their goals. Currently almost eight million employees in more than 35,000 organisations, based in 50 countries worldwide, are working with Investors in People. Of those organisations, 3,500 have been recognised for 10 or more years bearing testimony to the long term effectiveness of the Investors in People approach.

1990	1991	1993	1995	2001	2004
Investors in People is created when The Employment Department is tasked with developing a national standard that sets out a level of good practice for training and development to achieve business goals.	The first 28 Investor in People organisations – both large and small – are celebrated at the formal launch of Investors in People on 16th October.	Investors in People UK is formed as a business-led, non-departmental public body. The following year the first Investors in People Week is launched.	The first review of The Standard is carried out and an operation is established in Australia.	A total of 5,939,825 employees are in organisations working with Investors in People.	Investors in People launches the latest version of The Standard and The Champions programme is launched.

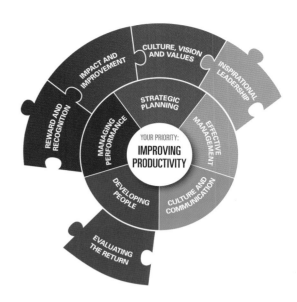

Promotion

Investors in People's marketing strategy focuses on the promotion and positioning of the brand as a business improvement tool. Investors in People thrives on word-of-mouth recommendation through trusted, respected sources and has two programmes recognising the value of advocacy: The Champions Programme and The Ambassadors Programme. Champions are organisations that disseminate and share best practice with employers of all sizes and sectors, engaging in additional promotional activity to extend understanding of Investors in People and its benefits. Currently over 50 organisations have gained the prestigious status of Investors in People Champion.

Ambassadors are individuals who promote and represent Investors in People, inspiring others to adopt best people management practices. They take part in a series of high profile events and speaking platforms.

Achievements

When Superbrands revealed its top 500 Business Superbrands for 2009, Investors in People had risen an impressive 207 places to sit at 210, making it the biggest year-on-year riser. Investors in People has consistently achieved high levels of consumer recognition and its listing as one of the top Business Superbrands is testament to its reputation as the UK's leading tool for business improvement through people.

Investors in People aims to be relevant, trusted and flexible. During its history, the framework has been through three extensive reviews to ensure it is at the forefront of best practice, challenging organisations to continuously improve. Furthermore, Investors in People delivers real results; it creates improved employee engagement, increased flexibility and better bottom line results. Independent research in 2008 from Cranfield School of Management shows a causal link between the adoption of the Investors in People Standard and improved financial performance. This research also showed that the more an organisation embraces the principles of Investors in People, the greater the benefits.

Recent Developments

Investors in People is introducing a Health and Wellbeing Good Practice Award in the spring of 2010. This award will help employers develop effective health and wellbeing strategies, ensuring that activity is linked to corporate objectives and the impact of interventions is evaluated. The award aims to build resilience and engagement with employees, enabling organisations to adapt and remain innovative in a continued climate of change.

Brand Values

Investors in People takes pride in offering an accessible, flexible and responsive service to customers, reflecting its promise to deliver real benefit to employers of all sizes and in all sectors throughout the UK. The brand aims to be confident, credible and energising – values which are underpinned by research findings and reflected in customers' pride in achieving success with Investors in People.

These values are expressed in a new identity and revised logo that Investors in People launched alongside its new approach and extended framework in May 2009. The laurel mark has been developed to make it work more effectively and the brand's regional delivery partners have rebranded using the new logo to present a seamless identity throughout the delivery network.

Essentially the Investors in People brand represents a promise; it is an expression of the positive performance improvement experience that everyone – customers, suppliers and its own people – expect and should receive.

investorsinpeople.co.uk

Things you didn't know about Investors in People

Investors in People has introduced a new approach that can transform performance by targeting an organisation's specific business priorities.

Since 1991 over 40 per cent of the UK workforce, more than 10 million people, have worked in an Investors in People recognised organisation.

Investors in People brings a wide range of benefits to organisations of all sizes. Any changes are always developed in consultation with customers so the framework remains universally relevant.

2007	2008	2009	2010
Investors in People Interactive, a free online support tool, is launched.	Some 7,771,357 employees are in organisations working with Investors in People.	Investors in People unveils an extended framework plus Bronze, Silver and Gold recognition for those who work beyond The Standard.	The Health and Wellbeing Good Practice Award is launched in spring 2010.

Already one of the leading forces in the UK design, print and copying market, Kall Kwik continues to add to the range of services offered by its UK-wide network of Centres and is rapidly gaining a reputation for creative design that makes business print even more effective. At the same time, the company has expanded into new markets including email communications and web-to-print.

customers with complex campaigns. By covering a wider range of print and design requirements in-house – including specialist print services, such as large-format print or outdoor banners – Kall Kwik provides a complete service, from just one supplier. With shorter lines of communication involved, projects are able to run more smoothly and there can be direct economic benefits as a result.

Quick to recognise the potential of new technologies, Kall Kwik continues to adopt the latest in digital print. Personalised print – whereby printed items include content that is personalised to individual recipients – is just one area where Kall Kwik helps customers to ensure that items, such as direct mail, stand out from the crowd.

Market

With virtually every UK business requiring professional design, print or copying services, the total market exceeds £1 billion per annum. Kall Kwik is the UK's largest design and print group – with a seven per cent market share – and the company is proactively helping franchisees to expand into new market sectors.

Today, as businesses and public sector organisations seek to improve efficiency and focus on their core activities, there's a growing need for suppliers that offer a wider range of services, so that administrative burdens are eased and fewer suppliers need to be briefed for each project. While building on its strong position in the traditional print market, Kall Kwik is introducing non-print products that help franchisees respond to customer demand for integrated communications services.

Product

For many design and print projects, 85 per cent of the total spend is used on creative design – leaving just 15 per cent for print. Therefore, by placing greater emphasis on selling design services, Kall Kwik is helping franchisees to increase order values. In addition, as the choice of printer often lies in the hands of a project's designer, Kall Kwik franchisees that work with customers at the design level have greater ownership of the entire project. This design-led sales strategy is helping to position franchisees as trusted advisors in design and print; franchisees are able to engage with customers from the outset of a project, contribute ideas on a consultative basis and oversee every aspect from design through to print.

This integrated capability, known as Design to Delivery™ (D2D), is of particular benefit to

Achievements

Over the years, Kall Kwik has won many awards for its franchise model. In 2008, Kall Kwik's parent company, On Demand Communications, committed more than £3.5 million of new investment for its two franchise businesses: Kall Kwik and Prontaprint. This resulted in the sale of existing Kall Kwik stores alongside the opening of new Centres.

Kall Kwik has also accelerated the development of its design services offering. During 2008, franchisees undertook record levels of design and consultancy work and the number of Kall Kwik's specialist kdesigngroup Centres grew by 20 per cent. This growth in design-related business was achieved through support programmes that helped Kall Kwik and kdesigngroup Centres to recruit and train skilled design personnel.

1978	1979	1999	2005	2007	2008
The company is founded by Moshe Gerstenhaber, who purchased the master franchise from the US Kwik Kopy organisation.	The first Kall Kwik opens in Pall Mall, London.	Kall Kwik UK is acquired by Adare Group, the leading provider of print, mailing and data management solutions throughout the UK and Ireland.	Kall Kwik UK is named Franchisor of the Year by the British Franchise Association. Kall Kwik also launches D2D and the first k design studio is opened in Winchester.	The 33rd k design studio is launched and the 154th Kall Kwik Centre is opened in Stockport.	Kall Kwik celebrates its 30th year of trading and the number of k design studios grows by 20 per cent.

Dynamic Design
Ideas with impact

Vibrant Print
The sky's the limit

Direct Mail
To suit you

Large Format
Big, bright ideas

Recent Developments

Long established in printed direct mail services, Kall Kwik is now helping clients to execute email-based communications. The emphasis is on offering an integrated service with help at every stage – from sourcing targeted email address lists, to design, copywriting, email distribution and monitoring click-through rates.

Kall Kwik Studio is an innovative service whereby Kall Kwik offers clients an online ordering facility and works with them to create a portfolio of standard templates for a range of printed items. The online templates enable clients to offer their employees a self-service facility for the generation of new brochures, business cards or promotional materials. Logos and key design elements are fixed within the template, in order to ensure consistent layout and branding. The customised items can then be checked online before the final order is placed. Kall Kwik Studio helps to streamline the entire design, proofing and ordering process, which helps customers to reduce administration overheads, cut costs and eliminate errors.

Promotion

Kall Kwik has steadily increased the resources it devotes to generating sales leads for franchisees. While many new campaigns promote specific products and services, Kall Kwik's marketing team has used a range of techniques to help franchisees publicise their consultative approach to solving business communications issues.

The company has expanded its Franchise Sales Team which works closely with potential franchisees. It selects only those candidates

who have the necessary qualities to build a successful business and support Kall Kwik's reputation for consistently high customer service. Once a franchise agreement has been signed, the sales team oversees Kall Kwik's Marketing Launch Promotion (MLP) programme, which provides business and marketing support. Following the 12-month MLP programme, Kall Kwik Centres continue to receive direct access to specialist marketing and business expertise in order to help generate demand and manage growth.

Brand Values

Brand image is vitally important – both in attracting new franchisees and promoting services to each franchise's customers. To franchisees, Kall Kwik represents an established, respected brand with a proven business model. For customers, Kall Kwik offers a convenient, local service that has access to nationwide resources.

The company strives to ensure consistency across the franchise network. Each Kall Kwik Centre provides customers with access to an approachable team of design, print and communications experts, capable of contributing ideas to transform a concept into a finished product that achieves better results.

kallkwik.co.uk

Things you didn't know about Kall Kwik

Kall Kwik arranged for its Putney Centre in south west London to print the 'Feed Me Better' petition that was presented to the then Prime Minister, Tony Blair, by TV chef Jamie Oliver.

Across the group, Kall Kwik employs more graphic designers than any other UK private sector company.

2009 sees the 30th anniversary of the opening of Kall Kwik UK's first franchised Centre, located in London.

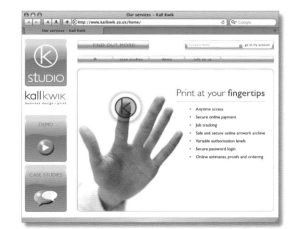

LandSecurities

As the leading commercial real estate brand for more than 60 years, Land Securities has focused on delivering a customer offering which provides its occupiers with quality accommodation and high levels of customer service. Three signature qualities exemplify the Land Securities brand: expert – recognisably an expert in commercial real estate; progressive – genuinely changing in a changing world; and accessible – easy to talk to and do business with.

Market

Land Securities is the UK's largest Real Estate Investment Trust (REIT). Its national portfolio of commercial property, worth many billions of pounds, includes some of Britain's best-known retail outlets, including Leeds' White Rose Centre and Gunwharf Quays in Portsmouth, as well as London landmarks such as the Piccadilly Lights and Westminster City Hall. Land Securities has a multimillion pound development programme with projects in Cardiff, Leeds and Glasgow city centres as well as key sites in central London. It is also involved in long term, large scale regeneration projects in the South East. Leading competitors in the market are institutional investors such as Prudential Property Investments Management, Legal and General, Standard Life and Morley Fund Management, quoted competitors such as British Land and Hammerson, together with private commercial companies such as The Crown Estate and Grosvenor.

Product

Land Securities operates mainly in the £500 billion UK commercial property market and, measured by market capitalisation, represents more than 20 per cent of the UK quoted property sector. Its business model is diversified, focused on retail property and London offices. In the core markets of retail property and London offices, the Group provides about 5.8 per cent and four per cent respectively of the market floorspace. Within its core market segments, Land Securities' activities include property management, investment, development and the provision of property related services.

Achievements

The Group's investment portfolio was valued at just under £9 billion at its half financial year on 30th September 2009, maintaining its position as one of the world's largest REITs. Land Securities is also a member of the FTSE4Good and Dow Jones Index, which acknowledge its commitment to corporate responsibility. The Group is a regular recipient of industry awards and recently Land Securities developments won the Supreme Gold at the British Council of Shopping Centres' awards for five consecutive years.

Recent Developments

In January 2009 Land Securities sold its property outsourcing arm Trillium for a total cash consideration of £750 million as it raised capital to manage through the testing market conditions. In 2009, the Retail team completed a major development project in the heart of Cardiff in conjunction with Capital Shopping Centres. The combined 1.4m sq ft centre, boasts the largest John Lewis department store outside London. The scheme showcases the best of the UK high street in a new two level grand arcade, a modern adaptation of the Victorian arcades which are a popular feature of the city. The development at One New Change, in the heart of London's financial district, will open for business in 2010. The mixed use scheme will bring a long awaited retail focus to the area to the east of St Paul's Cathedral, accommodating 70 retailers on the lower three levels and a roof terrace on the sixth floor which will open up new views of the Cathedral and its surroundings. In late 2009 Land Securities also became the first major

1944	1950	1968	1982	1987	1994
Harold Samuel buys Land Securities Investment Trust Limited, which at this point owns three houses in Kensington together with some Government stock.	Shares purchased for 44p in 1945 are now worth £6.15. The following year, Associated London Properties is purchased for £2 million. This marks the first big takeover by the company.	In Britain's biggest property deal of its time, Land Securities takes over City Centre Properties, which has assets of £155 million.	The name of the company is changed from Land Securities Investment Trust Limited to Land Securities PLC.	The total income of the Group exceeds £200 million and the portfolio valuation tops £3 billion.	Following the recession, the portfolio increases in value to more than £5 billion.

property company to announce the intention to start new developments in 2010. The three schemes will deliver 60,000 square metres of office, retail and residential space in the West End of London on some of London's most famous streets. The Park House scheme on Oxford Street and at Selborne House and Wellington House in Victoria will all aim for completion in 2012 or 2013.

Land Securities also became the first London Office business to take the lead on Display Energy Certificates by announcing the intention to certificate and display the energy a building is actually consuming instead of the less meaningful measure of energy a building is designed to consume. This action was taken to try and lead the industry to recognise the contribution it can make to reducing CO2 emissions.

Promotion
During 2009, the property market continued to be affected by the wider economic landscape with property values reaching a historic low

point in July 2009. Against this backdrop Land Securities sought to continue to build its brand at a business unit and individual scheme level using all aspects of the marketing mix. In London the Great British Summer consumer campaign unified three separate London properties at New Street Square, EC4; Bankside, SE1; and Cardinal Place, SW1, under one banner as the place to be, with bespoke caravans appearing with embedded

large screens showing live sporting events to the public who were able to relax in the deck chairs provided as part of the event. It allowed an estimated 107,000 visitors to not only watch sport but take advantage of the retail and leisure opportunities provided in the location. The campaign received notable media coverage as the fortunes of Andy Murray and the England cricket team thrilled the sporting public. In retail, as the whole sector suffered in the recession, Land Securities Retail continued to use sponsorship as a key tool, emphasising its market leadership and

expertise by sponsoring Retail Week's 'Stores' book, celebrating the best of retail interior design as well as sponsoring high profile retail awards and events.

Brand Values
Land Securities' values are: excellence – striving to achieve the very best; customer service – never forgetting that its customers are the source of its strength; innovation – new ideas inspiring the Group to new heights; integrity – people trust Land Securities; and respect for the individual – everyone has the power to help, to grow, to influence and to contribute.

These values are reinforced by the Group's People into Action initiative which recognises and rewards employees and key stakeholders whose behaviour reflects the core values. They are also reflected in all marketing and communication materials to ensure that the brand the Company presents and the brand that people experience, are aligned.

landsecurities.com

2000	2005	2008	2009
With the purchase of Trillium, Land Securities enters the new property outsourcing market. Pre-tax profits rise by 11.7 per cent to £327.7 million and the portfolio is valued at £7.5 billion.	Land Securities acquires Tops Estates – a quoted shopping centre company – and LxB, an out of town retail specialist. Its portfolio is valued at £14.5 billion.	Jointly developed with Hammerson, Bristol's Cabot Circus opens. It is one of the UK's largest retail-led city centre urban regeneration projects.	Land Securities sells Trillium for a headline consideration of £750 million.

The most successful club in English footballing history, Liverpool Football Club is among the most recognisable and aspirational sport brands in the world. Founded in 1892 and supported by millions of fans globally, the Club has a reputation for passion and authenticity. As the seventh most valuable club in the world, Liverpool FC is recognised as one of the true giants of the game.

Market

While football remains the world's most popular sport, the Barclays Premier League is widely recognised as its most professional, exciting and competitive football league. With an annual television audience exceeding three billion people, it is watched in more than 600 million households across more than 200 territories, making the Barclays Premier League and Liverpool Football Club ubiquitous globally.

Product

Alongside its burgeoning trophy cabinet, Liverpool Football Club (LFC) is a profitable business off the pitch with a variety of product extensions and assets for engagement with its fans. Anfield is one of the most iconic stadiums in world football and is regularly sold out on match days, filling its 45,482 capacity, while average annual footfall in the Club's UK retail outlets has grown to 3.5 million.

The Club uses international tours as a platform to engage with its fans around the world and is the only Barclays Premier League club to distribute a weekly magazine, keeping supporters across the globe up-to-date on Club news and stories. LFC TV, launched in 2007, provides Club content to almost three million viewers in the UK.

In 1998 Liverpool FC launched the Official Club Credit Card and between 2000 and 2006, annual revenue grew by a staggering 1,700 per cent as the number of credit card holders grew by 750 per cent. In accordance with the Club's ambition to develop young talent, a percentage of the proceeds contribute to the Club's Academy programme.

The Club's Official Website, liverpoolfc.tv, was launched in 2000 and currently receives up to 2.9 million unique visitors per month, with 1.6 million registered users and 52 million monthly page impressions. It is also home to the most successful football club video subscription service in the world, the e-season ticket. In 2008, liverpoolfc.tv was the most searched for football club website in the UK according to Yahoo!, the number one football website in the UK according to Hitwise, the second most frequently visited sports site in the UK according to comScore (second only to BBC Sport) and the fourth most searched for item on MSN UK.

Achievements

A British icon, Liverpool Football Club's accolades include 11 major European trophies and 18 League Championships, but its triumphs extend beyond the pitch with an enviable history of media firsts also to its name. For example, LFC appeared in the first edition of the BBC's Match of the Day in 1964, was the subject of the first colour football TV transmission, and was the first

1892	1901	1928	1959	1964	1965
Liverpool Football Club is formed by John Houlding when the board of his previous creation, Everton Football Club, walk out of Anfield stadium.	Liverpool FC wins the First Division League Championship for the first time.	The official Spion Kop Stand opens, replacing its predecessor of the same name. This soon becomes one of football's most famous stands – and sets of supporters.	Bill Shankly becomes manager; successful and charismatic, he plays a key role in creating a close bond between the Club and its fans.	The famous all-red strip is worn for the first time, in a European Cup game against Anderlecht at Anfield.	Shankly and his team win the Club's first FA Cup, beating Leeds United at Wembley.

top division team in England to have a shirt sponsor (Hitachi).

Football has changed considerably – both commercially and on the pitch – since Liverpool FC's 'golden age' of the 1970s and 1980s when it established itself as a truly global sporting institution, dominating competitions at home and in Europe. It's testament to the Club's business acumen that its brand is still recognised for being as passionate and spirited today as it ever was. 'Anfield', 'The Kop' and 'You'll Never Walk Alone' are considered valuable club assets, enjoying international fame and enabling Liverpool FC to extend its reach further. The Club's goal remains to replicate the golden age of footballing success and to match it with first-class commercial results.

Recent Developments
The Club's Official Website was redesigned and relaunched in May 2009, and a new user generated content channel called 'The Kop' provides even more opportunities for fans to interact with the Club.

Liverpool Football Club invests significantly in research to understand the needs of its

fans. Recent customer insight led to the restructuring of its Official Club Membership Scheme and the benefits received by Members. The Club relaunched its Membership Scheme in July 2008 and has since seen growth of 150 per cent year-on-year.

A new stadium is planned which will allow Liverpool FC to fulfil its potential for match day income while providing a world class facility for its fans and partners.

Promotion
With its strong brand values and diverse fan base, Liverpool Football Club presents an attractive proposition for brand association. Mutually beneficial partnerships see LFC further increase brand visibility while delivering measurable results for its associates in return.

Partnerships include the world's largest credit card issuer, MBNA/Bank of America; one of the UK's largest travel groups, Thomas Cook; and leading sports drink, Lucozade Sport. In addition, the official launch of the 2008 home kit in association with supplier adidas was named Best Club Marketing Campaign at the Northwest Football Awards.

Brand Values
Liverpool Football Club aims to maintain a reputation for being friendly, entertaining, exciting and passionate. The Club is committed to upholding its brand values of authenticity and community responsibility and seeks to remain one of the most valuable, powerful and enduring global sport brands.

liverpoolfc.tv

Things you didn't know about Liverpool Football Club

The Liverpool FC fans in the Kop end of the stadium are widely credited with starting the now ubiquitous practice of rhyming chants and songs in the late 1950s.

Bill Shankly's most famous quote is often miscited, his actual words being: "Some may say that football's a matter of life and death to you, and I'd say listen, it's more important than that. And that's true."

Carlsberg has been Liverpool Football Club's official shirt sponsor for 16 years – the longest such agreement in the Barclays Premier League.

Many fans that write to, or email the Club sign off with 'YNWA', the acronym for 'You'll Never Walk Alone'.

1973	1977	1989	2005
With the clinching of the UEFA Cup, the Club triumphs in Europe for the first time.	Bob Paisley takes Liverpool FC to Rome to win the first of five European Cups, watched by the 'travelling Kop'.	Tragedy strikes as 96 innocent fans lose their life at the Hillsborough Stadium disaster. Never forgotten, an eternal flame still burns at Anfield in their memory.	Under Rafa Benitez's management, Liverpool FC claims (and keeps) the Champions League Trophy after recovering from a three goal deficit against AC Milan to win on penalties.

LLOYD'S

Lloyd's is not an insurance company but a market of independent businesses where many of the world's most skilled and experienced underwriters come together to insure and reinsure risk. Business comes into Lloyd's from more than 200 countries and territories, and includes 88 per cent of FTSE 100 companies and 97 per cent of Dow Jones companies.

Market

Lloyd's has the capacity to underwrite a significant amount of business. Just under half of the business it writes is for UK listed and other corporate clients, but Lloyd's also underwrites significant amounts of business for the worldwide insurance industry, as well as private individuals.

The London insurance market is more than just Lloyd's alone. Of the world's 20 largest reinsurance groups, 18 have a physical presence in London. However, this is only part of the global picture. New competitor markets, such as Bermuda, are on the rise as well as other reinsurance markets in the US and Europe. All have to compete with alternative techniques for transferring risk, and deploying and redeploying capital, supported by an army of analysts and consultants.

Product

Like any market, Lloyd's brings together those with something to sell – underwriters, who provide insurance coverage – with those who want to buy – brokers, working on behalf of their clients who are seeking insurance.

Lloyd's is structured as a society of corporate and individual members, who underwrite insurance in syndicates. The make-up of Lloyd's underwriting membership has gone through a major change, today most of the capital supporting underwriting in the Lloyd's market comes from corporate bodies, while private individuals or 'Names' as they became known supply only 15 per cent of the market's capital backing. Lloyd's unique capital structure, often referred to as the 'chain of security', aims to provide excellent financial security to policyholders and capital efficiency to its members.

A member or a group of members form a syndicate. A syndicate's underwriting is managed by a managing agent, who employs underwriters to accept or decline risk. There are around 80 syndicates operating

within Lloyd's, covering many speciality areas, including: marine; aviation; catastrophe; professional indemnity and motor.

Businesses from all over the world can come to Lloyd's to find insurance, often for highly complex risks. There are 180 firms of brokers working at Lloyd's, many of whom specialise in particular risk categories.

Lloyd's underwriters are renowned for devising tailored, innovative solutions to complex risks. As a result, Lloyd's covers the world's most demanding and specialist risks – from insuring oil rigs, man-made structures and major sporting events through to new areas such as cyber-liability and terrorism.

Achievements

Lloyd's has been around for more than three centuries, helping communities and businesses to survive major world crises from the San Francisco earthquake of 1906 to the terrorist attacks of 9/11. During that time, many aspects of Lloyd's have changed, but its priorities and values have remained consistent.

This incredible history and reputation mean that Lloyd's is a truly famous global insurance brand.

It has earned this reputation through the expertise shown by its talented underwriters and the development of many pioneering and innovative insurance products. It's an offering that few can rival.

Key to Lloyd's dependable reputation is its financial solidity. Lloyd's strength and robust

1688	1871	1887	1904	1906	1998
Lloyd's coffee house is recognised as the place for obtaining marine insurance.	Lloyd's is incorporated by an Act of Parliament.	The first non-marine policies are underwritten at Lloyd's by Cuthbert Heath.	The first Lloyd's motor policy is issued, followed seven years later, by the first aviation policy.	San Francisco earthquake claims are met by Lloyd's underwriters establishing Lloyd's reputation in US.	The Government announced independent regulation of Lloyd's by the Financial Services Authority effective from midnight on 30th November 2001.

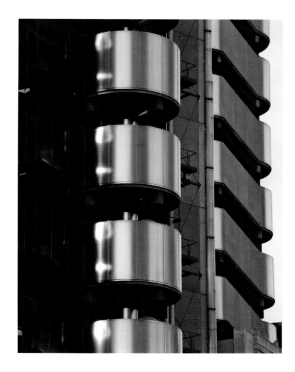

capitalisation is reflected in its ratings. Lloyd's currently holds A+ ratings from Fitch Ratings and Standard & Poor's, and an A rating from A.M. Best. These ratings apply to every policy issued by every syndicate at Lloyd's since 1993.

Recent Developments

After two years of exceptional hurricane activity with the Asian Tsunami and Hurricane Katrina devastating major regions in 2005, 2006 was exceptional for very different reasons. A lack of catastrophe activity meant that Lloyd's produced a strong profit.

In 2007 Lloyd's received the formal license document from the Chinese regulators for

its new reinsurance company in Shanghai, which enables Lloyd's to underwrite onshore reinsurance business throughout China.

A series of initiatives were then commenced in 2008, to continue to strengthen Lloyd's presence across emerging regions in Europe and Brazil. New offices were set up in Ireland and Poland. In addition Lloyd's became the first reinsurer to be granted 'Admitted status' in Brazil, which permits the market to underwrite Brazilian reinsurance business.

This trend continued into 2009 when Lloyd's secured an establishment license in Portugal.

Lloyd's has so far emerged relatively unscathed from the global financial crisis that has dominated the headlines over the past two years. Since the 1990s, Lloyd's has changed almost every aspect of its business – taking steps to improve the quality of business and stringency of governance. In addition, Lloyd's stuck to the traditional reinsurance and insurance products and did not seek to diversify into complex financial products and markets such as credit insurance. Notably, Lloyd's businesses have always maintained a conservative investment strategy which has meant that any fallout from the crisis could largely be dealt with through its normal course of business.

These challenging times have proven that Lloyd's is now better prepared than ever to manage the insurance cycle. Through a combination of underwriting for profit rather than market share, the use of state-of-the-art modelling tools, better availability and application of data – the flexibility, responsiveness, resilience and underlying financial strength of Lloyd's is greater than ever before.

Promotion

An important part of the promotion of Lloyd's is creating a high level of awareness of what Lloyd's is, how it works, what it stands for and what makes it different.

Over the last two years Lloyd's has launched two major campaigns to address key industry issues of Thought Leadership and Talent.

Lloyd's 360 Risk Insight brings together the views of the world's leading business, academic and insurance experts to analyse the latest material on emerging risk. Lloyd's 360 Risk Insight is focused on driving the global risk agenda as it takes shape and providing organisations with practical advice and information to help them turn risk into opportunity.

The attraction, development and retention of talent are key issues facing the insurance industry today. In response to this, Lloyd's launched a graduate programme in 2008 and is promoting it through a range of media, including its website, brochures, print and online advertisements, recruitment fair attendance and direct mail.

Brand Values

The Lloyd's brand is a massive asset, not just for the market itself, but for all the businesses associated with it. Today it is recognised all over the world as a leading global market which is able and trusted to take on the world's toughest risks.

It is a highly distinctive brand, known for its traditions, its unique way of doing business, and its ability to meet highly specialised requirements.

The core brand idea for Lloyd's is encapsulated in the phrase: Constant Originality. 'Constant' conveys its good faith, security, reliability whilst 'originality' conveys Lloyd's, creativity, individuality, authenticity and adaptability.

lloyds.com

2002	2005	2007	2009
Lloyd's Members approve the proposals of the Chairman's Strategy Group outlining major changes that will transform Lloyd's into a modern, dynamic marketplace.	In the aftermath of Hurricane Katrina, Lloyd's emerges with only a small market loss and reinforces its commitment to help a devastated region rebuild.	Lloyd's opens an onshore operation in Shanghai, enabling it to access one of the fastest-developing economies.	Lloyd's secures an establishment licence in Portugal.

Magnet TRADE
The Kitchen & Joinery specialists

Magnet Trade is dedicated to supporting the businesses of small builders and kitchen fitters throughout the UK via a growing network of more than 200 branches. Each offers an extensive, varied and high quality range of rigid cabinet kitchens, doors, windows and other joinery products, designed and priced to enable trade professionals to win business from those who want to improve their homes.

Market

Magnet Trade operates in the £4 billion trade kitchen and joinery market. Its main customers are small local builders typically one or two person businesses who undertake home improvement projects for private homeowners.

A strong trend in this sector is away from Do It Yourself towards Done For Me. Magnet Trade's mission is to enable small building firms to prosper by meeting this demand.

The company's principal competitors are Howdens Joinery and Benchmarx, plus general builders merchants such as Jewson and Travis Perkins.

Product

Magnet Trade defines itself as 'The Kitchen and Joinery Specialists' and the product offering reflects this with a range of more than 40 rigid cabinet kitchen designs, complemented by worktops, sinks and taps, handles and accessories ranging from lighting to storage solutions as well as cooking, washing and cooling appliances.

The joinery range encompasses internal and external doors, French and folding doors, windows, stair parts and flooring, plus general joinery items including hardware, sawn timber and sheet materials.

Trade professionals are further supported by expert advice from trade counter staff, free kitchen planning and design and the ability to offer bespoke joinery products via Magnet Trade's made-to-measure service.

Achievements

Magnet was founded in 1918 in Bingley, West Yorkshire, becoming Britain's largest joinery manufacturing company by 1975. It was also a founder member of the FTSE 100 share index in 1984.

Magnet established separate retail and trade divisions in 1990, recognising that the two markets had very different service requirements. The Magnet Trade brand was

1918	1920s	1960	1970	1990s	2001
Magnet is established in Bingley, West Yorkshire.	The company pioneers the mass production of joinery, doors and windows.	The first branch is opened in Birmingham, quickly followed by more across the UK.	Kitchen products are introduced. Only one style is offered for the next nine years.	Separate retail and trade divisions are formed. Magnet Trade launches a range of kitchens specifically for the small local builder market.	Magnet is purchased by Swedish kitchen company Nobia, for £134 million.

launched to specifically serve registered small builders and kitchen installers.

Magnet Trade kitchens and joinery products are manufactured at the Magnet Group's own UK factories in Keighley and Darlington. All kitchen cabinets and worktops have been awarded the British Standards Institute Kitemark and most also carry FIRA Gold Award Certification.

Magnet Trade takes its social and environmental responsibilities seriously. All softwood timber windows supplied are FSC certified. Kitchen cabinets are manufactured from wood sourced from a combination of sustainable forests and recycled materials. The company is actively working to reduce its carbon emissions by investing in more fuel-efficient vehicles and improving delivery fleet efficiency. This has resulted in 47,000 fewer miles being driven each year.

Magnet Trade also recognises the importance of supporting both customers' and colleagues' communities, providing sponsored kits for local sports teams and sponsoring the Northern Echo's Local Heroes awards, recognising the achievements of grassroots sport in the North East.

Recent Developments
In 2001 Sweden's Nobia Group, Europe's biggest kitchen company, purchased Magnet for £134 million and invested heavily, transforming Magnet Trade showrooms and adding more stock and branch staff.

The company's active customer base has doubled since 2006 and as demand for its products increases, further investment has resulted in the Darlington factory being converted into an ultra-modern 'assemble to order' facility, manufacturing around 20,000 kitchen cabinets a week. Twenty new trade

counters have been opened since 2008, creating more than 150 additional jobs.

New kitchen designs and joinery products are continually being added to the Magnet Trade range. Recent introductions include folding internal and external doors as well as curved kitchen cabinets.

Promotion
Magnet Trade provides its trade professional customers with a comprehensive range of printed and online resources, all designed to give them a genuine competitive edge over their rivals.

To help builders secure orders, Magnet Trade also produces a wide range of marketing collateral aimed at the end user, including its glossy product brochure, titled The Book, as well as a price guide for consumers called The List. There is also a version of The List which is aimed towards the trade but can be used in conjunction with the consumer edition.

In addition to this, the newly expanded Magnet Trade website includes a dedicated consumer section which enables the trade to reach the home improvers who prefer to choose their products online.

Regular discounts and promotions aim to further enhance the competitive edge of Magnet Trade's customers. Account holders are informed about this activity through regular communications, including a log-in, trade only section of the website, where customers can also pay their account bill.

Other communications material include monthly statement inserts, the quarterly

offers bulletin, titled The Deal, and the trade customer magazine, The Mag, which is distributed free to account holders and is available in branches, also on a quarterly basis. Point of sale displays in Magnet Trade branches still play an important role, highlighting offers and products that are available.

Recognising the increasing importance of new technology to trade professionals, the company also targets its customer base via media such as email and SMS.

Brand Values
Magnet Trade is a strictly trade only brand. Underlying all brand communications is the objective of enabling trade professionals to attain 'The Edge' over their rivals by offering high quality home improvement products at low and frequently discounted prices. This enables Magnet Trade customers to offer home improvers a better result at a lower cost, backed by the kudos of the Magnet name with its reputation for quality and design flair.

magnettrade.co.uk

2006	2009	2010	
The Darlington kitchen manufacturing facility becomes fully dedicated to assemble to order jobs.	Magnet Trade's website is relaunched with additional features to help its customers win new business.	The Magnet Trade kitchen range now includes 12 Contemporary styles, nine Modern Classics as well as five Traditional styles.	Meanwhile, its Joinery range encompasses doors, windows, flooring and stairs.

Things you didn't know about Magnet Trade

Magnet was established when Tom Duxbury swapped his horse (called Magnet) for a fire lighting company.

During World War II, Magnet helped the war effort by manufacturing munitions boxes.

If all the kitchen units sold by Magnet Trade each year were stacked on top of each other they would reach past the International Space Station, 350km above the Earth.

Each year, Magnet Trade sells more than 600,000 timber doors and more than one million sheets of plasterboard.

Magnet Trade is part of Nobia, Europe's largest kitchen company.

Marshalls

Transforming Britain's Landscapes

Marshalls is the UK's leading hard landscaping transformation company which has supplied some of the most prestigious landmarks in the UK with hard landscaping solutions since the 1890s. With its market leading position in the industry, Marshalls has become synonymous with quality and innovative product development whilst still caring for the environments and communities in which it works by actively operating a sustainable business model.

1,000 landscapers and ensures high standards of construction and training, giving homeowners peace of mind.

Product

The Marshalls Group operates its own quarries and manufacturing sites throughout the UK and, as a major plc, is committed to quality in everything it does. This includes environmental best practice and continual improvement in health and safety performance. Marshalls is making further advances by introducing an integrated management system to PAS99 which encompasses the already achieved standards of 9001, 14001 and 18001.

Marshalls' commercial product range provides the freedom to create powerful and practical solutions for building and landscape

Market

Sustained growth and diversification has seen Marshalls expand to become the market leader in its sector. It supplies superior natural stone and innovative concrete hard landscaping products along with street furniture and water management solutions to the construction, home improvement and landscape markets.

For the public sector and commercial markets, it satisfies the needs of a diverse customer base including local authorities, commercial architects, specifiers contractors and house

builders with constantly evolving products to meet the exacting standards and sustainable requirements to achieve better landscapes across a broad range of developments. These include public realm, education, infrastructure and healthcare.

For the domestic householder market, Marshalls provides the inspiration and the product ranges to create gardens and driveways that integrate seamlessly with peoples' lifestyles. Its approved contractor scheme, the Marshalls Register, covers over

1890	1947	1948	1955	1964	1972
Solomon Marshall starts to quarry in Southowram, Halifax and in 1904 establishes S. Marshall & Sons Ltd in Halifax, West Yorkshire.	A second production site is opened at West Lane in Halifax producing lintels, steps and fence posts.	An engineering division is established. The innovations of this division become fundamental in the development of the company.	The first wet cast product, Pennine Paving, is developed. This becomes another highly successful product for Marshalls.	Marshalls becomes a PLC with shares quoted on the London Stock Exchange.	New product development sees the introduction of block paving and the famous 'Beany Block' which combines drain and kerb in one unit.

projects. The company's expertise extends from surfacing to street furniture and water management, further enhancing its product offering to public sector and commercial users.

Its domestic range offers consumers Marshalls' unique flair for design, matched by its expansive, innovative product range and enables consumers to create unique spaces to enjoy all year round. From inspiration to project installation, a Marshalls' garden or driveway is an affordable investment which adds real value to a property. Backed by Marshalls' Register of Approved Installers and Contractors, homeowners can be secure in the knowledge that they have used the best products, installed by professionals from the Marshalls' Register, all backed by the Marshalls Hard Landscaping guarantee.

Achievements

Marshalls recently became the first company in the world to carbon label its entire domestic range, which consists of 503 products, by working with the Carbon Trust to create independently audited values using the PAS2050 methodology. Marshalls' carbon labelling programme has now extended to its commercial range with a further 1,565 products which will enable public and private bodies to understand the amount of embodied carbon dioxide in their landscaping project.

Marshalls was the first company in the hard landscaping industry to belong to the Ethical Trading Initiative (ETI), a diverse alliance of retailers, brands, trade unions and NGOs working collectively to tackle the complex questions posed by ethical trade.

The company has also received a record number of awards in 2009; a Big Tick was won at the Business in the Community Awards along with Marketing Society Awards for Ethical Marketing. Marshalls also won the International Award for Trade in Supply Chain Ethics and the Award for Sustainability, Business and the Built Environment at the Sustain Awards 2009.

Recent Developments

Marshalls is proud to support the Living Streets charity and has trained employees to become 'street auditors' to engage with local communities to better understand what people want to see on their street and in their community. By understanding and involving local people in the decision process, Marshalls can provide the hard landscaping solutions to truly transform the UK's landscapes for the better.

Promotion

Marshalls' sponsorship of the world's premier garden event, the prestigious RHS Chelsea Flower Show, has raised the profile of the Marshalls brand beyond all recognition. A potential audience reach of more than 141 million was achieved with Marshalls branding on TV, radio, online, social networking sites, the press and magazine coverage. Furthermore, a total of 50,000 Marshalls branded bags were handed out at the 2009 show – that's one in three visitors to Chelsea.

From its comprehensive corporate responsibility projects throughout the UK to eye-catching marketing campaigns, Marshalls' 23 award-winning marketing team use their skills to maximise media coverage, engage with consumers and promote its broad product range with a variety of marketing tools.

In 2009 the launch of Marshalls TV, via its popular website, brought a new dimension to its customers by providing a visual representation of Marshalls' products in a concise and visual way. This has been further enhanced by the introduction of Marshalls TV News, a new platform to deliver up-to-the-minute news, features and stories from across the Marshalls Group.

Brand Values

Marshalls' brand values are based on trust, honesty and integrity in all of its activities. Its vision is to be the supplier of choice to the landscape architect and contractor for architectural landscaping and to the consumer for garden and driveway improvement projects.

Customers are at the centre of its business and Marshalls supplies its consumers with high levels of customer service, which it measures monthly against a range of values. Marshalls is committed to conducting business in a manner which achieves sustainable growth, whilst incorporating and demonstrating a high degree of social responsibility with an experienced, qualified and flexible workforce.

marshalls.co.uk

Things you didn't know about Marshalls

Marshalls is the first company in the world to carbon label an entire product range.

Marshalls was the first company in its sector to join the Ethical Trading Initiative and leads the market in the development of ethical natural stone.

Marshalls became the UK's first landscape materials manufacturer to be accepted into the prestigious UN Global Compact – the world's largest corporate citizenship and sustainability initiative.

An ITN exposé into child labour in Indian quarries featured a Marshalls interview as the voice of Ethical Stone Suppliers.

In 2009 Marshalls won the prestigious Achievement in Sustainability Award at the PLC Awards.

1988	2000	2006	2009
George Armitage & Sons, a brick manufacturer, with three sites, is acquired and goes on to become Marshalls Clay Products.	The range now includes street furniture and in 2004 Compton Group is acquired, opening up the portable buildings and greenhouses markets to Marshalls.	Marshalls agrees to sponsor the prestigious RHS Chelsea Flower Show for three years, raising its profile.	More than 2,000 of Marshalls' commercial products now have a Carbon Trust Carbon Footprint label.

Microsoft®

Founded in 1975, Microsoft is the worldwide leader in software, services and solutions; its products power more than 90 per cent of the world's PCs. It has been at the forefront of the personal computing revolution that has transformed communications in recent decades. Its mission is to enable people and businesses to realise their full potential through the use of technology.

Market

Microsoft is the worldwide leader in software, services and solutions and its revenue is generated by developing, manufacturing, licensing and supporting a broad range of software products for computing devices. Its products include: PC operating systems, servers and mobile devices, server applications for distributed computing environments, information worker productivity applications, business solutions, software development tools and hardware including Xbox and computer accessories.

The company runs four operation centres globally in Ireland, Singapore and the USA and has subsidiaries in more than 100 countries around the world. Its global employees top 91,000 and it made US$14.57 billion in net income for the year ending June 2009.

Product

Microsoft's products are split into five key areas: client, server and tools, consumer and online services business, business division, and entertainment and devices division.

The client business includes Windows and is responsible for managing relationships with PC manufactures, while the business division covers Microsoft Office suites, desktop programmes, servers, and services and solutions; Microsoft Dynamics; and Unified Communications business solutions.

Microsoft is continually developing products and services driving the future shape of the immensely quick-paced market in which it operates. One highly visible launch for 2009 was Windows 7 which delivers on a simple premise: make it easier for people to do the things they want on a PC. The new operating system offers a streamlined user interface and significant new features that make everyday tasks easier and allow people to get the most out of computers of all styles and sizes.

Windows 7 was designed with the focus on quality, compatibility and performance and builds on Windows Vista with a high degree of compatibility with Windows Vista software and hardware. In terms of performance, Microsoft focused on improving key areas that affect user experience and productivity – from boot time to battery life to shut-down.

Windows 7 was designed to deliver enterprise value to customers in three ways: Making Users More Productive From Anywhere –

Windows 7 takes information access to the next level, enabling users to access the documents and data they need to get their work done from anywhere; Enhancing Security – Windows 7 builds on Windows Vista's security foundation, adding advanced capabilities to protect corporate data and enable low-cost compliance; Streamlining PC Management – Windows 7 provides IT with tools to further reduce costs and complexity of managing both physical and virtual environments on users' PCs.

In 2009, Microsoft launched Bing, its search engine designed to help internet users make faster and more informed decisions. It aims to offer a new approach to surfing with intuitive tools to help people gain better insight and knowledge from the web.

Also in 2009, Microsoft showcased its next generation of Windows phones as well as new mobile services to support Windows Live in line with its integrated PC, web and mobile strategy. These include Microsoft My Phone, which synchronises text messages, photos, video and contacts to the web.

In the online arena Microsoft offers an online advertising platform for publishers and advertisers as well as communications services such as email, instant messaging and the MSN portal. Its Xbox video game system is at the heart of its entertainment and devices division.

Achievements

Microsoft consistently wins awards around the world not only for its products but for the way in which it does business and acts as

1975	1981	1989	1990	1995	2001
Microsoft is founded in Seattle by Paul Allen and Bill Gates.	IBM introduces its personal computer with Microsoft's 16-bit operating system MS-DOS 1.0.	Microsoft launches the first version of its Office suite of productivity applications.	Microsoft becomes the first personal computer software company to exceed US$1 billion in sales in a year. In addition, Windows 3.0 launches.	Bill Gates outlines the company's commitment to supporting and enhancing the internet. Windows 95 launches and sells more than one million copies in the first four days on the market.	Office XP launches and is soon followed by Windows XP. Microsoft enters the gaming market for the first time with Xbox.

a responsible corporate citizen. In the UK, it was voted as one of The Sunday Times 100 Best Companies to Work For in 2009.

Microsoft has nearly 700,000 business partners, many of whom are small and medium sized enterprises that are deeply rooted in their local communities. It also partners with a diverse array of government agencies, non-governmental organisations, and inter-governmental organisations. These partners guide how it uses technology to address societal needs and help it to deploy software to benefit the millions of people they serve.

Recent Developments

Recognising that leading businesses need to do all they can to help people during the

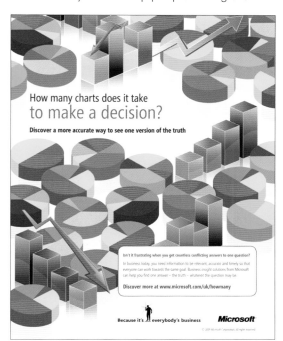

recession, Microsoft UK launched its flagship employment and skills campaign, Britain Works, in September 2009. Britain Works is a multi-year plan aimed at addressing one of the biggest challenges in the economy – unemployment. Over the next three years, through a series of partnerships with NGOs, community learning centres and public authorities Microsoft UK is aiming to help 500,000 people into jobs in the areas of the economy that will lead the recovery. These will be digital jobs requiring the use of computer skills but will be in a range of industries from manufacturing to services and the IT industry itself.

With over 77 per cent of all jobs in the UK requiring some form of IT skills, Microsoft believes that, given the rising issue of unemployment in the UK, its role as a responsible business leader is to provide access to vital IT skills that could improve the employability of UK citizens.

Promotion

'Because it's everybody's business' offers a fresh look at a range of technologies designed to empower people to build their own business success. The animated creative broadcast online and in print uses audio interviews with executives from Microsoft and leading organisations worldwide to show how their organisations are using technology to solve business problems and be more competitive. It highlights that everyone in an organisation is responsible for a company's success and that the essence of business is personal, with every individual playing an important role.

Keeping a pace with the current economic climate, some of the ads deal specifically with the problems of a recession for businesses. The campaign has its own dedicated website at www.everybodysbusiness.co.uk.

Brand Values

Microsoft aims to provide consumers and businesses around the world with the tools

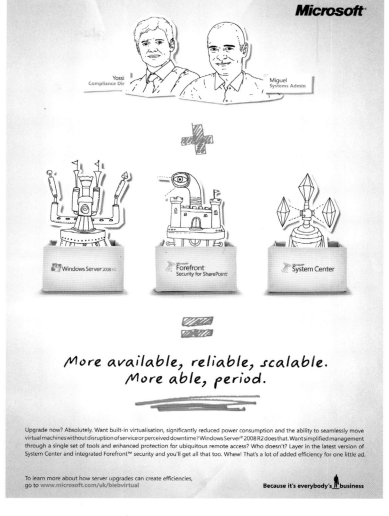

to fulfil their potential. By playing an active role in developing a safer computer environment, Microsoft helps people benefit from advances in technology. It is focused on improving quality and works with Government, law enforcement and industry partners to enable them to benefit from technological developments.

In the wider community, it is focused on raising awareness around security and child safety online through campaigns such as Get Safe Online as well as making an active contribution to the public policy debate.

microsoft.com/uk

2002	2007	2008	2009
Microsoft and its partners announce the launch of Tablet PC.	Microsoft launches Windows Vista and the 2007 Microsoft Office System to consumers worldwide.	Bill Gates steps down from the day-to-day running of the company to spend more time working with his charity foundation.	Windows 7 is launched.

Since its launch in 1977, Mini Babybel® has grown to become one of the cheese market's most iconic products. Its success can be attributed to a unique proposition: a natural cheese in a convenient individual portion size – with its red wax jacket adding a touch of play to the eating experience. The brand's consistent positioning as a healthy and fun snack has led to a strong visual identity and universal consumer appeal.

Market

Mini Babybel® is part of the £187 million cheese snacking category (Source: Nielsen 52 w/e 21st February 2009). It has coverage in 41 per cent of UK households and is a high frequency purchase, typically bought more than six times a year.

This highly competitive market includes a wide range of products in different formats and flavours and has experienced a high level of innovation from the leading brands in recent years. With the majority of products in the sector aimed towards children and mainly used as lunchbox items, brands seek to emphasise the interactive and 'fun' positioning of their products.

The category has been increasingly influenced by the UK's health debate and extended regulation on food advertising. However, with adults accounting for more than 50 per cent of consumption and its differentiated positioning as a natural product, Mini Babybel® has experienced continued growth.

Product

Mini Babybel® offers a range of portion-sized cheeses. Mini Babybel® Original, the brand's flagship product, accounts for 55 per cent of the brand's sales. In recent years, however, it has been joined by variants made from Emmental, Cheddar and Goat's cheese as well as a Light option, broadening its appeal to adult consumers. As consumers look towards healthier eating, Mini Babybel® Light has grown in popularity and now accounts for 30 per cent of sales.

The variants are distinguished through the use of different coloured wax jackets, which also serve to reinforce the playful brand character. The iconic red wax is reserved for its Original and Light versions, while purple defines Cheddar, yellow is used for Emmental and green indicates Goat's cheese.

Further brand extensions have included Christmas and Halloween sharing pots, which

1977	1981	1990	1992	1995	2000
Mini Babybel® is launched in France.	Mini Babybel® reaches the UK market.	Mini Babybel® Light hits UK shops, tapping into consumers' desires for lower fat options.	The brand advertises on UK television for the first time. The ad features a Mini car, a baby and a church bell.	The first 'rolling cheese' commercial appears. It goes on to become the brand's most recalled advertising signature.	Mini Babybel® Cheddar launches.

introduced a new seasonal uplift for the brand outside of traditional back-to-school periods.

The brand continues to attract new consumers looking for a healthy, savoury snack, appealing equally to children and adults. Naturally rich in calcium, essential for healthy bones, a single cheese provides children with one-third of their daily calcium requirement – a key benefit in the eyes of parents. Its convenient, portion-controlled packaging also ensures the brand is well placed to benefit from the trend towards snacking and eating on the go.

Achievements

Mini Babybel® has consistently outperformed its category with sales more than doubling since 2000. In 2009, the brand has achieved sales of more than £40 million (Source: Nielsen 52 w/e 21st March 2009). In 2008, Mini Babybel® was the best-selling cheese portion, achieving 21 per cent market share and finding its way into one-fifth of UK households, more than any other cheese snack.

Recent Developments

Mini Babybel® is a registered trademark and part of the Bel Group, which also markets Leerdammer, Boursin, The Laughing Cow and Port Salut cheese brands. Not only committed to delivering high quality cheeses, Bel Group takes its social responsibilities

seriously. In the UK, the company's corporate social responsibility policy has seen Mini Babybel® link up with Comic Relief – playing on the visual association between its red wax wrappers and the bright red noses. As an Official Partner for Red Nose Day (RND) 2009, Mini Babybel® raised more than £300,000 for the charity by donating a proportion of its sales for every special RND net of cheese sold.

In 2007 the Mini Babybel® Emmental variety was launched to join the portfolio. This option has proved popular with consumers and is already worth £1 million in value sales in the UK.

Promotion

The brand's most recent television advert, 'Tiny Factory', has set out to remind consumers that beneath Mini Babybel®'s playful exterior lies a real cheese, despite its small size. These brand attributes are being reinforced to appeal to consumers looking for reassurance of the wholesomeness of their family food choices, with the ad using the strapline: 'Real cheese, only smaller.' The concept, created by RKCR/Y&R, is of a tiny factory in the countryside where miniature people are producing Mini Babybel® as if it were a traditional, larger cheese. The playful brand personality is conveyed through the head cheese-maker explaining some of the

challenges the tiny workers face, such as milking the cows.

Over the years, Mini Babybel® has established itself as an advertiser that plays on the brand's element of fun. This started in 1992 with 'The Mini, the Baby, the Bell', a TV advert that quickly built brand awareness of the cheese and its unusual name.

In 1995 this progressed to 'The Rolling', aimed at the growing demand for more convenient products and positioning Mini Babybel® as a cheese that 'likes to get out'.

The well known television adverts 'The Chase in the Park' followed in 2003, which broadened the cheese's appeal to adults while reinforcing the health message with an 'active' storyline. This positioning continued with the next creative in 2006, 'Parachutes', which featured hapless sky divers, eager to get their hands on a Mini Babybel®.

Brand Values

Mini Babybel® is positioned as a healthy and playful cheese for snacking food occasions. The round red wax keeps the cheese fresh, makes it portable and aims to add a touch of fun to the eating experience. The brand's character, reflected in its advertising, is to be playful and cheeky.

babybel.co.uk

2005	2007	2008	2009
Mini Babybel® Cheddar Light and Goat varieties join the portfolio of cheese snacks.	An Emmental variant is introduced.	The 'Tiny Factory' TV commercial is launched.	Mini Babybel® joins Comic Relief as a National Partner to support its 2009 Red Nose Day campaign.

nutella®

From its beginnings in Italy in 1946, nutella has grown to become the world's leading hazelnut spread and is now marketed in 75 countries globally. Since its relaunch in the UK in 2007, nutella has enjoyed double digit growth, successfully altering perceptions and becoming increasingly accepted as a regular spread at family breakfast time. In February 2009 nutella became the UK's leading sweet spreads brand according to Nielsen.

Market

There are 16 billion in-home breakfast occasions a year in the UK which represents one in four of all meals eaten (Source: TNS Family Food Panel November 2008). According to nutritionists, breakfast is the most important meal of the day and yet many people still leave home without it. The key reasons for missing breakfast are a lack of time, followed by not liking what's on offer or simply not being hungry (Source: nutella Breakfast Time Report

2007). The breakfast foods most typically consumed in the UK are cereals and toast with spreads. Indeed, 74 per cent of all sweet spread consumption occasions are at breakfast time (Source: TNS).

The sweet spreads market is worth £310 million and is in nine per cent growth year-on-year (Source: ACNielsen 52 w/e 21st February 2009). Within this, nutella has an impressive 67 per cent value share of all hazelnut and chocolate spreads in the UK. nutella is also strong in sweet spreads worldwide and is worth US$1.2 billion, making it 10 times more valuable than its closest rival (Source: Euromonitor International Packaged Food 2007).

Product

Contrary to popular belief, nutella is a hazelnut rather than chocolate-based spread, containing almost twice the amount of hazelnuts to cocoa. In fact, in each 15g portion there are two whole hazelnuts and nutella contains no artificial colours, preservatives or hydrogenated fats.

nutella has been proven to release its energy slowly (Source: Leatherhead Food RA) and with no need to use an additional butter or fat-based spread, it is therefore a good alternative to jam or peanut butter at breakfast time.

In the UK nutella is available in three different jar sizes: 200g, 400g and 750g.

Achievements

Following the 2007 repositioning of nutella from an occasional treat to a breakfast spread, the brand has moved from being the third largest sweet spreads brand to become Britain's number one sweet spread brand in just 18 months (Source: ACNielsen).

Sales of nutella have grown sharply, up 26 per cent year-on-year, almost three times faster than the sweet spreads category itself. In the last year nutella has driven 77 per cent of all the value growth in the category (Source: ACNielsen March 2009). In fact, over the past 12 months, nutella has attracted 1.4 million new households and is now purchased by one in every four family households. Existing consumers have stepped up their buying frequency with repeat purchase rates increasing significantly from 34 per cent to 45 per cent (Source: ACNielsen).

Parents are now connecting more strongly with nutella than ever before, with the number naming it as their first choice of sweet spreads brands increasing almost fivefold.

Recent Developments

After spending years in the UK being perceived as a chocolate spread – and therefore an 'occasional treat' with limited penetration – in 2007 nutella

1946	1949	1964	2007	2008	2009
With cocoa beans in short supply due to post-war rationing, Italian patisserie maker Pietro Ferrero creates 'Pasta Gianduja' – a blend of toasted hazelnuts and cocoa.	Ferrero modifies the recipe so that it can be more easily spread on bread, creating 'Supercrema Gianduja'.	The product is renamed 'nutella' (thanks to the wide appeal of its hazelnut taste) and is launched in the UK.	In August, nutella is relaunched in the UK.	nutella becomes Britain's number one sweet spread brand (Source: ACNielsen).	nutella celebrates its 45th year in the UK.

wake up to...

nutella
FERRERO

was successfully relaunched to UK mums. Its bold repositioning moved the spread away from being an occasional 'chocolate' treat to become a breakfast spread.

nutella launched an all-encompassing campaign called 'wake up to nutella' with significant sales and marketing investment of £8 million. nutella was successfully repositioned by using all touch points – TV, press, consumer PR, online and packaging – to tell mums that nutella provides a good start to the day.

Promotion
At the heart of the nutella brand proposition lies the promise of an appetising taste and a good start to the day.

In order to encourage consumers to re-examine the suitability of nutella as a breakfast spread, the little-known fact that it is actually a hazelnut rather than chocolate-based spread – and therefore a good breakfast option when served as a 15g portion on wholegrain toast – formed the building blocks for an engaging communication platform. A consultant nutritionist was brought on board to ensure that the nutella ingredient story was conveyed in a way that was both credible and responsible, with the resulting 'wake up to

nutella' campaign positioning the spread as a suitable addition to the breakfast table alongside commonly seen spreads such as jam, honey and marmalade.

'Wake up to nutella' saw the brand utilise television advertising with slots showing mums choreographing their young families through the weekday breakfast ritual of toast popping and nutella spreading, accompanied by a voiceover explaining the ingredients and slow energy release message. New print adverts were also developed for women's weeklies while online, nutella targeted popular mums' websites and launched wakeuptonutella.co.uk, highlighting the importance of having breakfast before leaving home – and nutella's role on the breakfast table.

In stores, nutella's visibility significantly improved with new point of sale displays utilising the 'wake up to nutella' tagline and driving significant sales growth.

Brand Values
An iconic brand for millions of families worldwide, nutella is committed to offering a unique product through a blend of simple and uncompromised, high quality ingredients.

It aims to continue its mission to add value to the family breakfast table and to remain a trusted breakfast time staple.

wakeuptonutella.co.uk

Things you didn't know about nutella

If all the nutella bought in Britain in a year was spread on toast, it could cover more than 1,000 full-size football pitches.

There are two hazelnuts in each 15g portion of nutella and in the last year, 529 million hazelnuts were consumed in the spread in the UK alone.

On average, one jar of nutella is sold every 2.5 seconds and enough jars were sold in the last year to provide almost 50 per cent of UK households with one.

The nutella facebook page has more than 2.9 million fans, making it the second most popular brand fan site in the world.

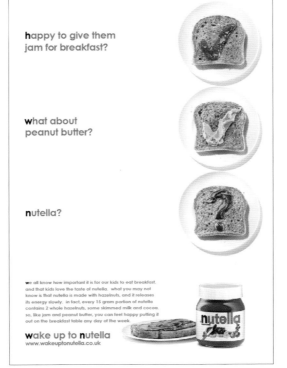

happy to give them jam for breakfast?

what about peanut butter?

nutella?

we all know how important it is for our kids to eat breakfast. and that kids love the taste of nutella. what you may not know is that nutella is made with hazelnuts, and it releases its energy slowly. in fact, every 15 gram portion of nutella contains 2 whole hazelnuts, some skimmed milk and cocoa. so, like jam and peanut butter, you can feel happy putting it out on the breakfast table any day of the week.

wake up to nutella
www.wakeuptonutella.co.uk

officeangels
RECRUITMENT CONSULTANTS

With 80 branches, Office Angels is one of the UK's leading recruitment consultancies specialising in secretarial and office support staff. Each week 8,000 people find short term assignments while more than 9,000 people are placed in permanent jobs each year. At every step candidates are guided through the recruitment process by experienced and qualified consultants.

Market

The UK recruitment market is dominated by temporary and contract business (88 per cent), with the industry turnover valued at £22.5 billion between April 2008 and March 2009. The total number of placements in both temporary and permanent sectors now equals 1.7 million (Source: Recruitment Employment Confederation (REC) Recruitment Industry Trends 2008/09). Unsurprisingly, the economic downturn has caused a contraction in the market from its peak in 2007, as the sector is closely linked to the strength of the economy. Even though 2008/09 has been tough for the industry as a whole, the downturn has created opportunities for recruiters to demonstrate the value they can provide to both their clients and candidates.

Product

Office Angels provides clients with both assignment and permanent staff across a wide range of secretarial, administrative, financial, call centre and customer service positions. Jobseekers follow a thorough and formal procedure from registration through to assignment which includes an in-depth interview, skills evaluation and online training courses.

To gauge candidates' abilities, Office Angels uses a skills evaluation system that allows consultants to assess the fundamentals, such as PC skills, but can also create tailored tests to reflect a client's requirements. Through working closely with candidates and providing them with continued support, Office Angels lives by its belief that it is in the business of finding 'jobs for people' rather than 'people for jobs'.

1986	2003	2005	2006	2007	2009
Office Angels is founded and the first office opens in London.	Office Angels joins Race for Opportunity (RFO), a government-backed initiative for UK organisations committed to race and diversity issues.	Office Angels is voted as one of The Sunday Times 100 Best Companies to Work For, sitting in eighth position.	Office Angels celebrates its 20th anniversary.	Office Angels organises its 10th Exectuary of the Year Awards.	Office Angels is voted seventh in The Sunday Times 100 Best Companies to Work For list and is ranked with three stars in the Best Companies scheme.

At office-angels.com candidates are able to view all current vacancies and obtain further information on the services offered. This is not a substitute for the personal, one-to-one service that remains the cornerstone of the Office Angels philosophy, it simply compliments the branch experience.

Office Angels' consultants are key to the brand's success and as such undergo training and development to ensure they are equipped with the latest and most relevant skills. This also helps to create a knowledgeable and highly motivated workforce.

Integral to Office Angels' commitment to its assignment staff is its ongoing employee care programme. Initiatives such as regular social and networking events, Angel of the Month and Year awards, pension schemes, competitions, and training ensure that candidates are rewarded for their dedication and professionalism.

Achievements

Office Angels is consistently regarded as one of the UK's best employers, as recognised in 2009 when it was ranked seventh in The Sunday Times 100 Best Companies to Work For survey. Based on employees' views, the company's success in the survey reflects its efforts to listen to its people and to create a strong and supportive organisational culture. It was also awarded the top three-star ranking in the Best Companies Accreditation scheme, which is designed to reward excellence in employee engagement.

Office Angels upholds the principles of equality and fair treatment for workers in and out of the workplace, operating a diversity monitoring and reporting system that complies with industry best practice.

Furthermore, Office Angels has made a conscious effort to minimise its environmental impact. In order to reduce its carbon footprint in the UK and Ireland, Green Policies are being

implemented that encompass travel, recycling, energy use, waste, stationery and carbon offsetting.

Recent Developments

In March 2009 Office Angels relaunched its website to include advanced job search functions, a quick branch locator and rotating news. The company utilises Broadbean's multi-posting tool to improve its job advert distribution and response tracking.

Office Angels has also launched a Virtual Branch at http://oavirtualbranch.com where visitors can find out more about Office Angels, read tips on jobs, play games, as well as follow the latest instalment of its own soap opera.

With the development of its colleagues in mind, Office Angels has created a suite of training opportunities to help its employees learn new skills and achieve their work ambitions. This includes Office Angels Training Solutions (OATS), which consists of more than 60 online courses such as MS Office packages, accountancy packages, languages, customer service, IT and psychometric testing. Ascent, a year-long programme, exposes potential management trainees to every aspect of the company to equip them with the necessary experience to become branch managers. Finally, the Aspire senior management development programme builds the skills required to manage an Office Angels region.

Promotion

The Office Angels marketing strategy aims to build on the brand's position as an industry leader. Recent activity has encompassed marketing campaigns, public relations, competitions and affiliate promotions such as film and theatre ticket offers.

It also uses awards such as the well-established Executary of the Year and Angel of the Year to create excitement and loyalty around the brand and incentivise good performance.

Further brand exposure is gained by conducting regular research studies and publishing reports on a range of employment-related issues, including flexible working, employee benefits and managing communications in the modern office.

Brand Values

The professional and contemporary style of Office Angels attracts clients and candidates alike. At the core of its brand values are fun, accountability, passion and knowledge. Its business proposition is based on sharing knowledge, teamwork, client and candidate satisfaction and quality of sales.

office-angels.com

Things you didn't know about Office Angels

Eighty six per cent of candidates would refer Office Angels.

Office Angels took part in the nation's first Learn More at Work Day.

Office Angels often hits the news – 204,683,692 people would have seen one of the workplace research pieces released in 2009 (figures are up to October 2009).

One in four of its candidates are male and one in five are more than 45 years old.

Office Angels' biggest research piece in 2009 focused on your desk neighbours annoying habits – this story was covered by two broadcast stations, seven nationals, one radio station, 14 online sites and nine regional press titles.

PHILIPS
sense and simplicity

Philips puts its customers at the heart of its product innovations and begins by understanding their needs and aspirations. Focusing on the health and well-being domain, the company serves professional and consumer markets through three overlapping sectors: healthcare, lighting and consumer lifestyle. Throughout its portfolio, it demonstrates its innovation capacity by translating customer insight into technology and applications that improve the quality of people's lives.

Market

Philips focuses mainly on the health and well-being domain, manufacturing products and services for the professional and consumer markets.

Its sales total more than 26 billion euros (US$33 billion) and it employs 121,000 people with sales and service outlets in 100 countries. Every day one million people buy a Philips product (Source: Philips UK). More than 30 per cent of the company's annual sales are from emerging economies. Philips is among the world's top 50 most valuable brands and its brand value has doubled to US$8.3 billion since 2004 (Source: Interbrand). Research and development is a vital part of its business and the company invests 1.6 billion euros – more than six per cent of sales – into it. It currently has 55,000 patent rights, 33,000 registered trademarks and 49,000 design rights. It also runs one of the largest design organisations in the world with eight studios across three continents.

It is market leader in cardiac care, acute care, home healthcare and energy efficient lighting. Its product portfolio also includes lifestyle products such as flat screen TVs, male shaving and grooming, and domestic appliances.

Product

Philips manufactures products across three core areas: healthcare, lighting and consumer lifestyle. The healthcare sector is dedicated to providing solutions designed around the needs of clinical care teams and patients and includes cardiac care equipment and home healthcare products. Its lighting sector aims to introduce innovative and energy efficient solutions and applications for lighting, for both the business and consumer markets. The consumer lifestyle products provide solutions to consumer needs, enabling people to live healthier and more fulfilled lives.

Achievements

Philips is making significant strides in sustainability and offers green solutions across its portfolio – from energy saving lighting to TVs, home theatres, kettles and more. In 2008 Philips invested approximately 282 million euros in Green Innovations and launched 91 new Green Products (those identified as having

1891	1910	1914	1927	1939	1983
Anton and Gerard Philips set up Philips & Co. in Eindhoven, the Netherlands. It begins by manufacturing carbon-filament lamps.	Philips is the largest single employer in the Netherlands, with 2,000 employees.	The company opens a research lab, which results in its first innovations in x-ray and radio technology. Four years later, a medical x-ray tube is introduced, marking its entry into healthcare.	Philips produces its first radios; by 1932 it is the largest producer of radios in the world.	Its first electric shaver is introduced and the company now employs 45,000 people.	A technological and cultural landmark, the Compact Disc is launched, illustrating Philips' dedication to innovation.

a significantly better environmental performance than competitors or predecessors). Sales of Green Products rose to around 25 per cent of total sales in 2008, compared with 20 per cent in 2007.

Winning 50 design awards each year, Philips' worldwide design branch won 22 iF product design awards in 2009 alone. One was for the Wake-up Light, an alarm clock which gradually brightens to simulate a natural sunrise, accompanied by natural sounds. In healthcare, the Kitten Scanner – which helps teach children what happens during a CAT examination to reduce their fears – and a handheld ultrasound system also won iF awards.

2009 also saw the IEEE, the world's largest technical professional society, honour Philips with an IEEE Milestone Award for its contribution to developing the Compact Disc (CD). This Milestone Award is only ever given to significant innovations that have stood the test of time for at least 25 years.

asimpleswitch.com

Recent Developments
Philips believes that demand for healthcare products – especially outside the hospital – and high quality, energy efficient lighting will grow by six per cent per year. As a result, it has focused activity on becoming the leading business within these markets. In 2006 it sold its semiconductor and electronic components-related businesses and invested half the proceeds in acquiring further businesses in the target markets. These included Genlyte and Respironics in 2008.

In the UK Philips is working with the charity Cardiac Risk in the Young (CRY) to raise awareness and provide screening to prevent Sudden Arrhythmia Death Syndrome (SADS). Twelve apparently fit and well young people

between the ages of 14 and 35 die every single week from undiagnosed heart conditions. By providing mobile screening equipment and getting its employees to volunteer, Philips is helping CRY tour England to provide free cardiac screening for up to 3,000 young people.

Promotion
In 2008, Philips launched a global brand campaign to highlight its health and well-being credentials among business influencers. The campaign includes partnerships with leading global media owners – such as CNN, Financial Times, The Economist Group, CNBC and Harvard Business Review – and drives Philips' vision and thought leadership in the health and well-being domain.

First staged in 2005, Philips' 'Simplicity Events' act as a platform for the company to demonstrate its commitment and leadership in delivering 'sense and simplicity' to people. Events have been held in Paris, Amsterdam, New York, London, Hong Kong, Sao Paolo and most recently, Moscow.

The company logo has been consistent since the 1930s. Until the mid-1990s its advertising

and marketing was focused at product level and varied for local markets. In 1995 Philips introduced its first global tagline with a unified company look.

Brand Values
The Philips brand promise to customers and consumers is 'sense and simplicity'. In a world where complexity increasingly touches every aspect of people's daily lives, Philips is committed to understanding the needs and aspirations of real people in order to deliver innovative solutions that are advanced and easy to experience – and that ultimately improve the quality of their lives.

philips.com

Things you didn't know about Philips

Every day one million people buy a Philips product.

Philips lights many international landmarks, including the Hermitage Museum in Saint Petersburg, the Eiffel Tower, Buckingham Palace, the National Theatre in London, the Pyramids, the National Stadium in Beijing and the ball at Times Square (which will use up to 20 per cent less energy in 2009 than 2007, thanks to the use of LED lights).

Although most people know Philips for TVs and shavers, Philips also holds leading positions in the lighting and healthcare markets: it is market leader in cardiac care, acute care, home healthcare and energy efficient lighting.

One in every three automobiles worldwide uses Philips lighting.

1995	1997	2004	2008
The company sells its 300 millionth Philishave electric shaver.	In co-operation with Sony, Philips introduces the DVD which becomes the fastest growing home electronics product in history.	Philips unveils its new brand promise of 'sense and simplicity', which marks a commitment to being a truly people-focused company.	Philips launches a global brand campaign to highlight its strong credentials in health and well-being.

Premier Inn is the UK's biggest hotel chain, with more than 580 hotels across the country. Premier Inn bedrooms feature king size beds, en-suite bathrooms with complimentary toiletries and flat screen digital TVs with Freeview. It offers all its customers a money-back 'Good Night Guarantee' which is unique amongst Britain's leading hotel chains. All Premier Inns feature a bar and restaurant, situated either inside the hotel or adjacent to it.

Market

The Budget Hotel Market has nine key players which, in addition to Premier Inn includes Travelodge, Jury's Inn, Holiday Inn Express, EasyHotel, Comfort Inn, Days Inn, Ibis and Innkeeper's Lodge.

Data from the BDRC Hotel Survey 2008 showed 107 million adult room nights for 2008, a year-on-year fall of 1.8 per cent. Due to the drop in the number of domestic leisure stayers, hotel staying penetration receded slightly to just under 36 per cent of all adults which equates to just under 16.5 million people.

Total UK business volume remained unchanged from the previous year at 59 million room nights while domestic leisure volume fell to 48 million room nights.

The development of the budget sector, led by Premier Inn, continues to grow. Furthermore, usage of budget hotels by business travellers exceeded that of mid-market and upper tier sectors for the first time, according to the BDRC.

Product

Premier Inn bedrooms feature en-suite bathrooms, TV with Freeview, and WiFi internet access. Customers are also offered a money-back 'Good Night Guarantee' and the promise of a good quality room, comfortable

1987	2004	2007	2008	2009	
The first Travel Inn is opened in Basildon, Essex.	Whitbread acquires Premier Lodge, and merges with the Travel Inn estate to create the Premier Travel Inn brand.	In October, Premier Travel Inn rebrands to Premier Inn.	In February the Premier Inn brand is unveiled with an £8 million media launch including, for the first time, TV advertising and an online and press campaign, featuring its new brand personality, Lenny Henry.	A new brand campaign launches in June, again featuring Lenny Henry in iconic scenes taken from films.	Also in 2009, Premier Inn is recognised as the Best Business Hotel Chain at the Business Travel World Awards for the second consecutive year.

surroundings and friendly service. All Premier Inns feature a bar and restaurant serving dinner, drinks and Premier Inn's renowned 'All you can eat' cooked breakfast.

Premier Inn also offers a Business Account for business travellers, a unique expense management solution which allows companies to control spend more effectively.

In 2008 Premier Inn introduced self check-in kiosks to a number of hotels, reducing check-in time to less than one minute, which has proved to be particularly popular with business guests.

Achievements

Over the past few years Premier Inn has won several awards. It was recognised as Best Budget Hotel at the Business Traveller Awards 2008 and in the JD Power European Economy Hotel Guest Satisfaction Survey 2008 and 2009 was voted the Leading Economy Brand. Premier Inn was also recognised as the BDRC British Hotel Guest Survey Most Improved Brand 2008 and was the winner of the HolidayCheck Awards in the same year. It was also recognised as the Best Business Hotel Chain at the Business Travel World Awards 2008 and 2009 and received the Leisure and Tourism Award at the Customer Satisfaction Awards run by the Institute of Customer Service.

Premier Inn supports WaterAid, the international charity whose mission is to overcome poverty by enabling the world's poorest people to gain access to safe water, sanitation and hygiene education. As part of Whitbread Hotels and Restaurants, Premier Inn aims to raise £1 million for WaterAid over the next two years.

In December 2008, Premier Inn opened its first 'green' hotel in Tamworth, Staffordshire. The technologies used in the hotel take radically different approaches to ventilation, heating, cooling and water wastage and have the potential to reduce energy use by 80 per cent.

Recent Developments

In 2009 Premier Inn launched 'Premier Offers' – a £29 special rate for leisure and business guests.

To date, two million rooms have been released at £29 with the promotion set to continue in 2010.

Premier Inn has also launched a new look website at www.premierinn.com with more hotel details, easier booking, interactive maps and increased functionality.

At the end of 2009, Premier Inn's parent company, Whitbread, announced that it plans, by 2020, to reduce its CO_2 emissions by 26 per cent. This is the company's first statement of intent on carbon reduction and will form an important part of its `Good Together' corporate sustainability strategy. At the same time, Whitbread reported that from 2007 to 2009, the company improved its carbon efficiency by four per cent which is equivalent to saving 8,562 tonnes of CO_2 or taking 2,446 cars off the road.

In recognition of this achievement, Whitbread has been awarded the Carbon Trust Standard which is the world's first award that requires organisations to measure, manage and reduce their carbon footprint and make real reductions year-on-year.

Premier Inn has launched its first hotel in India and at the end of 2009 and announced plans to open nine further hotels in India in the next five years. It aims to capitalise on the country's developing business traveller market. Currently there is a limited number of budget

hotel brands in India so this represents a good opportunity for Premier Inn, with its strong budget hotel model.

Promotion

Premier Inn uses famous comedian Lenny Henry in its advertising – for TV, press and online. The Premier Inn Lenny Henry campaign first launched in 2008, with the current version having been launched in June 2009.

The advertising focuses on iconic moments in famous movies contrasted against individual experiences in a Premier Inn to highlight the 'great quality experience' of the brand. The 2009 campaign has been a great success as it led to Premier Inn achieving its highest ever brand awareness among business and leisure travellers (Source: Hall and Partners ad tracking, September 2009).

Brand Values

The Premier Inn promise of 'Everything's Premier but the Price' sums up what the brand stands for and sums up the brand's positioning as 'quality meets good value'.

premierinn.com

Pret A Manger creates handmade, natural food, avoiding the obscure chemicals, additives and preservatives found in much of the 'prepared' and 'fast' food on the market today. For more than 20 years it has kept quality and service at the heart of its business, focusing on high standards for both its food and staff.

Market

First making its mark in city locations populated by workers, today Pret A Manger serves more than one million people a week in prime sites across the UK. Operating 225 shops in the UK, New York, Washington DC and Hong Kong, the company has an annual turnover in excess of £200 million.

Pret's competitors encompass sandwich bars, coffee shops and fast food outlets. The sandwich market has experienced significant growth over the last 10 years and is now estimated to be worth around £3.5 billion (Source: The British Sandwich Association 2007), while the coffee shop market was estimated to be worth £1.2 billion in 2008 (Source: Mintel).

Product

From the outset, Pret A Manger has built its business on two key ingredients: fresh food and professional people. Rather than operating as a franchise, each outlet runs like

a restaurant with almost every shop having its own kitchen and using organic and free-range produce wherever possible.

The brand's product offering focuses on simple, confident flavours. Available to eat-in or take-away, fresh sandwiches, salads, hot wraps and soups are prepared daily and sweet

treats such as chocolate brownies and carrot cake are also available. Attention to detail drives product development; the Pret Chocolate Brownie, for example, has changed 34 times with each alteration to the recipe designed to further improve the flavour.

Pret's Baristas serve a range of tea and coffee and use only organic, Fairtrade™ and Rainforest Alliance coffee beans which are used within two weeks of roasting to ensure freshness – a policy that sets Pret apart on the high street. In 2009, Pret's regional shops introduced filter coffee priced at 99p, offering the same 'Just Roasted' coffee but at a more accessible cost.

Achievements

The emphasis on staff and customer satisfaction has paid dividends for Pret A Manger. Its accolades include featuring in the Guardian's list of Britain's Top Employers in 2008; winning Best Vegetarian Sandwich of the Year 2007 from The Vegetarian Society; being named first in the Food Service Top 50

1986	1990s	2001	2007	2008	2009
On a mission to serve up freshly prepared, good, natural food, Julian Metcalfe and Sinclair Beecham open the first Pret A Manger at 75b Victoria, London.	Pret A Manger becomes the first retailer to replace plastic sandwich boxes with cardboard versions. Today, all its sandwich boxes are 100 per cent recyclable and compostable.	The McDonald's Corporation buys a 33 per cent non-controlling stake in Pret A Manger, facilitating expansion outside of the UK.	Eat With Your Head, Pret A Manger's proper eating campaign, is rolled out.	Pret A Manger is sold to Bridgepoint, bringing an end to the relationship with McDonald's. Pret A Manger management retains 33 per cent of the company.	Pret A Manger has 225 shops across the UK, New York, Washington DC and Hong Kong and the Passion Fact campaign is introduced.

awards in 2005, taking second place in 2006; and scooping two GreenFleet awards in 2006 for its electric vans.

The company is looking at all aspects of its business as it strives to be more sustainable, addressing packaging, recycling, food waste, energy and food. To name just a few of its initiatives, the majority of its shops have customer and back of house recycling facilities, the company uses electricity from 100 per cent green sources, and air freighting fruit and vegetables is avoided. In 2008 Pret reduced the number of plastic bags used in its outlets by 28 per cent simply by asking its customers if they needed one.

Pret's longstanding association with charities for the homeless remains an integral part of the company ethos. The Pret Charity Run operates a fleet of electric vans that deliver more than 12,000 fresh meals to shelters for the homeless in London each week.

Recent Developments
In response to the current financial situation, Pret A Manger has developed a range of affordable sandwiches to appeal to those watching their pennies. The range is focused on affordable, simple sandwiches using the

same high quality ingredients and includes Simply Ham & Mustard and Free-Range Egg & Bacon. A total of 10 options priced at less than £2.50 are available, including four 'kids only' variants such as Organic Strawberry Jam & Butter and Dolphin-friendly Tuna & Mayo. The 'kids only' sandwiches complement the colouring books and pencils currently available in Pret's regional shops.

Promotion
Pret A Manger's philosophy is to communicate with its customers without the aid of traditional PR teams. It doesn't use mass media and direct marketing, instead focusing on investing in its staff and the quality of its food. Its total communications expenditure is budgeted to be less than 0.4 per cent of sales, unlike many other food retailers who spend up to seven per cent of sales on communication.

The shops and packaging are used as channels through which the brand – known for its use of humorous and quirky images of food – is promoted. In 2008 Pret refreshed its communications to include Passion Facts. These give insights into the company's thinking and approach to food and include everything from the type of mozzarella it uses to how it trains its staff to slice vegetables.

As with many retailers, Pret's shop fronts are an important part of its promotion and in particular, its external menu signs are something of a billboard. Fully redesigned, they act as a signpost to the shops while also carrying the 'Just Made' menu, giving potential new customers – or less regular customers – a chance to see what it offers.

Brand Values
The Pret A Manger ethos is one of simple, delicious and flavoursome food served by staff who take pride in their work. The brand personality is underpinned by core values of: a passion for food, enthusiasm, integrity, honesty and belief in its convictions with an uncompromising stance on quality and commitment to innovation.

pret.com

Things you didn't know about Pret A Manger

In the UK, Pret A Manger's Baristas serve more than 400,000 hot drinks each week.

Each year, Pret donates more than 1.7 million products to homelessness charities across the UK, saving up to 250 tonnes of food from ending up in landfill.

Whenever a customer acknowledges the quality of their service, a member of staff is awarded a solid silver star designed by Tiffany & Co.

prontaprint
trusted to deliver, every time.

Prontaprint has maintained its position at the forefront of the corporate print-on-demand market by delivering distinctive design and print solutions, underpinned by a commitment to first class customer service. Through its ability to evolve and adapt to changing customer needs, Prontaprint has grown to become the largest and best-known brand in the business.

Market

In an age where design and print technology are rapidly developing, the business print world demands the very latest digital know-how the minute it hits the market.

Prontaprint is exploiting its commercial design and print expertise, concentrating on tailored communications for business clients – and the number of centres with turnover in excess of £1 million is growing rapidly.

Prontaprint is committed to taking a completely client-focused role to ensure that the network is in a strong position to capitalise on major changes within the B2B market. Understanding clients' businesses is crucial to satisfying a greater proportion of their needs. Delivering exceptional standards of client care and relationship management are key to the total service offering. In recent years, clients have increased in-house capabilities, becoming digitally enabled and web-smart. In response, Prontaprint has repositioned itself to provide an enhanced business offering comprising design, print, display, direct mail and finishing services.

Product

Prontaprint offers a comprehensive portfolio of business communication solutions to businesses of all sizes including design, print, display, direct mail and finishing services. An ongoing programme of investment in the latest digital technology ensures its centres feature the latest design, black and white and colour, high volume digital print equipment alongside traditional print capabilities.

With most documents now produced digitally, clients' original designs can be enhanced,

When you need to bring your ideas to life and tell your clients about them quickly — who do you turn to...

| Design | Print | Display | Direct Mail | Finish |

prontaprint...trusted to deliver, every time.

updated, and amended. Work can also be securely stored electronically at Prontaprint centres, where it can be easily accessed. The versatile nature of the Prontaprint digital network means that material can be supplied to one centre and sent out digitally across the network to be produced at different centres simultaneously, simplifying distribution and increasing capacity and efficiency. This not only saves the client time and money with reduced wastage and storage costs, but also improves competitive advantage by enabling clients to respond to market opportunities quickly.

Prontaprint's direct mail service focuses heavily on the use of variable data printing, enabling images and text to be customised to the recipient. This service, offering one-to-one marketing solutions, underpins Prontaprint's consultancy approach to servicing clients.

Achievements

Established more than 35 years ago, Prontaprint has a fully integrated European network of nearly 150 digitally linked centres across the UK and Ireland and employs more than 1,100 people with an annual turnover nearing £45 million.

The company is a founder member of the British Franchise Association (BFA) and played a crucial role in establishing a regulatory body for the franchise industry. A former winner of the BFA Franchisor of the Year award, Prontaprint remains a strong supporter of the BFA and was appointed to the board in 2005. It is also affiliated to the British Print Industry Federation, the British Association of Printers and Copy Centres, the Institute of Printers and XPLOR International (the Electronic Document Systems Association).

1971	1973	1980s	2000s	2009	2010
The first Prontaprint centre opens in Newcastle-upon-Tyne, aiming to overcome the high prices, large minimum orders and long lead times associated with traditional commercial printers.	Following the signing of the first Franchise Agreement, the Prontaprint business model goes from strength to strength.	The company continues to expand widely across the UK, as well as into international markets.	Prontaprint is now the largest design and print network in the UK and Ireland and repositions to consolidate its place at the forefront of the corporate print-on-demand market.	Prontaprint completes the roll out of a new brand positioning, following an investment of more than £3 million and almost two years of research into the market, brand development and training.	Prontaprint commences the roll-out of its bespoke web-to-print service, Prontaprint Gateway.

It was also the first national print-on-demand network to sign a formalised licensing agreement with the Copyright Licensing Agency. This allows licensed copying of specified material within agreed limits. Prontaprint is therefore able to offer clients advice on copyright issues and help protect businesses from potential copyright infringements.

In 2007, Prontaprint won a prestigious Franchise Marketing award for the work it had done repositioning the brand to appeal to higher value business clients; the Best Overall Marketing Campaign award was judged by a panel of experts from the Franchising Industry and the Chartered Institute of Marketing (CIM). In 2008, Prontaprint went on to win the Best Brand Management title in the Franchise Marketing Awards.

Recent Developments

Proud of its heritage, Prontaprint remains focused on consistently evolving the brand to meet changing client needs in the commercial design and print market. With a corporate client base including British Airways, NEXT, Hush Puppies and Dixons, Prontaprint has rolled out a new brand positioning to develop this market further, investing more than £3 million following almost two years of research.

In 2010, Prontaprint will be launching its bespoke web-to-print service across the UK and Ireland. The new system will be known as Prontaprint Gateway. Clients will have 24-hour access to an online gateway where they can personalise pre-approved artwork templates, view proofs and place print orders. This service has applications in many businesses but is especially suited to large organisations and multi-site operators who want individual outlets to be able to order customised printed materials at a local level, but also need the guarantee that their brand integrity is maintained at all times.

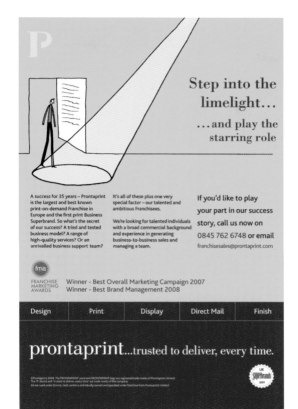

Promotion

Prontaprint has been transformed from a high street print and copy shop into a key player in the B2B print-on-demand sector through continual investment in the development and promotion of its brand on a local, national and international level. It has maintained its market leading position through a sustained and structured approach to business planning, sales and marketing strategy at both macro and micro levels.

Marketing activity is based on extensive client feedback and market research. Independent in-depth surveys of existing, lapsed and potential customers help to identify changing factors of importance among small, medium and large businesses when buying print and related products and services. Results provide Franchisees with a greater understanding of buyer behaviour as well as identifying new market opportunities.

Prontaprint believes that consistent and regular external sales and marketing activity is central to the ongoing profitable growth of each centre. This activity is focused on the acquisition, retention and development of business clients. It also provides franchisees with a wide range of central sales and marketing tools and resources to enable them to grow their businesses locally coupled with external sales support.

Brand Values

Prontaprint has four key brand values – Close, Connected, Can-do and Collaborative. 'Close' focuses on building long term relationships with clients on a one-to-one level. This is achieved through close contact with clients and close understanding of their needs.

'Connected' refers to Prontaprint's network of talented and experienced people as well as the use of technology. Prontaprint harnesses these connections, aiming to ensure clients get the best results with their business communications, on time, every time.

'Can-do' reflects the business culture of getting things done. Whatever the job, large or small, Prontaprint aims to go the 'extra mile' ensuring it is 'trusted to deliver, every time.'

Finally, 'Collaborative' reflects that talking to clients is the start of a two-way conversation, rather than a one-way sales pitch. By working in partnership with clients and each other, Prontaprint consistently guarantees distinctive design and print solutions.

prontaprint.com

Things you didn't know about Prontaprint

Prontaprint was the first print brand to be acknowledged as a Business Superbrand.

Prontaprint is a former winner of the British Franchise Association's Franchisor of the Year award.

In 2007, Prontaprint's central marketing support was accredited with a prestigious Franchise Marketing award by a panel of experts from the Franchising Industry and the CIM.

In 2008, Prontaprint's central brand management was also accredited with a prestigious Franchise Marketing Award.

RadioTimes

Radio Times is an iconic British brand, selling more than 15 billion copies since its launch in 1923. Offering unrivalled guidance and both comprehensive and easy-to-use listings, Radio Times features over 85 digital TV and radio stations, 10 pages of TV listings each day, a four-page weekly TV and film planner, 18 pages of digital and local radio and an insightful and exclusive features and interview package.

Product

Radio Times is continually evolving, fine-tuning its features and listings package to reflect the ever-changing digital landscape while ensuring ease-of-use remains top of the agenda.

Weekly TV, radio and film planners allow readers quick access to the week's best programming, while a listings team produces in-depth guidance with more than 12 pages of dedicated TV and radio listings per day. Radio remains core to the magazine's offering with no other title matching its depth of coverage and range of digital and local stations listed.

The listings are combined with an insightful features package that includes top contributors such as Andrew Collins, Stuart Maconie, Alison Graham and Barry Norman. An extended sports planner provides an at-a-glance guide to the week's sport; a comprehensive feedback page provides crucial information and guidance in the confusing digital arena; and a newly revised film section, overhauled in 2009, reflects the growing multichannel environment. Entering its 10th year, the Radio Times Guide to Films annual publication cements the brand's film credentials.

Market

Radio Times competes in the paid-for TV listings market where it sells 1,023,255 copies (Source: ABC July-December 2008), making it the highest revenue-generating title in the market, delivering more than £46 million retail sales value each year. Radio Times outsells the other four premium-priced listings magazines combined, a margin that has increased consecutively for the previous seven ABC periods.

With a readership of 2.63 million (Source: NRS January-December 2008) and the highest ABC1 profile of any paid-for magazine in the UK,

Radio Times is more closely aligned to quality supplements than to the paid-for listings market. With more than two million ABC1 readers and over one million AB readers, Radio Times is an invaluable advertising proposition for clients looking to reach a large upmarket audience on a weekly basis.

Selling in excess of 2.3 million copies and with 6.2 million readers, the Radio Times Christmas double edition is the market leader in volume and value. Delivering £4.6 million retail sales value in 2008, it enjoyed its best performance since 1991, increasing sales by 1.2 per cent year-on-year.

The Radio Times brand is extended online at radiotimes.com, which offers a fortnight of TV and radio listings for more than 400 channels. Users can personalise listings, browse a film database of over 24,000 films, and access blogs from Radio Times contributors and columnists. Since its launch in 1997, radiotimes.com has grown to a user base of 1.1 million, delivering 19 million page impressions each month.

1923	1936	1988	1997	2007	2009
In September, the first Radio Times is published after John Reith, BBC director general, refuses to pay newspapers to print details of BBC radio programmes.	BBC Television services open and Radio Times becomes the world's first television listings magazine.	Radio Times enters the Guinness Book of Records as its Christmas edition sells 11,220,666 copies – the biggest-selling edition of any British magazine in history.	Radio Times becomes the first television listings website, launching online with radiotimes.com.	Radio Times editor Gill Hudson is named PPA Editor of the Year.	Radio Times prints 21 different covers in celebration of the 21st anniversary of Comic Relief.

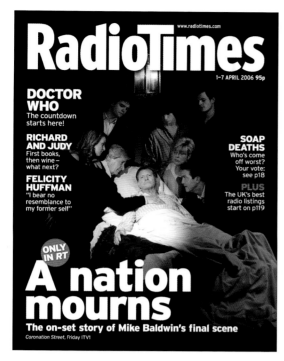

Achievements

The brand's commercial success is matched by reader recognition and in 2008, the Radio Times 'Vote Dalek' cover (published in the week of the 2005 general election) was named the best British magazine cover of all time in a poll organised by the Periodical Publishers Association. Radio Times covers have consistently made an impact with buyers, drawing attention at the newsstand. Recent notable covers include: the four-change Little Dorrit covers which, when placed together, linked to produce a panoramic scene from the programme; a specially commissioned three-change celebration of the 2008 Olympic Games, exclusively created by Gorillaz's Jamie Hewitt; a 21-change Comic Relief cover, celebrating its 21st anniversary in 2009; and a mountain of collectible Doctor Who gatefolds.

Recent Developments

Newly launched in 2009, a Radio Times application is now available to download to Apple iPhone and iTouch devices, allowing consumers to access TV and radio information on the move. Radio Times is also available through Panasonic and Sony electronic programme guides, providing a listings offering to viewers on screen.

Promotion

Radio Times manages a full programme of sales promotions each year. Over the last three years, Radio Times has featured free audiobook downloads, cover-mounted audio CDs featuring Doctor Who and The Chronicles of Narnia, free token-collect DVDs featuring classic BBC comedy and exclusive offers on digital TV.

Partnerships are key to Radio Times's promotional mix and throughout 2008/09, the brand has built relationships with the British Academy Television Awards, as the 2008 media partner and Classic FM, for the Nation's Favourite Music Poll. Each promotion has allowed Radio Times readers to interact at each of the events, while linking the brand with a salient partner.

Radio Times remains in the headlines of the national press with an inspired and sustained run of photography and news exclusives, creating widespread discourse about the magazine. Recent revelations from interviews with Terry Wogan, Ray Mears and Natasha Kaplinsky, for example, received wide coverage in the UK and international press. In total, 2008 saw more than 3,000 articles and 800 TV and radio interviews generated, a 25 per cent year-on-year increase in the brand's media coverage.

Brand Values

Radio Times is guided by five clear brand values, identified to ensure it best meets the needs of its customers. It aims to be consistently entertaining, intelligent, authoritative, comprehensive and accessible – the reliable, interesting and easy way for consumers to make choices.

radiotimes.com

Things you didn't know about Radio Times

Radio Times is the UK's third biggest-selling magazine, with more than a million copies sold each week.

When the BBC built Broadcasting House in 1932, a copy of Radio Times was placed under the foundation stone of the new building.

Radio Times has the largest subscription base of any weekly magazine in the UK, with more than 170,000 subscribers.

RIBA

As the voice of architecture in the UK since its foundation more than 175 years ago, the Royal Institute of British Architects (RIBA) champions good design to Government, the public and the construction industry. It believes that everyday life can and must be improved through better designed buildings and communities, and that the architect's role is crucial. RIBA Enterprises, the RIBA's principal commercial arm, is the leading information provider to the UK construction industry.

Market

The RIBA's founding mission, 'to advance architecture by demonstrating public benefit and promoting excellence in the profession', holds true to this day, but has evolved to meet the needs of its members and the society they serve. The growing demand for sustainable buildings, new-built and 'retrofitted', is currently transforming the market place for architects, while in today's uncertain economic times, the RIBA's role as a source of information and business guidance for its members remains key. The RIBA validates architecture courses around the world, with one third of the world's architects qualifying through an RIBA validation system.

Product

Although many architectural icons such as 30 St Mary Axe (The Gherkin), London Eye and Gateshead Millennium Bridge were created by RIBA members, most of the RIBA's work does

not centre on big design statements, setting out instead to raise the standards of buildings and spaces everywhere by supporting the designers of everyday architectural necessities. RIBA Client Services helps clients commission the right architect for their project, while the RIBA Competitions Office is dedicated to helping clients run competitions to select architects for their project. Clients are also benefiting from the RIBA Client Design Advisor scheme, which provides independent, expert advisors to guide clients through the, often complex, public sector procurement process. RIBA Awards, given to projects that have high architectural standards and make a substantial

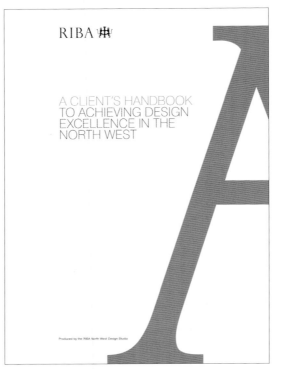

contribution to the local environment, are the industry's benchmark and culminate in the RIBA Stirling Prize.

RIBA Enterprises is the leading source of technical expertise and insight for those working within the built environment. Through the National Building Specification (NBS) sub-brand, it delivers the de facto standard specification system for buildings in the UK. It is also a key provider of a vast array of technical and regulatory information, including the Building Regulations' Approved Documents, as well as being a foremost innovator in essential learning services.

1834	1934	1996	1997	2004	2006
The Institute of British Architects is founded.	King George V and Queen Mary open the RIBA's new headquarters.	RIBA Stirling Prize is inaugurated.	The RIBA/Shelter collaboration, Architect in the House, is launched.	V&A + RIBA Architecture Partnership is established at the Victoria and Albert Museum.	The RIBA Library is designated as an Outstanding Collection by the Government.

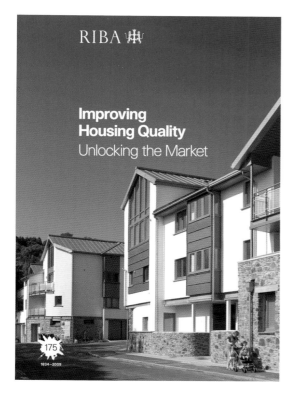

As RIBA Publishing and RIBA Bookshops, it is the industry's leading publisher and re-seller of books, contracts and forms. Finally, RIBA Enterprises is sought out for its unique marketing opportunities, enabling product manufacturers and service providers to interface with the architectural community and other construction professionals.

Achievements

The Institute continues to champion the long term benefits of good design to Government. RIBA Client Design Advisors, offering independent design advice, are soon to be appointed to every new project in the Government's £45 billion Building Schools for the Future programme. With society's growing awareness of the environment and its impact on the built world, RIBA's architects

have turned their problem-solving design skills to the subject of flooding. Working with the Environment Agency, the RIBA has produced a number of recommendations that are now being incorporated into local authorities' plans to alleviate flooding. In addition, the Government's 2009 'world class places' strategy, which recognised the role of the built environment on crime, health, community cohesion and prosperity, incorporated demands from the RIBA for a minimum design standard for public buildings and the involvement of local design review panels. From tackling the extremes of nature to everyday life, communities are benefiting from the expertise of the RIBA and its architect membership.

Recent Developments

Not all architects are 'RIBA' architects, with the Institute's own 'chartered members' practicing at the very top of their profession. The RIBA and RIBA Enterprises help them to excel by providing leading edge information. In uncertain economic times, the RIBA has developed a 'recession tool-kit', which includes information on those parts of the construction industry best tackling the recession, additional advice on client marketing, and the promotion of a skills audit, so that members can discover how to use their design skills in new, innovative areas. To broaden accessibility to membership, the Institute has recently created new categories that welcome a wider range of design professionals to the benefits of RIBA membership.

Promotion

The RIBA brand is driven through its press and marketing activity, the high-profile role taken by its presidents, as well as its lobbying of Government. In addition, its members play a central role in developing the brand as they trade using the 'RIBA' name. The RIBA works collaboratively with bodies such as the Construction Industry Council, Institution of Civil Engineers, Royal Town Planning Institute and, on the consumer front, with the housing and homelessness charity Shelter through the annual RIBA Architect in the House scheme.

The RIBA Trust, the Institute's cultural arm, partners with other organisations to help promote interest in architecture, as well as devising its own range of exhibitions and a talks programme which attracts speakers of world renown. The RIBA Library, housed at the RIBA headquarters and with free admission, holds one of the world's greatest collections of books, photographs and drawings, devoted to the study of architecture. This includes the world's finest holding of Palladio drawings, many of which will be heading to the USA for an RIBA Trust organised exhibition in 2010/11,

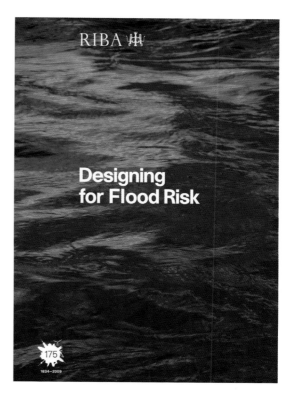

having already formed the core of a highly successful show touring Europe in 2009. The Library's virtual gallery RIBApix.com has a growing collection of more than 40,000 images to view and buy.

Brand Values

The brand is crystallised in the letters 'RIBA', which represent architecture's gold standard, and which are valued by RIBA members and the public alike. The RIBA aims to be responsive to its stakeholders and audiences; to be influential through its advocacy and campaigning; to be bold as it addresses 21st century challenges of design and construction; and to be authoritative at all times. In all that it does, it aims to inspire trust, demonstrate competence and show leadership.

architecture.com

Things you didn't know about the RIBA

First run in 1997, the RIBA and Shelter's Architect in the House scheme has now raised more than £1 million, helping Shelter to provide essential advice and support to those facing bad housing and homelessness in the UK.

Every year some 20,000 students emerge from schools of architecture, both in the UK and worldwide, whose courses have been validated by the RIBA.

The RIBA Library holds four million items devoted to the study of architecture. This includes 350 original drawings by renowned Italian Renaissance architect Andrea Palladio – more than 80 per cent of his total portfolio in existence today.

2007	2008	2009	2010
The RIBA Lubetkin Prize is founded.	Ruth Reed is elected as the RIBA's first female president.	The Institute celebrates its 175th birthday.	The Palladio USA exhibition tours four North American cities.

Rolls-Royce

Rolls-Royce is a global business, providing and supporting integrated power systems for use on land, at sea and in the air. The Rolls-Royce Group has a broad customer base including more than 600 airlines, 4,000 corporate and utility aircraft and helicopter operators, 160 armed forces, more than 2,000 marine customers, and energy customers in nearly 120 countries. With facilities in 50 countries, it employs 39,000 people worldwide.

Market

Annual sales for Rolls-Royce are more than £9 billion, half of which comes from services. The Group's order book by the middle of 2009 stood at £57.5 billion.

The Group operates in four long term global markets – civil and defence aerospace, marine and energy. These markets create a total opportunity worth some US$2 trillion over the next 20 years. The markets have a number of similar characteristics: they have very high barriers to entry; offer the opportunity for organic growth and feature extraordinarily long programme lives, usually measured in decades.

The size of these markets is generally related to world Gross Domestic Product (GDP) growth or, in the case of the defence markets, global security and the scale of defence budgets.

Product

Rolls-Royce is the world's number two aero engine manufacturer and its Trent family of engines is a leader in modern, widebody aircraft. Rolls-Royce is also a market leader for business jet engines.

In civil aerospace, Rolls-Royce powers more than 30 types of commercial aircraft from business jets to the largest widebody airliners. A fleet of 12,000 engines is in service with 600 airline customers and 4,000 corporate operators.

Rolls-Royce is also the leading military aero engine manufacturer in Europe and the number two military aero engine manufacturer in the world, powering approximately 25 per cent of the world's military fleet.

In the marine market, Rolls-Royce serves more than 2,000 customers and has equipment installed on 20,000 commercial and naval vessels operating around the world. Its products and services include established names such as Kamewa, Ulstein, Aquamaster and Brown Brothers, which together with a strong focus on research and development, have made Rolls-Royce a pioneer of many important technologies including aero-derivative marine gas turbines, controllable pitch propellers and water jets.

The Rolls-Royce energy business is a world-leading supplier of power systems for onshore and offshore oil and gas applications with a growing presence in the electrical power generation sector. It supplies products to customers in more than 120 countries and its main products include the industrial Trent and industrial RB211 gas turbines.

Achievements

Rolls-Royce is ranked in a number of external indices which benchmark corporate responsibility performance. It has retained its position in the Dow Jones Sustainability (World and European) Indexes for the sixth consecutive year.

It has been awarded Gold Company status in the 2008 Business in the Community Corporate Responsibility Index for the second year

1904	1914	1940	1944	1953	1966
Henry Royce meets Charles Rolls, whose company sells quality cars in London.	At the start of World War I, Royce designs his first aero engine, the Eagle, providing half of the total horsepower used in the air by the allies.	Royce's Merlin powers the Hawker Hurricane and Supermarine Spitfire in the Battle of Britain.	Rolls-Royce begins development of the aero gas turbine.	Rolls-Royce enters the civil aviation market with the Dart in the Vickers Viscount. It becomes the cornerstone of the universal acceptance of the gas turbine by the airline industry.	Bristol Siddeley merges with Rolls-Royce.

running. In particular, the Group's commitment to environmental management including reductions in greenhouse emissions and the promotion of behavioural change, has been recognised by being awarded platinum status.

Recent Developments
Among its ongoing CSR activities is the Rolls-Royce Science Prize, an annual awards programme that helps teachers implement science teaching ideas in their schools and colleges. There is a total of £120,000 in prizes to be won each year. The competition builds on the company's commitment to Project ENTHUSE, a £30 million partnership between industry, the Government and the Wellcome Trust, which provides teachers with funding to cover the cost of attending courses at the National Science Learning Centre.

At major Rolls-Royce sites the Group also sponsors a range of education projects. Employees get involved with local schools to support young people and promote STEM subjects – Science, Technology, Engineering and Maths.

Promotion
The strategy for the Rolls-Royce Group centres on five key elements: addressing the four global markets; investing in technology, infrastructure and capability; developing a competitive portfolio of products and services; growing market share and installed product base; and adding value to customers through product-related services.

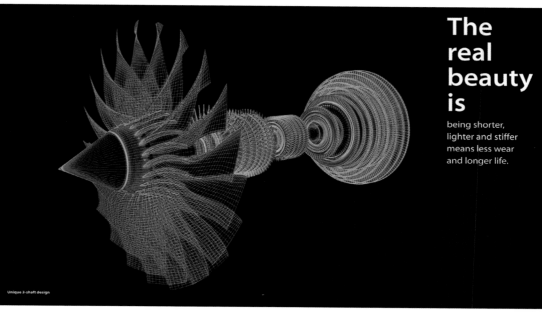

The real beauty is being shorter, lighter and stiffer means less wear and longer life.

Unique 3-shaft design

The Trent philosophy of continuous evolution and intelligent innovation delivers decisive business benefits.

Rolls-Royce

Over the past five years Rolls-Royce has invested £3.7 billion in research and development and it invests approximately £30 million annually in training.

The Group is determined to give an effective response to the problem of climate change and other environmental concerns and is committed to a programme of continuous improvement for its production and service activities around the world.

Similarly, it is committed to significant annual investments in research and development in order to provide leading-edge technologies that reduce fuel burn, emissions and noise across all its products. It is at the forefront of research into advanced technologies that could provide entirely new approaches to the problem of climate change.

Brand Values
Rolls-Royce is one of the most well-known brands in the world. The Rolls-Royce brand means more than engineering excellence – it is a standard of quality across all the company's activities. The brand is at the heart of everything Rolls-Royce does. Its brand values are reliability, integrity and innovation and its brand positioning statement is 'Trusted to deliver excellence'.

rolls-royce.com

Things you didn't know about Rolls-Royce

Rolls-Royce invests nearly £900 million annually in research and development.

The company celebrated its centenary in 2004.

It was the first to power the Airbus A380 into service with the Trent 900 engine.

The company has announced a new business to address the expanding market for civil nuclear power.

Its UT-Design of offshore vessel is the most successful in the world.

Rolls-Royce reactor plant designs power all of the nuclear submarines for the Royal Navy.

1976	1987	1999	2009
Concorde, powered by the Rolls-Royce Snecma Olympus 593, becomes the first and only supersonic airliner to enter service.	Rolls-Royce is privatised.	Rolls-Royce acquires Vickers for £576 million which transforms Rolls-Royce into the global leader in marine power systems.	Rolls-Royce Trent 1000 engines power the new Boeing 787 Dreamliner on its first flight.

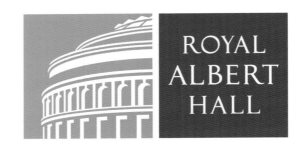

Since 1871, the Royal Albert Hall has had an unrivalled history of associations with some of the world's greatest artists. From contemporary to classic, world-class performances to tomorrow's stars, the Hall's flexibility and diverse programming showcases more than 350 events every year. From global broadcasts to intimate events, the Hall's breathtaking surroundings enhance the experience of the best live performances for well over one million people every year.

The Hall's founding Charter requires it to maintain this iconic Grade I listed building and through it to promote the understanding, appreciation and enjoyment of the Arts and Sciences. The Hall launched an extensive Learning & Participation programme in 2004, providing opportunities to experience and participate in live performance. This has now enabled more than 128,000 young people from many different backgrounds to explore and engage in the arts, science and the cultural industries.

Market

The Royal Albert Hall operates in the highly competitive entertainment, leisure and tourism sectors. It is a registered charity and receives no public funding. Its competitors are the other leading UK performing arts and entertainment venues and organisations, many of which receive central or local government funding. It also faces more general competition for a customer's leisure time and pound, especially in the age of digital media, home entertainment and the current economic situation.

Product

The Royal Albert Hall hosts live performances by artists from around the world and, with partners, promotes productions of opera, ballet, musicals and classical music. Each year, more than 350 events are held in the Hall's auditorium, including performances of classical music, jazz, folk and world music, circus, rock and pop, ballet, opera, comedy, tennis, film premieres, corporate dinners and award ceremonies.

Achievements

In 2008, the Royal Albert Hall was recognised by the music industry when it won International Theatre of the Year at the Pollstar Concert Industry Awards for the sixth consecutive year. The Hall also picked up its first International Live Music Conference Arthur Award.

Key Learning & Participation events during 2008 included Summertime, a music and dance project which enabled around 200 teenagers to learn different forms of dance and perform at the Hall; Last Standing, a project in which young offenders wrote a play based on the opera Tosca; and a press conference with The Wombats for young people.

The Hall supports other registered charities with their fundraising activities and offers itself free of charge to a charity each year, awarding the 2009 opportunity to Chickenshed. Recent highlights have included concerts in support of the Teenage Cancer Trust, featuring

1871	1912	1941	1963	1970	1996
The Royal Albert Hall is opened by Queen Victoria in March.	The Titanic Band Memorial Concert takes place at the Hall, encompassing 500 performers and conductors, Sir Edward Elgar, Henry Wood, Landon Ronald and Thomas Beecham.	The first BBC Proms season at the Hall takes place.	The Beatles and The Rolling Stones appear on the same bill on 15th September.	Tennis is first played at the Hall.	Work begins on the Royal Albert Hall's eight-year major building development programme and Cirque du Soleil premieres Saltimbanco at the Hall.

ENTERTAINING
THE WORLD

EVENTS APRIL 09

artists such as Stereophonics and Kasabian, RockCorps and a world music concert in support of VSO.

Recent Developments

The Hall's ignite series of free Friday lunchtime concerts by world music and jazz artists, held in the Café Consort, was bolstered with the launch of ignite brunch on Sundays in 2007. An ongoing success, it sold to 95 per cent capacity in its second year.

The Hall's engaging free exhibition series continued in 2008 with I am 90, photographs documenting Nelson Mandela's 90th birthday visit to London, and Counterpoint, an intriguing exhibition from the Science Photo Library.

hush, the intimate gigs for up and coming artists in the Hall's Elgar Room, launched in 2007, continued with five bands performing during 2008. In May, The Albert Sessions were launched by The Wombats; the series of discounted rentals for the main auditorium aims to encourage young artists and support new music.

The Hall jointly promoted a new dance spectacular, Strictly Gershwin, with Raymond Gubbay and English National Ballet in June 2008. It proved extremely successful, performing to audiences of over 96 per cent capacity and was followed in June 2009 by a new production of The King and I, starring Maria Friedman and Daniel Dae Kim.

The Hall extended its corporate and public hospitality opportunities during 2008, launching fine dining packages for the public and offering

a wider range of bespoke corporate packages across an increased range of shows.

Promotion

The Royal Albert Hall markets its own initiatives and works with its event promoters, assisting them with the ticket sales for their events through the Hall's marketing channels. In 2008, the Hall had more than 1.2 million people through its doors and the average attendance across the year was over 84 per cent – an all time record.

The Hall's brand positioning 'Entertaining the World' is designed to capture the magic of the Hall experience for customers, the wide range of leading artists from around the world that it plays host to, and its ambitions to continue to spread the reach of the Hall and its events beyond the building itself through broadcast and new media channels.

The Royal Albert Hall is a brand known around the world through extensive PR coverage, broadcasts and DVD releases. It also works in partnership with brands to

reach new audiences and is interested in exploring new business partnerships. Its current business partners include iTunes, Moët & Chandon and Häagen-Dazs.

Brand Values

The Hall's brand values are encompassed in the positioning statement, 'Entertaining the World'. It is the Hall's ambition that everyone, young and old, from every nation and culture, should feel welcome at the Hall and able to enjoy the shared experience of live performance by the best of today's global artists.

Built as part of Prince Albert's vision for a centre for the Arts and Sciences in South Kensington, the Royal Albert Hall is proud of the building and its heritage. It remains true to his founding ambitions to maintain and develop this magical building for future generations and to continue to promote the appreciation of the Arts and Sciences.

royalalberthall.com

2004	2006	2007	2008
The official 're-opening' of the Hall by Her Majesty The Queen takes place, celebrating the completion of the Hall's major building development programme.	President Bill Clinton speaks at the Hall about his vision for leadership in the 21st century.	Swarovski Fashion Rocks is broadcast to more than 40 countries around the world.	The UK premiere of Cirque du Soleil's Varekai takes place at the Hall.

Things you didn't know about the Royal Albert Hall

In 1909 a full indoor Marathon was run at the Hall – a total of 524 circuits of the Arena.

There are more than 13,500 letter 'A's in the Royal Albert Hall – featured on the banisters and in the terracotta and stonework throughout the building.

It took six million bricks and 80,000 terracotta bricks to build the Hall.

The Hall has hosted many world statesmen including Sir Winston Churchill, President FW de Klerk, Nelson Mandela, His Holiness the Dalai Lama and President Bill Clinton.

Ryman
stationery EST. 1893

Since Ryman was established in 1893 it has become a household name; recognised for its quality stationery products, value, reliability and famous for customer service. With a multi-channel and nationwide chain of 240 stores, Ryman is the high street's market-leading specialist stationery retailer. Turnover for the group is more than £140 million.

Market

Building on its longstanding history of stationery product innovation and customer service, Ryman combines high street accessibility with a much extended range of products available online and through in-store ordering for next day delivery. Targeting business, home office and consumer stationery markets, Ryman's range extends to more than 20,000 items, supported with newly introduced business services including DHL Servicepoints. In addition, Ryman offers a dedicated business account with optional credit facilities and bulk discounting.

Despite recent difficult trading conditions, the UK market for personal and office stationery remains relatively constant. According to Key Note research, it is valued at just over £3 billion, made up primarily of core products such as paper, writing instruments, filing and storage solutions. Digital storage, home printing and social categories are experiencing growth, as are security products such as shredders, tamper proof ink and forged note identification equipment, fuelled by rising consumer concern of identity theft. In 2008 the banking crisis generated marked growth in home safes and cashboxes.

Due to the wide appeal of stationery, Ryman has a broad spectrum of competitors ranging from electrical retailers to supermarkets as well as more traditional stationery retailers such as WHSmith, Viking and Staples.

Product

Ryman sells a wide range of stationery and office supplies, from writing equipment, paper and filing solutions to office furniture and technology, including large capacity external hard drives, A3 colour printers and a wide range of own-brand remanufactured, compatible and high capacity ink cartridges.

As a specialist stationer, Ryman is able to offer products not normally found in general stationery stockists, such as grades, colours and sizes of products to suit many specific needs. Ryman continually strives to be first to market with innovative new stationery products. A full business service is provided in a number of stores, including DHL Servicepoints, photocopying, binding, laminating, bulk printing and business and personalised stationery. Self-service photocopying is also available in most stores. In addition, business account holders are offered a credit facility which combines the benefits of bulk pricing and convenience of delivery for large orders with the flexibility of visiting any of its stores for smaller top-up purchases.

Achievements

Ryman continues to show strong performance in the stationery sector; since 1995 the business has increased fourfold and today, Ryman has a turnover in excess of £140 million. Not only diversifying into new product areas as the market changes, Ryman's success can also be attributed to consistent investment in its people, its store estate, information technology, warehousing and distribution.

In the last year, Ryman continued to follow a robust store opening programme with the most recent launch on Cheapside in the City of London in November 2009. Ryman has also maintained its refurbishment programme with over half the chain receiving significant shop floor improvements during 2009.

Theo Paphitis, Chairman, Ryman Limited

1893	1970s	1995	2001	2007	2009
Henry J Ryman opens his first store on Great Portland Street, London.	The family business is sold. Over the next 20 years its owners include Burton Group, Terence Conran, Jennifer d'Abo and Pentos.	Ryman is acquired by Chancerealm Limited (later known as Ryman Group Limited), in which Theo Paphitis is the controlling shareholder.	Ryman acquires Partners the Stationers, comprising 86 stores.	Ryman acquires 61 Stationery Box stores, which are rebranded to Ryman by October 2008.	Ryman partners with Red Nose Day 2009 raising more than £500,000 for Comic Relief through staff fundraising and the sale of exclusive product.

The Ryman website and online business has recently undergone a major transformation in preparation for the next generation of multichannel retailing. Furthermore, Ryman has continued to build on the benefits of the integration of three separate stationery businesses – Partners, Stationery Box and Ryman – into one national chain, implementing state-of-the-art store planning software to improve stock control and optimise on shelf presentation.

Recent Developments

It's not only the Ryman product offering that is driven by innovation and improvement but the business itself is in the midst of an initiative to lessen its impact on the environment by working closely with the Carbon Trust. Theo Paphitis, chairman of Ryman, has fronted a major campaign for the Trust, publicising its loan scheme to businesses.

In product development, Ryman is committed to growing its range of products using new technology, recycled paper and materials from sustainable forests. On the shop floor, meanwhile, biodegradable carrier bags have been introduced which, due to their light weight, have a smaller carbon footprint than the equivalent sized paper bag. A reusable carrier bag made from non-woven polypropylene is also available.

The company's warehouse, packaging and logistics operations compress and recycle cardboard and plastic waste, while the Ryman delivery fleet uses Euro 4 vehicles to reduce carbon emissions and developments in eco-friendly fuels are monitored. In addition, all Ryman suppliers must comply with guidelines from the Ethical Trading Initiative Base Code.

Promotion

Ryman's promotional strategy rests on its consistent 'value for money' offering across its ranges. Multi-purchase discounts are made available on key lines and special items, while price-led promotional activity features heavily during seasonal consumer peaks such as 'Back to School' and Christmas.

Charity work is a central part of the Ryman culture and includes Ryman's support of Comic Relief in 2009 which is being repeated in 2010 through an official partnership with Sport Relief, an initiative of Comic Relief.

For the Academic Year 2009/10 Ryman is sponsoring the Young Enterprise Company Scheme Marketing Award for the first time,

providing inspiration and encouraging the development of entrepreneurial skills in 3,000 schools across the UK. Ryman continues to sponsor the Ryman Football League, maintaining visibility for the brand in the south of England.

Brand Values

Acknowledged as a specialist in its field, Ryman has developed and nurtured its standards of quality, value, reliability and service over 115 years, building and retaining a loyal customer base. Ryman is proud of its record of investing in its people, training them to be able to deliver a high standard of service, backed by expert knowledge of Ryman's range of products and their applications.

ryman.co.uk

Things you didn't know about Ryman

Ryman recycles more than 150,000 cartridges every year on behalf of its customers. Many of its own-brand cartridges also use remanufactured materials.

Ryman opened its first stationery shop in 1893; sales were £50 in the first week.

Ryman sells two million pens every year; enough ink to draw along the length of the Great Wall of China almost 300 times.

At present there are 27 members of staff who have been with Ryman for more than 25 years, 49 members of staff who have celebrated at least 20 years' service and 118 members of staff who have been with the company for more than 15 years. Ryman's longest serving member of staff retired in 2009 following an impressive 53 years of service.

Saint-Gobain is the world-leader in the design, production and distribution of materials for the construction and habitat markets. Its corporate strategy is to achieve global leadership in providing innovative solutions for a more sustainable built environment, addressing the global challenges of our time – in particular, energy efficiency and environmental protection.

Market

Saint-Gobain has grown rapidly in the UK and Ireland over the past 20 years to gain leadership in the construction materials market. Since 2001 it has made over 70 acquisitions, adding more than 200 sites to its UK and Ireland operation which turned over more than £3 billion in 2008. Today it includes some of the best known and respected brands in the industry such as British Gypsum, Isover, Saint-Gobain Glass, Artex, Solaglas, Weber, Saint-Gobain PAM, Ecophon and Saint-Gobain Abrasives. Collectively they employ over 17,000 people at more than 1,000 sites.

Its businesses are structured into three core sectors: Construction Products; Innovative Materials, and Building Distribution. It is the world leader in ductile iron pipe systems, plasterboard and plaster, insulation, industrial mortars, abrasives and flat glass, as well as being Europe's largest distributor of building material. In the UK and Ireland it includes Jewson, the leading builders' merchant chain, Graham the plumbers' merchant and Pasquill – a specialist in engineered timber solutions.

Product

More than a quarter of the UK's carbon dioxide emissions come from the energy we use to heat, light and run our homes, while a further 19 per cent is generated by non-residential buildings. There is a clear need for urgent action to reduce this environmental impact by making our homes and buildings as energy efficient as possible. As a member of the UK-Green Building Council, Saint-Gobain's businesses offer an unrivalled range of high performance, energy-saving solutions. These

give architects and designers the ability to meet the most exacting performance and legislative standards, whilst creating comfortable and secure living and working environments.

Together they form a robust, integrated supply chain partner that has the strength and flexibility to support the most diverse range of customer requirements. This adds up to its unique capability to support everything from the biggest landmark projects, such as St Pancras International station and 30 St Mary's Axe (The Gherkin), to ongoing repair and maintenance programmes.

As well as fast, efficient access to a comprehensive range of products, Saint-Gobain can provide specialist technical expertise and resources backed by world leading R&D facilities. Last year it invested almost £400 million in R&D, employing 3,500 people in this crucial area and registering over 300 patents. This has enabled it to maintain a leading technical edge in each of its core markets.

Saint-Gobain's advanced range of construction materials includes high performance plaster and plasterboard which offer acoustic and energy saving benefits, plus external and internal insulation systems. Many of these use glass wool which has a very limited environmental footprint over its entire life cycle. Through the heat savings it makes possible, glass wool saves up to 1,000 times the amount of CO_2 emitted and energy used during its manufacture. Its portfolio also includes low emissivity glass and acoustic glazing, fire proof and bullet proof safety glass,

SGG ECOCLEAR® double glazed units and extra clear glass for photovoltaic systems.

Saint-Gobain also specialises in mineral ceramics, performance polymers and glass textiles, is the world's leading manufacturer of abrasives and the only one to supply each of the three major types of abrasives: Bonded Abrasives (resinoid and vitrified), Coated Abrasives and Diamond products.

Its advanced architectural membranes are used in high-performance roofs, for example Saint-Gobain Performance Plastics manufactured the PTFE coated fabric for The O2 arena in London's Docklands.

Achievements

Sustainability is at the core of Saint-Gobain's business strategy as recognised by its ranking in the Global 100 list of the most sustainable corporations. This evaluates companies according to how effectively they manage environmental, social and governance risks and opportunities relative to their industry peers. It was one of only 15 industrial corporations to feature in the list from MSCI World – the global stock market index from Morgan Stanley Capital International.

In December 2009 it was named one of the UK's best regarded businesses, ranking a close second in the Building Materials and Merchants category of Management Today's list of Britain's 50 Most Admired Companies. Corporate reputation is reviewed by industry peers with leading professionals in British companies assessing and nominating their most admired rivals.

1985	1990	1996	2000	2005	2009
Saint-Gobain enters the UK and Ireland market by acquiring Stanton from British Steel, now known as Saint-Gobain PAM UK.	The company buys Solaglas and builds its presence in the high-performance materials and flat glass sectors.	A General Delegation is formed to serve the needs of the UK and Ireland markets.	Meyer International is bought for £1.4 billion, now known as Saint-Gobain Building Distribution it is the UK's leading builder's merchant and owner of Jewson and Graham merchant chains.	Saint-Gobain Gypsum division is formed with the acquisition of BPB Group, which adds 12,500 people and 130 sites to the Group globally.	UK and Ireland continues to grow, employing 17,000 people across 1,000 sites.

This followed on the heels of Saint-Gobain Glass being voted one of Britain's Best Green Companies by The Sunday Times in both 2008 and 2009. One of its key achievements was the establishment of a scheme for customers to send waste glass (cullet) back to the factory. It leads the industry with 28 per cent of new products being made from returned cullet – double the amount of competitors.

Saint-Gobain also recently put its name to the Copenhagen Communiqué which calls for a fair global deal on climate change in recognition of the environmental crisis facing the world. The statement was officially handed over to Ban Ki-Moon, the UN general secretary, in advance of the Copenhagen summit.

Saint-Gobain also believes strongly that no business should pursue success at the expense of the communities in which it operates. Last year it launched the Saint-Gobain Initiatives Foundation which supports projects proposed by its employees in three focus areas: construction-related job training for young people; construction, refurbishment or renovation of community buildings or housing for low income or disadvantaged groups and individuals; and energy efficiency and environmental protection in housing and community buildings.

Recent Developments

Key developments include the insulation system, Vario, the world's most advanced solution for the management of interstitial moisture in timber construction; it uses a polymide-based membrane to allow timber to breathe and dry out naturally. It was developed to help meet new legislation on airtightness and the Government's Code for Sustainable Homes.

Other new products include a floating floor system by British Gypsum, SGG EcoClear® – the best energy efficient sealed unit on the market, a severe-duty partitioning system, GypWall Extreme, and the weber.therm XM external wall insulation (EWI) system which has achieved the 'Energy Saving Recommended' label from the Energy Saving Trust (EST).

The highly innovative range of GripTop™ access covers (manhole covers), produced by iron technology leader Saint-Gobain PAM UK, recently won the Motorcycle Award category at the 2009 Prince Michael International Road Safety Awards. GripTop significantly reduces the risk of skidding and skid-related road accidents caused by traditional metal access covers which become worn smooth over the decades.

Promotion

In 2009, Saint-Gobain showcased more than 70 of its products at its first exhibition in the UK, Ecobuild. This is the world's biggest event for sustainable design, construction and the built environment. With almost 35,000 visitors, the exhibition connects formal learning with practical experience, and with products and suppliers.

Saint-Gobain is also the main sponsor and technical partner for the Nottingham H.O.U.S.E – an energy efficient, zero carbon solar powered home designed and built by a team of students from the University of Nottingham's Department of the Built Environment (DBE). The H.O.U.S.E is the UK's only entry into the first International Solar Decathlon Europe competition to design and build Europe's most effective and energy efficient zero carbon solar powered house.

The Nottingham H.O.U.S.E has been constructed entirely from materials supplied by Saint-Gobain's UK companies including Saint-Gobain Isover, British Gypsum, Weber, Saint-Gobain Glass, Solaglas, International Timber, Pasquill and Greenworks, providing total solutions to optimise energy efficiency.

Demonstrating how low energy architecture can lend itself to the mass market, the building's versatile L-shaped, modular design can be worked into terraces, rows or stacked as apartments. The resulting concept is a highly marketable, zero carbon starter home for a new family – a major requirement in the UK.

Brand Values

Saint-Gobain is engaged in an innovation-led process of strategic refocusing on the habitat and construction markets. Research and development is the lifeblood of the company ensuring it can continue to innovate and introduce new products to the market that help the building industry become more sustainable as well as growing its business. It is committed to creating more comfortable, economical and sustainable living and working environments.

saint-gobain.co.uk

Things you didn't know about Saint-Gobain

Saint-Gobain products insulate half of all the homes in Europe.

The company has equipped 80 capitals and more than 1,000 major cities across the world with ductile iron water pipes.

One in every two cars uses glass manufactured by Saint-Gobain.

The company was founded in 1665 to deliver the world's first industrial scale glass for the Hall of Mirrors at Versailles, France.

Among the landmark buildings its materials have been used in are London's St Pancras International station, 30 St Mary's Axe (known as The Gherkin) and the Emirates Stadium.

For more than 70 years, Samsung has been 'dedicated to making a better world' through diverse businesses that today span advanced technology, semiconductors, skyscraper and plant construction, petrochemicals, fashion, medicine, finance, hotels, and more. Its flagship company, Samsung Electronics, leads the global market in high-tech electronics manufacturing and digital media.

Market

Samsung Electronics has grown from a small-scale manufacturer with a little known brand into one of the world's strongest and most powerful technology companies.

Boasting a diverse product portfolio, Samsung's success can be largely attributed to its strength in three core areas – memory chips, liquid crystal displays (LCDs) and mobile phones.

Samsung also attributes its success to: the production of innovative, reliable products and services; talented people; a responsible approach to business and global citizenship; and collaboration with its partners and customers.

Samsung's aim is to develop innovative technologies and efficient processes that create new markets, enrich people's lives and continue to make Samsung a trusted market leader. Samsung is guided by a singular vision: to lead the digital convergence movement. This vision is being delivered through Samsung Electronics' innovative product range that spans mobile phones, TV, audio and video, PCs, cameras and camcorders, monitors, printers, home appliances and more. Samsung is a leader in all of these markets.

Product

From stylish mobile phones to semiconductors, from DRAM to digital TVs, Samsung encompasses a variety of products in its various business divisions that harness speed, creativity and efficiency to invent and develop market-leading products. Samsung's commitment to being the world's best has won the company number one global market share for 13 products

including semiconductors, TFT-LCDs, monitors, and CDMA mobile phones.

Samsung is divided into several different affiliated companies, with Samsung Electronics being the best known and most profitable. It manufactures a wide range of products including audio/visual, computer related and telecommunications products as well as home appliances and various components.

Samsung sold more than 2.5 million LED TVs globally in 2009; in 2010 Samsung expects to sell 10 million.

Achievements

Samsung has won many awards and gained recognition for its products in recent years. In 2009 this included awards for TV of the Year at T3 Gadget Awards for the Samsung UE40B7000; TV/AV Product of the year for the UE46B8000 at the Stuff Awards 2009; Best Laptop Under £400 for the R519 on Five TV's The Gadget Show. The R519 went on to become Samsung's best selling notebook of the year; Best Multimedia Device for the i8910HD mobile phone, establishing Samsung as a top Smartphone manufacturer; Best Multimedia Phone at the Mobile Choice

1938	1950s	1960s	1970s	1990s	2000
Samsung General Store opens in North Kyungsang Province, Korea.	Samsung becomes a producer of basic commodities such as sugar and wool.	Samsung expands overseas and is one of the first Korean companies to do so.	The foundations for the present day Samsung are laid. Investment grows in the semiconductor, information and telecommunications industries.	Significant change in relation to Samsung's approach takes place.	A Digital Management approach is adopted to ensure that Samsung maintains its leading position in the Information Age.

Awards for the i8910 HD; a top industry accolade for Samsung as Monitor Manufacturer of the Year came from PC Pro with the PC Pro 2009 Reliability & Service Awards for Monitors; it also received a Which? Magazine Best Buy accolade for the WB1000 camera, positioning Samsung Digital Imaging as a 'premium' brand amongst the competition.

Samsung's premium brand image has powered its growth in the telecommunications category. It is the number one handset manufacturer globally and leads the telecommunications industry with the widest range of mobile phones currently available in the market. Samsung has also led the standardisation of mobile phone technologies with products such as mobile WiMAX.

Samsung was awarded 23 prestigious CES 2010 Innovation Awards including: three Best of Innovations; three eco-design honours; three awards for its LED back-lit HD TVs; one for its Plasma HD TV; three for blue-ray players; one for its home theatre system; two for its digital audio players; two for its digital cameras; one for a refrigerator; six awards for mobile phones; and one for a monitor with multi display functionality.

Recent Developments

More than a quarter of Samsung employees are engaged in research and development. This is a hallmark of the company and each year the business is focused on discovering new technologies, products and services in order to keep Samsung at the cutting-edge of innovation.

At the 2010 Consumer Electronics Show in Las Vegas which took place in January 2010, Samsung showcased an abundance of product launches in the home entertainment arena. Highlighted products included its new 3D TV line-up, the widest product range ever and the innovative LED9000, which is as thin as a pencil. In addition to LED TV the full line-up also includes LCD TV, Plasma TV, Blu-ray players and home theatre systems. The first complete 3D eco-system with an advanced 3D television, sophisticated 3D Blu-ray player, stylish active shutter 3D glasses and a home theatre system was also launched. In addition, an HD TV-based internet applications store was also launched; the first application store to be designed to work across all of Samsung's

What colour is your life? Samsung GENIO touch

devices from TVs and laptops to mobile phones as well as two innovative e-Book readers.

Reflecting further innovation, Samsung showcased concept products in the form of the world's first transparent MP3 player with an AMOLED display.

Samsung has launched the world's first multi-device applications store – a single destination to browse, buy and manage apps for Samsung

devices, beginning with mobile phones, TVs and Blu-ray players. Already launched in the UK, France and Italy, it will expand to approximately 50 countries worldwide in 2010. Content partners will include Accedo Broadband, AccuWeather.com, The Associated Press, Blockbuster, Fashion TV, Netflix, Picasa, Pandora, Rovi, Travel Channel, Twitter, USA TODAY, Vudu and YouTube. Samsung Apps will eventually be open to developers and Samsung will offer a software development kit.

Promotion

Samsung's marketing aim is to drive profitable growth with a focus on brand preference and loyalty. By adopting a holistic approach to the various Samsung businesses, it is able to leverage the full strength of the Samsung brand.

Nurturing brand loyalty is a key pillar of Samsung's marketing. Its consumers continue to remain

loyal to the brand as a result of a range of initiatives including product experience, customer service and support as well as an ongoing active dialogue through a broad range of communications programmes.

Samsung continues to drive a brand-led consumer-centric approach to marketing, building emotional engagement across a range of product businesses.

Samsung aims to create some of the world's most innovative and inspiring communications and advertising campaigns that bring its product propositions and brand to life. Recognised by consumers and the industry as an award winning advertiser, Samsung continues to build rapid brand preference and aspiration.

Samsung's product research and development is world-class, driving the company to build a brand that is best-in-class in technology and entertainment.

Samsung is concerned with managing its business processes to produce an overall positive impact on society. Its Corporate Responsibility (CR) strategy includes; business ethics, public and community affairs, investor relations, governance, stakeholder engagement, brand management, environmental affairs and corporate philanthropy.

Brand Values

The Samsung brand is based around core values of technology, design and innovation as well as efficient processes that create new markets, enrich people's lives and maintain Samsung's position as a digital leader.

samsung.co.uk

2006	2008	2010	
World firsts include the launch of an 82 inch full HD TV TFT-LCD and a 10 mega pixel 8GB HDD camera phone.	The Olympic Games in Beijing offer Samsung a prime sponsorship opportunity.	Samsung is a worldwide Olympic partner and sponsor of the 2010 Winter Olympics in Vancouver.	Also in 2010, Samsung will introduce a full-range of 3D ready HD TVs and the world's first transparent MP3 player with an AMOLED display.

Sandals

THE *Luxury Included* HOLIDAY

Since opening its first resort in 1981, Sandals Resorts has been at the forefront of the Caribbean all-inclusive travel sector by offering luxury, innovation and choice. In an industry brimming with new contenders, the combined knowledge and experience of Sandals' management team and resort staff has kept the company at the head of the expanding all-inclusive market by introducing the Luxury Included® holiday experience.

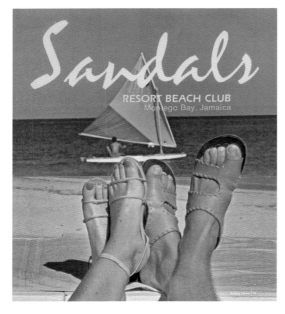

Market
In recent years the concept of luxury travel has steered away from conservative off-the-shelf five star packages towards tailor-made individualism. The market remains people focused and it is people skills, along with an emphasis on personal choice, that Sandals Resorts sees as key in setting it apart from its competitors.

Right from the outset, the brand aimed to offer more; where others had inclusive meals and rooms at a set rate, Sandals' prices covered premium drinks, tips and taxes, in addition to all recreational and water sports activities. Furthermore, while it was common within the market for meals to be served as buffets, Sandals built its reputation on gourmet specialty restaurants and silver service.

Sandals Resorts International (SRI) is now the largest operator of Luxury Included® resorts in the Caribbean. Currently there are 12 Sandals Resorts aimed at 'two people in love' located in Jamaica, Antigua, St Lucia and The Bahamas and four of its sister chain, Beaches Resorts, catering for couples, families and singles.

Product
Sandals prides itself on its top-of-the-range products; from à la carte restaurants, benefiting from the brand's established partnership with California's Beringer Vineyards, to an extensive range of water sports – Sandals Resorts is now one of the largest dive operators in the Caribbean. Its butler service, offered in partnership with the Guild of Professional English Butlers, represents the ultimate in luxury pampering; from private in-suite check-in to unpacking and packing as well as any special request, such as a moonlit dinner, that individual customers may require.

Sandals was one of the first operators in the Caribbean to offer European-style spas. Red Lane® Spas now feature prominently in all of its establishments, with their scenic beachside locations being an enduring signature of the brand.

Achievements
Both Sandals Resorts and the more family-oriented Beaches Resorts continue to accrue industry awards that reaffirm the brand's leading position across the luxury travel market – for the last 14 years the brand has been voted the World's Best at the World Travel Awards.

Notable accolades in recent years include winning at the 2008 TripAdvisor Travellers' Choice Awards, where Beaches Boscobel Resort & Golf Club was recognised as one of the Top 10 Hotels for Families in the Caribbean and Latin America. In 2007, Travel + Leisure Family Magazine singled out Beaches Turks & Caicos Resort & Spa as the second best overall

1981	1985	1988	1991	1993	1994
Gordon 'Butch' Stewart buys a dilapidated hotel in Montego Bay, Jamaica. Despite no prior hotel experience he opens Sandals Montego Bay several months later.	Sandals unveils its signature swim-up pool bar, enabling guests to order refreshments without having to leave the swimming pool.	Cuisine becomes sophisticated with gourmet meals prepared by international chefs served 'white-glove' style. Sandals Negril also opens its doors.	Sandals becomes the largest operator of all-inclusive resorts in the Caribbean and opens its first resort in Antigua.	Sandals St Lucia is launched in April offering guests the opportunity to split their stay between two islands, Sandals Antigua and Sandals St Lucia.	WeddingMoons® is launched – a concept combining a holiday wedding with an inclusive honeymoon.

Caribbean resort. A trio of Sandals Resorts, the Sandals Negril Beach Resort & Spa, the Sandals Dunn's River Villaggio Golf Resort & Spa and Sandals Whitehouse European Village & Spa, made it onto Condé Nast Traveller's Gold List for 2007, an accolade that reinforces the brand's continued dominance within the luxury travel sector.

Recent Developments

Sandals recently introduced the concept of the Luxury Included® holiday through a collection of suites in Jamaica, Antigua, St Lucia and the Bahamas. The new experience features an extended range of premium services and amenities that include private plunge pools and Jacuzzi baths, as well as a selection of exclusive partnerships with the likes of celebrity designers Preston Bailey and Sylvia Weinstock.

Sandals Resorts' new Mediterranean Village at the Sandals Grande Antigua Resort & Spa is the first all-suite property to offer guests the new Luxury Included® experience and in doing so, signifies a shift in direction for the company away from the all-inclusive label towards a more contemporary approach.

Promotion

Brand promotion comes in the form of a multimillion-pound advertising campaign that supports the efforts of travel agents and tour operators to market both the Sandals Resorts and Beaches Resorts brands. The campaign encompasses a broad range of media: flyers, property-specific brochures, posters, signage and window displays for travel agents, in

addition to the more high profile television and ecommerce activities, consumer and trade advertisements, newspaper advertising and national billboards.

Sandals has often been recognised by the strong, vivid and colourful aesthetics that flow through its various media campaigns. However, this visual brand identity is evolving to suit global markets in the ever changing face of luxury world travel. The new brand image is more sophisticated and lifestyle focused, hence able to deliver the Luxury Included® ethos with more success.

Sandals Resorts and Beaches Resorts operate a sophisticated CRM programme which includes a highly attractive loyalty scheme, Sandals Select.

In addition, in 2006 an exclusive partnership was developed with Crayola, defining Beaches Resorts as the first in the Caribbean to offer younger guests Crayola Art Camps. Beaches Resorts is also a sponsor of Sesame Street®, with an exclusive Caribbean Adventure Programme where children benefit from character activities and weekly shows.

Furthermore, Beaches Resorts collaborated with Microsoft® Xbox to create the Xbox 360 Game Garage Video Game Centres.

Brand Values

Sandals is one of the best-known luxury resort brands in the world. It continues to build on its leading position in the Caribbean hotel industry with innovations such as the Luxury Included® concept, making it well positioned to address consumers' growing demands for luxury choices to be included in their package holiday. Throughout its history the company has strived to create the ultimate Sandals experience: luxury, service and uncompromising quality delivered in picturesque beachside locations.

sandals.co.uk

1995	1996	2004	2008
The first Beaches resort, Beaches Negril – catering for singles, families and 'two people in love' – opens in Jamaica.	Sandals Royal Bahamian Resort & Spa opens, and readers of Condé Nast Traveller name it one of their top 10 spa resorts.	A butler service is introduced to Sandals' top suite categories – an ultimate all-inclusive pampering service.	Sandals Negril is the first hotel in the world to be awarded Green Globe Platinum Certification in recognition of more than 10 years' dedication to sustainable practices.

Things you didn't know about Sandals

It took seven months and US$4 million to renovate the first Sandals Resort in Montego Bay to transform it into Sandals' flagship property.

Sandals was the first Caribbean brand to offer Jacuzzi baths, satellite television, swim-up pool bars and to equip every room with a king-size bed.

Chairman Gordon 'Butch' Stewart donated US$1 million worth of holidays to military personnel who served in the Gulf War.

Although best known as a resort for 'two people in love', Sandals Resorts also offers family holidays with its Beaches Resorts brand.

Silver Cross®

Silver Cross is passionate about offering parents the highest levels of quality, baby comfort and safety with chic, contemporary design. A British brand with more than 130 years of heritage, Silver Cross now operates distribution channels throughout Asia, the Middle East, North America, Russia and Europe, offering fashionably designed wheeled, home and car safety goods.

Market

The UK baby market, which is defined as households with babies and children under the age of four years old, is currently worth an estimated £1 billion. Already a world leader in the design, development and production of high-quality nursery products, Silver Cross is aiming for an increased share in sales of nursery goods in both domestic and international markets. Indeed, the particular focus for Silver Cross in 2009/10 is to offer new parents across the globe a truly international selection of quality nursery products.

Product

All Silver Cross products are created by in-house designers and product development specialists in the UK, with the aim of making mums' and dads' lives as simple as possible. Along with recent product launches, the Silver Cross brand is famous for its Lifestyle and Heritage Collections.

The highly acclaimed Lifestyle Collection, launched in 2003 with the Classic Sleepover, now encompasses: the best selling 3D Pram System, which is a pram, pushchair and travel system in one; an updated Sleepover, which comprises a pram, pushchair and carrycot; and the Linear Freeway – the sleekest, lightest, combination pushchair Silver Cross has ever made. The collection also includes a range of lightweight strollers with the Dazzle, Pop and Fizz pushchairs.

The car safety range includes four car seats: the multi-award-winning Ventura Plus; the Explorer Sport, a two-stage car seat that grows with the child; the Explorerfix, using a push

click ISOFIX installation; and the Navigator, a fully adjustable group 2-3 car seat.

The Heritage Collection features two traditional coach-built prams for newborns. The Balmoral pram has become a global style icon, highly favoured by the Royal Family and A-list celebrities; it sets the highest standard for handmade luxury. In addition to this, the

Silver Cross Kensington pram comes from the same line and is defined by a sweeping, curved, hand-painted steel body and highly polished chrome chassis. All Heritage prams are handmade to the same high standards employed in the early 19th century. Each comes with an individually numbered plaque and certificate of authenticity, including the craftsman's signature.

1877	1920s-30s	1951	1977	1988	2002
Silver Cross is founded by William Wilson, a prolific inventor of baby carriages who created a reputation for producing the world's finest carriages.	Silver Cross becomes incorporated and is crowned the number one baby carriage for royals, supplying its first baby carriage to George VI for Princess Elizabeth.	Silver Cross launches a new shape; the forefather of the Balmoral, it becomes synonymous with the name 'pram'.	Silver Cross celebrates its centenary by flying customers and buyers around the world in its new centenary aircraft and by presenting a baby carriage to Princess Anne.	The Wayfarer is launched. It becomes Britain's best-selling pushchair for a decade, selling more than 3,000 a week.	Entrepreneur and businessman Alan Halsall purchases Silver Cross and relaunches the famous Balmoral.

The Silver Cross children's Heritage toy range includes: the Baby Balmoral, an exact miniature replica of the full size Balmoral; the Toy Rose, featuring a ceramic plaque with a rose design; and the Oberon which comes in a choice of scarlet, navy or white.

Achievements

Silver Cross' leading British design and high manufacturing quality has been put through its paces by parents across the country in the last two years. The brand's Lifestyle range has won 16 high profile parenting magazine awards in this time, which stands as proof of what parents really think about Silver Cross.

The brand's popularity in the UK has aided growing recognition of its products internationally. Worldwide demand has resulted in global expansion with the development of new markets in Australia, China, Russia and the Middle East, as well as a deal to supply Babies 'R' Us in the US, meaning that Silver Cross is now a truly global brand.

Recent Developments

In 2009, Silver Cross continues to drive forward with groundbreaking modern designs. Spearheading this activity is the new Halo, a stroller and travel system with an ultra compact fold, which combines with the Ventura Plus car seat to create the ultimate travel system, suitable for use from birth.

There are also two new additions to the Silver Cross Home Collection. The Doodle high-low chair features a unique design which enables it to be converted from a high chair into a chair and play table featuring a toy basket and crayon cups. This significant development extends the Doodle's working life by approximately six years, compared to a traditional high chair. The second newcomer, the Halo Rocker for newborns, combines a stylish design with luxurious fabrics and a smooth rocking motion.

2009 will also see developments in new areas for Silver Cross, with ranges of soft activity

and collectible toys further diversifying the brand's product range.

Promotion

Silver Cross invests heavily in marketing, with consumer advertising featuring in lifestyle and parenting titles, a presence at major nursery trade events and consumer shows, point of sale promotions and online activity.

Silver Cross' marketing communicates in a straightforward, frank and honest way about its products. Indeed, its strongest marketing tool has always been word-of-mouth. From trendsetters in the film and music world to

everyday British mums, the brand is endorsed by those who have first-hand experience of Silver Cross products.

Brand Values

Silver Cross is one of the UK's most loved and established brands. In 2009, more than 130 years after its launch, Silver Cross still stands for elegance, fashion and cutting-edge British design. It strives to be known worldwide for its experience and passion in producing stylish and innovative products that deliver genuine value for money while making the lives of modern parents easier.

silvercross.co.uk

2006	2007	2008	2009
Silver Cross goes global, forging partnerships with distributors in Europe, America, Canada and Japan.	Silver Cross launches its Home Collection and the combination stroller, Dazzle.	Silver Cross launches the lightweight stroller Fizz, with £5 of every purchase donated to The Meningitis Trust.	Silver Cross launches the new Halo pushchair, Halo Rocker, Doodle high-low chair and a range of toys.

Things you didn't know about Silver Cross

Founded in 1877, Silver Cross is the oldest nursery brand in the world.

Silver Cross prams have been used by royalty for nearly 100 years; it supplied its first baby carriage to George VI for Princess Elizabeth.

Every Balmoral pram is painstakingly made, with more than 1,000 individual hand operations required during the manufacturing process.

Silver Cross sells prams in more than 30 countries worldwide.

SKANSKA

Skanska UK has operations in building, civil engineering, utilities, infrastructure services, piling, M&E, facilities management, PFI/PPP, ceilings and steel decking and delivers ModernaHus, a low energy residential solution. Skanska likes to integrate its core disciplines to deliver project solutions across its chosen markets, working with its clients, partners and supply chain to make a difference to the way construction is normally delivered.

Market

Skanska is a multinational construction and development company headquartered in Sweden. It is a local player in many countries, with expertise in construction, development of commercial and residential projects and public-private partnerships. Primary markets are the Nordic region, the UK, the US, Central Europe and Latin America. The Group's operations are based on local business units which have good knowledge of their respective markets, customers and suppliers. These local units are backed by Skanska's common values, procedures, financial strength and Group-wide experience. Skanska is thereby both a local construction company with global strength and an international constructor and developer with strong local roots. All business units work strictly in accordance with the Skanska Code of Conduct.

Product

Skanska UK is a leading Privately Financed Initiative (PFI) provider. From the successful completion of the country's first PFI scheme in the late 1980s when it built the Queen Elizabeth II Bridge, Skanska's portfolio is now in excess of £3 billion, covering healthcare, custodial, education, transportation and defence.

Complex civil engineering projects are often involved in developing and improving Britain's physical environment for living, working and travelling. The need to improve the infrastructure of our roads, railways and utilities has led to upgrades that draw upon a wide range of expertise and experience.

In the market of commercial construction, Skanska UK's capability and experience, encompassing the entire scope of construction, is unique. Skanska offers its clients more than just a traditional construction service.

Skanska combines its main contracting expertise with its expertise in utilities, infrastructure services and a wide-range of in-house specialist skills, to provide total solutions to both its building and civil engineering clients.

Achievements

Skanska UK undertakes approximately £1.5 billion worth of work each year and prides itself on being able to draw on a combination

of the best in British engineering with the best in Swedish innovation and design. As a construction company, it has recognised that almost everything it does affects both the environment and the lives of people and the communities in which it works, now and in the future. Skanska appreciates that this brings with it a moral and ethical duty to ensure that it is considerate and responsible in all it does.

Skanska has undertaken some of the most technically challenging infrastructure schemes across the UK. Current projects include the new Docklands Light Railway extension to Stratford, which is expected to play a key role in transport plans for the 2012 games, the widening of the

1887	1897	1927	1965	2000	2009
Aktiebolaget Skånska Cementgjuteriet, later renamed Skanska, is founded by Rudolf Fredrik Berg.	Great Britain's National Telephone Company places Skanska's first international order; more than 100km of hollow concrete blocks are supplied to hold telephone cables.	Sweden's first asphalt-paved road is constructed in Borlänge in central Sweden – a milestone in Skanska's role in building Sweden's infrastructure.	Skanska is listed on the Stockholm Stock Exchange.	Skanska enters the UK construction market by acquiring Kvaerner's construction business, which had previously been part of the Trafalgar House Group.	Skanska announces it aims to be the leading green constructor and developer. This is followed by Skanska in the UK being named the forth Best Green Company across all industries.

in a collaborative style in order to provide a construction service to its clients that delivers real benefits.

Skanska has worked on a wide range of notable contracts. In London, a few recent examples include Palestra on London's Southbank, Heron Tower and a world-class cancer centre for University College London Hospitals.

Promotion

While the company does occasionally promote its services and skills in the traditional way with advertising and exhibitions, this is secondary to the way in which the company prefers to be seen and recognised.

At Skanska, it's much more about being truly recognised for the way it lives up to its brand values. This is by the performance and behaviour of its people – Skanska people are 'team players who care and want to make a difference to the way construction is

M25, which it is carrying out as a joint venture and the Weymouth Relief Road set to ease traffic congestion for the local community.

Skanska is currently undertaking the UK's largest hospital development – Barts and The London. The company is also one of the largest providers of utilities and infrastructure services in the UK.

Skanska is proud of its third party recognition, which it considers a true measure of the value and performance of the company and the brand. In the last few years, Skanska has received more than 100 external awards not only for the projects it has constructed, but also for key areas of its performance including health and safety, the environment, and sustainability. In 2009 Skanska received a string of awards from the Considerate Contractors Scheme, was named as the UK's fourth Best Green Company across all industries (2008: fifth) and has achieved Business Superbrands status for the third consecutive year.

Recent Developments

Skanska UK currently employs approximately 5,000 people and operates across building, civil engineering, utilities, infrastructure services, piling and ground engineering, design, mechanical and electrical, facilities management, PFI/PPP, ceilings and decorative plasterwork, steel decking, and communities, which delivers ModernaHus, Skanska's low energy MMC residential solution.

The company works throughout the UK, integrating the skills of its operating units

Skanska's Green Initiative

delivered' – creating projects that its staff, clients, partners and the communities in which it works, are proud of.

Every office and major Skanska construction site in the UK is planned using a bespoke approach to meet the needs of its teams, partners, and clients – creating a 'shop window' for the company's visual brand identity.

Brand Values

Skanska's key responsibility is to develop and maintain an economically sound and prosperous business. It is committed to the countries, communities and environments

in which it operates, and at the same time, its employees and business partners.

Skanska stands for technical know-how and competence combined with an understanding of its customers' needs. The ability to apply these skills to new areas enables it to produce the innovation that its customers demand. Skanska aims to develop, build and maintain the physical environment for living, working and travelling. The company aims to be the leading green developer and constructor and by achieving this, Skanska believes it will be the client's first choice in construction related services and project development.

skanska.co.uk

Things you didn't know about Skanska

Miniland London at LEGOLAND Windsor was built with the help of Skanska.

Skanska is the only Swedish contractor in the UK.

Skanska globally undertakes approximately £12 billion of work a year.

In 2009, Skanska was declared the UK's fourth Best Green Company across all industries as reported in The Sunday Times.

Making every day a better day

Sodexo UK and Ireland is a leading provider of Quality of Daily Life Solutions for its clients in the corporate; education; healthcare; leisure, defence and justice sectors. Its 43,000 people at more than 2,300 locations have the professional expertise to deliver a diverse range of On-site Service Solutions. Sodexo Pass in the UK provides Motivation Solutions, such as Childcarepass and SayShopping vouchers.

Market

The Sodexo Group is the world leader in Quality of Daily Life Solutions. Its 380,000 employees in 80 countries provide an unrivalled array of comprehensive service solutions with its unique offer composed of On-site Service Solutions (previously food and facilities management services) and Motivation Solutions (previously service vouchers and cards).

With relatively low outsourcing rates in many of the markets in which it operates, Sodexo's activities offer considerable growth potential, with estimated markets of more than 650 billion euros in On-site Service Solutions and more than130 billion euros in issue volume for Motivation Solutions. The Group is listed on Euronext Paris.

With an annual UK turnover of approximately £1 billion, Sodexo leads the way in creating added value for its clients and in its ability to support them in resolving their business challenges and achieving their objectives.

More and more organisations are recognising the benefits of outsourcing many of their activities to one supplier. Sodexo's heritage is built on its catering expertise, but today more than 40 per cent of its turnover comes from other services, illustrating just how many clients recognise Sodexo's ability to effectively handle a comprehensive range of services.

Product

Sodexo believes that Quality of Daily Life contributes to the progress of individuals and the performance of organisations. For this reason Sodexo has become the strategic partner of businesses and organisations, creating, delivering and managing comprehensive Quality of Daily Life service solutions that improve its clients' performance in three areas: People; increasing satisfaction and motivation by helping them to be more effective at what they do. Processes; enhancing the quality, efficiency and productivity. Infrastructure and equipment; through optimised asset utilisation, profitability and reliability, and contributing to the attractiveness of living and work environments.

Achievements

Sodexo is proud of its many achievements and for being recognised as a responsible global business.

In the UK Sodexo has achieved silver status for the third year running in Business in the Community's (BITC) Corporate Responsibility Index as published in the Financial Times' Responsible Business special report in June 2009. It is the fourth year Sodexo has featured in the Index.

The Sodexo Group has been ranked third among the world's leading outsourcing services companies by the International Association of Outsourcing Professionals®

1966	1971-1978	1983	1985-1993	1995	1997
Pierre Bellon launches Sodexo, in Marseille, founded on the Bellon family's experience of more than 60 years in maritime catering.	International expansion begins with a contract in Belgium. Development of the Remote Site Management business takes place, first in Africa, then in the Middle East.	An initial public offering of Sodexo shares takes place on the Paris Bourse.	Sodexo establishes activities in the Americas, Japan, South Africa and Russia, and reinforces its presence in the rest of central Europe.	Sodexo becomes the world market leader in food service, thanks to alliances with Gardner Merchant in the UK and Partena in Sweden.	The group's holding company changes its name to Sodexo Alliance.

(IAOP®). It is the fourth consecutive year that Sodexo has been ranked in the top five of the Global Outsourcing 100® and the second year in a row as the highest-ranked company in its industry category, facility services.

For the fifth time Sodexo has been included in the Dow Jones World Sustainability Index (DJSI) and as a super sector leader for four years.

Recent Developments

Over the last 12 months the Sodexo Group has made a number of targeted acquisitions, enabling it to reinforce its global leadership positions in high potential markets.

It acquired Score Group, the fourth-largest provider of foodservices in France; Zehnacker in Germany, a specialist in facilities management services in the healthcare segment. Radhakrishna Hospitality Services Group (RKHS) in India to establish its leadership in comprehensive services solutions in one of Asia's largest markets, and finally Comfort Keepers, one of the leading providers in the North American market of non-medical in-home services for seniors and persons in need of support.

Promotion

In December 2009, the Sodexo Group reinforced its sustainability commitment with the launch of The Better Tomorrow Plan. The objective of which is to consolidate Sodexo's sustainability performance and provide a framework to measure the impact of the company's actions worldwide.

Sodexo's strategy for the plan is built around three pillars: 'We are' – which embraces values and ethics, 'We do' – which sets out 14 commitments to action on sustainability

challenges, and 'We engage' – which recognises the dialogue required to translate commitments into action.

The 14 key commitments span across three areas of focus; health, nutrition and wellness, local communities and the environment. For each, Sodexo is developing phased plans and indicators to measure the degree of implementation and impact across the business.

The plan's approach is collaborative, encompassing Sodexo's own employees as well as its clients and suppliers in carrying out its commitments. Finally, The Better Tomorrow Plan is a long term process, which provides tools for measuring its progress and sets dates for progress assessments in 2012, 2015 and 2020.

Sodexo's mission is to improve the quality of life for the people it serves and contribute to the economic, social and environmental development of the areas where it operates. Through this 10-year sustainable development strategy, Sodexo is committing to continuous improvement through a challenging but robust and structured approach.

Brand Value

Sodexo views its values as the foundation of its success – both in the past and for the future. In pursuing its strategic goal to become the global expert in Quality of Life services,

three enduring values guide Sodexo's business and its 380,000 employees; service spirit, team spirit and the spirit of progress. These values reflect the brand's aim to both grow organically and contribute to the development of countries in which it operates.

sodexo.com

Things you didn't know about Sodexo

Sodexo has extensive experience in the Private Finance Initiative (PFI) market and is currently involved in 17 PFI projects across the defence, healthcare, education and correctional services sectors.

At the Chelsea Flower Show 2009 Sodexo served 5,400 glasses of champagne, 20,500 cakes and pastries and 46,500 glasses of Pimm's.

Since 2008 Sodexo has saved 58,000 food miles and 60 tonnes of CO2 through 160,000 fewer deliveries.

Sodexo has been providing school meals for more than 55 years and is committed to improving the diet of school children.

In the UK Sodexo Motivation Solutions processes and reimburses more than 60 million vouchers a year.

Sodexo provides remote site management in more than 40 countries in various market segments, including oil and gas, mining, and construction.

1998	2005	2008	2009
Sodexo Marriott Services is founded with Sodexo holding 48.4 per cent of the outstanding shares.	On 1st September 2005, Michel Landel becomes chief executive officer while Pierre Bellon continues as chairman of the board.	Sodexo Alliance becomes Sodexo and a new modern, dynamic logo is adopted globally.	Sodexo launches The Better Tomorrow Plan, sustainability strategy which provides a framework to measure the impact of the company's actions worldwide.

Specsavers is the largest privately-owned opticians in the world and the market leader in the UK (Source: Mintel 2008). Furthermore, one in three people who wear glasses in the UK buy them from Specsavers (Source: Mintel). Run by husband and wife founders Doug and Dame Mary Perkins, Specsavers is also a success abroad. There are now more than 1,350 stores in 10 countries including Australia and New Zealand.

Market

The current UK market for eyecare products and services is estimated at more than £2.6 billion, with less than 49 per cent still being provided by small independent opticians. Specsavers currently has a 39 per cent share of all transactions within the opticians' market (Source: GfK December 2008), twice that of its two nearest competitors combined.

While the demand for glasses has flattened out with sales barely ahead of inflation (Source: Mintel), Specsavers continues to expand, celebrating record like-for-like increases in 2008 and record sales of nearly £19 million in one week.

Expansion in Europe, where Specsavers is one of the few British retail success stories, continues to be brisk with the acquisition of a 26-store chain in Finland and further stores opening in Spain.

Product

Specsavers has maintained the Perkins' philosophy of providing affordable, fashionable eyecare for everyone. The company keeps its prices low but does not stint on quality,

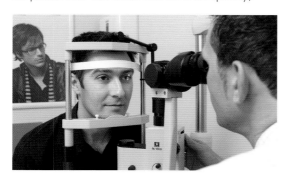

JASPER CONRAN

investing in new technology and continuing to scour the world for fashionable frames to suit all ages.

Specsavers offers its customers more than 1,000 frames to choose from, including designer brand names such as Jasper Conran, Tommy Hilfiger, FCUK, French Connection, Red or Dead, Missoni, Quiksilver, Roxy, Bench and the best-selling Osiris.

All Specsavers glasses include Pentax lenses as standard and pricing is kept as simple and clear as possible so that there are no hidden extras, proving that high quality and low price can go hand in hand. Specsavers also offers a store voucher for employers, meaning companies can now offer their staff more affordable eyecare.

The largest retail provider of home delivery contact lenses in Europe, Specsavers was one of the first optical retailers to introduce a direct debit scheme for contact lens wearers. Its own-brand easyvision lenses include daily disposables, monthly disposables and

continuous wear lenses, which can be worn for up to 30 days and nights without removal.

Achievements

Specsavers turnover reached a record £1.2 billion in 2008 across all markets. In the UK alone, more than £7 million was invested in upgrading and expanding stores. Specsavers now employs nearly 26,000 people throughout its global business.

The optical company performed close to six million eye tests in the UK in 2008, 67 per cent of which were through the NHS. A further 272,000 eye examinations were conducted in Republic of Ireland stores and 16,000 in the Channel Islands, where there is no NHS.

Much of Specsavers' success can be attributed to its joint venture concept. Stores are owned and run by the opticians and retailers based in the stores, while a full range of support services, from accounting to marketing, are provided by a team of professionals, freeing the opticians to do what they do best – provide the highest quality customer service.

1984	1997	2002	2004	2008	2009
Specsavers Optical Group is founded by Doug and Mary Perkins, who open the first Specsavers Opticians in Guernsey, Bristol, Bath, Plymouth and Swansea.	The first overseas store opens in Haarlem, Holland. Two years later, its flagship store in London's Tottenham Court Road opens.	Specsavers expands into hearing, acquiring the Midlands-based Hearcare chain.	Specsavers celebrates 20 years of business and record profits, with expansions into Sweden, Norway and Denmark, as well as the opening of the 500th store in the UK.	Specsavers opens 150 stores in Australia and 10 in New Zealand. The new UK website allows customers to browse frames and try them on using a digital 'mirror'.	Specsavers is named Most Trusted Brand of Opticians for the eighth year in a row by Reader's Digest.

Achieving exacting standards in a high volume business requires state-of-the-art operations, so Specsavers has invested heavily in new systems and equipment to ensure that its supply chain partners attain world-class standards.

Recent Developments

Specsavers is bringing its core offers to its rapidly expanding hearing service, which is now doing for hearing what the retailer has already achieved in optics – dramatically reducing prices and waiting times and making audiology services more accessible for everyone. Specsavers is already the largest retail dispenser of digital hearing aids in the UK and offers a hearing service from more than 400 locations.

The future continues to look bright for Specsavers' core optical business: a new store opens somewhere every week and turnover target is set at £1.4 billion by the end of 2009.

Specsavers has expanded its website by offering customers the chance to order or buy online but still have the benefit of having their glasses professionally fitted in-store.

Promotion

Specsavers' marketing has helped revolutionise the optical market with its Two for One promotion and Clear Price policy that other opticians have struggled to replicate.

Indeed, Specsavers has been the largest advertiser in the optical sector for many years, with a total gross spend of more than £30 million per annum to promote its special offers and build its brand.

The company's 'Should've Gone To Specsavers' campaign was the first to win Retail Week's Marketing Campaign of the Year award two years running and the phrase has been adopted by the nation. Its sponsorship of football and rugby referees has also attracted much support as it reflects a sense of humour appreciated by consumers.

In addition, Specsavers runs an annual Spectacle Wearer of the Year competition to find the UK's sexiest specs wearers and the nation's favourite specs-wearing celebrities.

The company also respects its duty of care to inform people when their next eye examination is due, which was done through more than 23 million letters in 2008.

To keep customers informed, Specsavers' in-store customer magazine is published three times a year and is available free of charge and online.

Brand Values

Specsavers is still very much a family-run business with family values to match and over the past few years the company has donated more than £1 million to various charities. Recipients include Diabetes UK, Guide Dogs, Deafness Research UK, Fight for Sight and Hearing Dogs. In 2008 Specsavers raised £250,000 for Vision Aid Overseas to help fund a new eyecare clinic and optometry school in Zambia.

specsavers.com

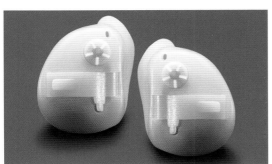

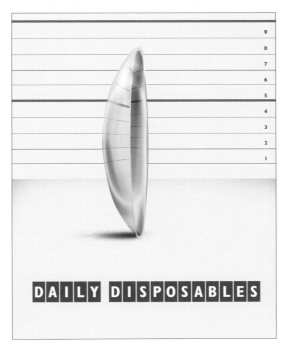

DAILY DISPOSABLES

Things you didn't know about Specsavers

Specsavers carried out nearly six million eye examinations in the UK in 2008.

Approximately 26 per cent of all hearing aids sold in the UK are dispensed by Specsavers and its own brand, Advance, is the best-selling brand in the UK.

More than 9.5 million frames in 2,000 different styles were exported from the warehouse and transported to stores during 2008.

Specsavers sells a pair of glasses every three seconds.

If all the glasses ever sold by Specsavers were laid end to end they would wrap around the world more than three times.

STANLEY

Stanley is the largest global manufacturer of hand tools, with nearly 170 years of history in tool innovations and manufacturing excellence. The Stanley brand name is recognised as a guarantee of quality and value, and is synonymous with hand tool stalwarts such as the Stanley Knife and Stanley PowerLock® tape. Stanley currently holds the number one brand position in hand tools (Source: BRG 2008) and has manufacturing and sales offices around the world.

Market

Stanley is a worldwide manufacturer and marketer of tools, hardware and speciality hardware products for professional, home improvement and industrial use. The company still bears not only founder Frederick T Stanley's name but also the spirit and passion which drove him to success where others have failed.

It has maintained a competitive advantage through continued investment in its team of industrial designers, process engineers and material scientists – The Discovery Team – and ongoing investigation into how professional tradesmen use their tools. New products are tested 'in field' by professional tradesmen and refined accordingly. In this respect, Stanley's new product innovation is designed from the inside out.

Product

As a world leader in the design, development and delivery of tools, Stanley aims to bring to market the strongest and most innovative tools available. With thousands of products on the market and hundreds introduced each

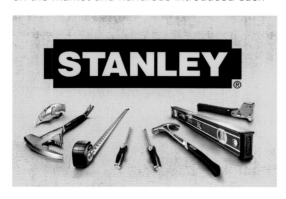

year, Stanley develops the tools people require to get a job done. Since 1857, Stanley has produced some of the most iconic tools ever made. Among these are the PowerLock® tape rule, the famous Stanley Knife and FatMax anti-vibe hammers.

In 2006, Stanley introduced its most ingenious tool range to date, FatMax XL. This responds to the needs of professional users and the demands of today's construction methods and materials. As a result, these are not only the toughest, most durable hand tools available on the market but they have also turned some traditional thinking on its head. For example, the FatMax XL screwdriver becomes a Demolition Driver, the FatMax XL

tape reaches new levels of strength and stand out, while a new type of hand tool, the Functional Utility Bar – or FuBar, for short – creates a unique tool category of its own. The FatMax FuBar II followed, designed to build on the success of its older sibling while offering benefits such as a lighter weight and neater dimensions, making it better suited to repetitive striking and work in confined spaces.

Testament to Stanley's strength of new product development, 2009 sees it welcome a new member to the FuBar family of demolition tools, the FuBar III, which is bigger and stronger than its predecessors and is designed for a host of professional demolition and refurbishment applications.

1902	1926	1937	1966	1980	1990
Stanley makes its first exports.	Stanley's first overseas location is established in Germany.	Stanley enters the UK market via the acquisition of JA Chapman.	Stanley is first listed on the NYSE.	Stanley acquires MAC Tools, Proto and Bostitch.	Stanley acquires ZAG Industries.

Other recent product launches include the new Stanley FatMax Blade, the sharpest the company has ever made. Stanley invested in a special heat treatment, which provides an induction-hardened edge to create a new generation of blade: 35 per cent increased sharpness, 20 per cent improved strength and 75 per cent longer life than a conventional Stanley heavy duty blade.

Further investment in new product development will continue throughout 2009, with the introduction of new products in all major hand tool categories. The focus is on tools that offer improved productivity or deliver more than one function, ensuring value for money for professional and DIY users.

Achievements

Stanley continues to be awarded for both its product and marketing innovation. Indeed, it

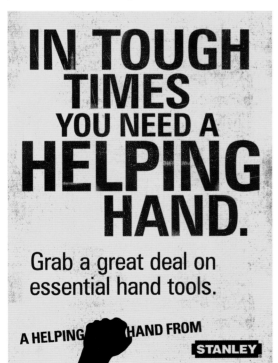

received the high profile Grand Prix accolade at the 2008 B2B Marketing Awards.

Promotion

Stanley has long been a brand that professional users trust to help them get their jobs done quickly and professionally. The brand can also be relied on during tough times, which is why Stanley has this year launched its 'Helping Hand on Essentials' promotional campaign. It asked its customers which hand tools are key to their daily work and is offering deals on these essential tools – such as hammers, knives, tapes, saws and screwdrivers – through three seasonal sales promotions.

Also being unveiled in 2009 is an innovative website, where the content is generated as much by users as it is by Stanley. Alongside the usual product and availability information, 'The Site' has been designed to provide professional tradesmen with advice on staying ahead of the game in the current commercial climate. More importantly, it will also allow them to share their own tips with others.

Stanley will also continue to invest in its 'Judgement Day' events, which were launched in 2007. This experiential activity was designed to give professional users the chance to road-test Stanley FatMax XL tools

in a number of extreme challenges, allowing tradesmen to really get to know the products before purchasing.

A fully integrated media campaign including advertising within key trade, national and consumer media titles as well as an ongoing programme of PR activity ensures that Stanley stays front of mind with professional and DIY users and retains its number one brand position in hand tools.

Brand Values

Throughout its 160-year history, innovation has been the driver of new product development at Stanley. It continually tests and improves its products to ensure quality and maximum function for professionals – and those who think like professionals – and as a result, has gained a reputation for excellence.

stanleyworks.co.uk

2000	2006	2007	2009
Stanley acquires Blick.	Stanley acquires Facom and Britool, and the FatMax XL range launches.	The experiential 'Judgement Day' events take to the road for the first time.	The FuBar III launches and a new website is unveiled.

Stannah
The Stairlift People

Stannah is a family-owned British company with a reputation for safety, reliability and design. Joseph Stannah began his crane and hoist manufacturing business in the 1860s and it has grown into today's Stannah Group of companies – Stannah Stairlifts, Stannah Lifts, Stannah Microlifts and Stannah Lift Services. Its name is synonymous with stairlifts and Stannah is committed to providing customers with a tailored solution.

Market
According to consumer research by Hall & Partners, Stannah Stairlifts continues to dominate the market in terms of brand awareness. Both spontaneous consideration and awareness have increased since 2007.

In a highly competitive market Stannah has built a reputation for safety, quality of service and product design. It now operates in 40 countries including the US, France, Holland, Italy and Germany.

While consumers know the brand best for its stairlifts, it also produces vertical platform lifts and passenger lifts in a range of sizes and capacities.

Product
Stannah has continued to innovate in its market with its most recent concepts in stairlifts being the Sofia and Solus. The chairs are the culmination of research by international product designers SeymourPowell and reflect crucial consumer insights.

Designed to be tailored to the individual, both seats include features such as a seat load sensor so the lift cannot accidentally move until the user is safely in the chair; adjustable arms with 'grab' handles for improved support and comfort; seat-to-footrest height adjustment; a choice of fabrics; and a 'one-step' fold away system.

The Sofia and Solus can be used on straight and curved stairs, and the choice of rail colour has been extended to allow consumers to more effectively incorporate their stairlift into their home interior.

Stannah always considers the environmental impact of its operations and products. It aims to make all its products energy efficient and uses working practices and techniques that produce the lowest possible levels of noise and waste. It also works towards ensuring its products are easy to reuse, dispose of and recycle. Stannah offers reconditioned stairlifts and will buy back products no longer required by customers to help reduce waste.

Achievements
Stannah is a member of the British Healthcare Trades Association (BHTA). The BHTA is the UK's oldest and largest healthcare association (founded in 1917) and has a strict Code of Practice for its member companies to ensure

1860s	1975	1993/94	2003	2005	2008
Joseph Stannah starts manufacturing hoists and cranes in London, adding hand-powered lifts soon afterwards.	Stannah produces its first stairlift and begins exporting the range in 1979.	Subsidiaries open in the US and Holland and Stannah produces its 100,000th stairlift. The division also wins its second Queen's Award for Export Achievement.	Stannah Stairlifts wins awards from the Department of Trade and Industry for the best UK manufacturing and engineering factory, and a subsidiary opens in Slovakia.	Stannah Stairlifts' new Solus chair wins the Golden Trophy Award for design. The division also purchases its distributor in Ireland and sells its 300,000th stairlift.	Stannah Stairlifts is awarded Superbrand status for the first time.

they trade ethically and professionally. The Code has been granted stage one approval under the Office of Fair Trading's Consumer Codes Approval Scheme.

Stannah has achieved environmental management certification ISO 14001:2004. It was the first company to become compliant with PAS 2050, created by the Carbon Trust, Defra and BSI to measure embodied greenhouse gas emissions. This adds to Stannah's portfolio of compliances which includes ISO 9001, OHSAS 18001 and the Investors in People Standard.

In 2009 it won a Gold award at the Royal Society for the Prevention of Accidents (RoSPA) Occupational Health and Safety Awards.

Recent Developments

Stannah has developed a Mobility Partner Scheme which allows consumers to test-ride a stairlift before committing to a purchase; bespoke demonstration units have been installed in-store in selected mobility shops.

The website – stannahstairlifts.co.uk – has also been redesigned and has received the Royal National Institute for the Blind's accessible websites seal of approval as a result. Improved navigation means that visitors to the website are able to access all pages by following keyboard navigable links, rather than having to rely on using a mouse to access hidden menus.

Offering the best service has been at the heart of the company's recent developments and Stannah Stairlifts has extended its warranty from one to two years as standard on all new stairlifts. The warranty covers all call outs, parts and two service visits. It has also introduced a 100 per cent Money Back Guarantee on all direct sales of new or reconditioned products within 14 days of installation.

Promotion

The Think Again Fund was set up in March 2007 with the aim to help people over the age of 50 to realise a life-long dream. In March 2009 a dedicated website was launched to extend the fund to a wider audience. Thinkagainfund.co.uk makes the process of applying for an experience more interactive while also allowing friends and family to play a part. The site features photographs and video and allows winners to create blogs about their experiences.

Stannah's new advertising campaign hit TV screens in March 2009 to highlight the caring nature of the brand with humour and character, promoting its friendly, tailored service. The adverts were directed by Paul Weiland who has directed award-winning commercials for more than 20 years for clients such as Hamlet Cigars, Heineken, BT and Levi's 501. 'Tidy Up' features a woman busily making cakes for her local Stannah engineer who is coming to service her husband's stairlift. 'Shapes and Sizes' observes the relationship between Stannah and its customers by showing a sales representative taking the measurements of their home in order to fit a new stairlift.

Brand Values

Stannah's values are leading, caring, crusading and experienced. The company upholds strong ethical principles – a dedication inextricably linked to the values passed down through generations of the Stannah family. It sees ethical practice as vital and aims to follow the highest possible standards of responsible behaviour in all its dealings with employees, suppliers, customers and the wider community.

stannahstairlifts.co.uk

Things you didn't know about Stannah Stairlifts

Before purchasing, consumers can test-ride a Stannah stairlift at their local Stannah-selected mobility shop.

Stairlift installers visit customers' homes with two pairs of shoes – one pair solely for use indoors so that they won't dirty the carpet.

All Stannah Stairlifts' personnel who go into customers' homes undergo a Criminal Records Bureau (CRB) check.

Stannah employs 1,672 people worldwide and its products are available in 40 countries.

The Stannah Think Again Fund allowed 63-year-old Pamela Shaw and her husband to fulfil a lifelong dream to go sledging with huskies.

Stannah's stairlifts are now available to buy through The Southern Co-operative's newly launched home shopping catalogue, co-operative Xest.

Starbucks Coffee Company is one of the leading retailers, roasters and brands of specialty coffee in the world. It is committed to offering customers the highest quality coffee and the finest coffee experience, while operating in ways that produce social, environmental and economic benefits for the communities in which it does business. Starbucks entered the UK market in 1998 and now employs more than 9,000 'partners' (employees) in over 700 coffeehouses.

for Starbucks VIA™ Ready Brew to be available in other markets around the globe, online and in stores, in late 2009 or early 2010.

Market

Throughout 2008 the branded coffee chain market continued to expand rapidly in the UK, with more than 3,700 outlets and an estimated £1.53 billion turnover. Despite the recent economic slowdown, the market is expected to almost double in the next decade to an estimated 6,000 outlets and £2.5 billion turnover. Starbucks remains the UK's leading branded coffeehouse, with 31 per cent of UK coffee shop visitors rating Starbucks as their favourite coffee shop brand (Source: Allegra Strategies).

Product

The Starbucks coffeehouse offering comprises high-quality whole bean coffees, fresh, rich-brewed, Italian-style espresso beverages, a variety of pastries and confections, and coffee-related accessories and equipment. In addition, Starbucks retails whole bean and ground coffees through selected UK supermarkets and has a well established business in the UK foodservice sector. Starbucks also retails Starbucks VIA™ Ready Brew, an instant coffee, at selected outlets in London, Illinois and Seattle. There are plans

Achievements

Since the company opened its very first store, Starbucks has been committed to doing business responsibly. Building on years of expertise, in 2008 it launched Starbucks™ Shared Planet™, setting out a series of global goals in the areas of ethical sourcing, environmental stewardship and community involvement.

In the UK, Fairtrade™ Certified coffee and chocolate have been available in all Starbucks stores since 2002. In November 2008, Starbucks UK announced that by the end of 2009, 100 per cent of the espresso coffee sold in its stores in the UK and Ireland will be both Starbucks™ Shared Planet™ verified and Fairtrade™ Certified. This forms part of

1971	1982	1991	1998	2000	2003
Starbucks is founded in Seattle by three friends who met at the University of San Francisco in the 1960s.	The first store is a success and catches the attention of Howard Schultz, who joins the company. With the backing of local investors he purchases Starbucks in 1987.	'Bean Stock' is introduced – a stock option scheme for all employees to make them 'partners'.	Starbucks enters the UK market through the acquisition of 60 stores from Seattle Coffee Company.	The Starbucks Christmas Bookdrive is first launched with the National Literacy Trust. In the same year, Starbucks begins to sell Fairtrade™ Certified coffees in-store.	The Starbucks Coffee Master Programme is launched.

a broader global commitment with Fairtrade™ Labelling Organizations International (FLO) that builds on the organisations' shared history of support for small-scale coffee farmers. Starbucks is now the largest purchaser of Fairtrade™ Certified coffee in the world.

2008 marked the seventh anniversary of Starbucks UK's partnership with the National Literacy Trust (NLT) and saw the fifth Starbucks Book Drive take place. More than 200,000 books, collected from local customers, partners and businesses were donated to local primary schools. Since the partnership began, more than 460,000 books have been distributed to communities throughout the UK.

Additionally, Starbucks continues its longstanding relationships with Conservation International (CI) and humanitarian and development organisation, CARE International.

In a five-year partnership, Starbucks is working with CI to address climate change, contributing to the search for global climate solutions while also aiming to help coffee farmers ensure their coffee is responsibly grown and ethically traded.

The Starbucks Foundation has contributed to CARE International since 1992. Most recently it has committed US$500,000 for a three-year social development project with the coffee-growing community of Gewgew Dingete in West Hararghe, Ethiopia. The project aims to improve economic and educational prospects for more than 6,000 people, providing farmers and their families with better food, safe drinking water and a greater income, as well as enabling communities to work together to invest in their businesses and plan for the future. Starbucks UK & Ireland committed a further US$350,000 to support initiatives for improved water resources, sustainable farming and life-long learning, with Starbucks partners helping to generate additional funds for the project through fundraising events.

Starbucks believes its policy of enabling its partners to get involved in community

projects has contributed to its reputation as an admired employer. In 2008 the company was recognised by the Great Place to Work® Institute for the third consecutive year and in 2009, was included in the Fortune 100 Best Companies to Work For ranking.

Recent Developments

Starbucks continually strives to improve the 'Starbucks Experience' for its customers. In 2008 it launched mystarbucksidea.com, an online community that enables customers to play a role in shaping the company's future.

In 2009, Starbucks UK & Ireland introduced Starbucks Card Rewards. The new programme offers Starbucks Card holders extra value and benefits whenever they use their registered Starbucks Card, such as free everyday extras and exclusive offers throughout the year. The Starbucks Card is accepted in participating Starbucks coffeehouses in many countries around the world (from the UK to Australia and Thailand), offering increased convenience for customers.

2009 also saw the launch of Starbucks VIA™ Ready Brew, a rich, flavourful instant coffee. Starbucks VIA™ Ready Brew is available in selected stores in the UK and the US and has been named Most Innovative Product this Year by Allegra Strategies. The coffee is made with the highest quality, ethically sourced 100 per cent arabica beans and is produced by a natural process that includes micro-grinding the coffee in a way that preserves its essential oils and flavour.

Promotion

Storytelling is part of the Starbucks culture and, as part of a non-traditional marketing model, the success of the company's communication strategy is rooted in its partners' passion for and involvement in its innovative product and experience.

The company has established seasonal favourites in the UK and Ireland, promotes individual beverage customisation and has been at the forefront of innovating the coffeehouse experience in the UK over the last 10 years. Starbucks coined the phrase

the 'third place' – a restful environment between home and work in which to relax, take time for yourself and enjoy a freshly brewed cup of high quality coffee. Partnerships with BT OpenZone and the Guardian newspaper further enhance the 'Starbucks Experience'.

Brand Values

The Starbucks mission is to 'inspire and nurture the human spirit – one person, one cup, and one neighbourhood at a time', which is supported by a passionately held set of principles that guide how partners in the company live every day.

starbucks.co.uk

Things you didn't know about Starbucks

Starbucks is the largest purchaser, roaster and distributor of Fairtrade™ Certified coffee in the world, offering it in 28 countries.

Starbucks offers more than 87,000 possible beverage combinations.

Starbucks buys only the finest arabica coffee beans, and selects only the top 10 per cent of these, which are grown at an altitude of between 900 and 1,500 metres.

2006	2007	2008	2009
Starbucks is awarded a Business in the Community Big Tick for excellence in CSR – for the second consecutive year.	Starbucks is named as one of the top 10 Best Workplaces in the UK by the Great Place to Work® Institute.	Starbucks reaches its 10th year of operation in the UK and Starbucks™ Shared Planet™ launches.	The Starbucks Card Rewards programme and Starbucks VIA™ Ready Brew are introduced. Starbucks is ranked as one of the 100 Best Companies to Work For by Fortune.

Sudocrem®
ANTISEPTIC HEALING CREAM

Sudocrem's heritage spans 70 years, during which time it has proved itself as a brand that can be trusted to soothe, heal and protect babies' skin from nappy rash. Instantly identifiable, thanks to its familiar grey tub, the multiple award-winning treatment is recognised as the nation's favourite nappy rash cream and has been market leader in its sector for decades. Sudocrem's versatility has made it a medicine cabinet staple for the whole family.

Market
The UK baby nappy rash market is worth £21 million and is on the increase; between 2007 and 2008 market growth was 12 per cent (Source: IRI December 2008). Forest Laboratories' Sudocrem has dominated this category for the past 20 years; it holds more than 70 per cent of volume sales and its share continues to grow. Even with the increasing popularity of disposable nappies, Sudocrem remains as popular today as ever.

Product
Sudocrem is clinically proven to treat nappy rash, however the cream's combination of ingredients makes it a versatile product for use by the whole family. As well as treating a baby's nappy rash, it can help teenagers treat their acne, and older people treat skin problems such as incontinence dermatitis. Sudocrem is also recommended as a first aid box treatment for minor burns, sunburn, cuts and grazes.

Sudocrem is available both over the counter (OTC) and via prescription. Generations of healthcare professionals have put their trust in Sudocrem and in 2008, more than 600,000 prescriptions were written for Sudocrem.

The antiseptic healing cream is available in a range of sizes from a 400g tub down to a portable 30g tube.

Achievements
Sudocrem has been the market-leading nappy rash cream in the UK for more than 20 years and has achieved total penetration across the UK's pharmacies.

It has carved a niche as an essential first aid item with lifelong usage appeal. Indeed, Sudocrem's market research shows its spontaneous brand awareness recall to be more than 90 per cent. As well as being a mother's staple it has earned recognition among healthcare professionals.

Thanks to its consistent and reliable positioning, the Sudocrem brand has earned a plethora of awards over the years.

Recent Developments
In 2007 Forest Laboratories broadened the brand message. It has established a strong

1931	1950s	1960s	1977	1985	2007
Thomas Smith develops Smith's Cream in his Dublin pharmacy.	The product's name changes to Sudocrem.	Sampling to parents and healthcare professionals, to broaden the cream's appeal, begins.	Sudocrem is launched across the UK.	A new manufacturing facility opens in Dublin.	Sudocrem celebrates its 30th birthday in the UK and continues its reign as the number one selling nappy rash cream.

positioning with parents for helping to ease nappy rash, but its unique formulation also allows it to be positioned as a useful first aid cream. The brand's marketing was therefore extended to relay the message that other minor complaints such as sunburn and cuts can be treated with the cream.

Plans are afoot for 2009 to be a year of new activity for Sudocrem, including another fresh approach to marketing the brand. The launch of a portable plastic tube is aimed at attracting a wider audience to the product, specifically targeting men for the treatment of minor cuts and the travel market for sunburn and first aid purposes.

In response to requests to provide more training to pharmaceutical assistants, Forest Laboratories has also embarked on an educational programme that focuses on therapeutic approaches to skin care.

Promotion

The brand makes use of a diversified range of promotional activities in order to communicate the product's unique selling points and brand heritage.

Consumer-facing promotion takes the form of traditional, above the line media such as television, outdoor and parenting press. Indeed, in 2007 the brand embarked on its first national TV advertising campaign to highlight its multiple uses. In 2009 Sudocrem will continue to invest in TV advertising aimed at mothers with young children (from babies up to five years of age) to communicate the product's many uses. The campaign will be broadcast across terrestrial, digital and satellite channels.

In addition to the television adverts, the 'Bottoms Up' print campaign will continue to run in leading parenting magazines. Online campaigns on leading parenting websites have been added to the promotional mix.

To complement the consumer strategy, a full programme for promotion within the medical community sees the brand actively engage with primary care healthcare professionals and pharmacists. Forest Laboratories attends more than 50 nursing and specialist exhibitions, reaching thousands of health visitors, midwives and district nurses. Forest also arranges bespoke symposia, providing education and support. In addition, a dedicated sales team visits nursing homes nationwide to promote the benefits of Sudocrem in caring for elderly skin.

Brand Values

Through its consistent and robust formula, Sudocrem has become a consumer stalwart with a strong brand heritage. A clinically proven cream that can soothe, heal and protect, its key brand values are: gentle, effective and trusted.

sudocrem.co.uk

Always read the label.

When you get to the bottom of it there is only one Sudocrem

It's easy to see why Sudocrem is the most popular nappy rash cream in the UK. Gentle, effective and easy to use, Sudocrem soothes, heals and protects baby's delicate skin. And as your baby grows you will find that Sudocrem can also be used for cuts, grazes, minor burns and sunburn. All good reasons to make Sudocrem your number one choice.

The nation's favourite nappy rash cream

Available from supermarkets & pharmacies nationwide. www.sudocrem.com Always read the label.

TRUST IN A GREY TUB

Generations of healthcare professionals have put their trust in Sudocrem. And generations of parents have found that a little Sudocrem goes a long way to soothe the soreness of nappy rash and protect delicate skin from further irritation.

Soothes, heals, protects

Things you didn't know about Sudocrem

Although it's best known for helping to ease babies' nappy rash, Sudocrem can also be used for treating sunburn, minor burns, cuts, grazes, eczema, chilblains and acne.

Seven million tubs of Sudocrem were sold in the UK in 2008.

Many athletes such as runners and cyclists use Sudocrem to treat minor cuts and grazes.

Sudocrem is used by a range of celebrities as part of their beauty regime to treat acne.

TATE

Tate's impressive pedigree dates back to the 19th century, but in recent years it has built an unparalleled reputation for increasing public access to national collections of both home-grown and international modern, contemporary art. This ambitious and trailblazing agenda has been achieved through challenging traditional ideas of gallery-goers and embracing innovation across its four sites: Tate Britain, Tate Modern, Tate Liverpool and Tate St Ives.

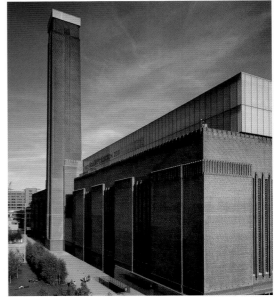

Market

Tate defines itself through a commitment to making art more accessible, moving away from the view of galleries as 'elitist' – a legacy from the past. Opening up the market in this way is key to the brand's ethos of making visiting galleries and exhibitions a more social, people-focused experience.

Tate works hard to ensure it appeals to and attracts new audiences. It has been particularly successful at making gallery attendance attractive to young audiences and family visitors, with London's Tate Modern boasting one of the youngest global visitor profiles. Around 35 per cent of Tate Britain's visitors in 2008 came from overseas but its four galleries remain popular with indigenous audiences.

1897	1917	1932	1988	1993	2000
The National Gallery of British Art opens at Millbank, London – commonly referred to as the Tate Gallery in honour of its founder, Sir Henry Tate.	The Tate Gallery is given responsibility for the national collection of international modern art and for British art dating back to about 1500.	The Gallery is officially renamed 'Tate Gallery'.	On 24th May, Tate Liverpool is opened by HRH The Prince of Wales.	Tate St Ives opens. Within its first six months the 'Tate of the West', as it was dubbed by the press, received 120,000 visitors, almost twice the expected number.	Tate Modern is created in a former London power station and the gallery at Millbank relaunches as Tate Britain.

Product

At one time simply known as the Tate Gallery, expansion has seen the brand evolve with a family of four galleries now united under the Tate umbrella: Tate Britain, Tate Modern, Tate Liverpool and Tate St Ives.

The new Tate brand was developed in partnership with Wolff Olins for the launch of Tate Modern and Tate Britain in 2000. The brief was to create a distinctive, worldwide brand that broadened the appeal of Tate's four gallery sites and conveyed its forward-thinking approach to experiencing art. It needed to unify the collection through the notion of 'one Tate but many Tates'. The galleries were joined together under the single powerful idea of 'look again, think again', offering both an invitation and a challenge. This is epitomised by an ever-changing, four-faceted logotype. In a design that mirrors Tate's approach, a simply written 'TATE' is modelled to provide a range of logos that reflect the fluidity and dynamic nature of the brand.

But Tate's product offering is not limited to its four galleries; one of its many brand extensions is its subsidiary, Tate Catering, that places an importance on food not only tasting good but also being impeccably sourced and honestly priced. The Tate Modern restaurant benefits from impressive views across London and a wine list chosen by sommelier Hamish Anderson.

In addition, Tate Entertaining runs indoor and outdoor events that reinforce the brand mantra: open, inviting, challenging and fresh. The Long Weekend, for example, is a four-day music and art extravaganza that takes place over the last May bank holiday weekend each year. Featuring musicians, performers and young people's activities, it attracts around 100,000 visitors regularly.

Achievements

Since opening the new Tate Modern gallery in 2000, visitor figures to the four Tate galleries have risen from four million to 7.7 million. A key factor in achieving this significant increase has been the brand's emphasis on differentiation. Tate was the first major gallery in the UK to establish a distinct brand appeal through a pioneering approach to art that focuses on increased accessibility. It continues to lead the field internationally in regard to arts communication, through the democratisation of gallery-going (without dumbing down) and a shift of focus from 'the collection' to 'the experience', putting people before art.

Recent Developments

In a recent example of brand innovation, Tate Modern asked the public to respond to the futuristic elements of its Turbine Hall exhibition, 'The Unilever Series: Dominique Gonzalez-Foerster TH. 2058,' by writing their own 1,500-word science fiction story inspired by the installation. The Sci-Fi Short Story Competition was judged by a panel comprising Dominique Gonzalez-Foerster, the exhibition's curator, actor Christopher Eccleston (of Doctor Who fame) and celebrated science fiction writer, Jeff Noon. Blurb, an online self-publishing platform, produced a book of the six winning stories while an audio version was voiced by Christopher Eccleston. In addition, a recording of Jeff Noon reading his essay from the exhibition catalogue was posted on the Tate website.

Promotion

Tate runs a number of campaigns throughout the year, some linked to its programme of events and exhibitions and some to the permanent collection. Core promotional activity centres on high profile press campaigns, underground advertising and innovative strategies.

Tate started working with advertising agency Fallon in 2004 and has since developed a number of groundbreaking and award-winning campaigns. Targeting younger Londoners who rarely visit galleries, Tate and Fallon developed Tate Tracks, 'an experiment between art and music'. Tate invited high-profile bands such as The Chemical Brothers, Klaxons, Union of Knives and The Long Blondes to choose a piece of artwork from the gallery and pen an

exclusive track about it. Over a period of four months, each track was available through headphones placed beside the artwork that inspired it – the gallery was the only place in the world where each track could be heard. Promotion took a range of forms such as via music channels, flyers outside gigs, blogs, Xfm radio, band fansites and legal flyposting – all designed to appeal to a new, younger audience.

Tate Tracks culminated in the autumn of 2008 with a competition in conjunction with MySpace that encouraged members of the public to write their own tracks inspired by Tate artworks. The winning track was played in the gallery.

Brand Values

Tate's brand values are imbued throughout the organisation and include elements outside the presentation of art. The way Tate speaks in any form of communication reflects the spirit of the brand: inviting – it makes you curious and interested; intelligent but not academic – it doesn't underestimate your intelligence, but it's never obscure; challenging but not intimidating – it makes you think; and fresh – it has a contemporary point of view.

tate.org.uk

Things you didn't know about Tate

Tate Britain was built in the 1890s on part of the site of the old Millbank Penitentiary, a vast 19th century prison.

Tate has a collection that currently consists of some 67,000 works of art by more than 3,000 artists.

The **co-operative**
good for everyone

As the UK's largest mutual retailer, wholly owned by its members, The Co-operative's winning formula is built on trust and sound ethics. Under the master brand, its family of businesses from food retail to financial services is experiencing a renaissance as consumers increasingly see the value in The Co-operative's integrity. The acquisition of Somerfield in 2009 and merger with the Britannia Building Society are taking the Group from strength to strength.

Market

The Co-operative is now the clear leader in the community food sector – the fastest growing area of the grocery market. Furthermore, since acquiring Somerfield, The Co-operative has become the fifth biggest food retailer in the country, accounting for eight per cent market share. In its Food arm alone, its 3,000 stores generate annual sales of more than £7 billion.

With interests in food, funerals, travel, pharmacy, online electrical, motors, financial services and legal services, The Co-operative's broad portfolio has helped the Group negotiate a difficult climate. Its operating model, which means it doesn't answer to stock markets and speculators, has appealed to those mistrustful of the way in which big businesses operate, especially in light of the current economic downturn.

Over three million new members have joined The Co-operative since it relaunched its membership scheme and reintroduced the famous dividend scheme in 2006. This takes the current membership base to 5.5 million. Members receive a payment based on points earned every time they trade with any of the Group's businesses; the dividend amount varies according to the Group's performance. In 2008, the Group's members earned £38.6 million as a share of profits.

Product

Now united under the The Co-operative's umbrella brand, its businesses embrace multiple sectors and offer unparalleled reach across all areas of the country. Best known for its food stores, The Co-operative is also the country's largest independent travel agency, the third largest pharmacy and its Funeralcare concern has become Europe's leading funeral business. The Co-operative Bank is featured overleaf.

Perhaps less well known among its activities is that The Co-operative is one of the UK's largest farmers with more than 50,000 acres in England and Scotland. It is also diversifying into wind farms with a target to generate 15 per cent of its own energy by 2012 through these and other renewable energy sources such as hydropower, biomass and ground-source heat.

In 2006, The Co-operative set out on the largest rebranding exercise in UK corporate history when it began the task of converting its entire estate to 'The Co-operative'. The £1.5 billion upgrading exercise involves refitting and rebranding its stores; to date, 3,445 of its 5,300 outlets have undergone this transformation.

Achievements

In November 2009, Group chief executive, Peter Marks, was named Leader of the Year at the Orange National Business Awards. He was recognised for his outstanding achievements and demonstration of exceptional business acumen and vision over the past 12 months. In addition, The Co-operative won the People's Choice Supermarket Award at the RSPCA's Good Business Awards. This recognises The Co-operative's track record in animal welfare initiatives and achievements, in particular for its commitments to Freedom Food, free range eggs and responsible fish sourcing.

In July 2008, The Co-operative was awarded the International Climate Change Award by Business in the Community for its strategic,

1863	1872	1942	1965	1985	2000
The Co-operative Wholesale Society (CWS) is established with the Scottish CWS following in 1868.	The Co-operative Bank is set up, initially as the CWS Loan and Deposit Department.	The first self-service shop is opened by the London Co-operative Society. By 1950, 90 per cent of all the self-service stores in the UK are operated by co-operatives.	Dividend Stamps are introduced as an alternative to the traditional methods of paying the 'divi'. The CWS launches the national Dividend Stamp Scheme in 1969.	The CWS stops all animal testing on its own-brand toiletries and household products. It co-sponsors a Private Member's Bill to improve labelling for products tested on animals.	Co-operative Retail Services (CRS) and CWS merge, creating the world's largest consumer co-operative.

comprehensive and innovative approach to tackling climate change. Other accolades have included being named Most Ethical Brand in the UK in the Consumers & Ethical Brands survey conducted by GfK NOP. Its ethical credentials have been further reinforced by The Co-operative brand claiming two of the top 10 places in the annual independent Ethical Reputation Index (ERI) – for two consecutive years.

In 2009, retail analysis experts IGD highlighted The Co-operative as one of the top 10 worldwide businesses whose 'innovative and exciting approaches' mark them out.

The Co-operative's corporate social responsibility activities are extensive and pervade all aspects of its business. Notably, it was the first major retailer to champion Fairtrade and now accounts for over 16 per cent of all UK Fairtrade sales. In February 2008, it became the first and only retailer to convert its entire own-brand hot beverage range to Fairtrade.

The Co-operative Group has seen unprecedented growth. Interim results for 2009 showed Group revenues were up 17 per cent and Group profit was up 33 per cent. The Food business total year-on-year sales grew by 66 per cent, boosted by the acquisition of Somerfield and the business has reported 14 consecutive quarters of like-for-like sales growth.

Recent Developments
In February 2009, the Somerfield supermarket chain was acquired by the Group for £1.56 billion, propelling The Co-operative up the food retailer ladder to become the fifth biggest player in the UK grocery market. The Co-operative is combining the 'best of the best' of both businesses, maximising the talents of both teams towards the common goal of becoming the UK's top community food retailer.

The merger with Britannia and on-going consolidation in the co-operative sector means the Group is going from strength to strength.

Promotion
In February 2009, The Co-operative launched a £10 million national master-brand marketing campaign to raise awareness of its family of businesses and re-assert itself as the pioneer of ethical business. Led by an iconic two-and-a-half minute TV advert set to Bob Dylan's 'Blowin in the Wind', the integrated campaign clearly demonstrated the organisation's leadership values and 'Good for Everyone' qualities. Results have been outstanding and show the campaign to have delivered significant uplifts against key brand awareness and perception measures.

Brand Values
The Co-operative's vision is to be 'Good for Everyone' with five key components forming the core of its brand: consistent quality, trustworthy, rewarding, championing and community.

A consumer-owned business where its members have a democratic say in the way the business is run and how its profits are distributed, collective action lies at the heart of The Co-operative. In 2008, it again polled its members to determine the causes and campaigns that it will support. Three priorities emerged which have become the focus of the Group's Community Plan: inspiring young people, combating climate change and tackling global poverty.

Just £1 allows anyone to join The Co-operative and each member has an equal say in how the business is run and how it achieves its social goals.

co-operative.coop

2003	2006	2007	2009
The Co-operative switches all own-brand coffee to Fairtrade, generating an extra £1 million each year for coffee farmers in the developing world.	The Co-operative becomes the most trusted retailer among UK consumers (Source: AccountAbility and National Consumer Council).	The Co-operative Group and United Co-operatives merge, successfully becoming one business within one year – ahead of schedule.	The Co-operative acquires Somerfield, creating a powerful fifth player to challenge the established big four retailers.

The **co-operative** bank
good with money

The Co-operative Bank continues to stand strong and adhere to the brand values – value, fairness and social responsibility – which lie at the heart of its business. These have enabled the bank to weather the prevailing financial storm successfully, not least because customers recognise that it has a responsible attitude to banking and their money. It is also the only UK high street bank with an Ethical Policy shaped by its customers.

The **co-operative** bank
good with money

Your money Our commitment

To provide banking services to suit your needs, free from the demands of shareholders or speculators.
Just as we've been doing for all our customers and members **since 1872.**

0800 783 7717
Lines open Mon-Fri 8am to 9pm, Sat/Sun 9am to 6pm

goodwithmoney.co.uk

Part of The **co-operative** financial services

Market

During the banking crisis of 2009, many consumers lost confidence in shareholder and government-owned banks. The Co-operative Bank continued to be successful thanks to its prudent approach to banking and its unique member-owned structure that originated in 1872. It's not wholly reliant on money markets, and all lending is funded from customer deposits.

Over 2009 it experienced a distinct upturn in business. Share of the current account market grew to five per cent (Source: GFK NOP) and there was a 68 per cent increase in current account switching from other banks compared to 2008. In the first half of 2009 average customer deposits grew by 21 per cent and average customer lending grew by 12 per cent.

The Co-operative Bank is part of The Co-operative Financial Services (CFS), which also operates through the brands The Co-operative Investments, The Co-operative Insurance, The Co-operative Asset Management, Britannia, Platform and the internet bank, smile. CFS offers a comprehensive range of financial products and has more than nine million customers.

Product

During 2009, The Co-operative Bank promoted its packaged current account, an innovative way for customers to manage their day-to-day banking, with a choice of features and benefits to suit individual requirements. Customers can choose from one of three benefit bundles relating to travel, personal safety and gadgets. This joins a range

of products and services – current and savings accounts, credit cards, loans and mortgages.

The Co-operative Bank also provides a comprehensive portfolio of corporate banking services. Its corporate customers include a wide cross-section of businesses and organisations, across a broad range of sectors. The assets managed in this particular area total £17 billion in customer loans, and £15 billion in funding.

Members of The Co-operative are able to earn membership points on a range of banking products. The Co-operative is the only mutual organisation that enables its members to earn financial rewards for the products they hold, as well as giving

1844		1867	1872	1992	1997
Twenty-eight weavers – the 'Rochdale Pioneers' – create a local store to avoid exploitation by unscrupulous shopkeepers.	Other groups follow suit and co-operative businesses spring up, first in the north, then throughout the country.	The Co-operative Insurance Society is formed. It goes on to build a broad customer base with a wide portfolio of insurance services and a reputation for social responsibility.	The Co-operative Wholesale Society's Loan and Deposit Department is founded – the origins of The Co-operative Bank.	The Co-operative Bank becomes the world's first bank to introduce a customer-led Ethical Policy.	In partnership with Greenpeace, The Co-operative Bank launches the world's first biodegradable credit card.

them the opportunity to have a say in how the business is run.

Achievements

Amongst recent awards, The Co-operative Bank came top of the high street banks in customer polls for Watchdog and Which? magazine, the latter voting it Best Financial Provider 2009.

CFS also won the Best Large Company category at the UK Customer Experience Awards, which recognised performance against a wider market beyond financial services.

Following its success as Business in the Community's (BITC) Company of the Year in 2008, CFS has now been awarded Platinum

Plus status. This is the highest ranking in the BITC Corporate Responsibility Index and relates to a company's attitude to long term sustainability.

The Co-operative Bank has also won the Your Mortgage award for Best Direct Mortgage Lender 2009/10. The award recognises and rewards mortgage providers that have excelled in their field. The judging criteria included – friendliness, speed of picking up the phone, explanation of products, costs and processes, speed of literature being received and overall impression.

The Co-operative Bank also received two prizes at the Card Awards 2009. The Woodland Trust Credit Card was named the Best Charity Credit Card, while the Customers Who Care scheme was voted Best Corporate Social Responsibility (CSR) Programme.

Recent Developments

In 2009 The Co-operative Bank merged with Britannia Building Society to form one of the most diversified financial mutual businesses in the UK. The merger has created a business of real scale with £70 billion of assets, nine million customers, 12,000 employees, more than 300 branches and 20 corporate banking centres. The new and stronger CFS aims to be a pioneering business, providing high quality financial products to its customers and members.

Promotion

The bank's 2009 award winning advertising campaign, Your Money, recognises that it is there for the sole benefit of its customers and Co-operative members, not shareholders.

The activity promoted specific messages around stability and reassurance, reflecting the needs of financial services consumers in the current climate.

The campaign built on The Co-operative's investment in awareness-building as it launched its biggest ever advertising campaign. The high-profile TV campaign promoted a range of initiatives including; community projects, renewable energy and Fairtrade products; that demonstrated why The Co-operative is 'good for everyone'. The ad also highlighted the family of businesses – Food, Travel, Pharmacy, Bank and Insurance – and memorably, used the Bob Dylan classic Blowin' In The Wind as its soundtrack.

Brand Values

The Co-operative Bank can rightly claim to be 'good with money' by always keeping true to principles rooted in its origins as a co-operative movement. It is dedicated to upholding its proud heritage of being customer focused, community orientated, socially responsible, and its willingness to champion causes.

co-operativebank.co.uk

2002	2007	2008	2009
The Co-operative Financial Services is launched, encouraging a stronger relationship between The Co-operative Bank and The Co-operative Insurance.	The Co-operative Group and United Co-operatives become one organisation, known as The Co-operative, the world's largest consumer co-operative.	The Co-operative Bank and Co-operative Insurance Society (CIS) re-brand under The Co-operative Bank, Insurance and Investments brands.	The Co-operative Bank merges with Britannia Building Society and The Co-operative ad campaign is launched.

The Daily Telegraph

The Daily Telegraph, established in 1855, is the UK's best-selling quality newspaper, with an audited circulation of 836,541 (Source: ABC average daily circulation September 2008-February 2009). In its broadsheet format, the newspaper offers home and international news coverage, a stand-alone business section, which is highly respected in the City, and a compact daily sport section.

Market

The UK's quality daily newspaper market comprises The Daily Telegraph, The Times, the Guardian and The Independent which together account for more than two million copies per day (Source: ABC average daily circulation September 2008-February 2009). The Daily Telegraph is the market leader with a 41.5 per cent share, approximately 217,000 copies ahead of The Times.

Product

The Daily Telegraph is known for its line-up of distinguished journalists and columnists, who lend the paper its distinctive voice and personality. Delivering lively and challenging comment on the issues of the day, The Daily Telegraph boasts such unique contributors as Boris Johnson, Con Coughlin, Andrew Pierce and Simon Heffer. The Sport team includes football writer Henry Winter as well as sporting luminaries such as Alan Hansen, José Mourinho and James Cracknell. The Daily Telegraph Business section is famous for its accurate, bold and insightful coverage, provided by an award-winning team of journalists including business commentator Jeff Randall.

'Get your hands off me!
I'm not the Queen, you know'

The Daily Telegraph's fashion director, Hilary Alexander, is a stalwart of the world's catwalk front rows. She brings her flair and experience to the fashion pages not only in the newspaper and online, but also in her own Telegraph TV programme, Hilary & Co, talking to top designers and taking viewers behind the scenes of the fashion industry.

The Daily Telegraph has been home to the Matt cartoon – created by award-winning cartoonist Matt Pritchett – since 1988, while one of the most popular features of the Business section is the Alex cartoon, which comments on the wheeling and dealing of the business world. In December 2007, Alex was brought to life on stage in London's West End in the form of Alex the Play.

September 2006 saw a design revamp of The Daily Telegraph on Saturday, introducing a new technology section, Digital Life. The redesign extended to other sections including Motoring – featuring James May's column and advice from Honest John – Weekend and the award-winning Telegraph Magazine.

Achievements

At the 2008 British Press Awards, The Daily Telegraph's theatre critic, Charles Spencer, was named Critic of the Year while Matt Pritchett was awarded Cartoonist of the Year, taking his tally of honours (which includes an MBE) to

1855	1897	1987	1994	2006	2007
The first Daily Telegraph & Courier is published, having been founded as a vehicle for its proprietor, Colonel Sleigh, to wage a vendetta against the Duke of Cambridge and his conduct in the Crimean War.	A young Winston Churchill reports from the North West Frontier for the Telegraph.	The Telegraph moves from Fleet Street to the Isle of Dogs then to Canary Wharf five years later.	The Telegraph becomes the first British newspaper to launch an internet presence – the Electronic Telegraph.	The Telegraph Group rebrands to become Telegraph Media Group and moves from Canary Wharf into state-of-the-art offices in Victoria, central London.	Telegraph TV is launched.

13 during his 20 years with the newspaper. In October 2007 The Daily Telegraph was named Best Consumer Online Publisher at the Association of Online Publishers' awards and in March 2007, was awarded Best Newspaper Sport Coverage at the Sports Industry Awards. Michele Lavery, the editor of Telegraph Magazine, was named Newspaper Magazine Editor of the Year at the British Society of Magazine Editors' 2008 awards; the second time in three years that the Telegraph has won.

Recent Developments

In 2006, Telegraph Media Group embarked on a momentous shift in the way it published news. Where previously stories were broken in the newspaper and subsequently posted online, stories are now reported as they happen and published across several platforms. In order to provide the state-of-the-art newsroom required for this new approach, the Telegraph moved to new offices in central London. It now occupies one of the biggest open office spaces in Europe, accommodating the new 'hub and spoke' editorial system.

This move also reflects the Telegraph's commitment to offering its customers quality news content when – and how – they want it. The Telegraph has constantly innovated in bringing new features to its audience in the digital environment. Recent advances include a portfolio of widgets and online applications that allow users to place Telegraph content within their own social network profiles and homepages, such as Facebook and iGoogle.

Launched in September 2007, Telegraph TV has taken The Daily Telegraph's journalists from pages to programmes. There are now 11 shows produced exclusively for Telegraph.co.uk. These include the travel show, Real Trips; the daily Business Bullet; and Lloyd Grossman and Xanthe Clay's cookery show, 10 Minutes to Table. A recent highlight was James Cracknell's Beijing Olympics coverage, a daily sideways look at the Olympics which included Cracknell and Olympic champion Sir Chris Hoy racing each other on the two worst bicycles in Beijing.

As Telegraph.co.uk continues to bring new audiences to the Telegraph portfolio, so a constant programme of product development is helping to build distinct communities, each with particular interests. These now range from a crossword community to those centred on dating and genealogy. The MyTelegraph online blogging community also invites users of Telegraph.co.uk to create their own blogs, post their views and contribute to an array of online discussions.

Promotion

The Daily Telegraph creates dedicated events for its customers, ranging from an exclusive performance of The Sound of Music to nationwide shopping evenings held in collaboration with major brands, including Jaeger and Fenwick.

The Daily Telegraph is the official media partner to the Orange British Academy Film Awards, a partnership highlight of the year. Other events in which the Telegraph has been involved include the RHS Chelsea Flower Show, the CLA Game Fair, the Bath Children's Literature Festival and the Ways with Words Literary Festival.

Each year, thousands of readers and online users compete to

manage the best team of the season in Telegraph Fantasy Football. Fantasy Football fans can also fill the off-season void with Fantasy Cricket. In addition, The Daily Telegraph supports a grassroots Junior Golf programme, attracting more than 41,000 entrants in 1,000 regional competitions.

Brand Values

The Daily Telegraph brand values are defined as: accuracy, honesty, integrity, quality and heritage.

telegraph.co.uk

The Law Society

The Law Society is the representative body for more than 130,000 solicitors, qualified in England and Wales, practising both at home and across the globe. The Society's aim is to protect and promote the interests of the profession by providing advice, training, products and services to its members as well as developing new legal markets and international networks. It also influences law and policy through representation to governments, regulators and the wider community.

Market

The Law Society has more than 130,000 members. Private practice remains the biggest sector of the profession, encompassing firms of all sizes from sole practitioners in high street firms to global law firms. A large and growing number of solicitors work in the employed sector in commerce and industry as well as in local and central government.

Product

The Law Society engages with and meets the diverse needs of solicitors through special interest groups. More than 10,000 solicitors take advantage of the specialist help provided by the Law Society's sections which includes CPD accredited events, online seminars, e-alerts, websites, magazines with free CPD,

discounts, campaigns, publishing, discussion forums and networking opportunities.

Generic products and services include a range of helplines, a comprehensive website, a weekly e-newsletter, the Law Society Gazette, Law Gazette Jobs online, a library/information service and titles from Law Society Publishing. It continues to provide extensive support during the recession including lobbying, advice and practical help.

More than 16,000 solicitors belong to the Law Society's accreditation schemes, benefiting from free promotion online and in print. Customers can be confident that members' skills, knowledge and experience have been thoroughly tested and certified.

The Lexcel quality mark is a sign of excellent client service, cost efficiency and minimum risks. More than 800 practices are already accredited with more continually applying. Implementing the Lexcel framework across a practice can help a firm manage itself more effectively, providing the potential to secure lower professional indemnity insurance premiums.

Achievements

The Law Society is a major player on the international legal stage and uses its influence to create opportunities for solicitors and law firms from England and Wales operating in markets overseas. Its market opening efforts have resulted in important advances in jurisdictions including Japan, China, South

1825	1903	1922	1983	2007	2009
The Society of Attorneys, Solicitors, Proctors and others not being Barristers, practising in the Courts of Law and Equity of the United Kingdom is formed.	The name is changed to the Law Society.	Carrie Morrison becomes the first woman solicitor admitted to the roll.	The Law Society establishes the Office for the Supervision of Solicitors to deal with complaints about solicitors.	The Law Society refocuses to work on helping, supporting and promoting solicitors as independent boards established for regulation and complaints-handling.	The Law Society leads the debate on the future for legal businesses under the Legal Services Act.

Korea and Singapore. The Society promotes England and Wales as the jurisdiction of choice for dispute resolution.

At home, the Law Society represents solicitors' interests by lobbying the Government, parliament and thought leaders at all levels. It campaigns for better legislation and has successfully represented its members on a wide range of issues that directly affect them. These include the new regulatory regime, threats to legal professional privilege, the funding of legal aid, bureaucracy around stamp duty, proposed changes to small claims and problems around professional indemnity insurance.

Lawyers are determined, committed, challenging, resourceful and innovative. Many have extraordinary stories to tell and the Law Society is proud to showcase the best of them at its annual Excellence Awards ceremony. In 2009 Jason McCue from H2O Law LLP won the Solicitor of the Year – Private Practice category for his exceptional contribution to securing the rights of victims of the Omagh bombing, and for his efforts to promote peace and equality in Darfur. The winner of the Solicitor of the Year – In-house category, Roger Clayson, was selected for his groundbreaking work at the Nuclear Decommissioning Authority.

There is a long tradition of pro bono work in the legal profession, which is estimated to be worth around £340 million per year. Two-thirds of private practice solicitors undertake such work at some point during their careers. The Law Society is proud to have been involved in the organisation of National Pro Bono Week, which raises awareness of the free advice that is available. Since its inception in 2002, it has encouraged more solicitors to get involved.

In 2007 the Legal Sector Alliance was launched in association with DLA Piper and the charity, Business in the Community. This partnership of leading law firms aims to drive environmental sustainability in the legal sector, promoting positive steps that all solicitors and firms can take to conserve natural resources. The Alliance currently has 139 members, representing more than 25 per cent of solicitors in private practice in England and Wales.

The Law Society's Diversity and Inclusion Charter, developed with BT and the Society of Asian Lawyers, is the bedrock of its work to develop best practice across the legal sector. The Society launched a Procurement

Protocol alongside the Charter and together they are gathering widespread support from private practice firms, in-house lawyers and large consumers of legal services alike.

It also campaigns in support of solicitors in jurisdictions where human rights and the rule of law are under threat. In 2007 it set up an international action team through which solicitors and law students can get involved with human rights work.

Developing legal systems are also supported in jurisdictions such as Nigeria. Working in partnerships with bar associations, NGOs and overseas governments, schemes that support the rule of law, access to justice, and which encourage economic development, are delivered.

Recent Developments

The establishment in 2007 of independent boards to handle regulation and complaints-handling freed the Law Society to become a modern and responsive representational professional body that offers activities and services which meet the needs of all parts of its membership. Since then, the Society has established a strong record in lobbying robustly and campaigning successfully for its members, and providing relevant, valued products and services.

The Legal Services Act 2007 presents both opportunities and threats for solicitors. The Law Society lobbied to improve the proposals in the original Legal Services Bill, which led to significant changes to the legislation.

A new regulatory regime is central to the Act, and the Society continues to lobby for proportionate regulation. Legal disciplinary practices, in which up to 25 per cent of partners in a law firm can be non-lawyers, came into being in March 2009. The Law Society provides comprehensive support to enable solicitors to understand and benefit from the changes.

Promotion

'Qualified to answer' is the strapline used in recent consumer campaigns developed with DML Marketing. The campaigns aimed to persuade consumers that solicitors are the best choice for legal advice. As part of the campaign, ads ran on 280 taxis in London and other major cities (pictured far left).

Advertising and PR resulted in more than 100 million 'opportunities to see' during the 2009 campaign alone. Many law firms joined in, taking out supporting advertising and displaying the campaign logo. More than half a million copies of the Society's consumer guides to common legal problems were ordered.

The Society's Lawyers For Your Business scheme generates 500 new leads for members each month.

For business-to-business communications, electronic and traditional face-to-face techniques are used. Generic and specialist e-newsletters and e-alerts allow the Society to communicate instantly with its members, while events and regionally-based staff provide opportunities for more direct interaction.

Brand Values

The Law Society's brand values are defined as professional, authoritative, influential, forward-looking, modern, accessible, responsive, transparent, accountable and value for money.

lawsociety.org.uk

Things you didn't know about the Law Society

The Law Society supports an international team of volunteers who campaign on human rights abuses around the world.

The Law Society's Hall contains many unusual architectural features including five clocks by Benjamin Lewis Vulliamy and stained glass from Serjeants' Inn.

Women now constitute 60 per cent of new entrants to the solicitors' profession.

Black and minority ethnic solicitors currently make up 22.6 per cent of new entrants to the profession.

The Law Society owns the only known copy of the Law List from 1775 (first edition).

Since Thomas Cook's inaugural trip in 1841, his name has come to represent a pioneering approach to tourism. Introducing the first overseas package tour in 1855, today Thomas Cook takes six million British holidaymakers abroad each year. Thomas Cook Group plc has a network of more than 3,400 stores across 21 countries and over 22.3 million customers, making it one of the world's leading leisure groups.

Don't just book it. Thomas Cook it.

Market

Formed from the merger with MyTravel Group in 2007, the new Thomas Cook Group delivered strong results in its first full year of trading; against an unsettled economic backdrop, it has laid firm foundations for the future. To maintain its industry-leading margins, the Group's focus lies on continued tailoring of its offering to meet the needs of its customers.

In the UK and Ireland, Thomas Cook continues to deliver strong results in a market where capacity has been reduced by around 25 per cent over the last two years.

Product

Thomas Cook boasts a diverse portfolio of brands that continue to evolve in line with changing market trends and consumer buying habits. Through its leading mainstream brands such as Thomas Cook, Airtours, Cruise Thomas Cook and Direct Holidays as well as niche brands including Thomas Cook Signature, Cresta and Club 18-30, it is able to offer a holiday or service to suit a myriad of tastes and budgets. The Group recently added hotels4u.com, Elegant Resorts, Gold Medal and Med Hotels to its portfolio, increasing its profile in the rapidly expanding independent travel sector.

Through Thomas Cook Sport – the largest UK provider of team and supporter travel – sports packages to major sporting events around the world are on offer, as are holiday clubs for supporters of more than 60 UK football clubs.

Achievements

In November 2008, Thomas Cook celebrated the 200th birthday of its founder. Regarded as the pioneer of popular tourism, Thomas Cook described himself as "the willing and devoted servant of the travelling public" and today the company maintains many of his original values.

It is an approach that has stood the company in good stead, with several Thomas Cook brands recognised with industry accolades in 2008/09. Its retail network was named Large Travel Retailer of the Year at the British Travel Awards and Thomas Cook was named Favourite Package Holiday Provider at the 2009 Globe Travel Awards. Furthermore, Thomas Cook Airlines was listed as the Most Punctual Charter Airline for the winter 2008/09 season (Source: Flightontime.info February 2009).

Thomas Cook scooped two awards at the inaugural Econsultancy Innovation Awards for ecommerce activity: winner of Innovation in Online Conversion, thanks to a personalised approach to user activity on its website; and winner of Innovation in Email Marketing, for its interactive magazine, Holiday Hotspot.

1841	1855	1872/73	1874	1939	2003
Thomas Cook's first excursion, a rail journey from Leicester to a temperance meeting in Loughborough, takes place.	Thomas Cook's first continental tour takes place: Cook leads two parties from Harwich to Antwerp, then on to Brussels, Cologne, Frankfurt, Heidelberg, Strasbourg and Paris.	Cook guides the first around-the-world tour and is away from home for 222 days, covering more than 25,000 miles.	Cook's Circular Note, the first travellers' cheque, is launched in New York.	Holidays by air on chartered aircraft are included in the summer brochure for the first time.	Thomas Cook rebrands its airline to Thomas Cook and launches a tour-operating brand under the same name.

The company not only works towards providing an award-winning offering for its customers but is also committed to being a responsible business; Thomas Cook works with the Travel Foundation, contributing towards sustainable tourism projects worldwide and in January 2009 launched its own charity, The Thomas Cook Foundation. A major part of the foundation is the Thomas Cook Children's Charity, raising money for sick and disadvantaged children.

Prior to this, Thomas Cook raised £2.3 million to refurbish the critical care wards in the Variety Club's Children's Hospital at King's College Hospital, London. Following three years of customer donations and the fundraising efforts of its employees, the Thomas Cook Critical Care Centre opened its doors in 2008.

Recent Developments

Thomas Cook himself invented the Circular Note in 1874 – the forerunner to the travellers' cheque – and today the company is placing renewed focus on ancillary services including foreign exchange, the Thomas Cook credit card and travel insurance. Every Thomas Cook store offers a travel money service and the Group operates 17 foreign exchange

bureaux across Manchester Airport and Heathrow's Terminal 5.

With more than 1.5 million passengers in the UK opting to holiday at sea every year, cruising has become one of the fastest growing holiday choices – doubling its share of foreign inclusive package holidays over the past 10 years. Cruise Thomas Cook is the biggest selling cruise retailer in the UK, accounting for one in every seven bookings made by UK passengers in 2008.

Promotion

Created in 1984 by advertising agency Wells Rich Greene, 'Don't just book it. Thomas Cook it' rapidly became one of Britain's best-known advertising slogans. Indeed, in research carried out by YouGov in 2008, 60 per cent of respondents could complete the strapline, with this recall rising to 75 per cent in the 35-44 age bracket. Last used in the 1990s, the strapline was reintroduced in 2008 and ran alongside the company's 24-hour money back guarantee which was promoted in Thomas Cook's January campaign.

Thomas Cook actively markets its 'four ways to book' message – driving customers to its stores, sales centre, online and to Thomas

Cook TV. Press, radio, television, outdoor and point-of-sale merchandising are also used alongside a significant direct marketing programme to communicate with new and existing customers.

Campaigns for core holiday products are based around the key sales periods of post-Christmas and high season summer months. Tactical activity is increasingly used throughout the year, particularly in growth areas like independent travel and financial services which are less seasonally driven. In 2009, for example, Thomas Cook Foreign Exchange sponsored ITV's Saturday night primetime show, The Colour of Money.

Brand Values

Committed to keeping the customer at the heart of everything it does, Thomas Cook believes that its people are its greatest asset and key differentiator in a highly competitive marketplace.

A modern, forward-thinking business dedicated to finding new ways in which to pioneer, Thomas Cook takes pride in its heritage and trusted brand to drive results and add value.

thomascook.com

Don't just book it.

Thomas Cook it.   Thomas Cook

2007

Thomas Cook Group plc is formed after merging with MyTravel Group.

Also in 2007, Thomas Cook UK & Ireland becomes a FTSE 100 company listed on the London Stock Exchange for the first time in the company's history.

2008

The Thomas Cook Children's Critical Care Centre officially opens at King's College Hospital, London.

Also in 2008, Thomas Cook reintroduces its classic slogan, 'Don't just book it. Thomas Cook it'.

Tommee Tippee is the UK's number one brand in the baby accessories market (Source: IRI 2009) and has been trusted by parents worldwide for more than 50 years. Known for its cups and tableware, in 2006 the brand's leading position was reinforced with the launch of Closer to Nature, an infant feeding range now credited with revolutionising the way mothers feed their babies.

Market

The baby accessories market is estimated to be worth more than £150 million in the UK (Source: IRI) and encompasses everything from bibs and bottles to monitors and harnesses. It does not include nappies, wipes, toiletries, formula milk or baby food.

Tommee Tippee is the leading brand in a fiercely competitive market: it has nearly one-third of the total market share by value and volume and is growing at twice the rate of the market. The brand has more than 96 per cent distribution through all channels including specialist baby stores, nursery shops, supermarkets, independent chemists and department stores. Internationally, it is sold in more than 40 countries.

Product

There are more than 100 different products in the Tommee Tippee range, making it the only baby accessory brand to cater to parents' and children's needs from pregnancy through to the reception class gates.

The brand prides itself on its commitment to innovation and has patents in place on most products. Its offering is enhanced by a promise of quality, safety, simplicity, convenience and value. Tommee Tippee was the first to introduce a non-spill cup in the 1980s (Sip 'n' Seal); a groundbreaking bottle which babies could hold themselves (Nipper Gripper); and a teether filled with purified water that can be cooled to provide effective relief from the discomfort of teething and which is still on sale today.

In recent years, significant additions to the product portfolio have included the Closer to Nature range and Sangenic, a patented nappy disposal system. Closer to Nature products have been specifically designed to mimic the natural flex, feel and movement of a mum's breast, making it easier for her to combine breast and bottle feeding, while Sangenic hygienically and conveniently twists and

1965	1985	1986	1988	1995	1997
Manufacturing rights are acquired for Tommee Tippee baby products in the UK and Europe.	Tommee Tippee moves into headquarters at Cramlington, Northumberland.	Tommee Tippee introduces Pur, the first silicone teat, to the market.	Sip 'n' Seal, the first non-spill baby cup, is launched.	Maws, one of the oldest names in British babycare, becomes part of the Tommee Tippee stable.	Tommee Tippee buys Sangenic – a patented nappy disposal system.

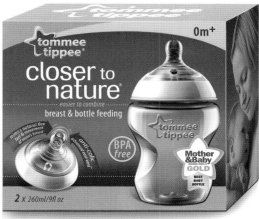

seals away the smells and germs from used disposable nappies, wrapping them individually in antibacterial film.

Achievements

Tommee Tippee is now the fastest growing baby accessories brand in the UK (Source: IRI) and is rated the sixth biggest baby accessories supplier globally. It is estimated that every household with a baby has at least four Tommee Tippee products.

In 2001, Tommee Tippee Easiflow became the first baby cup to be endorsed by the British

Dental Health Foundation; its natural action spout helps to reduce the potential for dental problems that are associated with other non-spill cups.

In 2006 Tommee Tippee's Sangenic system won the Queen's Award for International Trade in recognition of the outstanding growth achieved in overseas markets.

The Closer to Nature range has won Best Buy awards from all the leading parenting titles in the UK including the Mother & Baby Gold Award for the Best Bottle in 2006/07 and 2008/09. Also in 2008, Closer to Nature soothers were added to the range. Designed by a leading paediatric dentist, the soothers support healthy oral development.

Recent Developments

In 2009 a 'star' was born, with the launch of a new Tommee Tippee brand identity and dramatic new grey and silver packaging for Closer to Nature.

In April the brand introduced Explora, a patented range of seven cups and beakers, which take a child from early weaning through to independent, active drinking – in and out of the home.

2009 has also seen the launch of two new patented nappy disposal systems from the Sangenic stable, with Hygiene Plus and Nursery Essentials succeeding in more than 40 markets worldwide.

Promotion

Tommee Tippee is one of the key partners in the Baby Shows, a series of consumer exhibitions attracting more than 75,000 parents and pregnant women every year. The brand also works closely with the top parenting titles and employs a practicing midwife as its health liaison manager, enabling a strong relationship with health professionals directly involved with the care and welfare of newborn babies.

Brand Values

With a range stretching from pregnancy to toddler, Tommee Tippee aims to make it easier for parents to do what's best for their children.

Tommee Tippee's established reputation and continuing commitment to quality and innovation ensures that brand loyalty is passed not only from generation to generation, but also from mum to mum.

Social responsibility is important to Tommee Tippee and as a result, the brand donates products to support vulnerable communities at home and overseas, such as Women's Aid refuges, feeding projects in Africa and orphanages in Romania.

tommeetippee.com

Things you didn't know about Tommee Tippee

Tommee Tippee's first product was a weighted base cup, so named because it didn't tip over.

Its Sangenic products wrapped up more than 350 million nappies in the UK and Europe in 2008.

In the UK in 2008, a Tommee Tippee product was bought on average every three seconds and Closer to Nature bottles delivered 861 million feeds.

On average, every household in the UK with a child under two owns more than 15 Tommee Tippee products (Source: IRI April 2009).

2001	2006	2008	2009
Easiflow cups are introduced to the UK market.	The launch of Closer to Nature changes the face of newborn feeding through radical product innovation.	The Closer to Nature bottle wins the Mother & Baby Gold Award for Best Bottle for the second time.	Tommee Tippee's new 'star' brand identity is introduced and Explora – a new drinking system for babies and children – is launched.

TONI&GUY™

TONI&GUY has long been renowned as a pioneer and innovator within the hair industry, changing the face of the British high street and providing the link between high fashion and hairdressing. The Mascolo family's franchise model has maintained the company's high education and creative standards, protected the brand and made successes of thousands of TONI&GUY hairdressing entrepreneurs worldwide. It is widely regarded as the number one global hairdressing brand.

Market

In the 46 years since the birth of TONI&GUY, hairdressing has become a sophisticated industry worth billions, spawning some of the most influential and creative artists in the beauty and fashion sector. From individual salons to global chains, competition is fierce, with both men and women now seeking quality as well as service from their hairdresser.

Product

TONI&GUY aims to offer a consistent level of service, guaranteed quality and affordable hairdressing throughout the world with simple but well-designed salons offering high levels of customer care, exceptional cutting and innovative colour. All the techniques practiced by its hairdressers are taught by highly trained and experienced educators in 28 academies around the world.

Within the salons, clients can watch TONI&GUY.TV, read TONI&GUY's award-winning Magazine and take away samples of luxury brands.

In addition to the salon experience, TONI&GUY offers two ranges of haircare products – label.m and TONI&GUY – and a collection of electrical styling tools.

Achievements

TONI&GUY has helped to change the face of the hairdressing industry on an international scale, dominating the UK high street. There are now 406 TONI&GUY and 67 essensuals salons in 43 countries worldwide, while annual turnover exceeds £185 million.

TONI&GUY has an unsurpassed worldwide brand presence with a strong education network, currently operating 28 teaching academies globally – three in the UK and 25 internationally. An average of 100,000 hairdressers are trained each year, with more than 5,500 employees in the UK and a further 3,500 worldwide. A philosophy of motivation and inspiration is seen as fundamental to the brand's success.

TONI&GUY has won in excess of 100 awards, 48 of which are British Hairdressing Awards, including Best Artistic Team a record 11 times.

1963	1980s	1990	1997	2001	2003
TONI&GUY is launched from a single unit in Clapham, south London by Toni Mascolo and his brother, Guy.	In 1982 the TONI&GUY Academy launches. At the end of the decade, the first TONI&GUY franchise opens in Brighton.	TONI&GUY's first international salon opens in Tokyo, Japan. Three years later, the first International Academy launches in Stuttgart, Germany.	Toni's eldest son, Christian, co-launches essensuals with his sister, Sacha.	The TONI&GUY signature haircare range is launched.	Toni and Pauline Mascolo launch the TONI&GUY Charitable Foundation and begin raising money for a TONI&GUY Ward in the Variety Club Children's Hospital, London.

To date, TONI&GUY is the only hairdressing company to have achieved both CoolBrand and Superbrand status. In addition, in 2008 the company was voted Hair magazine's Nationwide Salon Group of the Year for the second time.

Co-founder and chief executive Toni Mascolo is a former winner of London Entrepreneur of the Year and was awarded an honorary OBE in 2008 for his services to the hairdressing industry. His daughter, global creative director Sacha Mascolo-Tarbuck, was the youngest ever winner of Newcomer of the Year at just 19 and has since won numerous accolades including London Hairdresser of the Year and, most recently, Hairdresser of the Year 2008/09 (as voted for by readers of Hair).

TONI&GUY haircare products have won numerous awards from magazines such as FHM, Hair and Grazia. Its electrical range has also achieved recognition: the Joystick Control Dryer won the coveted title of Best Appliance at the Pure Beauty Awards in November 2007; the Wave Soc Pro was voted Best Hairdryer on the Market by the Which? Report 2009; and four products have been short-listed in the 2009 Cosmopolitan Beauty Awards, Company Hair Awards and Your Hair Best Buys.

Recent Developments
July 2008 saw a redesign and upgrade of the label.m professional haircare range. Fusing a new luxurious design aesthetic with an interactive categorisation system, special patent-pending complex, website and eight additional product innovations, this distinctly trans-cultural range has now successfully launched in 48 countries.

2009 will see the continued growth of both TONI&GUY.TV and Magazine across all territories, further enhancing the client experience globally.

Promotion
As a brand, TONI&GUY juggles the need for consistency, the desire to be fashionable and the reassurance of solid service values, supported by its philosophy of continual education.

TONI&GUY.TV launched in 2003 and was the first private network of its type. Containing up-to-the-minute content, from music to high fashion footage and interviews with the TONI&GUY artistic team, it adds an extra dimension to a client visit that can last anything from 45 minutes to two hours. With more than 90,000 viewers per week in the UK it has also become an outlet for associated, appropriate brands to communicate to this sought-after audience.

TONI&GUY Magazine was also launched in 2003 to echo and communicate the brand's heritage and philosophy, focusing on key trends in fashion, the arts, beauty, grooming and travel. Distributed in salons across Europe and as far afield as Australasia, the magazine promotes an inspirational and yet accessible face of the company to customers, employees and franchisees alike. In November 2004 it was recognised with the Association

of Publishing Agencies' (APA) Launch of the Year award.

TONI&GUY's sampling initiative has seen it form mutually beneficial relationships with carefully selected partners, while giving clients free samples of products and adding to their in-salon experience.

TONI&GUY remains committed to its vision to link the fashion industry with hairdressing through its sponsorship of London Fashion Week and Weekend, which began in September 2004. Having completed 10 successful seasons, the TONI&GUY session team works on almost 50 shows a year in the UK alone, supporting key British design talent including Paul Costelloe, Betty Jackson and Giles Deacon.

Brand Values
TONI&GUY's reputation has been built on the foundations of education, fashion and friendly, professional service. It aims to provide local, individually tailored, customer-led service, promoting an authoritative, cohesive and – most importantly – inspiring voice.

TONI&GUY is one of the most powerful hairdressing brands in the world, offering some of the best education, cutting and colour available. By being pioneering, passionate and inspirational, it seeks to provide the ultimate link between fashion and hair.

toniandguy.com

	2005	2007	2008
Also in 2003, Sacha's husband, James Tarbuck, launches TONI&GUY's own TV channel – TONI&GUY. TV – TONI&GUY Magazine and the TONI&GUY Media division.	The professional haircare range, label.m, launches, growing to include more than 45 products distributed in over 47 countries internationally.	The Model.Me haircare range and TONI&GUY's electrical line are launched.	The company comprises two global, franchised hair salon groups (TONI&GUY and essensuals), with 294 salons in the UK and 197 internationally.

Virgin is known for applying its brand values across many sectors, making it arguably one of the most diverse brands in the world. Throughout its 40-year history, it has continued to stand out from its rivals through an unwavering focus on quality, outstanding customer service and industry innovation. That three of its brands – Virgin Atlantic, Virgin Media and Virgin Mobile – have attained Superbrand status in 2009 is testament to its ongoing success.

Market

Since it was established by Richard Branson in 1970, the Virgin Group has gone on to encompass sectors ranging from mobile telephony and music to travel, financial services, leisure, publishing and retail. There are more than 200 Virgin-branded companies worldwide.

In recent years, the Group has implemented a successful global expansion programme with launches of Virgin Mobile in India and Virgin Radio in France, Canada and Dubai as well as a low-cost, high-quality airline in the US, Virgin America.

By focusing its businesses around the needs of the customer and staying true to its values, Virgin remains one of the UK's most admired brands (Source: HPI Research 2007 and 2005).

Product

The Group's flagship airline, Virgin Atlantic, serves the long-haul flight market and despite having just three per cent of take-off and landing slots at Heathrow, carries around six million people annually on its 38 aircraft. In comparison, its main competitor (British Airways) holds a 41 per cent share of take-off and landing slots and carries 40 million across its total network. Virgin Atlantic operates three cabin classes on board its flights: Upper Class, Premium Economy and Economy.

Throughout its history, Virgin Atlantic has focused on quality and service and strives to offer industry innovation. It was the first to introduce seatback televisions

in Economy and a fully flat bed in Upper Class. Unlike many rivals, it continues to offer frills such as Oscar-winning films, drinks and a choice of three meals at no extra cost. Its new Upper Class Wing at Heathrow's Terminal 3 has been dubbed the world's fastest check-in by Wallpaper* magazine and along with its multi-award-winning Heathrow Clubhouse, demonstrates how Virgin Atlantic continues to strive for exacting standards within the airline industry.

Virgin Media – incorporating Virgin Mobile – launched in 2007 and now employs more than 14,000 staff, bringing broadband, television, phone and mobile services to almost 10 million people nationwide.

Through Virgin Media, the Group has become the first to provide for all of its customers' digital needs by offering television, broadband, phone and mobile services in one

package – and therefore offering better value. It is also the only major provider to offer services through a state-of-the-art fibre optic cable network. Using technology tailor-made for high speed internet, it delivers a revolutionary television service to accommodate shifting trends in viewing habits.

Mobile phone services are key to Virgin Media's strategy to develop fully integrated entertainment and communications services. Improved Pay As You Go and Pay Monthly tariffs, internet services on mobiles, and mobile broadband to complement home broadband are all designed to offer better value for customers.

Achievements

Virgin Atlantic has won an array of awards for its service and product innovation, including Best Business Class, Best Premium Economy, Best Economy and Best Airline

1984	1992	1999	2003	2006	
Virgin Atlantic is established. The inaugural flight takes place on 22nd June, from London to Newark.	Virgin Atlantic introduces the revolutionary Premium Economy class, which goes on to be replicated by several other airlines.	Richard Branson sells a 49 per cent stake of Virgin Atlantic to Singapore Airlines.	The new Upper Class Suite is launched, complete with the longest fully flat bed in any business class.	Virgin Atlantic adds Montego Bay and Dubai to its list of destinations and an industry-leading environmental strategy is unveiled.	Also in 2006, Casino Royale sees Virgin Atlantic replace British Airways as James Bond's airline of choice.

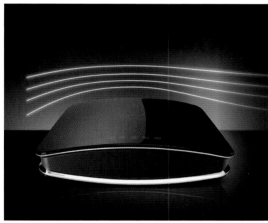

Lounge from the likes of Business Traveller, SkyTrax and Travel Weekly, to name but a few. It has also been commended for leading the way in environmental air travel and was the world's first airline to successfully fly biofuel at 30,000ft.

Formed by the merger of ntl:Telewest, virgin.net and Virgin Mobile, Virgin Media faced a substantial task to turn around customer perception. Since its relaunch, brand awareness has more than tripled and perceived brand warmth doubled. In 2008 Virgin Media climbed from 140th place to number six in the Joshua G-2/Marketing Brands We Love survey.

Putting the customer at the heart of the business is critical to Virgin Media's success. More than 500,000 individual customer comments and Net Promoter® scores have been collected, mobilising the company around the issues that customers themselves say are most important. Virgin Media's 14,000 staff have been central to the company's transformation; a leadership team was developed to take the business to the next level and implement a 'change' programme, focusing on Virgin values and behaviours.

Recent Developments
In celebration of its 25th birthday, Virgin Atlantic introduced its 'Still Red Hot' campaign. Recreating the airline's launch in June 1984, the TV advert incorporated classic 1980s imagery and themes. Virgin Atlantic has also

focused heavily on building its social media presence through social networking sites such as Facebook and Twitter. The airline is now one of the most positively perceived and talked-about brands in social media, according to the independent Kaizo Advocacy Index.

Since its launch, Virgin Media has continually looked for ways to improve its service. In 2008 customers on 4Mb broadband were upgraded up to 10Mb, and in spring 2009 customers on 2Mb followed. Further recent developments include a range of value-added services to enable customers to get the most out of their broadband, such as free file sharing, backup, storage and photo prints.

Promotion
Virgin Atlantic has recently revamped its advertising approach, concentrating on different aspects of each of its cabins and highlighting the product benefits of each, from the no-extra-cost frills in Economy to the wider legroom in Premium Economy and the fully flat bed in Upper Class. Its promotional strategy has been clearly designed to differentiate Virgin from other airlines that may fly the same planes from the same airports but don't offer the same standard of service.

As a brand, Virgin has successfully used traditional promotional media such as television, radio and cinema as part of its ongoing strategy and over the last year, in line with its digital diversification, has also used online advertising effectively.

For example, Virgin Media made its first foray into the world of in-game advertising through the appearance of outdoor posters in online games. It also sponsored the web drama 'Sam King', which integrated key messages about its Mobile Broadband product and V Festival sponsorship into the plotline.

Brand Values
Virgin has an appealing youthful personality and since its inception has endeavoured to adhere to its brand values: Fun, Value for Money, Quality, Innovation, Competitive Challenge and Brilliant Customer Service. These brand values focus on putting Virgin customers' needs first, constantly challenging the status quo by putting innovation at the heart of its philosophy and always encouraging staff to think the impossible, with resulting benefits for its customers.

virgin.com

2007
ntl:Telewest merges with Virgin Mobile and virgin.net, relaunching as Virgin Media. An internal brand and culture programme is rolled out.

Also in 2007, Virgin Atlantic places an order for 23 fuel-efficient Boeing 787 Dreamliners – the largest order in Europe – and its new Terminal 3 facility opens at Heathrow.

2008
Virgin Media launches its 50Mb broadband and is ranked the sixth Most Loved Brand in a survey carried out by Joshua-G2 and Marketing magazine.

2009
Virgin Media upgrades 4.2 million customers from 2Mb to 10Mb and Virgin Atlantic celebrates its 25th birthday.

Things you didn't know about Virgin

Virgin Atlantic's aircraft are all female and have carried more than 65 million passengers since the airline launched in 1984.

Virgin Media's V+ HD box lets viewers pause, rewind and record live TV. Unlike those supplied by other service providers, it allows two programmes to be recorded while a third is watched.

VISA

With more than 1.9 billion cardholders worldwide, Visa is the world's leading consumer payment brand (Source: The Nilson Report). In Europe alone, there are more than 360 million Visa-branded payment cards and these cards can be used in more than 30 million locations across the world. By providing consumers with a convenient, secure and globally accepted electronic payment solution, Visa's goal is to be the preferred alternative to cash and cheques.

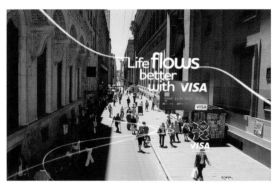

Today, recognising that every day and every person is different, Visa offers three cashless payment models to suit individual needs and circumstances: pay now – the debit card; pay later – the credit card, charge card and deferred debit card; and pay in advance – the prepaid card.

Market

In October 2007, Visa Europe became independent of the new global Visa Inc, with an exclusive licence to operate in Europe. Visa Europe operates in 36 countries, however Visa cardholders can use their cards in more than 30 million locations across the world. In addition, Visa/PLUS is one of the world's largest global ATM networks, offering cash access in local currency in over 170 countries.

Every year, Visa facilitates 19 billion point-of-sale transactions. Its 4,600 member banks issue 360 million Visa-branded debit, credit and commercial payment cards to European consumers. Each bank has access to the same powerful Visa brand, a range of products and services, marketing and other support, plus advanced technological systems to authorise, secure and process Visa transactions.

Visa competes with rivals in the field of electronic payments as well as cash and cheques.

Product

From the creation of the credit card in 1958 through to the invention of the dial-up terminal, the move to magnetic stripe, the shift to chip and pin and the creation of contactless payments, Visa has been at the forefront of change in the payments sector.

Achievements

Regular tracking research conducted by Visa shows that consumers know, like and trust the brand, which is seen as setting the standard among its competitors. Indeed, in a 2009 independent survey of more than 23,000 European subscribers of Reader's Digest, Visa emerged as the 'most trusted credit card brand' in 14 out of 16 countries.

For its member banks, the strength of the Visa brand brings tangible business value. In the UK, for example, it is reported that Visa-branded debit cards generate seven times more international usage than other competitor branded debit cards (Source: Apacs). 2009 saw Visa make its debut in the BrandZ Top 100 Most Valuable Global Brands ranking, taking 36th place.

1958	1976	1979	1983	1986	1993
Bank of America launches BankAmericard, the first successful general purpose credit card.	BankAmericard changes its name to Visa.	Visa introduces the first point of sale electronic terminal.	Visa launches the world's first 24-hour ATM network. The following year the 'dove' hologram is introduced to cards for the first time.	Visa becomes the first card payment system to offer multiple currency clearing and settlement and begins its worldwide sponsorship of the Olympic Games.	Visa issues the first smart card to accrue loyalty points, plus corporate business and purchasing cards.

Recent Developments

With its history as a pioneer in payment options, recent years have been as prolific as ever for Visa.

Visa payWave is a contactless method of paying. By removing the need to insert the card into a terminal, provide a signature or enter a PIN, transactions are completed in less than a second – cards are simply 'waved' in front of a special reader.

Visa Mobile takes contactless technology further by allowing consumers to use mobile phones equipped with near field communication (NFC) technology to complete transactions, instead of using a card.

Prepaid Visa payWave combines the speed of contactless payments with the convenience of a prepaid card and offers consumers an alternative way to control their everyday spending.

Life **flows** better when you can **win** a month's worth of **groceries*** every day

For your chance to win, simply use your Visa card for any purchase. Visit visa.co.uk for more information.

VISA WORLDWIDE PARTNER

*5 prizes of prepaid Visa cards worth £300 each to be won for each day of the promotion. Prize value based on average monthly spend of UK consumers. Ends 17 May 2009. To find out how to enter without making a purchase and to view terms and conditions visit visa.co.uk

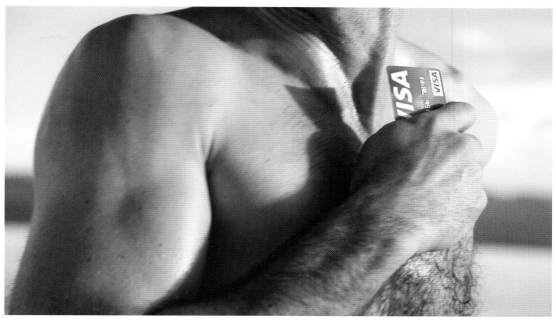

Verified by Visa provides security for consumers shopping online, requiring a password to confirm the transaction is being made between the genuine cardholder and a genuine retailer.

Visa's new one-time code card (pictured above left) features a built-in battery keypad and digital display and offers an even greater level of security when shopping online or over the phone. A consumer simply enters their PIN into the keypad to generate a unique security code which must be entered into the merchant's website to confirm identity and process the transaction. Five banks began trialling the card in 2009: Barclaycard and MBNA in the UK, Cornèr Bank in Switzerland, Cal in Israel and IW Bank in Italy.

Promotion

In 2008 the 'Life flows better with Visa' brand campaign launched across Europe with the 'Running Man' TV advertisement. The campaign aims to show how Visa can make life simpler for consumers and to encourage people to look at Visa in a new way – not as just a credit or debit card provider but as a trusted alternative to money which can bring convenience to their lives.

The latest TV ad, 'Bill', follows a man as he shops using his Visa card for all types of purchase, big and small. The ad features dance and media artist, Bill Shannon, who has developed a unique technique for dancing on crutches, which acts as a visually engaging representation of the brand's 'flow' message. Visa supported this activity with a national promotion to encourage consumers to use their Visa card instead of cash for all types of purchase, large or small.

In sponsorship, Visa builds high profile associations to drive brand awareness and deliver relevant and engaging consumer benefits. Its extensive partnership portfolio comprises some of the world's biggest names in sporting events and entertainment, including the Olympic and Paralympic Games, FIFA World Cup, The O2 in London, Berlin's O2 World, Twentieth Century Fox and Disneyland Resort Paris.

Brand Values

Visa provides trusted services and products which facilitate millions of financial transactions every day. Visa aims to help life flow better by taking the friction out of those transactions, by providing a product that is safe, quick and easy to use, and accepted in 30 million merchant outlets and 1.4 million ATMs worldwide.

visaeurope.com

Things you didn't know about Visa

On the first day of the 2008 Beijing Olympic Games, nearly US$10 million was spent on Visa cards in Beijing – an 11 per cent increase on the previous year.

In the 12 months ending June 2008, Visa cards were used to make purchases and cash withdrawals to the value of more than 1.3 trillion euros.

One in every nine euros is spent on a Visa card.

On the busiest shopping day before Christmas 2008, Visa Europe processed 731 transactions every second, with a total of 24.5 million in that one day to a value of 1.4 billion euros.

At point of sale, 11.3 per cent of consumer spending in Europe is with a Visa card.

1999	2000	2004	2008
Visa conducts the world's first euro transaction using a payment card.	A world first, Visa issues its one billionth card.	Visa is incorporated into Europe and becomes Visa Europe. The following year it revitalises its brand identity for the first time in its history.	Visa celebrates its golden anniversary.

From the classic P1800 coupe to the contemporary design of the sporty new C30, Volvo has a long tradition of producing progressive, innovative cars. This rich heritage has, over the years, led to the production of some of the world's safest cars, epitomised by the invention of numerous features now standard in modern vehicles. Today, this vigour for innovation continues to result in dynamic design, like the sleek new S60 concept car and groundbreaking technology, such as City Safety.

Achievements

When the first Volvo was produced in 1927, the company's founders announced that, "cars are driven by people, therefore the guiding principle behind everything we make at Volvo is, and must remain, safety".

Eighty-two years later, the improvement of everyone's environment through innovation remains the cornerstone of production and Volvo is consistently recognised for its achievements. Indeed, at the 2009 What Car? awards, the new Volvo XC60 crossover was named SUV of the Year with the jury commenting: "Volvo is renowned for two things – making some of the world's most family-friendly cars, and some of the safest. The XC60 reinforces that reputation."

The new XC60 is the only car on the market to feature the groundbreaking City Safety technology, capable of automatically applying the brakes when it senses that a collision with the rear of the vehicle in front is likely. Introduced in 2009, the technology could soon be extended further to include the ability to sense and stop for pedestrians.

Market

In 2008 the UK's total car market represented 2.1 million cars, of which Volvo sold 33,358, increasing its market share from 1.4 per cent to 1.6 per cent year-on-year. This 0.2 per cent gain in market share represents a significant achievement in a market that saw an overall decline of 11.3 per cent (Source: Society of Motor Manufacturers and Traders).

Product

Traditionally renowned for its luxury family estates, today Volvo is equally well known for its contemporary and distinctive range, from the C30 SportsCoupe to the rugged versatility of its Sport Utility Vehicles (SUV).

Designed to be driven and experienced – whether as a driver benefiting from the latest driver technology and responsive engines, or a passenger experiencing the intelligent and functional design and interiors – all vehicles within the range remain true to Volvo's guiding principles of innovative and stylish design, safety and compatibility with consumers' needs and lifestyle.

1927	1959	1970	1980	2000	2008
On 14th April, the first Volvo rolls off the production line in Gothenburg.	Volvo invents the three point seat belt and chooses not to patent it, so that all manufacturers can increase passenger safety and save lives.	The Volvo Accident Research Team is established, to attend the scene of real life accidents involving Volvo cars and learn more about their performance.	The Volvo Safety and Environmental concept car, a fully-functioning hybrid using gas turbine, electric motor and high-speed generator technology, is displayed at the Paris motor show.	The Volvo Cars Safety Centre opens. It is the only crash laboratory that allows two-vehicle crash tests to be staged at almost any speed and angle.	The lower emissions, higher mpg DRIVe range is launched. The following year, the unique City Safety system is launched on the new XC60.

The S40 DRIVe model, with start/stop technology and capable of up to 72.4mpg (miles per gallon), became a double What Car? award winner, picking up Best Small Family Green Car of the Year and the prestigious Green Car of the Year accolades in 2009.

Recent Developments

The striking new S60 concept car, unveiled at the end of 2008, has received critical acclaim at motor shows the world over. Designed with an aim to inspire and impassion, the new S60 combines a saloon with a coupe-style look and with its glass roof (extending the length of the car) and striking body, is set to further enhance Volvo's progressive style and modern Scandinavian design credentials.

With style and its customers' needs very much on the company's agenda, Volvo's R-Design package allows drivers to have the best of both worlds. A sporty body kit, R-Design comprises front and rear spoilers, a lower door trim and side skirts as well as roof and lip spoilers, 17-inch alloy wheels, a leather interior and blue instrument dials. The iconic C30 R-Design with its eye-catching 'youthful' looks and dynamic characteristics has proven particularly popular with a younger market. In 2008 it made its Hollywood debut as the car of choice in blockbuster movie Twilight.

2008 also saw the launch of Volvo's new lower emissions, higher mpg DRIVe range, designed to deliver all the financial and environmental benefits of more environmentally conscious motoring without sacrificing on style and safety. Each car in the range is based on its original model but incorporates a series of small design adjustments that together, add up to noticeable real life savings in efficiency and cost. For example, a lower chassis, reduced drag alloys, rear end spoilers, reduced friction tyres and the new start/stop technology all deliver performance of up to 72.4mpg with CO_2 emissions as low as 104g/km.

Volvo's vision has always been that 'safety' encompasses the environment in which we live: a cleaner environment is also a safer one. By designing cars that combine innovative style, safety and environmental technology, Volvo aims to produce cars that help create a better life, thus the brand line 'for life'.

Promotion

Since 2001 Volvo has sponsored the Volvo Ocean Race, the world's leading round-the-world yacht race. Volvo is also a proud sponsor of the Volvo Masters and the Volvo China Open golf tournaments, as well as having a longstanding commitment to the International Sailing Federation (ISAF) and the World Youth Sailing Championships.

Embracing social media and moving with the times, in 2008 Volvo partnered with Yahoo!, The Independent and Vice Magazine to launch a new national competition, 'Creative30'. Inspired by the C30, the campaign set out to uncover young creative talent. It generated more than 900 submissions to the creative30.net website, while more than 22,000 votes were cast by the public to select the winners.

Continuing its policy of interacting and engaging with consumers, 2008 also saw Volvo take the C30 to music festivals including Hard Rock Calling, T in the Park and V Festival.

Brand Values

Throughout its history, Volvo has stood for innovation through design and safety. Today it continues to strengthen this innovative reputation by producing cars with bold distinctive looks and contemporary Scandinavian style – inside and out. Volvo's vision of the future states that by 2020, no person will be injured in or by a Volvo.

Be it through safety, reducing emissions, contemporary design or seamless functionality, Volvo aims to always design cars 'for a better life'.

volvocars.co.uk

Things you didn't know about Volvo

The name 'Volvo' is derived from 'volvere', the infinitive form of the Latin verb 'to roll', while the brand's logo is an ancient chemical symbol for iron – bringing with it associations of strength, safety, quality and durability.

Volvo is the only car maker to have a specialist crash research centre and to use a 'pregnant' crash test dummy.

Volvo is the only car manufacturer that attends the scene of real life accidents involving its vehicles, in order to learn more about how they perform and how they can be improved.

August 19th 2009 will represent the 50th anniversary of Volvo's invention of the three point seat belt, a groundbreaking safety advance. Recognising its fundamental importance in saving lives, Volvo purposely chose not to patent it, instead sharing the design with rival manufacturers.

WARWICK
BUSINESS SCHOOL

Warwick Business School (WBS) is a leading thought-developer and innovator, in the top one per cent of global business schools. Its students come from over 148 countries to learn at undergraduate, masters, MBA and PhD levels. WBS educates and develops global citizens, and promotes new knowledge to benefit business and society, through its executive education and applied research. WBS is consistently top-rated for teaching quality and research.

...for the journey ahead

wbs.ac.uk/go/ahead

required. WBS was the first among fewer than 35 schools to be endorsed by all three international business school accreditation schemes.

WBS academics work to produce world-leading research in all fields of management. With recognised research leaders across disciplines as diverse as pensions, industrial dispute resolution, business strategy, customer service, enterprise, corporate social responsibility, sports management, public sector governance, sales marketing, and energy policy, people go to WBS to explore grounded, well researched ideas that work in the real world. WBS research and expert opinion is valuable, sometimes crucial, to the success of corporations, not-for-profit organisations, Government and society.

Product
Warwick Business School has something to offer individuals at every stage of their career. It provides a range of business and management undergraduate degrees; ten specialist masters courses; both a full-time and a new blended learning route to a general MSc in Management; the new Warwick Global Energy MBA as well as the popular and flexible Warwick MBA; its public sector equivalent, the Warwick MPA; and one of the world's most respected PhD programmes.

For corporate clients and individuals, it also offers a range of diplomas, short courses and customised programmes. WBS consults with industry to keep its programmes fresh, relevant and accessible. The fact that many graduates return for further study at WBS later in their careers demonstrates its effective blend of

Market
There are more than 3,900 business schools across the world, aiming to develop the next generation of business leaders. Warwick Business School is one of the largest in Europe, ranked at number 22 in the world (Source: The Economist 2009) and is in the top one per cent worldwide. As the largest department of the University of Warwick, WBS aims to offer its students both excellent facilities and a prestigious reputation.

A high quality business education is valued by employers and employees alike; employers can gain competitive advantage by recruiting and developing talent with knowledge and critical thinking skills, while individuals can gain new options for career progression, both sideways and upwards. With literally thousands of schools offering MBAs worldwide, the business school market is incredibly competitive. To be a success, and to attract successful people, a respected brand is

1965	1981	1986	1989	1997	1999
The University of Warwick is founded by Royal Charter. In 1967 WBS is created as the School of Industrial and Business Studies, with just three courses.	The Warwick MBA brand is launched.	The Warwick MBA by distance learning launches.	WBS achieves five star rating for research excellence.	On its 30th anniversary, WBS has 3,160 students, 263 staff, and a turnover of £12.4 million.	WBS becomes the first business school in the world to hold accreditation from all three global management education bodies: AMBA, EQUIS and AACSB.

academic research with the practicalities of the workplace. Learning by sharing experience and insight is key to the student experience at WBS. Alumni members, which number 24,500 in total, have cited the combination of a highly intelligent and internationally diverse cohort as being a major benefit of their learning experience as well as their future careers.

Achievements

WBS has achieved a global reputation for excellence in just 40 years. It has one of the broadest subject bases and most highly regarded faculty of any business school in the world. The latest Research Assessment Exercise (December 2008) rated 75 per cent of WBS research at 3* and above, placing it third in the UK. WBS submitted 130 academics for assessment, a real reflection of high quality, running across the breadth and depth of research at WBS. These research credentials are fundamental to its culture and differentiate it from teaching colleges and commercial training companies.

The performance of its degree programmes continues to excel; its undergraduate programme is ranked in the top five business and management degrees in the UK.

In addition, its portfolio of 12 masters courses provides highly specialised learning in areas of business that are increasingly important in the search for sustainable competitive advantage.

More than 20 years of combined learning experience enables WBS to deliver the Warwick MBA to nearly 2,600 experienced managers each year, wherever they are in the world. In 2009, WBS launched the Warwick

Global Energy MBA, a groundbreaking new programme that is developing strategic leadership for the future energy industry.

Its long standing commitment to work across the private, public and voluntary sectors created the Warwick MPA – the first MBA for the public sector in the UK.

Warwick Business School's reputation means WBS graduates are highly sought after by business leaders and can be found in senior positions around the world. Its expertise is clear from its diverse list of clients and sponsors, including Accenture, The Bank of England, BP, Capgemini, Deloitte, Deutsche Post, E.ON, GlaxoSmithKline, HSBC, IBM, Islamic Bank of Britain, Johnson & Johnson, J.P.Morgan, The National Health Service, Nestlé, PepsiCo, Procter & Gamble, PZ Cussons, Rolls-Royce, Santander, Siemens, UBS Investment Bank, Unilever and Vodafone.

Recent Developments

WBS celebrated its 40th anniversary in 2007. It has grown from offering three courses to 28, and now has more than 8,500 students enrolled, with a turnover of £40 million. The course portfolio continues to refresh, expand and diversify, with an ongoing contract to customise delivery of the Warwick MBA for IBM, as well as new courses in global energy, international management, and its unique blended learning route to the MSc in Management which allows inexperienced graduates to study as they work.

WBS has recently established a Fund for Academic Excellence to invest in future leaders, faculty, and its learning environment. Since August 2003, the fund has helped to support many students, recruit 16 new

professors and expand facilities with a £9 million building recently completed and £20 million earmarked for further development. WBS recognises that to retain competitive advantage, it is essential to continue to gain funding for growth.

Promotion

WBS maintains a solid global presence with a range of below- and above-the-line segmented international marketing. Its 'extremely usable' website (Source: WebWorks 2007) attracts around 2,600 visitors daily and is an essential communication platform. However, its brochures are still an important channel, providing tangible evidence in a knowledge-based sector.

WBS uses creative advertising channels but ultimately, its highly successful graduates are its best adverts and its best advocates.

Brand Values

WBS has simple core values: excellence in all it does, nurturing fresh-thinking in staff and students, ensuring a positive impact from the ideas it creates, and continuing to be international in outlook and approach. From these foundations WBS aims to continue to challenge minds, change lives, and create tomorrow's leaders.

wbs.ac.uk

2003	2006	2009	2010
The Guardian survey of top employers rates WBS graduates as the most employable in the UK.	The Times Good University Guide rates WBS as the best overall undergraduate business education provider in the UK.	Warwick Global Energy MBA is launched.	MSc in Management by blended learning launches.

WEBER SHANDWICK

Advocacy starts here.

Weber Shandwick is a full service public relations agency, helping clients to manage their reputation and achieve their business goals. Serving clients locally, nationally and globally, Weber Shandwick puts its creative talent, communications expertise and specialist teams to work for some of the biggest companies and most innovative brands across the private, public and not-for-profit sectors.

Market

It's been a tough 12 months for everyone in the PR industry but, despite the economic climate, the UK public relations market continues to steadily grow in size and diversity, with an estimated 50,000 people now working in the industry.

With many companies and organisations continuing to switch their marketing resources from traditional advertising to PR, key growth areas for the industry over the next 12 months

include corporate responsibility, multi-cultural and digital communications, public health, technology, sports marketing and corporate reputation.

The consultancy sector varies from one-man bands to UK-only agencies and international players. Weber Shandwick maintains the largest public relations network in the world, measured both in terms of number of employees and geographic coverage. With a core of 83 owned offices in 40 countries and affiliates that expand the network to 124 offices

in 77 countries, Weber Shandwick operates in virtually every major media, government and business centre on six continents.

Product

Weber Shandwick is a full service public relations agency. Its policy of recruiting the best media and PR professionals means it now possesses some of the strongest teams of experienced senior ex-journalists and industry specific communications specialists in the business.

In the UK, Weber Shandwick has six specialist practice groups in technology PR, healthcare PR, financial communications, corporate communications, consumer marketing and public affairs and also offers cross-practice consultancy in digital, multicultural and internal communications, crisis and issues management, corporate social responsibility, strategic planning, lifestyle marketing, over-50s marketing, broadcast PR, sports PR and market research.

The UK and Ireland business employs around 300 people across eight regional offices in London, Manchester, Glasgow, Edinburgh, Aberdeen, Inverness, Belfast and Dublin. Globally the company is part of the InterPublic Group network with a strong PR presence across the US, Europe, Asia Pacific and in the emerging economic giants of China, India, Russia and Brazil.

Achievements

In 2009, Weber Shandwick won outstanding international praise from its peers when it was named an Agency of the Decade by Advertising

Age. The firm was also recognised as: gold medal winner for PRWeek's inaugural Global Agency Report Card; Global Agency of the Year by The Holmes Report; Agency of the Year at the European Excellence Awards; and was the first-ever agency to be honoured International Agency of the Year by both PRWeek and the UK Public Relations Consultants Association (PRCA) within the same year.

In the UK alone, the agency won more than 30 industry accolades for client work

during 2009 including: Best Multicultural Communications Campaign at the European Excellence Awards; five European SABRE Awards including Platinum PR Campaign of the Year and Best PR-led Campaign at the inaugural Cannes Lions Advertising Festival award for BPEX's 'Pigs are Worth It!' campaign.

Weber Shandwick's Public Affairs practice was also honoured as Public Affairs Agency of the Year by Public Affairs News and the agency's Technology team was recognised as Specialist

1974	1987	1998	2000	2001	2009
Shandwick International is founded in London with a single client and a global vision.	The Weber Group is founded in Cambridge, Massachusetts as a communications agency for emerging technology companies. In less than a decade it goes on to become a top 10 PR firm.	Shandwick International is acquired by The Interpublic Group.	Shandwick International merges with The Weber Group and becomes Weber Shandwick.	BSMG Worldwide merges with Weber Shandwick.	Weber Shandwick continues to win leading industry awards and is recognised for its work internationally.

Consultancy of the Year and PR Company of the Year at the 2009 PRCA Awards and SC Magazine Awards, respectively.

High-profile assignments have included: helping to save the British pig industry by developing the integrated 'Pigs are worth it!' campaign for BPEX and the National Pig Association; demonstrating Barclays Wealth's knowledge and understanding of the Resident Non-Domiciled (RND) community; celebrating the achievements of professional British Muslim women with the launch of the first Muslim Women Power List for the Equality and Human Rights Commission; helping discount retailer Aldi become a national phenomenon as the credit crunch led to consumers being more savvy with their grocery shopping; delivering the Know Before You Go media campaign for the Foreign & Commonwealth Office, encouraging British nationals to prepare for foreign travel; creating a global water-cooler moment for African telecoms company Zain by engaging customers, employees and partners in what was the biggest corporate rebrand ever in Africa; and helping the Work Foundation demonstrate the social and economic benefits of early intervention in the treatment of musculoskeletal disorders.

Recent Developments

During 2009, Weber Shandwick continued to build on the agency's reputation for excellence in traditional PR by setting a new agenda for the future of the public relations industry. Advocacy remained at the heart of Weber Shandwick and the agency continued to invest in innovation and thought-leadership.

Leading the way in digital excellence, Weber Shandwick created INLINE Communications to provide a simple and straightforward solution to planning and executing 21st century public relations. INLINE Communications are not independent offline, online and experiential activities – but are campaigns that tell a consistent story across the spectrum of media that most influence the audience targeted.

Recognising that 2009 would also be remembered as the year when video on the internet truly came of age, the agency introduced Weber Shandwick Vision, a new offering dedicated to digital storytelling through the creation and promotion of online video content.

In October, Weber Shandwick also strengthened its Technology PR offering with the launch of a UK Cleantech practice, a dedicated specialist group with experience of creating lasting advocates for new energy and sustainability companies.

Promotion

Following the launch of its 'Advocacy starts here' positioning in 2007, which illustrated the agency's shift in focus to communications programmes that forge emotional bonds and higher levels of involvement with stakeholders, Weber Shandwick has continued to embed

advocacy into all of its agency work with the aim of creating an army of believers and fans for every client.

The agency's investment in its specialist offerings has also led to a number of high-profile new hires and internal promotions including a new worldwide chief digital creative officer, a strategic insight and planning specialist, a head of government and public sector and a vice chair of public affairs.

Brand Values

Weber Shandwick's values are: creativity, passion and commitment.

With a pool of specialist talent and strong European and international networks, the consultancy's clients are among some of the top brands, companies and organisations in the UK and around the world.

Every year, Weber Shandwick makes a significant investment in staff development to ensure the consultancy continues to develop added-value services and to deliver real business results for its clients. In 2009, the agency introduced its Future Leaders Academy, a year-long programme designed to equip employees with the skills and knowledge to make them the most respected professionals in the industry. The Weber Shandwick Digital University, a training initiative to drive digital PR skills across the agency, was also launched across the consultancy's EMEA network.

webershandwick.co.uk

Things you didn't know about Weber Shandwick

Part of the Interpublic Group of marketing companies, Weber Shandwick works closely with sister companies McCann Erickson (advertising), FutureBrand (branding consultancy), Jack Morton (event management) and Octagon (sports marketing).

Weber Shandwick's Client Relationship Leader (CRL) programme was selected as a case study by Harvard Business School for making a substantial contribution to management education.

In 2009, European and UK CEO Colin Byrne was named one of GQ's Most Powerful men in Britain for the eighth consecutive year. Byrne also authors a blog (byrnebabybyrne.com) that has been named by The Times as one of its Top 50 Blogs for Business.

Weber Shandwick is one of the biggest graduate recruiters in the UK public relations industry.

West Cornwall Pasty Co. was established in 1998 with the aim of selling top quality handmade Cornish pasties outside their traditional Cornish heartland. Opening its first store with just £40,000 start-up capital, today it has nearly 70 stores and sells over eight million pasties a year, making it the UK's largest specialist retailer of Cornish pasties. Its distinctive pirate logo in the Cornish county colours of black and gold creates an instantly identifiable brand image.

Geographical Indication (PGI) status, the overseas market could also experience growth.

2009 will see WCPCo. pursue an extensive shop opening and refurbishment plan to help maintain its position as the UK's largest specialist Cornish pasty retailer in terms of branch network and workforce.

Market

West Cornwall Pasty Co. (WCPCo.) has helped transform the traditional pasty into a modern-day food and competes with baking giants such as Greggs, high street coffee shops, premium sandwich chains and global fast food brands.

WCPCo. is positioned at the upper end of the bakery market with a range of premium quality products. The success of the WCPCo. formula has seen a rise in other smaller Cornish pasty retailers expanding out of Cornwall, including Cornish Bakehouse and Oggy Oggy.

The rise in popularity of the Cornish pasty saw it take 30 per cent of the savoury pastry snacking market in 2007 compared with only 20 per cent five years earlier (Source: TNS Superpanel). With so many high streets in towns and cities around the UK currently without a Cornish pasty shop, there is potential for further growth in the UK market. As the Cornish Pasty Association seeks Protected

Product

In the 11 years since the company was formed, the success of WCPCo. has been built on its traditional pasty which is based on a centuries old Cornish recipe: freshly diced potato, swede and onion, lightly seasoned and mixed with lean diced steak.

To cater for a variety of modern tastes, WCPCo. quickly developed its offering which today comprises 18 different varieties all handmade in Cornwall, including vegetarian

1998	2000	2004	2007	2008	2009
The company is formed by six Cornish school friends and family and opens its first store in Chippenham, Wiltshire.	Now with 15 stores, WCPCo. makes its millionth pasty.	The company launches its VW Camper Van mobile units, with destinations including Lords Cricket Ground and Twickenham Stadium.	CEO Richard Nieto leads a management buyout of the original founders and Fairtrade™ coffee and tea are introduced to all stores.	WCPCo. opens a new distribution centre, cold room and administration office, to meet future national demand.	The company opens 20 new stores across the UK, introduces free WiFi for customers and sells its 50 millionth pasty.

and – new for 2009 – vegan options. Modern twists on the original include: chicken balti; lamb and mint; pork and apple; steak and stilton; cheese and vegetable; and cheese, tomato and basil. Wherever possible, ingredients are sourced from Cornish farmers and growers.

A complementary range of savoury baked products is also available, including sausage rolls and pizza baguettes, as are items such as spicy potato wedges and hot and cold drinks.

The Cornish county colours of black and gold are used across all signage and packaging, with many stores featuring reclaimed beach wood alongside memorabilia, pictures and surf boards sourced from Cornwall – adding to the authentic Cornish atmosphere. Two specially commissioned mobile catering units in the form of 1960s VW Camper Vans – iconic symbols of the Cornish surf scene – extend the brand's reach further.

Achievements

Over the last few years the company has received numerous business accolades in recognition of its growth, including being named Fastest Growing Business (50+ employees) at the Sage/The Daily Telegraph Business Awards 2005; Best Emerging Brand in 2005 in The Sunday Times/Virgin Fast Track 100; and achieving Superbrands Brand to Watch status in 2006/07. Its ongoing success has seen WCPCo. enter the Superbrands top 500 for the first time in 2009/10.

Recent Developments

Since the management buyout in October 2007, the company has significantly increased its offering with the aim of broadening its appeal. Several new varieties of pasty have been introduced, including salmon, vegetable Provençal and wholemeal vegetable (suitable for vegans), while a limited edition turkey and cranberry pasty is produced for the six-week pre-Christmas period. WCPCo. has also linked

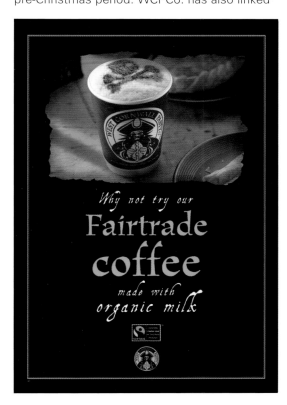

up with the award-winning St Austell Brewery and now uses the Cornish brewer's Tribute Ale in its steak and ale pasty.

The company made a strategic decision to target the breakfast market as a new growth area and in 2008 three varieties of 'Brekkies' were introduced, featuring a mixture of savoury breakfast fillings – such as scrambled egg, ham, bacon, sausage, mushrooms and cheese – wrapped in pastry. Traditional breakfast items were also added to the menu, including bacon rolls, muffins and Danish pastries, while the drinks offering was revamped to feature Fairtrade™ organic coffee and tea, organic milk and own-brand bottled mineral water.

A store refurbishment programme is currently underway to provide increased indoor seating and free WiFi.

Promotion

WCPCo.'s communications focus on conveying its core brand message: traditional Cornish products, handmade daily in Cornwall and baked freshly in store.

Over the last 18 months the company has significantly increased awareness of its products via an extensive campaign of internal and external POS and signage. A newly launched 'Cornish pirate' themed website was introduced and in response to customer demand, a range of WCPCo. branded merchandise is due to go on sale during 2009.

The company's oversized and branded Cornish pasty costumes have been used widely to help promote the company, from running in the

London Marathon to meeting royalty.

Brand Values

WCPCo. is governed by four core values: 100 per cent Cornish – made in Cornwall, by Cornish people; truly traditional – made to traditional recipes; quality and convenience – premium ingredients in a handy package for consumers on the move; and innovation – responding to customer tastes, introducing new products to meet changing needs.

SENSING THE DIFFERENCE

Whirlpool's emphasis on innovation has made it one of Europe's leading household appliance brands. The strategic investments it continues to make in design, manufacturing and the community lie at the heart of its commitment to maintaining customer loyalty and retaining its prominent position within such a competitive industry. Technological advancements are at the core of its product offering.

Market
Whirlpool is a leading producer of major home appliances in North America and Latin America with a significant presence in markets throughout India, China and Europe. It is the number one brand in Europe, where it is experiencing growth in the premium brand segment, and is continuing to expand into emerging markets.

As with many other industries, 2008 was a challenging year for home appliances. The volatile economic climate and decline in consumer demand naturally had an impact on Whirlpool; net sales for the year totalled US$18.9 billion, a three per cent drop on the previous year. Latin America and Asia delivered strong sales and operating profit but North America and Europe were hit harder.

However, while the company has had to reduce costs in some areas, it is maintaining investment in product innovation. It has been following a strategy of redesigning parts and components to global standards to lower costs and improve quality and speed to market.

Product
Today's consumer expects space-conscious kitchen appliances that integrate function and design. Whirlpool, which manufactures and markets a full range of home appliances, has consistently been at the forefront of innovative technological solutions to better meet consumers' evolving needs.

Whirlpool's range of built-in products offers high-specification, anti-fingerprint stainless steel ovens, wine cellars, coffee machines, extractor fans and under-counter cooling drawers.

The brand's range of built-in products plays a vital role in its growth strategy. The range offers style combined with intelligent functionality and customised features such as text-assisted displays and its patented '6th Sense' technology designed to sense, adapt and control.

Achievements
With 14,000 employees, a sales presence in more than 30 European countries and manufacturing sites in seven, Whirlpool

1911	1919	1989	2006	2008	2009
Upton Machine Corporation is founded in St Joseph, Michigan, to produce electric motor-driven wringer washers. In 1929 it merges with the Nineteen Hundred Washer Co.	Gottlob Bauknecht starts a small electric workshop in Taillfingen, Germany, eventually establishing his first factory in 1933. Philips acquires the Bauknecht business in 1982.	Whirlpool Corporation and Philips form a European joint venture; Whirlpool Corporation becomes the sole owner in 1991.	In March, Whirlpool completes the acquisition of Maytag.	GREENKITCHEN, a prototype for a sustainable integrated kitchen and an industry first, is launched. It is scheduled to enter the marketplace in 2010.	Whirlpool's freestanding design line is launched while its Glamour range brings a new dimension to built-in kitchens.

Europe is a wholly owned subsidiary of Whirlpool Corporation, the world's leading manufacturer and marketer of major home appliances. Globally, Whirlpool Corporation has 70,000 employees and 69 strategically located manufacturing and technology research centres. The company markets Whirlpool, Maytag, KitchenAid, Jenn-Air, Amana, Brastemp, Bauknecht and a host of other major brands around the world.

It was awarded two iF product design awards in 2009 for the Whirlpool Glamour Oven and for GREENKITCHEN, its eco-system design concept. This is the second award for GREENKITCHEN; it won a Gold SPARK Award in October 2008.

In April 2008, Whirlpool gained an Honorary Mention in four categories at the ninth Annual Process Excellence Summit in London. The awards were for Best Project Contributing to Innovation, Best Fast Track Project, Best Process Improvement in Manufacturing Project and Best Design for the Six Sigma Project.

Recent Developments
Whirlpool recently unveiled GREENKITCHEN, its prototype for a sustainable integrated kitchen and an industry first. GREENKITCHEN – scheduled to enter the marketplace in 2010 – was designed in response to increasing consumer demand for more eco-friendly products and is a key part of the brand's environmental strategy.

The concept is to deliver ecological benefits through adapting, recycling and reducing. These are achieved with a range of integrated appliances that optimise the use of heat and water and increase energy efficiency by up to 70 per cent. With green living at the forefront of today's consumers' minds, GREENKITCHEN focuses on four distinct areas to achieve energy savings: products, eco-system,

behaviour and co-generation – where domestic electricity is generated via systems producing hot water and electricity at the same time.

Its latest washing machine range includes Whirlpool's innovative AquaSteam technology. The design is modern and minimalist, featuring soft edges, crisp lines and a smooth integration of features for an overall sleek, modern feel combined with maximum ease of use.

For kitchens, its built-in Glamour Line aims to be luxurious while providing outstanding performance, superior quality and ease of use. It employs some of the most advanced engineering technologies, resulting in innovations such as a full glass door structure. The oven and the hood are made of the finest quality glass to offer flawless precision and aesthetics, lending a striking look to the entire kitchen.

Promotion
Whirlpool pursues its business objectives while helping to improve the lives of people in the communities in which it operates. Its most important corporate social responsibility project is its partnership with Habitat for Humanity, a charity that is committed to providing simple, decent, affordable houses for families in need in more than 100 countries. Whirlpool has supported this global, non-profit organisation in many ways for a number of years. As well as providing products, to date more than 3,500

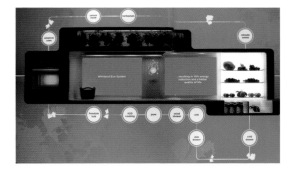

employees have volunteered to help physically build new homes.

In 2001, the charity recognised Whirlpool Corporation for its commitment as the largest corporate donor to the project; since the beginning of the programme, Whirlpool has supported Habitat for Humanity with an investment of more than US$25 million and donated 62,000 appliances.

Brand Values
Whirlpool strives to make intelligent appliances that make people's lives more efficient and pleasurable. The brand is about relentless inquiry and innovation, to produce industry-leading design and technological solutions to better meet consumers' needs. New design trends, technological advances, evolution in society and changes in domestic behaviour have all played a part in the development of its groundbreaking designs.

whirlpool.co.uk

Things you didn't know about Whirlpool

A refrigerator in the GREENKITCHEN range is designed to save up to 46 per cent more energy than regular models.

Whirlpool operates three of Europe's seven largest factories.

Whirlpool products can be found in more than 200 million households worldwide.

Whirlpool has been a specialist in home appliances for 98 years.

Innovation in Internet Marketing

By Damon Segal
Founder and MD
Emotio Design Group

So where are we now?

Consider these amazing statistics:
There are over one trillion unique URLs
on the web at any one time – that's one million
million pages. Globalisation is becoming
more relevant as more than 25 per cent of the
world's population has access to the internet
and the importance of consumer personal
engagement is all the buzz. In the UK
18.3 million households (70 per cent) have
access to the internet. More than 150 million
people access their Facebook account every
day, 65 million of these via their mobile device.
People are watching hundreds of millions
of videos a day. In fact, every minute, 20 hours
of video is uploaded to YouTube. So with these
facts in mind, how do you take an innovative
approach to creating and marketing
a web presence?

How the money flows

It has been reported that online retail
spend reached £21 billion in the UK last
year with that figure expected to triple over
the next decade. Over the same timeframe,
traditional spending will fall from £265 billion
to £247 billion, or so says the crystal ball that
is Reuters.

According to Paypal, 2010 will see a 235 per
cent growth in online grocery shopping to
£6.25 billion. On Christmas Day 2008, with all
the shops closed, online shoppers spent over
£100 million, and in November and December
2009 Americans spent US$29.1 billion online
(Source: comScore).

As a response to this demand, we have also
seen UK online advertising spend increase
to £17.5 billion in 2008, representing almost
20 per cent of all media spend in the UK.

So what does this mean?

It means businesses and retailers need
to get smarter in the way they attract
customers and generate sales. Competition
is going to be fiercer and margins are going
to be attacked even more with consumers
being able to compare prices quickly and easily.
The focus must be on brand trust, loyalty and
differentiation in order to influence market share.

The best way to predict the future
is to invent it

In just six years Apple's online music store
iTunes has picked up 25 per cent of the US
retail music market, selling over five billion
downloads. Facebook has gained more than
300 million users and Twitter grew 1,382 per
cent between February 2008 and February
2009. One of the reasons for Twitter's amazing
success was its open architecture, this is
creating the conditions for users to innovate
and shape the way twitter is used.

Innovations like these change our
understanding of how the world works.
Ten years ago, if I wanted to find a song that
a friend told me to listen to I had to go to a
shop and buy the track. Now, I can see what

my friend is listening to on his Facebook post then click and hear it immediately free of charge on a site like Spotify.

To keep up-to-date with the latest trends and technologies is almost a full time job in itself. Even more important is having the foresight and understanding of where future internet trends might head.

To understand this we need to examine the environment

- Personal profiling and community advertising will start to target customers more effectively than ever before.

- The growth in broadband and connection speed will allow more rich media to be delivered, bringing on the rapid growth of Web TV and premium content. This will allow personalised advertising to be delivered via this new exciting medium.

- Consumers will be more informed than ever before with live search becoming a growing trend, allowing people to find real time information and reviews.

- Web semantics will enable search engines like Google to improve their understanding of words and documents, therefore producing better results.

- More prominence will be put on personalisation and localisation. With a large increase in global urbanisation these factors will heavily affect online sales and customer engagements.

- The growth of smart mobile phones will mean that consideration for mobile content must be given when creating a website.

- The importance of site speed and usability will factor in search engine friendliness. Faster, better-structured sites will be looked at in a favourable way.

- Google personalised search will have an effect on site rankings as Google shows results to searchers based on their last 180 days of search history and behaviour,

although my understanding is that top rankings will retain a high position even if they may be displaced by one or two positions. The trick will be to look for ways to take advantage of personalised search – for example, making sure your locality is set correctly or that you have a broad spectrum of on-page optimisation that will cast a bigger net.

- Social media spheres will influence consumer trends whilst social media monitoring will provide an insight into your brand and sector. Engaging consumers on an emotional level will help grow loyalty and communicate brand differentiation.

- An integrated approach to managing social media will need to be defined and adopted in order to streamline management and keep messages consistent. With so many platforms now available, attracting literally billions of visits each month, solutions are being created so that accounts can be linked, allowing single posts to gain the maximum reach.

In Summary

"Only the paranoid will survive." said Andy Grove, chairman of Intel, adding "The more successful you are, the more people want a chunk of your business and then another chunk and then another until there is nothing left." This kind of paranoia leads to constant innovation in order to stay ahead.

Innovation should not be confused with change or creativity. Change is not always innovation, changing your website for a better-looking new one is not innovating. Being creative is only having the ideas for innovation, whilst innovation is actually taking those ideas and making them real.

Many of you have creative agencies and creative directors but the real question is how many of you have innovative agencies and innovation directors?

We should be taught not to wait for inspiration to start a thing. As Frank Tibolt says "Action always generates inspiration. Inspiration seldom generates action."

It's good to talk

By Raoul Shah
CEO
Exposure

Remember when we used to make time to sit and talk to each other? We'd talk with meaning and energy. Face to face, or by telephone, every conversation was as important as eating, drinking and sleeping. Each communication was part of our social evolution and intellectual validation amongst our peers. Often, we would write to each other and commit some true feelings and deeper thoughts to paper. Remember the wonderful art of writing and receiving letters? Now that was a welcome delivery from the postman.

Today we don't really need to move much to communicate. We can type, send, and receive from just about anywhere. A short form txt, a pointless "yes, great" reply to an email, or a Facebook invite to all your friends, and we can go and put the kettle on with plenty of time to spare. But actually we now seem to have less time. The tea gets cold because of the deluge of emails we need to read. We are distracted by so many incoming communications devices, that we toy with the idea of switching off. But we can't – we removed the landline since everyone calls the mobile (hopefully, BT's new campaign will reverse this trend). So we are now always on. The working week just became 24/7. The work/life balance just became life.

SAVE THE CHILDREN: 'Make Your Mark' campaign to sign up 250,000 new consumers up to support the charity.

Now this is not meant to be a rant about the last decade's digital onslaught, or a sad reflection on how good it once was. I love the enabling facility that technology has brought us. The speed, the efficiency, the freedom to control our own lives and personalise them is wonderful! One click and the groceries are ordered whilst also paying bills in the comfort of my own lounge. Booking hotels and actually knowing what my room will look like in advance. The cab driver sending me a text message to say he's outside (and the make, model and registration of the car, just in case). But all this is devoid of depth and lacks the personal touch. I actually miss the sound of "thank you, have a nice day."

My case here is for the revival of the good old art of conversation. And not just down the pub on a Friday night. My actual point is more serious than that. Brands and businesses have a critical requirement to connect with their consumers in a personal, relevant and engaging manner. And, whilst digital technology goes a long way to fostering strong relationships and dialogue, nothing beats the power and emotion of an actual conversation. If your brand's communication can successfully establish an emotional engagement with your consumer, you may benefit from merely being remembered – you may actually get talked

WRIGLEYS: Launch of 5 gum in France, featuring Augmented Reality music mixer (www.5gum.fr).

COCA-COLA: The limited edition bottles designed by Matthew Williamson, currently seen in the World of Coca-Cola, Atlanta, and available to buy on eBay for US$50.

about. Beyond just being the flavour of the month, if consumers can't stop talking about you, and your story is amplified by word of mouth, you may have found the holy grail of a future communications' model… welcome to the world of never ending conversations.

Today, the art of conversation goes beyond the realms of traditional communication between multiple people. The environments in which to converse are limitless. The need to be close is no longer mandatory. The speed at which a single conversation can lead to a million is very fast and, often, inexpensive. Our ability to say the right thing, edit our content, and even choose our audience is made possible with the wealth of digital technology and innovative platforms that continue to proliferate. If word of mouth now has a competitor, it's actually a friend called word of mouse.

Yet with speed, access, and low barriers to entry, comes a whole plethora of risks and challenges for brands. An over populated media environment requires even better editing and navigation. Attention to detail gets over-looked in our desire to get lots done, quickly. The abundance of information via the internet tells us a little about lots. Virtually anything you want is available at your convenience. Our time to digest, discuss and experience is rarely available.

As always, there is an exciting counter culture to the mainstream – creative excellence and brilliant ideas continue to stand out in such a cluttered environment. The improved quality of creative writing and self-taught journalism means the tabloid and disposable nature of a lot of media is balanced with intelligent and stimulating content from a rich variety of sources. Many of these sources are individuals

not organisations, each providing valuable information with spontaneous regularity. Specialist media outlets are focused and targeted, with less need for promiscuity in the face of ever-changing consumers. The influence of honeyee.com, hypebeast.com, Monocle or National Geographic is no longer confined to a handful of experts. In fact, specialists have become even more special, except they now have a global lens through which to focus.

The advance of digital technology and changing media also gives us a clue about the dynamics of Superbrands in the future. Expertise, knowledge and authenticity will continue to be valuable

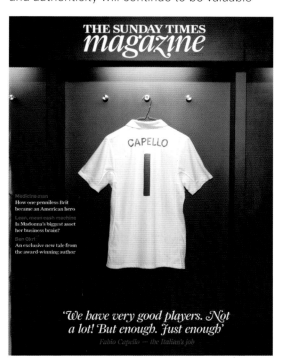

UMBRO: The Sunday Times Magazine exclusive front cover and brand feature to support the launch of the new England home shirt 2009.

brand assets, but align them with sensory experiences and the flexibility to engage consumers on their own terms, and the next Apple, Nike iD, or Twitter may be just around the corner. A personal touch, a memorable sound, and an arresting image will all enhance a brand's magnetic consumer appeal, and its ability to generate conversations that may fuel a never-ending cycle of consumer desire.

In conclusion, the new marketing landscape is dominated by the disproportionate influence of word of mouth versus traditional media channels. Our friends and family have a credibility and an honesty that no advertising campaign can supercede. The role of personal influence is paramount for building Superbrands, and the access to relevant networks that spread influence is highly valued. The art of conversation is top of the brand noise charts. A walk to the Post Office is worth the time. It really is good to talk. It's good for business. It's good for a change. It's even good for your health!

Branding by Stealth

By Neil Taylor
Creative Director
The Writer

Let's say you're the chief financial officer of a big brand. Or maybe of a company that owns a big brand. You think that there must be something in this branding malarkey – a lot of people in black-rimmed specs keep telling you there is, anyway – but you've never really got the, ahem, bang for your buck.

Or you're the HR director. People in the marketing department keep banging on about brand, and paying lip service to it being just as important internally as externally. But culture's your thing, and you know a ream of brand guidelines won't make the blindest bit of difference to the way people behave.

Or you're the head of customer service. It's your job to make customers happy. Quickly. Cheaply. The brand team produce some nice posters, but getting other stuff signed off by them is a pain, and frankly, doesn't help you make your numbers.

Sound familiar? Big brand agencies spend their lives telling people the brand is 'more than just a logo'. And it is. But they often struggle to persuade much of the rest of the company, who are busy trying to make things more efficient, hit their targets, or make their people do more with less. Brand doesn't get a look-in.

The brand manager's secret weapon
We would say this, wouldn't we (we're writers, after all), but language – specifically, tone of voice, which is about how brands use language – can be the secret weapon of the beleaguered brand manager; the bit that stops being a nice-to-have and becomes an essential. Why? Two reasons.

First, every part of the business uses language. While the details of logos, colour palettes and advertising segmentation might be a long way off from what most people think about in their day-to-day jobs, language isn't. Almost everyone in a business these days writes, from the CEO to the person manning your email helpdesk overnight. And they write a lot: yes, emails, but letters, too; bid documents; presentations; internal communications; health and safety policies. Every single time someone puts pen to paper (or more likely, typing finger to mucky keyboard), they're representing your brand.

If you're a brand manager, this vast quantity of writing can be scary. All the expensive work you do on your brand, or even its tone of voice, can be thrown away with some dodgy proposal or customer letter you're never even likely to see. So language can be a threat, but it's also an opportunity to make your brand relevant to everyone in the business.

That opportunity is obvious if your people are writing to other people outside the company; they're shaping the brand's reputation. But it's just as true if they're writing for people internally. They're either shaping or reinforcing the corporate culture. That's why, when we run a brand language project, we obsess about every bit of internal writing we can find. Done properly, your brand's tone of voice should apply just as much to the language your CEO uses to explain this year's corporate strategy as the words on the back of a visitor's pass. Language is the most basic and all-pervasive brand element there is.

Words mean numbers
The second reason why language is your secret weapon is that it's so supremely measurable. Proving 'return on investment' with something like branding is notoriously difficult. Even pseudo-scientific approaches to things like

© Katrin Solansky

Look for things with lots of people on the receiving end of them, and how you can gauge how successful they are (eg do customers ring in and take up a special offer? Do employees do their compulsory online training? Or do customers call up if they're confused?).

3. Rewrite each bit of writing, in line with your brand's tone of voice.

4. Measure the effect of improving each of those bits of writing. Did more people ring in, or not?

5. Put a financial value on that effect. For instance, if you cut the number of calls to a call centre, how much does each call cost?

6. Take your figures to your financial director. And show how you got a return on your brand investment in cold, hard cash, while also making your brand consistent and distinctive. Ask for more money to do even more.

brand valuation typically involve some brand consultant sticking their finger in the air and making a subjective judgement. It ain't like that with writing.

Write a better e-newsletter, and you can see how many more people click through to a website. Write better responses to complaints, and watch scary things like 'repeat complainants' and 'escalations' drop. Write better disciplinary procedures, and see fewer employees go to tribunals.

Start collecting these stats, and you'll have a much better chance of proving that branding doesn't have to be fluff and nonsense. We've been dealing with a CFO who was, unsurprisingly, initially sceptical about the benefit of tone of voice. But once we started shortening and simplifying customer emails and letters (as well as his own internal emails about procurement!), the benefits of less paper, less postage, less printing, and less writing time made the rest of the project a no-brainer.

A big part of the brand programme had just paid for itself. And in the process, we get to make the brand more consistent and more distinctive in all the little nooks and crannies that usually get overlooked.

That's why language refreshes the parts of your brand other elements cannot reach. It's time to stop policing your brand, and start releasing it.

The language action plan
So, if you're up for proving the value of a tone of voice programme to your business, how do you do it? Here are six steps.

1. Define how you want to sound.
Make sure it's a true reflection of what your organisation is really like (or could be and would like to be). Believe it or not, that's the easy bit.

2. Identify the most measurable bit of writing in each part of your business.

TheWriter ™

The Writer
The Writer does three things.

1. Writing. Everything from Guinness cans to huge corporate websites. And they manage big writing projects, too.

2. Brand language. Helping brands define their tone of voice, and coming up with names.

3. Training. They help people become more confident, creative writers at work.

The Writer is on a mission to save clients from tedious corporatespeak. In its place, it looks for language that helps clients sell, persuade, inspire, amuse, or whatever it is they need to do. And it does it with people like the BBC, Virgin, Barclays and Tate.

thewriter.com

The Centre for Brand Analysis

The Centre for Brand Analysis (TCBA) manages the research process for all Superbrands programmes in the UK. It compiles the initial brand lists, appoints each Expert Council and manages the partnership with the panel providers, whose panels are used to access consumer or business professionals opinion.

About TCBA

TCBA is dedicated to understanding the performance of brands. There are many ways to measure brand performance. TCBA does not believe in a 'one size fits all' approach, instead it offers tailored solutions to ensure the metrics investigated and measured are relevant and appropriate. Its services aim to allow people to understand how a brand is performing, either at a point in time or on an ongoing basis, and gain insight into wider market and marketing trends. Services fall into three categories:

Brand analysis – principally measuring brand strength and/ or values. This might require surveying the attitudes of customers, opinion formers, employees, investors, suppliers or other stakeholders.

Market analysis – for example, providing intelligence, trends and examples of best practice from across the globe.

Marketing analysis – reviewing brand activity, including: campaign assessment; image/brand language assessment; marketing/PR review; agency sourcing and ROI analysis.

TCBA works for brand owners and also provides intelligence to agencies and other organisations. It utilises extensive relationships within the business community and works with third parties where appropriate.

tcba.co.uk

Superbrands
Selection Process

The annual Superbrands and Business Superbrands surveys are independently administered by The Centre for Brand Analysis (TCBA). Brands do not apply or pay to be considered; rather, the selection processes are conducted as follows:

- TCBA researchers compile lists of the UK's leading business-to-consumer (B2C) and business-to-business (B2B) brands, drawing on a wide range of sources, from sector reports to blogs to public nominations. From the thousands of brands initially considered, between 1,200 and 1,400 brands are shortlisted for each survey.

- Each shortlist is scored by an independent and voluntary Expert Council, which is assembled and chaired by TCBA's chief executive. Each survey has a separate Council, refreshed each year. Bearing in mind the definition of a Superbrand or Business Superbrand, the council members individually award each brand a rating from 1-10. Council members are not allowed to score brands with which they have a direct association or are in competition to, nor do they score brands they are unfamiliar with. The lowest scoring brands (approximately 40 per cent) are eliminated after a council meeting to discuss the results and ratify the scores.

- The remaining brands are voted on by a YouGov panel. For the Superbrands survey, the panel comprises a nationally-representative sample of more than 2,100 British consumers aged 18 and above. For the Business Superbrands survey, the panel comprises more than 1,700 individual business professionals – defined as those who have either purchasing or managerial responsibilities within their organisation.

- For the Superbrands survey, the number of consumer votes received by each brand determines its position in the final rankings. For the Business Superbrands survey, the views of the council and the business professionals are taken into equal account when determining each brand's position in the official league table. In both cases, only the top 500 brands are deemed to be 'Superbrands' or 'Business Superbrands'.

Definition of a Superbrand:

All those involved in the voting process bear in mind the following definition:

'A Superbrand or Business Superbrand has established the finest reputation in its field. It offers customers significant emotional and/or tangible advantages over its competitors, which customers want and recognise'.

In addition, the voters are asked to judge brands against the following three factors:

Quality. Does the brand represent quality products and services?

Reliability. Can the brand be trusted to deliver consistently against its promises and maintain product and service standards at all customer touch points?

Distinction. Is the brand not only well known in its sector but suitably differentiated from its competitors? Does it have a personality and values that make it unique within its marketplace?

Superbrands
Expert
Councils

Stephen Cheliotis
Chairman, Expert Councils
& Chief Executive,
The Centre for Brand Analysis (TCBA)

In 2007, Stephen founded TCBA, which is dedicated
to understanding the performance of brands,
and runs the selection process for Superbrands'
annual UK programmes.

Stephen works with a variety of brands and agencies
on brand, market and marketing analysis whilst delivering
brand insights at conferences and for international media.

Business Council

Jaakko Alanko
Managing Director
McCann Enterprise

Jaakko merged his independent B2B agency, Anderson & Lembke, with McCann Erickson in 2001 and established McCann Enterprise as a division of McCann's London base. His focus is on Enterprise Branding, which is based on the belief that an organisation whose people are emotionally connected and behaviourally aligned, has a sustainable competitive edge.

James Ashton
Media and Telecoms Editor
The Sunday Times

James writes primarily for the business pages of The Sunday Times about companies such as Vodafone, Google and ITV. He joined from the Daily Mail in October 2007 where he was chief city correspondent and has also written for The Scotsman and Reuters.

Richard Bush
Founder & Managing Director
Base One Group

Richard is the driving force behind the multi-disciplined agency, Base One Group. In addition, he is a regular presenter at the Institute of Direct Marketing and writes and speaks frequently for a number of industry publications and institutions, including B2B Marketing, the Internet Advertising Bureau and the Association of Business to Business Agencies.

Chris Clarke
Chief Creative Officer
Lost Boys international (LBi)

In his current role, Chris is responsible for the creative output of the network and its 500+ creative staff in 12 countries. Chris loves to stay close to the work, developing creative ideas with teams across the network for clients as varied as Electrolux, BT, M&S, US National Gallery of Art, Vodafone and Kraft.

Paul Edwards
Chairman
TNS-Research International UK

Paul joined Research International UK in 2007. Prior to this he was group chief executive and chairman for Lowe & Partners, taking particular responsibility for serving clients' integrated marketing needs. He has also been chairman and chief executive of The Henley Centre, working on future strategic direction for a wide range of clients.

Pamela Fieldhouse
Managing Director
Edelman UK

Pamela is a senior communications consultant with over 18 years' experience in corporate reputation, issues and crisis management, brand strategy and business communications. She provides strategic counsel to senior executives from both the public and private sector and currently advises clients across a wide range of industry sectors.

Clamor Gieske
Manager
Vivaldi Partners London

Clamor manages the UK office of Vivaldi Partners, a global management consultancy headquartered in New York. He has a mix of international experience from working on strategy, innovation, marketing and brand consulting projects. This has involved him advising clients across the UK and Europe but also in countries as diverse as Saudi Arabia and Russia.

Richard Glasson
Chief Executive
GyroHSR

Richard is chief executive of GyroHSR, one of the world's leading independent integrated marketing companies. With 600 employees in 17 offices around the globe, GyroHSR works with top international brands such as Virgin Atlantic, American Express, Sony and Hewlett Packard. Richard has been with GyroHSR for seven years.

Richard Groom
Head of Consultancy
Groom Associates

With a strong background in brand development, Richard has worked in leading marketing roles for more than 15 years with companies such as United Biscuits, Délifrance and McCain Foods. In 2004 he co-founded Groom Associates, a brand and design agency. Based initially in Leeds, it now also has an office in Beijing.

Joanna Higgins
Consultant Editor and Writer
CBSi

Prior to her current role, Joanna was senior editor at BNET UK. Before this, she was group editor of the Institute of Directors' publications. Here Joanna led a highly praised and radical redesign, launched the website, and oversaw the development of new editorial products such as leisure and lifestyle publication After Hours.

Darrell Kofkin
Chief Executive
Global Marketing Network

Darrell formed the worldwide membership association for marketing and business professionals, Global Marketing Network, in 2005. It is now supported by a world-class global faculty comprising many of today's widely respected and most-published marketing thought-leaders. Darrell also regularly speaks, lectures and writes on the subject of global marketing strategy.

Kate Manasian
Managing Director
Manasianandco

Kate runs a small strategic brand consultancy together with a team of experienced associates. An ex-owner of Saffron and Wolff Olins, her work primarily involves working with boards to find their point of difference and designing programmes for expressing it internally and externally.

Ruth Mortimer
Associate Editor
Marketing Week

Ruth is associate editor for Marketing Week. In addition to her current role, she often appears on CNN, Sky and the BBC as an expert on business issues and is author of two books about marketing effectiveness. She is also a regular speaker at marketing conferences.

Marc Nohr
Managing Partner
Kitcatt Nohr
Alexander Shaw

Marc is a founding partner of integrated agency Kitcatt Nohr Alexander Shaw. He is an honorary life fellow of the Institute of Direct Marketing, and regularly contributes to debates on marketing in the media. Marc was named number one in Marketing Direct's Power 100 Agency Players in 2007 and 2008.

Phil Nunn
Executive Media Director
TBWA UK Group

Phil's experience includes working at BBC Worldwide, Publicis's Optimedia and launching Interactive@Optimedia globally in 1998. In 2003 he became MG OMD managing partner and went on to launch Trinity Communications in 2007/08 with clients including Talk Talk and Lexus. Phil is now executive media director at TBWA UK Group.

Andrew Pinkess
Strategy &
Marketing Director
Lost Boys international (LBi)

Andrew has 20 years' experience in brand and marketing consultancy. His specialisms include: brand strategy and development; digital strategy; integrated communications; and internal communications as a catalyst for organisational change. His client experience spans business to business, business to consumer and the public sector.

Russell Place
Chief Strategy Officer
UM London

Russell has worked at UM for seven years creating ROI focused, award winning work for clients such as Sky, Autoglass, Nickelodeon and Bacardi and has overseen UM London's wider awards success in recent years. He has also led a number of highly successful new business initiatives, most recently the £13 million UK Dairy Crest win.

Shane Redding
Managing Director
Think Direct

Shane is an independent consultant with more than 20 years' international business to business and consumer direct marketing experience. She provides strategic direct marketing advice and practical training to both end-users and DM suppliers. Shane also has an honorary fellowship of the IDM.

Elizabeth Renski

Editor

CEO Today

Elizabeth, who has 13 years' experience in the B2B magazine publishing sector, became the editor of CEO Today in 2004, shortly after its launch. Elizabeth is also the editor of Climate Change – an ambitious publishing initiative providing a platform for collaboration between governments, businesses and NGOs in tackling climate change and creating a low-carbon economy.

Matthew Stibbe

Writer-in-Chief

Articulate Marketing

In his current role, Matthew's clients include HP, Microsoft®, eBay and HM Government. He helps them talk to non-techies about technology and also writes the popular blog, BadLanguage.net. Before starting the agency in 2005, he worked as a freelance business and technology writer and was a regular contributor to Wired, Popular Science and Director magazine.

Giles Thomas

Chief Operating Officer

Branded

Giles has been advising a broad range of clients, including Orange, Yahoo!, EA, Channel 4, and Transport for London, during the last eight years that he has spent at Branded. He is an experienced international marketer, having earned his credentials as marketing director at MTV Networks Europe and European marketing director at Sega.

Richard Williams

Founding Partner

Williams Murray Hamm

Richard founded Williams Murray Hamm, with Richard Murray, in 1996. A fellow of The Royal Society of Arts and a member of the Design Council, Richard often acts as a spokesman for the design community, appearing on Radio 4's Today programme as well as speaking at Ashridge Management College, Warwick Business School and New York's FUSE.

Chris Wilson

Managing Director

Earnest

Chris has spent 15 years in B2B marketing, working with organisations in the technology, telecommunications and financial sectors. Chris founded Earnest in 2009 to help B2B marketing step out of the shade and stop being a poor cousin to FMCG. Chris also chairs the Association of Business to Business Agencies.

Andrew Worlock

Director

Insidedge

Andrew heads up the UK IPG agency Insidedge, a specialist internal communications consultancy based in London. Working with multinationals and blue-chip organisations across Europe, he advises those facing the eternal dilemma of how to maximise resource and budget in order to achieve corporate goals internally.

Simon Wylie

Founding Partner
& Managing Director

Xtreme Information

Simon is a founding partner of Xtreme Information and has more than 20 years' experience within the field of advertising, media intelligence, research and insight. Throughout this period he has worked with major global brands as well as a number of European NGOs, the European Commission and other regulatory bodies.

Consumer Council

Nick Blunden
Managing Director
Profero London

Nick joined the Profero group as client services director in 2004. In this capacity he successfully developed the agency's relationships with key clients such as AstraZeneca, Channel 4, COI, Johnson & Johnson and Western Union, by providing them with both digital leadership and strategic marketing expertise.

Tim Britton
Chief Executive, UK
YouGov

Tim has more than 15 years' experience working directly and indirectly in the research industry in the UK, culminating in his current role as chief executive of YouGov UK.

His experience in research is both on and offline, in areas ranging from financial services and business to business research, through to work on public policy.

Vicky Bullen
CEO
Coley Porter Bell

Vicky has built her career in the design industry, joining Coley Porter Bell from Graphique (now Vibrandt), becoming chief executive in September 2005. She has led some of the agency's largest business, winning a Design Effectiveness Award and a Marketing Grand Prix for Kotex. Vicky also sits on the Ogilvy UK Group Board.

Colin Byrne
CEO, UK & Europe
Weber Shandwick

Colin is one of the UK's leading PR practitioners with more than 20 years' experience spanning domestic and international media relations, politics, global campaigns and issues management. Colin joined Weber Shandwick in 1995 and is now CEO of the global agency's European network and a member of the global management team.

Leslie de Chernatony
Professor of Brand Marketing
Università della Svizzera
Italiana, Lugano,Switzerland
& Aston Business School, UK

Leslie has written extensively for American, European and Asian journals and is a regular presenter at international conferences.
He has written several books on brand marketing and is a Fellow of the Chartered Institute of Marketing and Fellow of the Market Research Society. He also frequently advises corporations internationally on brand strategy.

Jackie Cooper
Founding Partner
Jackie Cooper PR

Jackie is one of the pre-eminent voices and influencers in UK brand marketing today.

Jackie sold Jackie Cooper PR to Edelman in 2004 and now serves as creative director and vice chair of Edelman. She continues to deliver strategically powerful campaigns across the myriad of Edelman practices.

Peter Cowie
Managing Partner
Oystercatchers

Peter is a founding partner of Oystercatchers, a consultancy specialising in helping marketers achieve efficiency and effectiveness from their agencies. Peter has 28 years of experience working in advertising and marketing both agency and client side.

Tim Duffy
Chairman & CEO UK
M&C Saatchi

Tim joined Saatchi & Saatchi in 1986 as a strategic planner. In 1995 he was one of the founders of M&C Saatchi, now a top five UK agency with 16 offices in 12 countries. Tim was made UK chief executive in 2004 and chairman of the UK group in 2008.

Stephen Factor
Managing Director –
Global Consumer Sector
TNS

At the beginning of 2006, Stephen took global responsibility for TNS' FMCG business, supporting the world's leading brand owners in 70 countries. With some 25 years' experience in global market research agencies, he blends hands-on corporate management experience with a deep understanding of FMCG markets and brands.

Peter Fisk
Founder,
GeniusWorks
& Author,
'Marketing Genius'

Peter is an inspirational author, speaker and consultant. GeniusLab is an accelerated innovation process helping companies to deliver new brand experiences that make people's lives better and drive more profitable growth. Other books include the bestselling Customer Genius and People, Planet, Profit.

Avril Gallagher
Group Client Managing
Director
EMEA
Starcom MediaVest Group

Avril joined Starcom MediaVest Group in 2004 as a business director, was appointed UK client services director in 2005 and client managing director in 2006, extending her role to cover business in EMEA in 2007. She was appointed to her current role, group client managing director EMEA, in 2009.

Cheryl Giovannoni
European President
Landor Associates

Cheryl's role embraces managing Landor London and its European offices. A leading presence in the branding community and a strong advocate for the transformational power of design, Giovannoni enjoys hands-on involvement in a wide range of client business. Cheryl commented "For Morrisons we reinvented the brand which delivered huge growth and I'm very proud of that".

Martin Hennessey
Co-Founder
The Writer

Martin is a former journalist and co-founder of language consultancy, The Writer. Martin and his team are on a mission to rescue business and brands from the tyranny of linguistic mediocrity, training, writing and developing tone of voice for brands. Martin is also co-founder of not-for-profit organisation 26.org.uk.

Graham Hiscott
Deputy Business
Editor
Daily Mirror

Graham was appointed consumer editor of the Daily Express, in March 2005. In March 2008 he moved to the Daily Mirror as deputy business editor, covering City as well as consumer stories. A string of exclusives earned Graham the London Press Club Awards' Consumer Journalist of the Year 2007 accolade.

Mike Hughes
Director General
ISBA

Following a career in marketing and general management at Coca-Cola, Guinness and Bulmer, Mike assumed his current role as director general of ISBA, The Voice of British Advertisers, in 2007. A member of all key UK industry bodies, Mike also sits on the Executive Committee of the Worldwide Federation of Advertisers.

Paul Kemp-Robertson
Editorial Director &
Co-Founder
Contagious

Paul co-founded Contagious in 2004. This quarterly magazine, DVD and online intelligence resource reports on marketing innovation and the impact of new technologies on brands. Paul has written numerous articles, co-edited D&AD's The Commercials Book, appeared on BBC radio and has spoken at numerous events around the world.

Sophie Lewis
Group Planning Director
JWT

Sophie began her career at DFGW and moved to BBH in 1999, where she worked on Rolling Rock, Levi's, Baileys and Flora/Becel. She then joined Mother to work on Boots. Sophie joined JWT in May 2008 and now works across the Nestlé Confectionery Portfolio and Debenhams.

David Magliano MBE
Director of Commercial
and Marketing
England 2018

David is director of commercial and marketing at England 2018, the organisation bidding for England to host the 2018 FIFA World Cup. His previous roles include director of marketing for London 2012, sales and marketing director of easyJet, and sales and marketing director of Go, of which he was also a founder.

John Mathers
Managing Director
Holmes & Marchant

John joined Holmes & Marchant in late 2009 as the group's managing director, prior to which he has held senior roles at Blue Marlin, The Brand Union and Fitch. An active member of the design industry, John was president of the Design Business Association for three years and still works with the Design Council.

Crispin Reed
Managing Director
Brandhouse

Crispin has a rounded perspective on brands having worked in leading global advertising and design agencies, brand consultancy and client-side in the fragrance and beauty sector. In addition to his current role, Crispin is an associate of Ashridge Management College and sits on the Advisory Board of the Global Marketing Network.

Professor Robert Shaw
Honorary Professor,
Cass Business School
& Director, Value Based
Marketing Forum

As a consultant, businessman and bestselling author of Marketing Payback, Improving Marketing Effectiveness and Database Marketing, Robert is a top authority on value based marketing and customer relationship management. He is in demand both in the UK and overseas as a conference chairman and keynote speaker and also teaches on in-company executive education programmes.

Raoul Shah
Joint CEO
Exposure

Raoul launched communications agency Exposure in October 1993. It now employs 180 individuals in London, Tokyo, New York, San Francisco, and Los Angeles. In 2007 Raoul was top of the Guardian's ethnic minority media power list, and in October 2008 he was appointed as a trustee of the British Council.

Mark Sweney
Media Correspondent
Guardian Newspaper

Mark joined Guardian Newspapers in March 2006 as advertising, marketing and new media correspondent at MediaGuardian.co.uk. He is currently a media correspondent across the Guardian newspaper, weekly media supplement and online. Prior to this, Mark was a reporter on Campaign magazine before moving to Marketing as chief reporter in March 2004.

Alan Thompson
Founding Partner
The Haystack Group

Alan co-founded The Haystack Group in 2001 and has since built it into one of the most recognised agency engagement and management consultancies in the country. Alan advises brands on how to structure and manage their marketing resources, both internally and through agency partners.

Lucy Unger
Managing Partner, EMEA
Fitch

Lucy has a proven track record of working with large organisations and global clients to deliver strategic brand and design projects. Lucy's current role, which she began in 2006, sees her play an active role in London based client and project work as well as new business, while overseeing Fitch's operations in the EMEA region.

Harry Wallop
Consumer Affairs Editor
The Daily Telegraph

Harry is The Daily Telegraph's consumer affairs editor. He has been at the paper since 2004, when he joined as a business reporter, before moving across the title to write consumer stories. His work was recognised by the London Press Club in 2008 when he was named Consumer Affairs/Personal Finance Journalist of the Year.

Andrew Walmsley
Co-Founder
i-level

Andrew co-founded i-level in 1999 and the company has since won more than 40 awards. It has been Agency of the Year eight years out of 10 and in 2007 became the first digital agency to win a Queen's Award for Enterprise. Andrew writes for Marketing magazine and is also frequently quoted in the national media.

Mark Waugh
Deputy Managing
Director
ZenithOptimedia

In his career Mark has amassed experience across almost every market category, from motors to luxury goods and financial services to FMCG. This, coupled with his agency's £700 million UK spend, allows him a uniquely scaled perspective on the behaviour of some of Britain's biggest brands.

About YouGov

YouGov – What the world thinks

YouGov is the authoritative measure of public opinion and consumer behaviour. It is YouGov's ambition to supply a live stream of continuous, accurate data and insight into what people are thinking and doing all over the world, all of the time, so that companies, governments and institutions can better serve the people that sustain them.

YouGov's full service research offering spans added value consultancy, qualitative research, field and tab services, syndicated products such as the daily brand perception tracker BrandIndex, and fast turnaround omnibus.

YouGov's sector specialist teams serve financial, media, technology and telecoms, FMCG and public sector markets.

In the UK, YouGov operates a panel of over 250,000 members representing all ages, socio-economic groups and other demographic types, with excellent response rates. The quality of its panel allows YouGov to access difficult to reach groups, both consumer and professional.

YouGov has developed an extensive B2B offer, owing to its ability to access thousands of business decision makers on its panel. Clients can research specialist markets or get an overview with the YouGov Small Business Omnibus, a fast, cost-effective way of interviewing 500 decision makers of small businesses every week.

YouGov dominates Britain's media polling and is one of the most quoted research agencies in the UK. Its well-documented track record demonstrates the accuracy of its survey methods and quality of its client service work.

YouGov Panels are accessed to survey British consumers and business executives as part of the selection process. More details on the full research methodology can be found on page 180.

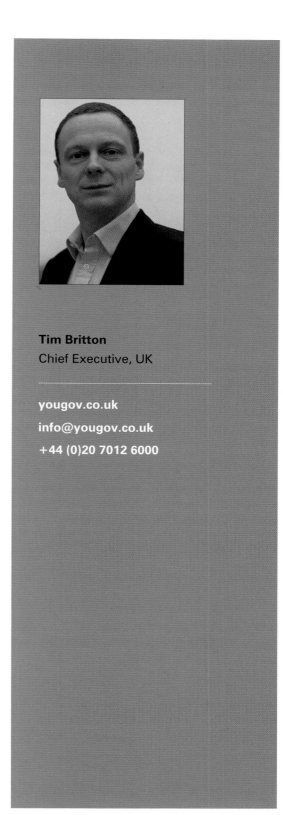

Tim Britton
Chief Executive, UK

yougov.co.uk
info@yougov.co.uk
+44 (0)20 7012 6000

What the world thinks

Superbrands and Business Superbrands Results Highlights 2010

Stephen Cheliotis

Chairman, Expert Councils
& Chief Executive,
The Centre for Brand Analysis (TCBA)

Introduction

For the forth consecutive year, Superbrands (UK) commissioned The Centre for Brand Analysis to independently administer the selection process for its high profile Superbrands, Business Superbrands and CoolBrands surveys. The results do not reveal the most powerful brands as such, whilst it is clear that the results equally, and thankfully, do not simply reflect either brand size or marketing spend. Rather the results reveal the degree to which the British public, in the case of Consumer Superbrands, and British business professionals and experts, in the case of Business Superbrands, feel that each brand deserves Superbrand status. The results do not correlate precisely to financial success but they do reveal the degree to which those surveyed believe, respect and indeed are fond of each brand and therefore indirectly may indicate future brand and financial performance. What is certain is that the rankings offer an invaluable snapshot of the UK brand landscape across a wide variety of sectors.

The surveys measure brands based on three criteria; quality, reliability and distinction. The criteria of quality reflects whether individuals believe that the products or services offered under the brand name are of high quality. Whilst this does not result in the Superbrands list being dominated by premium brands it might of course impact on the performance of those competing on a high volume low margin strategy. As such, the absence of brands such as easyJet and Ryanair, who are positioned as low price alternatives to competitors, might in part be attributed to this, although clearly the list still constitutes predominately mass market brands.

The criteria of a brand being reliable reveals the degree to which individuals trust each brand to deliver against their promises, and in an age when trust in brands continues to shrink, is an important component of brand potency.

Finally the criteria of distinction aims to investigate whether those surveyed believe that each brand stands out from its peers. As such the survey purposefully reiterates that this investigation is not just about fame and awareness, indeed many of the brands who are enjoying the highest awareness in the UK do not even make the top 500 because whilst people know of them, they do not believe that they are truly distinctive in comparison to their rivals.

Measuring brands against these three criteria offers an insightful picture of the UK landscape and allows the survey to produce results that do not simply mirror advertising spend figures or awareness. As such brands that otherwise deserve praise, but tend to miss out to the usual candidates in other surveys, might enjoy success (e.g. the likes of Encyclopædia Britannica or Royal Doulton in the Consumer Superbrands survey). Conversely those that are simply ubiquitous or shout loudly do not necessarily guarantee a high place, or a place at all in many cases, in the top 500.

Brands are able to track their performance in the rankings in order to gauge their success or failure. Clearly for many brand owners and managers, gaining a view of their place in the overall 'brandscape' is an interesting benchmark, although understanding performance relative to competitors is even more insightful in measuring progress or lack of in ones marketplace.

This Superbrands Annual contains case studies on many of the brands that achieved Superbrands status, based on either their position in one or both of the surveys. These case studies reveal in more detail the story behind those brands earning praise and how they have built their brand equity. This article highlights the overall winners in both surveys, together with some of the biggest movers and shakers. Clearly in this space we merely reveal some of the top line results, without being able to go into detail as to why certain brands might be succeeding and why others are not having as positive an impact. More details on the top 500 rankings for both programmes can be found online. Detailed analysis is available through The Centre for Brand Analysis (TCBA), including comprehensive information by sector, information on those brands that failed to make the top 500 and a segmented evaluation of specific brands' performance over the four year period of investigation undertaken by TCBA.

CONSUMER SUPERBRANDS

Top Consumer Superbrands Performers

This year's consumer rankings reveal changes aplenty in the UK consumer brand landscape. Yet there are also consistencies with last year's results, reaffirming the steady performance of many brands, which is perhaps the truest sign of a powerful Superbrand.

The 2009/10 top 10 contains five of last year's top 10, including Microsoft® and Google which continue to occupy two of the top three positions. Number one in 2007/08, Microsoft® slipped into second last year, behind Google, but reclaims the top spot in 2009/10. Google in third place sits in the same position as in the 2007/08 rankings.

Other brands to retain their top 10 positions this year include British stalwarts the BBC and British Airways (BA) in fourth and fifth position respectively, although they swap places from last year as the BBC rises one position and British Airways falls one place.

The last of the brands to retain a top 10 position year-on-year is Mercedes-Benz, although it falls from third to sixth place. Interestingly, all five brands retaining their top 10 status do so for a third year. LEGO® was almost as consistent; in seventh in 2007/08, it fell to 16th last year before regaining its top 10 place in 2009/10, taking eighth place.

Falling from their 2008/09 top 10 positions are Royal Doulton, BMW, Bosch, Nike and Sony, although all remain within the top 50. Indeed, the top 50 tends to be fairly static with this elite group appearing fairly impenetrable. The lowest placed brand from this collection of fallers is Bosch in 34th position. Royal Doulton drops from sixth to 33rd, BMW from seventh to 16th, Nike from ninth to 29th and Sony from 10th to 22nd place.

New entries to the top 10 in 2009/10 are Rolex, Coca-Cola, LEGO®, Apple and Encyclopædia Britannica (it should be noted that Rolex was considered in the survey for the first time). Like LEGO®, Coca-Cola regains its top 10

PUBLIC/OFFICIAL CONSUMER SUPERBRANDS TOP 20		
Rank	2008/09	2009/10
1	Google	Microsoft®
2	Microsoft®	Rolex
3	Mercedes-Benz	Google
4	BBC	British Airways
5	British Airways	BBC
6	Royal Doulton	Mercedes-Benz
7	BMW	Coca-Cola
8	Bosch	LEGO®
9	Nike	Apple
10	Sony	Encyclopædia Britannica
11	Apple	Virgin Atlantic
12	Duracell®	Duracell®
13	Jaguar	Marks & Spencer
14	Coca-Cola	Philadelphia
15	AA	Dulux
16	LEGO®	BMW
17	Marks & Spencer	Colman's
18	Thorntons	Dyson
19	Cadbury	Ordnance Survey
20	Hilton	Nintendo

EXPERT COUNCIL CONSUMER SUPERBRANDS TOP 20		
Rank	2008/09	2009/10
1	Google	Google
2	Apple	Apple
3	Nike	BBC
4	BMW	innocent
5	BBC	Rolex
6	innocent	BMW
7	Audi	Nike
8	Coca-Cola	YouTube
9	Marks & Spencer	Manchester United Football Club
10	Waitrose	Disney
11	MINI	Facebook
12	John Lewis	Financial Times
13	Manchester United Football Club	Green & Black's
14	Facebook	Waitrose
15	Green & Black's	Eurostar
16	BlackBerry	John Lewis
17	Financial Times	Dyson
18	Microsoft®	The Economist
19	Selfridges	Coca-Cola
20	Agent Provocateur	Marmite

position from two years ago (when it sat in second place), proving that they are both firmly entrenched in the top 20. Apple, is ninth this year, having just missed out on a place in the top 10 last year, when it sat in 11th place. Encyclopædia Britannica was 29th last year and is no doubt the surprise entry in the top 10 for 2009/10.

Revelations such as the appearance of Royal Doulton and Encyclopædia Britannica may surprise many in the top 10 and although the former was unable to retain its position within the top 10, both are firm fixtures in the top 50. The fact is that in the case of both brands, the vast majority of the UK public, when judging against the specific Superbrands factors of quality, reliability and distinction, believe these brands meet the requirements.

Consumer Superbrands Risers and Fallers

In terms of risers and fallers within the Consumer Superbrands top 500, there are some big swings this year. The fast food chains seem to have bounced back from a pretty torrid year in 2008/09. McDonald's, Burger King and KFC all rise substantially in this year's rankings; McDonald's is up 227 places, Burger King

CONSUMER SUPERBRANDS TOP 10 HIGHEST NEW ENTRIES*	
Brand	Rank
Krispy Kreme	68
Peperami	141
Macleans	144
L'OCCITANE	146
Jordans	166
Petit Filous	179
Pantene	192
Weight Watchers	200
RoC	236
Royal Caribbean International	271

*excluding those added to the research for the first time

rises 189 places and KFC climbs by 164, while Domino's Pizza also shows considerable gains, jumping 144 places.

The retail grocery sector has also recovered from a surprisingly bad year last year when, despite their ubiquity and substantial marketing spend, the three biggest players in the category struggled to reach the top half of the 500. Only Sainsbury's, which was placed in 232nd in 2008/09, was above the halfway mark. The sector was perhaps affected by negative stories from the media that focused on their treatment of suppliers, market dominance and impact on the wider retail market.

This year these brands have recovered most of the places they lost in 2008/09, although they are still below their record high. ASDA rises 213 places, Tesco 185 and Sainsbury's 140; those that have risen the least started higher in the rankings last year, where the gap between each position is more marked than lower down. Morrison's enters the top 500 for the first time, coming in at 451st position. This confirms the continued progress and growth of Britain's fourth biggest supermarket chain.

Staying in the retail sector, some old high street favourites also seem to have had a pretty good year with brands such as HMV jumping 118 places, B&Q up 168, Boots climbing 117 and Argos storming up the rankings by 230 places, making it the eighth biggest riser overall in the top 500.

These risers are consistent with the companies faring reasonably well in the economic downturn. The fast food industry has certainly been one of the winners with profits rising sharply, while the multiple supermarket chains have also fared comparatively well. While the retail environment has been severely impacted, the largest value retailers have generally outperformed weaker rivals. It also reveals that consumers are turning back to large, trusted brands that have considerable heritage in the UK.

Where the rankings don't necessarily start tallying with general preconceptions of how certain brands might have faired in this turbulent

CATEGORIES REPRESENTED IN THE CONSUMER SUPERBRANDS TOP 500

Category	Number of brands in the top 500	Category leader	Category leader's rank
Food – General	48	Philadelphia	14
Toiletries & Cosmetics	43	Oral-B	142
Retail – General	31	Marks & Spencer	13
Pharmaceutical	25	Durex	83
Clothing & Footwear	23	Calvin Klein	112
Technology – General	22	Sony	22
Drinks – Spirits	20	Jack Daniel's	76
Household – Cleaning Products	18	Fairy	32
Household – Appliances	16	Dyson	18
Household – General	15	Royal Doulton	33
Leisure & Entertainment – Games & Toys	15	LEGO®	8
Financial	14	Visa	91
Food – Chocolate & Confectionery	14	Thorntons	45
Household – General Consumables	13	Duracell®	12
Media – Newspapers & Magazines	13	National Geographic	123
Automotive – Vehicle Manufacturer	12	Mercedes-Benz	6
Drinks – Beer & Cider	11	Guinness	31
Drinks – General	11	Robinsons	49
Restaurants & Coffee Shops	11	Starbucks	67
Leisure & Entertainment – Destinations	10	Royal Albert Hall	36

CATEGORIES REPRESENTED IN THE CONSUMER SUPERBRANDS TOP 500 (Continued)

Category	Number of brands in the top 500	Category leader	Category leader's rank
Sportswear & Equipment	10	Nike	29
Automotive – General	8	AA	43
Drinks – Coffee & Tea	8	Twinings	38
Technology – Computer Hardware & Software	8	Microsoft®	1
Travel – Hotels & Resorts	8	Hilton	27
Household – Child Products	7	Pampers	77
Media – Reference	7	Encyclopædia Britannica	10
Watches & Accessories	7	Rolex	2
Drinks – Wine	6	Jacob's Creek	168
Drinks – Carbonated Soft Drinks	5	Coca-Cola	7
Internet – General	4	Google	3
Leisure & Entertainment – General	4	Manchester United Football Club	37
Media – TV Stations	4	BBC	5
Mobile Telecommunications	4	Vodafone	151
Leisure & Entertainment – Gambling	3	The National Lottery	124
Oil & Gas	3	BP	23
Travel – General	3	Cunard	41
Travel – Agents & Tour Operators	2	Thomas Cook	26
Travel – Airlines	2	British Airways	4
Travel – Bus & Rail Operators	2	Eurostar	52

period is in the movement of the financial services brands. One might have expected that with the recapitalisations of the banks and the nationalisation of others – together with the general storm surrounding banking bonuses and the role of the banks in the economic downturn – their image would be at an all-time low. Yet in these rankings the majority of the banks improve their position. Lloyds TSB leads the way jumping 178 places while Barclaycard and Barclays climb 157 and 134 places respectively. NatWest and HSBC also improve their standings going up 86 places each.

Out of the entire top 500 only four brands remain in exactly the same position as the previous year. They are Duracell®, Dell, Yellow Pages and Kwik-Fit whose positions respectively are 12th, 63rd, 89th and 421st. Eighty brands remain within 10 positions of their previous year placing, while 129 remain within 20 places of their last entry.

Consumer Superbrands New Entries and Fallers

There are 106 new entries in the top 500 with 106 unlucky brands therefore making way. Some of these brands were removed or entered into the process for the first time, which slightly over exaggerates the changes. Our researchers constantly add in new brands for consideration in the process while others make way due to rebranding and corporate activity such as takeovers – and of course we have an unprecedented number of brands that simply no longer exist.

The biggest genuine new entry – i.e. excluding those brands considered in the process for the first time – is Krispy Kreme. It enters not only the top 500 but the top 100, joining the Superbrands ranking in 68th position. This is a rise of an incredible 650 places.

Peperami and Macleans are the next highest genuine new entries, coming in at 141st and 144th and rising 564 and 391 places respectively. L'OCCITANE also enters for the first time in 144th place, up 433 positions, while cereal brand Jordans, which just missed out on the top 500 last time, rises 337 to enter in 166th place.

Toiletries and cosmetics is one of the sectors struggling this year with major players in the category such as Estée Lauder, Chanel, Dior and Lancôme falling out of the top 500.

A number of the brands that are now insolvent or have been in administration have been in the research process during the last two years. The likes of Woolworths, SCS, MFI, Barratts, Miss Sixty and Adams did not make the top 500 over that period. While not the only reason for their demise or troubles, perhaps their lack of brand strength and the protection this affords companies during an economic downturn was one of the issues that contributed to their plight.

BUSINESS SUPERBRANDS

Business Superbrands Top Performers

After two years at the top of the Business Superbrands ranking, search engine giant Google falls to sixth place, leaving Microsoft® to top both the consumer and business to business brand lists.

In addition, we can reveal that similar to the pattern seen in the Consumer Superbrands rankings, half of last year's top 10 business brands once again make this grade. This reiterates their strength while simultaneously demonstrating the difficulty faced by other brands wishing to challenge the top tier. Rolls-Royce one of Britain's largest engineering concerns and one of the few to remain UK-owned, remains in second place this year. In addition the London Stock Exchange and GlaxoSmithKline retain their top 10 placing.

Sony, Nokia, Michelin and Bupa all new entries to the Business Superbrands top 10 last year fall back out of the top group. In addition, BP also dropped out of the top 10 for the first time in four years, although it only missed out by one place. These five brands are replaced this year by BlackBerry, Visa, PricewaterhouseCoopers and both Virgin Atlantic and British Airways, the latter returning to the top 10 after a one year absence. It should be noted that Sony's listing

in the ranking was changed to its specialist B2B brand, Sony Professional, which would undoubtedly have affected its performance in the survey. Equally, the tire brands were removed from the business to business rankings leaving them just in the Consumer Superbrands process, where they continue to perform strongly. Thus the demise of

Sony and Michelin from the top 10 of the B2B rankings is not a reflection of how they are perceived.

Like BP, Shell just misses out on the top 10 coming in one place below its rival in 12th, four places ahead of its position last year. BT which just missed out on a top 20 placing last time,

TOP 10 BUSINESS SUPERBRANDS RISERS, 2009/10			
Brand	2010 Position	2009 Position	Rise
Premier Inn	240	437	197
Aviva	144	315	171
Management Today	317	477	160
Bombardier	334	494	160
DHL	37	187	150
BDO	173	319	146
GKN	217	359	142
Pitman Training	301	441	140
Initial	299	438	139
Veolia Environmental Services	267	399	132

TOP 10 BUSINESS SUPERBRANDS		
Rank	2009	2010
1	Google	Microsoft®
2	Rolls-Royce	Rolls-Royce
3	Sony	BlackBerry
4	Microsoft®	Virgin Atlantic
5	Nokia	Google
6	GlaxoSmithKline	London Stock Exchange
7	London Stock Exchange	GlaxoSmithKline
8	Michelin	British Airways
9	BP	Visa
20	Bupa	PricewaterhouseCoopers

TOP 10 CATERGORIES REPRESENTED IN THE BUSINESS SUPERBRANDS TOP 500 2010			
Number of Brands in Top 500	Category	Catergory Winner	Average Rank
34	Technology - Hardware & Equipment	Apple	253
21	Support Services - Associations & Accreditations	The Law Society	249
18	Construction & Materials - Tools / Equipment	Bosch	224
17	Software & Computer Services	Microsoft®	229
17	Support Services - General	AA	295
16	Industrial Engineering - General	Siemens	199
15	Construction & Materials	Pilkington	260
15	Executive Education, Training & Development	London School of Economics and Political Science	237
15	Travel & Leisure - Business Hotels	Hilton	219
14	Aerospace & Defence	Rolls-Royce	233
14	Insurance	Lloyd's of London	214
14	Retailers - Office Equipment & Supplies	Staples	268

in 21st place, climbs five places to 16th.Bosch, Mastercard and Hertz can be found rising from the thirties to the twenties.

More widely in the top 500 topping the biggest risers list is the rapidly expanding Premier Inn, which has also been one of the relative winners in a recession hit corporate hotel industry. Aviva is the second strongest riser year-on-year, showing that its brand is now becoming firmly established, having replaced the traditional Norwich Union name in 2009. Another relative newcomer to these shores, Veolia Environmental Services, is certainly on the rise, although sector compatriots such as Shanks Group also enjoyed fairly significant gains.

The biggest faller was credit rating agency Moody's, which dropped a significant 168 places. Its brand and those of the other credit rating agencies were not without criticism in the financial crisis, although Standard & Poors only falls a modest 26 places. Not surprisingly,

and unlike the pattern seen in the Consumer Superbrands survey, many financial brands suffer in the ranking with many in the top 10 biggest fallers; these include Dresdner Kleinwort, UBS, Morgan Stanley, and JP Morgan. Perhaps showing the UK's dwindling love affair of the green movement the Carbon Trust is the second biggest faller.

In terms of the top 500, there are 80 new entries this year, although this includes many yo-yo brands that made the top 500 two years ago, fell out last year and just regained their place again this year. Such brands range from law firm Simmons & Simmons to stationery brand Niceday.

In terms of categories, once again the Technology Hardware and Equipment category is the most represented in the top 500, with 34 brands. The Association and Accreditations sector, a sub-sector of support services, comes second with 21 brands in the top 500.

Construction and Equipment falls from the second to the third most represented sector in the top 500, although it increases its representation from 17 brands by one to 18. As with last years' survey sectors that have traditionally not been considered to be brand focused actually perform very well in the survey with, for example, Industrial Engineering General being represented by 16 brands topped by Siemens and Aerospace & Defence, with 14 representatives, topped by the Rolls-Royce.

Conclusions

As ever, the Superbrands ranking, both consumer and business to business, generate an excellent snapshot of those brands highly thought of in the UK market. Once again both rankings reveal steady performances by many top brands, who have clearly established powerful and market-leading positions in the minds of their customers. Other brands continue to fail to maintain this consistency as they move up and down the rankings year-on-year based on short term influences. A third group are as consistent as the first, but are either on a straight line down or up in the rankings over the four-year period. As ever within this short analysis we can only reflect some of the headline results and with little supporting theoretical or factual arguments. As always TCBA is able to provide additional analysis and insights on request. In the meantime I hope that you find these top line findings interesting.

Qualifying Business Superbrands

3
3663
3COM
3I
3M
AA
ABB
ABTA
ACCA
ACCENTURE
ACCOUNTANCY AGE
ACER
ACNIELSEN
ADDISON LEE
ADECCO
ADOBE
ADT
ADVISORY, CONCILIATION
    & ARBITRATION SERVICE
AIM
AIRBUS
AKZONOBEL
ALAMO
ALLEN & OVERY
ALLIANZ INSURANCE
ALLIED IRISH BANK
ALSTOM
AMD
AMEC
AMERICAN EXPRESS
AMV BBDO
ANGLO AMERICAN
APPLE
ARMITAGE SHANKS
ARRIVA
ARUP
ASHRIDGE BUSINESS SCHOOL
ASKJEEVES UK
ASTON BUSINESS SCHOOL
ASTRAZENECA
ATKINS
AUTOCAD
AVERY
AVIS
AVIVA
AXA
AXA PPP HEALTHCARE
BAA
BABCOCK INTERNATIONAL
BACS
BAE SYSTEMS
BAIN & COMPANY
BAKER TILLY
BALFOUR BEATTY
BARCLAYCARD
BARCLAYS
BASF
BASILDON BOND
BAYER
BBC WORLDWIDE
BBH
BDO
BG GROUP
BHP BILLITON
BIFFA
BLACK & DECKER
BLACKBERRY
BLOOMBERG
BLUE ARROW
BLUETOOTH
BMI
BMRB OMNIBUS
BNP PARIBAS
BOC GASES
BOEHRINGER INGELHEIM
BOEING
BOMBARDIER
BOOKER
BOOZ & CO
BOSCH
BOSTIK
BOSTON CONSULTING GROUP
BOURNEMOUTH INTERNATIONAL CENTRE
BP
BRISTOL-MYERS SQUIBB
BRITISH AIRWAYS
BRITISH DENTAL ASSOCIATION
BRITISH GAS BUSINESS
BRITISH GYPSUM
BRITISH LAND
BRITISH RETAIL CONSORTIUM
BROOK STREET
BROTHER
BRUNSWICK
BSI
BT
BUDGET
BUPA
BUSINESS DESIGN CENTRE
BUSINESS WEEK
CABLE & WIRELESS

CALOR
CAMBRIDGE JUDGE BUSINESS SCHOOL
CAMPAIGN
CANARY WHARF GROUP
CANON
CAPGEMINI
CAPITA
CARBON TRUST
CARILLION
CARLSON WAGONLIT TRAVEL
CARPHONE WAREHOUSE
CASIO
CASS BUSINESS SCHOOL
CASTROL
CATERPILLAR
CB RICHARD ELLIS
CBI
CHARTERED MANAGEMENT INSTITUTE
CHEVRON
CHUBB
CIMA
CIPD
CISCO
CITI
CITY & GUILDS
CITY LINK
CLEAR CHANNEL OUTDOOR
CLIFFORD CHANCE
CNBC
CNN
COMPASS GROUP
CONOCOPHILLIPS
CONQUEROR
CONSTRUCTION NEWS
CORUS
COSTAIN
COSTCO
CRANFIELD SCHOOL OF MANAGEMENT
CREDIT SUISSE
CROWN TRADE
CROWNE PLAZA
D&B
DATAMONITOR
DE LA RUE
DE VERE VENUES
DELL
DELOITTE
DEUTSCHE BANK
DEWALT
DHL
DOW CHEMICALS
DOW CORNING
DRAPER
DRAPERS
DRESDNER KLEINWORT
DTZ
DULUX TRADE
DUPONT
E.ON UK
EADS
EASYJET
EBAY
EDDIE STOBART
EDF ENERGY
ELI LILLY
ELSTREE STUDIOS
ENTERPRISE
EPSON
EQUIFAX
ERNST & YOUNG
ESTATES GAZETTE
EUROPCAR
EUROSTAR
EUROTUNNEL
EVERSHEDS
EXCEL LONDON
EXPERIAN
EXXON MOBIL
FEDERATION OF SMALL BUSINESSES
FEDEX EXPRESS
FIRST GROUP
FLIGHT INTERNATIONAL
FLYBE
FREIGHTLINER
FRESHFIELDS BRUCKHAUS DERINGER
FT
FTSE GROUP
FUJITSU
FUJITSU TECHNOLOGY SOLUTIONS
G4S
GALLUP
GARMIN
GATWICK EXPRESS
GE
GENERAL DYNAMICS UK
GETTY IMAGES
GFK NOP
GKN
GLAXOSMITHKLINE
GOLDMAN SACHS
GOOGLE

GRANT THORNTON
GREAT PORTLAND ESTATES
GREEN FLAG
GROSVENOR
GULFSTREAM
HANSON
HAPAG-LLOYD
HARRIS
HARROGATE INTERNATIONAL CENTRE
HAYS
HEATHROW EXPRESS
HENLEY BUSINESS SCHOOL
HERTZ
HEWLETT-PACKARD
HILL & KNOWLTON
HILTON
HISCOX
HITACHI
HOLIDAY INN
HONEYWELL
HOTELS.COM
HOWDENS JOINERY
HRG
HSBC
HSS HIRE
IBIS
IBM GLOBAL SERVICES
ICAEW
IDEAL STANDARD
IMAGINATION
IMPERIAL COLLEGE BUSINESS SCHOOL
INGERSOLL RAND
INITIAL
INMARSAT
INTEL
INTERBRAND
INTERLINK EXPRESS
INVENSYS
INVESTORS IN PEOPLE
IOD
IPSOS MORI
J.P. MORGAN CAZENOVE
JANES
JC DECAUX
JCB
JEWSON
JOHNSON & JOHNSON
JOHNSON MATTHEY
JOHNSTONE'S TRADE PAINTS
JONES LANG LASALLE
JP MORGAN
JWT
KALL KWIK
KELLY SERVICES
KIER GROUP
KIMBERLEY-CLARK PROFESSIONAL
KING STURGE
KITEMARK
KNIGHT FRANK
KPMG
KUEHNE & NAGEL
LAFARGE
LAING O'ROURKE
LAND SECURITIES
LANDOR ASSOCIATES
LATEROOMS.COM
LEGAL & GENERAL
LENOVO
LETTS
LEXMARK
LEYLAND TRADE
LG
LIFFE
LINDE GROUP
LINKEDIN
LINKLATERS
LLOYD'S OF LONDON
LLOYDS TSB
LOCKHEED MARTIN
LOGICA
LOGITECH
LONDON BUSINESS SCHOOL
LONDON CITY AIRPORT
LONDON METAL EXCHANGE
LONDON SCHOOL OF ECONOMICS
    AND POLITICAL SCIENCE
LONDON STOCK EXCHANGE
LOVELLS
M&C SAATCHI
MAERSK LINE
MAGNET TRADE
MAKITA
MAKRO
MALMAISON
MANAGEMENT TODAY
MANCHESTER AIRPORTS GROUP
MANCHESTER BUSINESS SCHOOL
MANPOWER
MARKETING
MARKETING WEEK
MARRIOTT

MARSHALLS
MASSEY FERGUSON
MASTERCARD
MBNA
MCAFEE
MCCANN-ERICKSON
MCKINSEY & COMPANY
MERCK
MICHAEL PAGE INTERNATIONAL
MICROSOFT
MICROSOFT ADVERTISING
MILLENNIUM & COPTHORNE
MILLWARD BROWN
MINTEL
MISYS
MITSUBISHI ELECTRICS
MOODY'S
MORGAN STANLEY
MOTHER
MOTOROLA
MUNICH RE
NATIONAL
NATIONAL EXPRESS
NATIONAL GRID
NATWEST
NEC
NETGEAR
NETJETS
NICEDAY
NOKIA
NORTHROP GRUMMAN
NORTON
NOVARTIS
NOVELL
NPOWER
O2
OBSERVER
OFFICE ANGELS
OFFICE DEPOT
OGILVY
OLYMPUS
ORACLE
ORANGE
OXFORD BLACK N' RED
OXFORD INSTRUMENTS
OXFORD SAID BUSINESS SCHOOL
PA CONSULTING
PALM
PANASONIC
PARCELFORCE WORLDWIDE
PARK PLAZA
PAYPAL
PC WORLD BUSINESS
PEARL
PEARL & DEAN
PFIZER
PHILIPS MEDICAL SYSTEMS
PICKFORDS
PILKINGTON
PINEWOOD STUDIOS GROUP
PITMAN TRAINING
PITNEY BOWES
PORTAKABIN
POW WOW
PRATT & WHITNEY
PREMIER INN
PRESS ASSOCIATION
PRICEWATERHOUSECOOPERS
PRONTAPRINT
PRUDENTIAL
QINETIQ
QUARK
RAC
RADISSON EDWARDIAN
RAMADA JARVIS
RAYTHEON SYSTEMS
REED
REED ELSEVIER
REGUS
RENTOKIL
RETAIL WEEK
REXEL
RIBA
RICOH
RIO TINTO
ROCHE
ROLLS-ROYCE
ROYAL INSTITUTE OF
    CHARTERED SURVEYORS
ROYAL MAIL
RYMAN
SAATCHI & SAATCHI
SAGE
SAINT-GOBAIN
SAMSUNG
SANDISK
SANOFI-AVENTIS
SAP
SAVILLS
SCHRODERS
SCOTTISH & SOUTHERN ENERGY

SCOTTISH POWER
SCREWFIX
SEAGATE TECHNOLOGY
SECURITAS
SERCO
SEVERN TRENT WATER
SHANKS GROUP
SHARP
SHELL
SHERATON
SIEMENS
SIMMONS & SIMMONS
SIR ROBERT MCALPINE
SKANSKA
SKYPE
SLAUGHTER & MAY
SMITH & NEPHEW
SMITHS
SNAP-ON
SODEXO
SOIL ASSOCIATION
SONY ERICSSON
SONY PROFESSIONAL
SOPHOS
SPECTATOR
STAEDTLER
STAGECOACH
STANDARD & POOR'S
STANDARD LIFE HEALTHCARE
STANLEY
STAPLES
STRUTT & PARKER
SUN MICROSYSTEMS
SWISS RE
SWISSPORT
SYMANTEC
TARMAC
TDK
TETRA PAK
THALES
THAMES WATER
THE BANKER
THE BRIGHTON CENTRE
THE CO-OPERATIVE BANK
THE DAILY TELEGRAPH
THE ECONOMIST
THE FAIRTRADE FOUNDATION
THE GROCER
THE GUARDIAN
THE ICC BIRMINGHAM
THE LAW SOCIETY
THE LAWYER
THE NEC BIRMINGHAM
THE OPEN UNIVERSITY
    BUSINESS SCHOOL
THE QUEEN ELIZABETH II
    CONFERENCE CENTRE
THE SUNDAY TIMES
THISTLE
THOMSON LOCAL
THOMSON REUTERS
THYSSENKRUPP
T-MOBILE
TNS
TNT EXPRESS
TOMTOM
TOPPS TILES
TOSHIBA
TOTAL
TRAVELEX
TRAVELODGE
TRAVIS PERKINS
TWYFORD BATHROOMS
UBS
UNIPART
UNISYS
UNIX
UPS
VELUX
VEOLIA ENVIRONMENTAL SERVICES
VIKING
VIRGIN ATLANTIC
VIRGIN TRAINS
VISA
VODAFONE
WALES MILLENNIUM CENTRE
WARWICK BUSINESS SCHOOL
WEBER SHANDWICK
WESTFIELD
WICKES
WINCANTON
WOLFF OLINS
WOLSELEY
WOOLMARK
XEROX
XSTRATA
YAHOO! NETWORK
YALE
YELLOW PAGES
ZENITH-OPTIMEDIA
ZURICH

Please note that some brand names have been changed since the research was conducted. These lists reflect the brands as they are generally marketed (at the time of going to press) and may differ slightly from the name analysed in the survey.

Qualifying Consumer Superbrands

AA
ABBEY
ADIDAS
ADOBE
AEG
AFTER EIGHT
AGA
ALFA ROMEO
ALKA-SELTZER
ALPEN
ALTON TOWERS
AMAZON.CO.UK
AMERICAN EXPRESS
AMOY
ANADIN
ANDREX
APPLE
ARGOS
ARIEL
ARSENAL FOOTBALL CLUB
ASDA
AUDI
AUTOGLASS
AVON
A-Z MAPS
B&Q
BACARDI
BAILEYS
BANG & OLUFSEN
BARCLAYCARD
BARCLAYS
BAXTERS
BBC
BECK'S
BELL'S
BEN & JERRY'S
BEN SHERMAN
BENDICKS
BENYLIN
BERGHAUS
BIRDS EYE
BISTO
BLACK & DECKER
BLACKBERRY
BLAUPUNKT
BLOSSOM HILL
BMW
BOBBI BROWN
BOLD
BOMBAY SAPPHIRE
BONJELA
BOOTS
BOSCH
BOSE
BP
BRAUN
BRITA
BRITAX
BRITISH AIRWAYS
BRITISH GAS
BRYLCREEM
BT
BUDWEISER
BUPA
BURGER KING
CADBURY
CALPOL
CALVIN KLEIN
CANON
CARLING
CARLSBERG
CASTROL
CHAMPNEYS
CHANNEL 4
CHARLES WORTHINGTON
CHELSEA FOOTBALL CLUB
CHIVAS REGAL
CHUBB
CIF
CILLIT BANG
CLAIROL
CLARINS
CLARKS
CLEARASIL
CLINIQUE
COCA-COLA
COINTREAU
COLLINS
COLMAN'S
COMFORT
COSMOPOLITAN
COSTA
COURVOISIER
COW & GATE
CRABTREE & EVELYN
CRAYOLA
CROWN
CUNARD
DAIRYLEA
DEEP HEAT
DELL
DERMALOGICA
DETTOL

DIESEL
DISNEY
DKNY
DOMESTOS
DOMINO'S PIZZA
DORITOS
DOUWE EGBERTS
DOVE
DR MARTENS
DULUX
DUNLOP
DURACELL
DUREX
DYSON
E&J GALLO
E45
EA
EARLY LEARNING CENTRE
EBAY
EDEN PROJECT
ELASTOPLAST
ELECTROLUX
ELIZABETH ARDEN
ENCYCLOPÆDIA
    BRITANNICA
ENERGIZER
EUROSTAR
EVIAN
FACEBOOK
FAIRY
FAMOUS GROUSE
FERRERO ROCHER
FINANCIAL TIMES
FINISH
FISHER-PRICE
FLASH
FLORA
FLYMO
FORD
FOSTER'S
FOUR SEASONS HOTELS
    & RESORTS
FRENCH CONNECTION
GALAXY
GAP
GARNIER
GAVISCON
GILLETTE
GLENFIDDICH
GOOD HOUSEKEEPING
GOODYEAR
GOOGLE
GORDON'S
GRAND MARNIER
GREEN & BLACK'S
GROLSCH
GÜ
GUINNESS
HÄAGEN-DAZS
HABITAT
HALFORDS
HALIFAX
HAMLEYS
HARD ROCK CAFÉ
HARDYS
HARPIC
HARRODS
HARRY RAMSDEN'S
HARVEY NICHOLS
HEINEKEN
HELLY HANSEN
HENNESSY
HERBAL ESSENCES
HEWLETT-PACKARD
HIGHLAND SPRING
HILTON
HIPP ORGANIC
HMV
HOLIDAY INN
HOLLAND & BARRETT
HONDA
HOOVER
HORLICKS
HORNBY
HOTPOINT
HOVIS
HP
HSBC
HUGGIES
HUGO BOSS
HUSH PUPPIES
IBM
IKEA
IMODIUM
IMPERIAL LEATHER
INNOCENT
INTEL
INTERFLORA
J2O
JACK DANIEL'S
JACOB'S CREEK
JAEGER
JAGUAR

JAMESON
JOHN FRIEDA
JOHN LEWIS
JOHN WEST
JOHNNIE WALKER
JORDANS
KAREN MILLEN
KENCO
KENWOOD
KENWOOD KITCHEN
    APPLIANCES
KFC
KICKERS
KIEHL'S
KIT KAT
KLEENEX
KNORR
KODAK
KP
KRISPY KREME
KRONENBOURG 1664
KUONI
KWIK-FIT
LA SENZA
LADBROKES
LAND ROVER
LE CREUSET
LEGO
LEGOLAND
LEICA
LEMSIP
LENOR
LEVI'S
LEXUS
LG
LINDEMANS
LINDT
LIVERPOOL FOOTBALL CLUB
LLOYDS TSB
L'OCCITANE
LONELY PLANET
LONGLEAT
L'ORÉAL PARIS
LUCOZADE
LURPAK
MAC
MACLAREN
MACLEANS
MADAME TUSSAUDS
MAGNERS IRISH CIDER
MALTESERS
MAMAS & PAPAS
MANCHESTER UNITED
    FOOTBALL CLUB
MARIGOLD
MARKS & SPENCER
MARMITE
MARRIOTT
MARS
MARTINI
MASTERCARD
MATTEL
MCCAIN
MCDONALD'S
MCVITIE'S
MERCEDES-BENZ
MICHELIN
MICHELIN TRAVEL GUIDES
    & MAPS
MICROSOFT
MIELE
MINI BABYBEL
MIRACLE-GRO
MISS SELFRIDGE
MOLTON BROWN
MONOPOLY
MONSOON
MORPHY RICHARDS
MORRISONS
MOTHERCARE
MOTOROLA
MR MUSCLE
MR SHEEN
MTV
MÜLLER
NATIONAL EXPRESS
NATIONAL GEOGRAPHIC
NATIONWIDE
NATWEST
NECTAR
NEFF
NESCAFÉ
NEW SCIENTIST
NEXT
NICORETTE
NIGHT NURSE
NIKE
NIKON
NINTENDO
NIVEA
NOKIA
NUROFEN
NUTELLA

O2
OCEAN SPRAY
OLAY
OLYMPUS
OMEGA
OPTREX
ORAL-B
ORANGE
ORDNANCE SURVEY
ORIGINAL SOURCE
OXFORD UNIVERSITY PRESS
OXO
P&O FERRIES
PAMPERS
PANADOL
PANASONIC
PANTENE
PATAK'S
PAUL SMITH
PAYPAL
PC WORLD
PEDIGREE
PENTAX
PEPERAMI
PEPSI
PERRIER
PERSIL
PETIT FILOUS
PG TIPS
PHILADELPHIA
PHILIPS
PIMM'S
PIRELLI
PIZ BUIN
PIZZAEXPRESS
PLAY-DOH
PLAYSTATION
POLYFILLA
POST OFFICE
POT NOODLE
PRET A MANGER
PRINGLE
PRINGLES
PRUDENTIAL
PUMA
QUAKER OATS
QUALITY STREET
RAC
RACHEL'S ORGANIC
RADIO TIMES
RADISSON HOTELS &
    RESORTS
RALEIGH
RAY-BAN
RED BULL
REEBOK
REMY MARTIN
RENNIE
RIBENA
ROBINSONS
ROC
ROLEX
RONSEAL
ROTARY
ROYAL ALBERT HALL
ROYAL BANK OF SCOTLAND
ROYAL CARIBBEAN
    INTERNATIONAL
ROYAL DOULTON
RUSSELL & BROMLEY
RUSSELL HOBBS
RYVITA
SAAB
SAGA
SAINSBURY'S
SAMSONITE
SAMSUNG
SANATOGEN
SANDALS
SAVLON
SCALEXTRIC
SCHOLL
SCHWARZKOPF
SCHWEPPES
SEIKO
SELFRIDGES
SENSODYNE
SEVEN SEAS
SHARWOOD'S
SHELL
SHERATON HOTELS &
    RESORTS
SHREDDED WHEAT
SILENTNIGHT
SILVER CROSS
SIMPLE
SKY
SLAZENGER
SLUMBERLAND
SMEG
SMIRNOFF
SONY
SONY ERICSSON

SOUTHERN COMFORT
SPECSAVERS
STANLEY
STANNAH STAIRLIFTS
STARBUCKS
STELLA ARTOIS
STREPSILS
SUDAFED
SUDOCREM
SWAROVSKI
SWATCH
TAG HEUER
TAMPAX
TATE & LYLE CANE SUGAR
TATE GALLERIES
TCP
TED BAKER
TEFAL
TERRY'S
TESCO
TETLEY
THE BODY SHOP
THE CO-OPERATIVE
THE DAILY TELEGRAPH/
    SUNDAY TELEGRAPH
THE ECONOMIST
THE INDEPENDENT/
    INDEPENDENT ON
    SUNDAY
THE LONDON EYE
THE NATIONAL LOTTERY
THE NORTH FACE
THE O2
THE SANCTUARY
THE TIMES/SUNDAY TIMES
THERMOS
THOMAS COOK
THORNTONS
TIFFANY & CO.
TILDA
TIMBERLAND
TIMOTEI
TOBLERONE
TOILET DUCK
TOMMEE TIPPEE
TOMTOM
TONI&GUY
TOSHIBA
TOYS 'R' US
TRESEMMÉ
TRIVIAL PURSUIT
TROPICANA
TUPPERWARE
TWIGLETS
TWININGS
TY.PHOO
UMBRO
VAIO
VANISH
VANITY FAIR
VICKS
VIRGIN ATLANTIC
VIRGIN MEDIA
VIRGIN MOBILE
VISA
VO5
VODAFONE
VOGUE
VOLKSWAGEN
VOLVIC
VOLVO
VTECH
WAGAMAMA
WAITROSE
WALKERS
WALL'S ICE CREAM
WATERFORD
WATERSTONE'S
WEDGWOOD
WEETABIX
WEIGHT WATCHERS
WELLA
WEMBLEY STADIUM
WEST CORNWALL
    PASTY CO.
WHICH?
WHIRLPOOL
WHISKAS
WHITTARD OF CHELSEA
WILLIAM HILL
WINALOT
WOLF BLASS
WONDERBRA
XBOX
XEROX
YAHOO!
YELLOW PAGES
YOUTUBE
ZANUSSI
ZOVIRAX